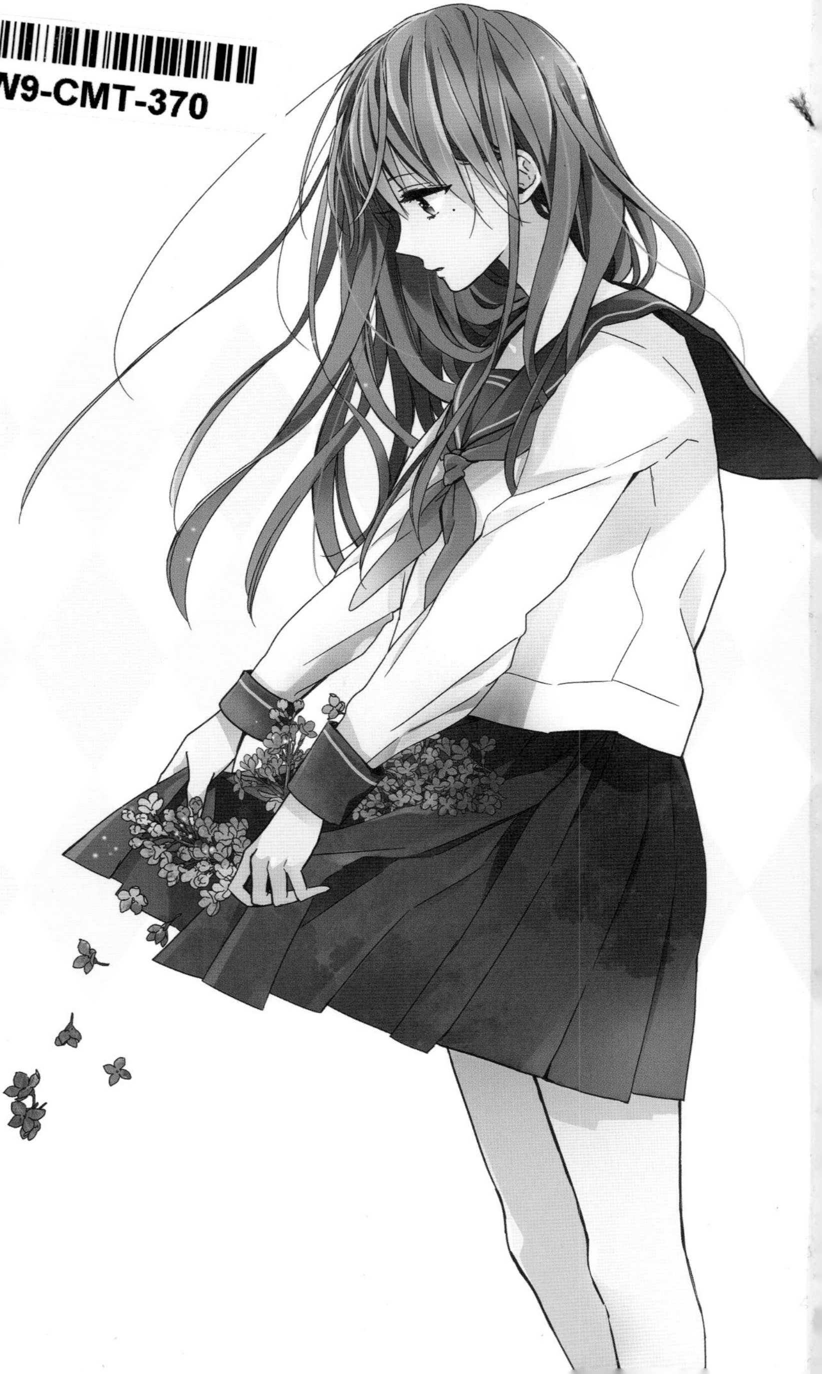

That Wolf-Boy is Mine!

Contents

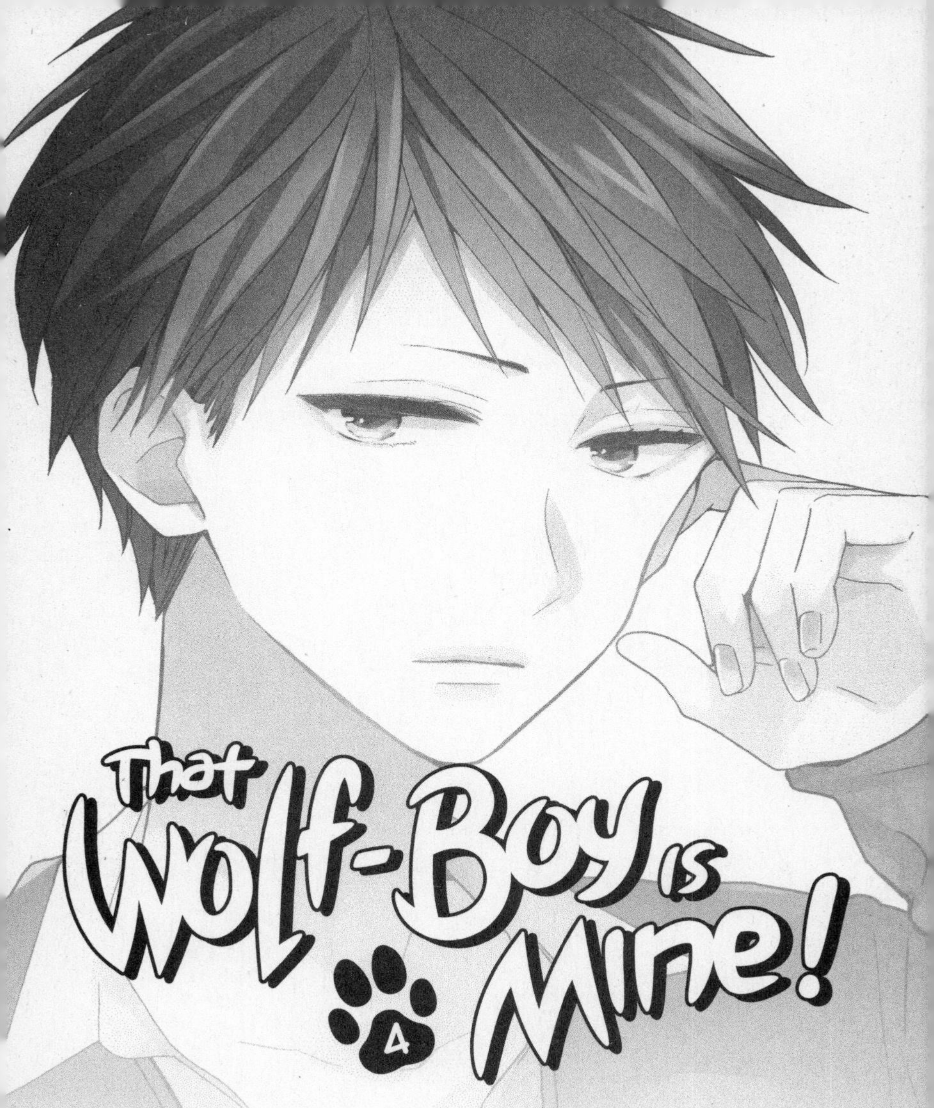
That Wolf-Boy is Mine!
4

Yoko Nogiri

CHARACTER & STORY

Sharing a secret with extraordinary boys?!

If you say no, I'll eat you up.

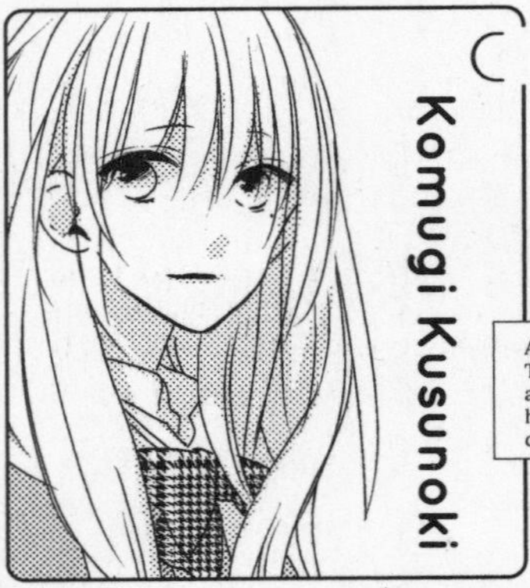

Komugi Kusunoki

A first-year high school student who transferred from Tokyo to Maruyama High School in Hokkaido. The one and only person who knows Ōgami's secret. She told him that she loves him, but he decided to pretend he didn't hear it.

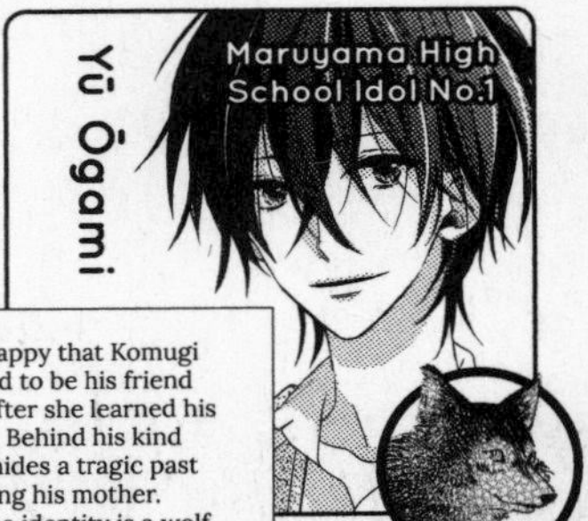
Maruyama High School Idol No.1

Yū Ōgami

Very happy that Komugi decided to be his friend even after she learned his secret. Behind his kind smile hides a tragic past involving his mother. His true identity is a wolf.

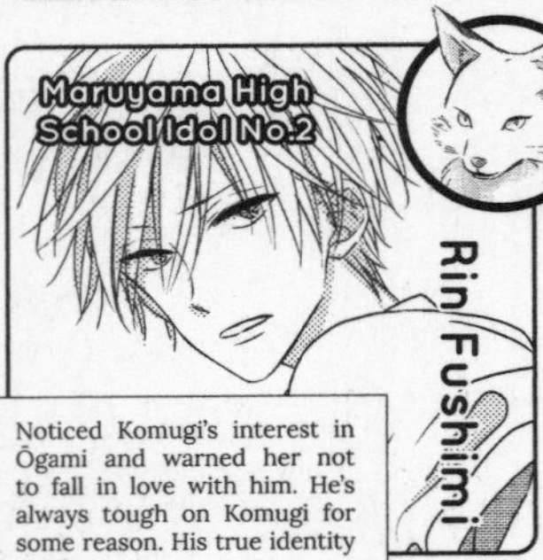
Maruyama High School Idol No.2

Rin Fushimi

Noticed Komugi's interest in Ōgami and warned her not to fall in love with him. He's always tough on Komugi for some reason. His true identity is a fox.

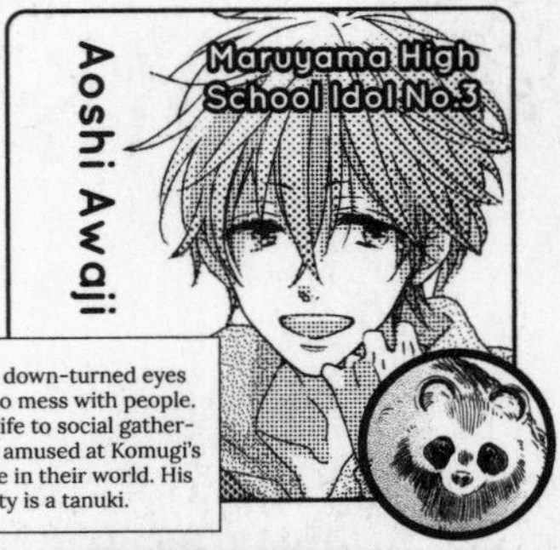
Maruyama High School Idol No.3

Aoshi Awaji

A boy with down-turned eyes who likes to mess with people. He brings life to social gatherings and is amused at Komugi's appearance in their world. His true identity is a tanuki.

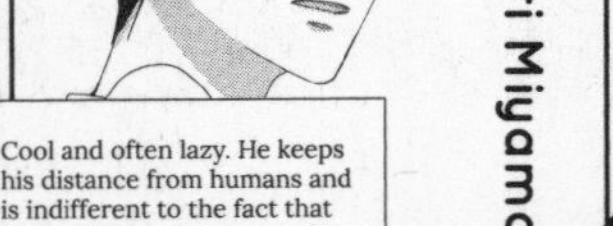
Maruyama High School Idol No.4

Senri Miyama

Cool and often lazy. He keeps his distance from humans and is indifferent to the fact that Komugi knows his secret. His true identity is a cat.

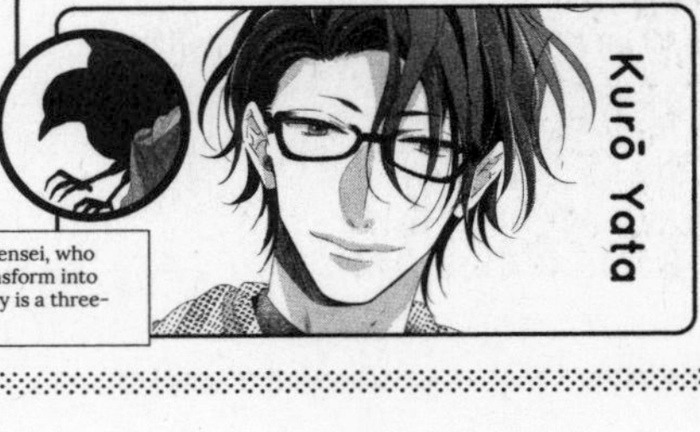

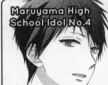

Kurō Yata

Ōgami and his friends' Sensei, who taught them how to transform into humans. His true identity is a three-legged crow.

At her new school, Komugi meets Yū Ōgami, who turns out to be a wolf!! Despite knowing his true identity, she confesses her love to him, but he rejects her. Komugi says that they can still be friends and puts a respectful distance between herself and Ōgami.

Meanwhile, when Ōgami learns that Yata is trying to keep Komugi away from him and his friends, he realizes how he really feels about her. When Komugi and Ōgami are finally on the same page about their mutual feelings, Yata learns that the two of them had met when they were young. Then, Yata makes a drastic move...

Finally, he can be true to himself. Finally, they can understand each other.

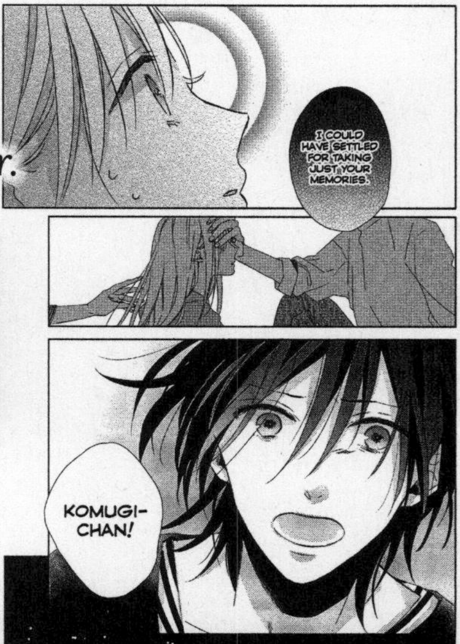
I COULD HAVE SETTLED FOR TAKING JUST YOUR MEMORIES.
KOMUGI-CHAN!

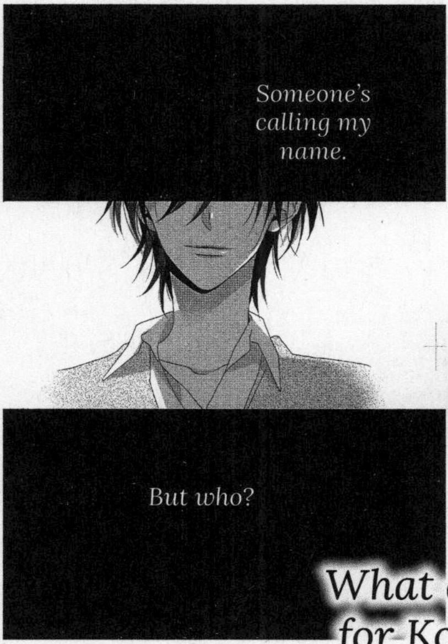
Someone's calling my name.
But who?

But...

What does the future hold for Komugi and Ōgami?!

That Wolf-Boy is Mine!

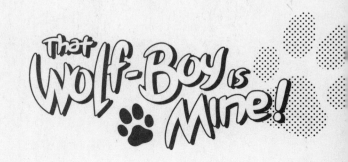

Chapter 14

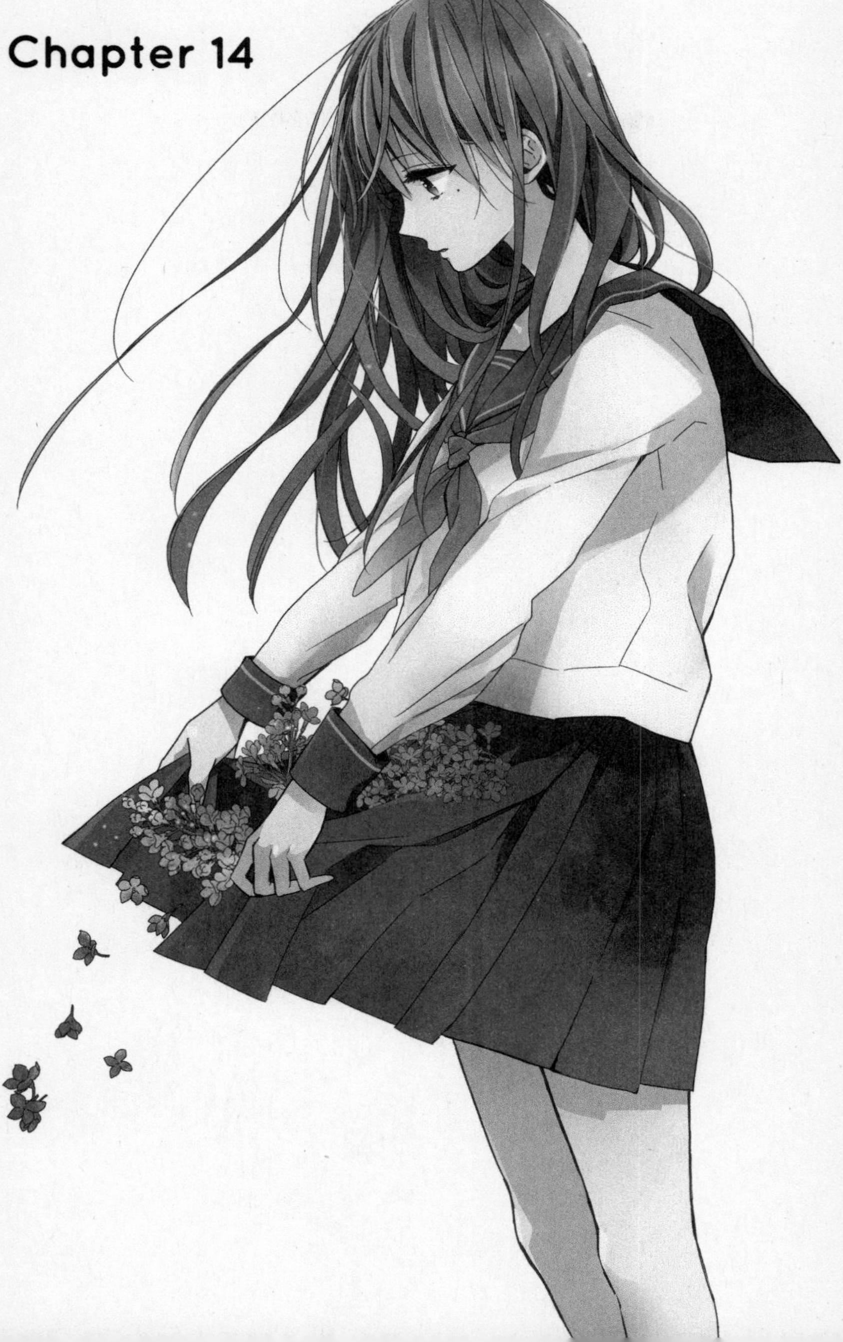

That Wolf-Boy is Mine!

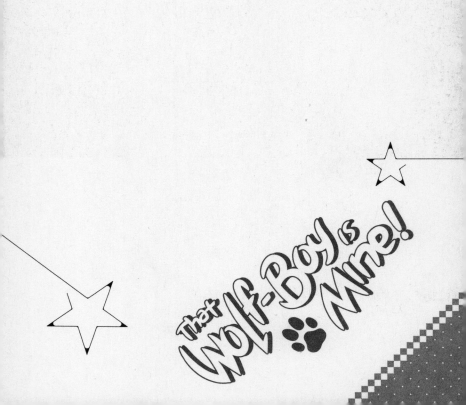

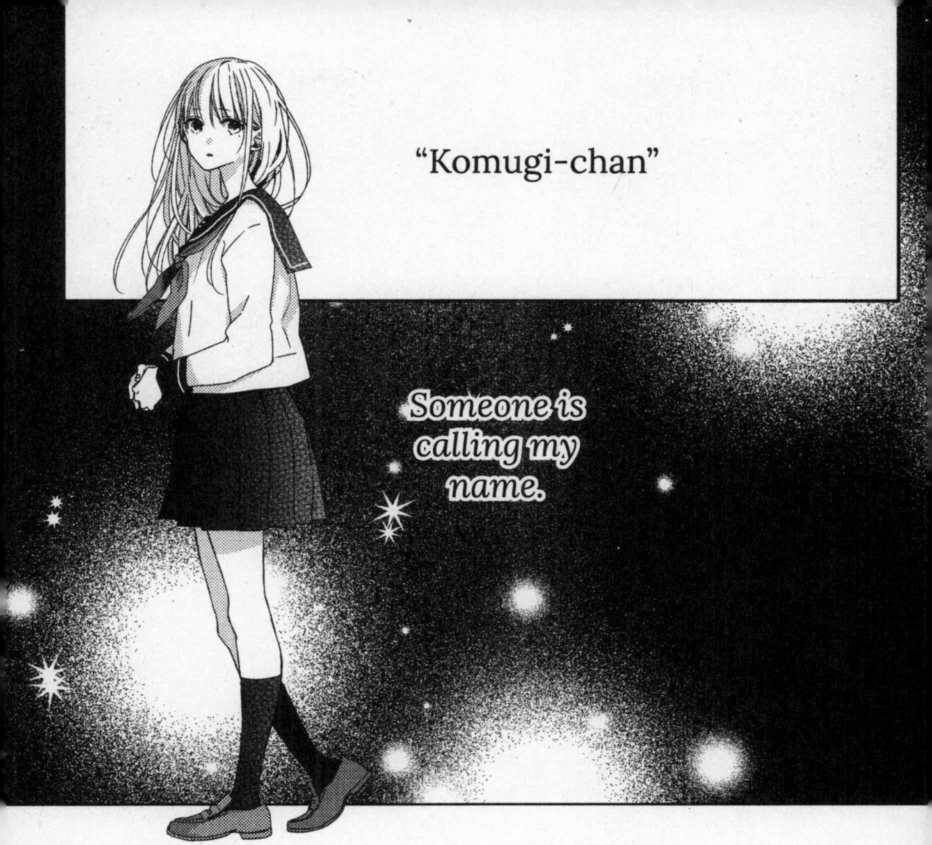
"Komugi-chan"
Someone is calling my name.

That Wolf-Boy is Mine! ☆

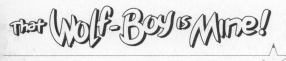

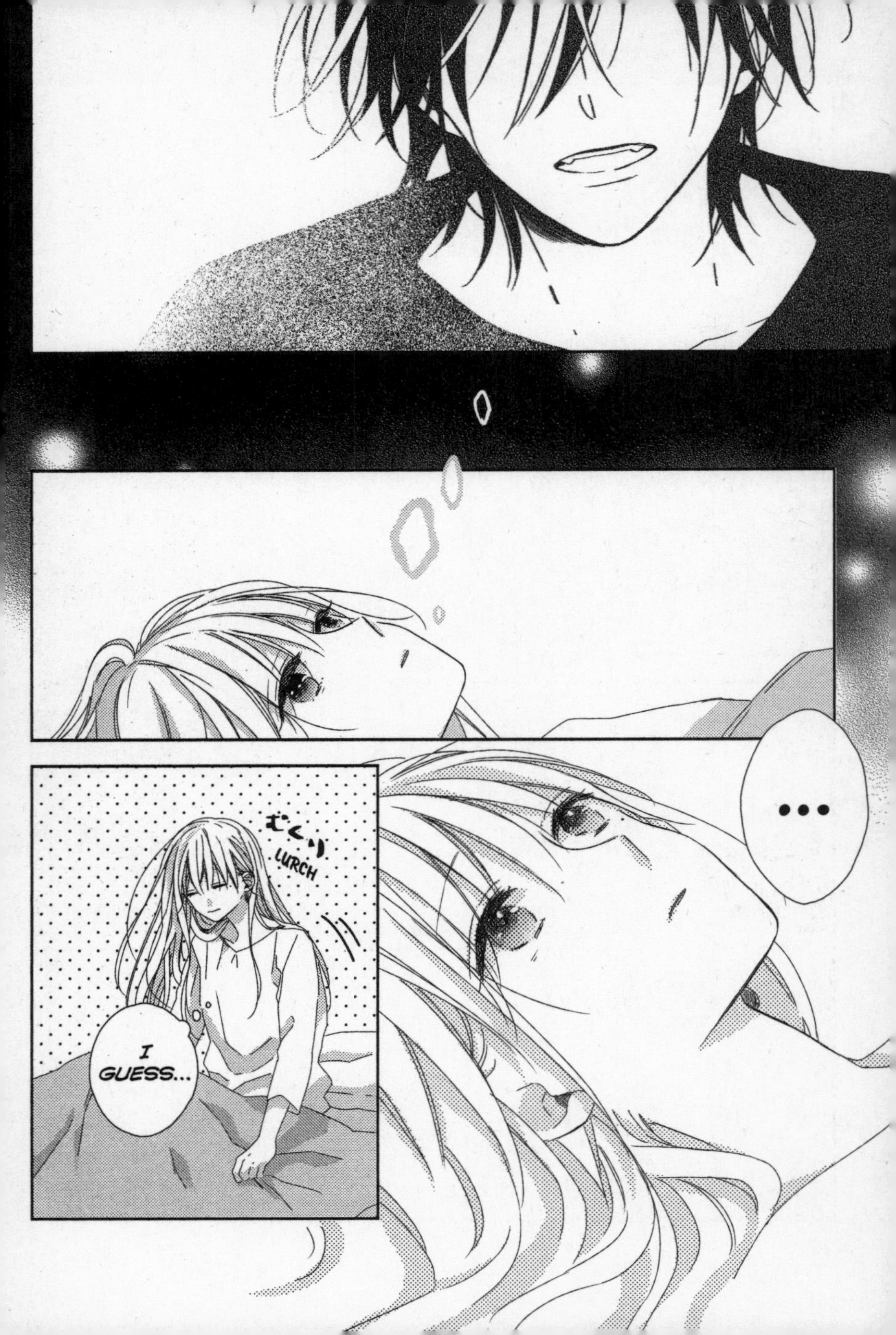
...
むくり
LURCH
I GUESS...

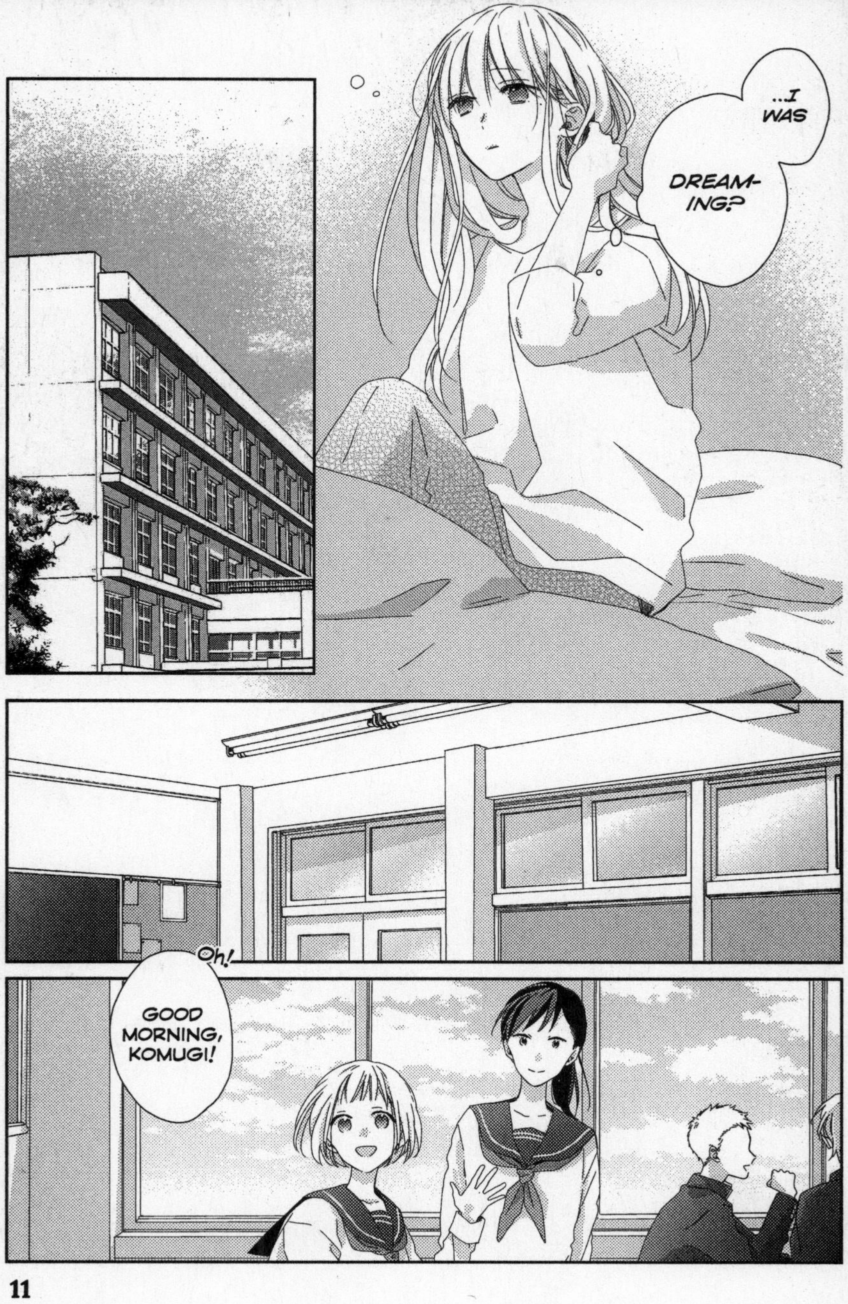
...I WAS DREAMING?
Oh!
GOOD MORNING, KOMUGI!

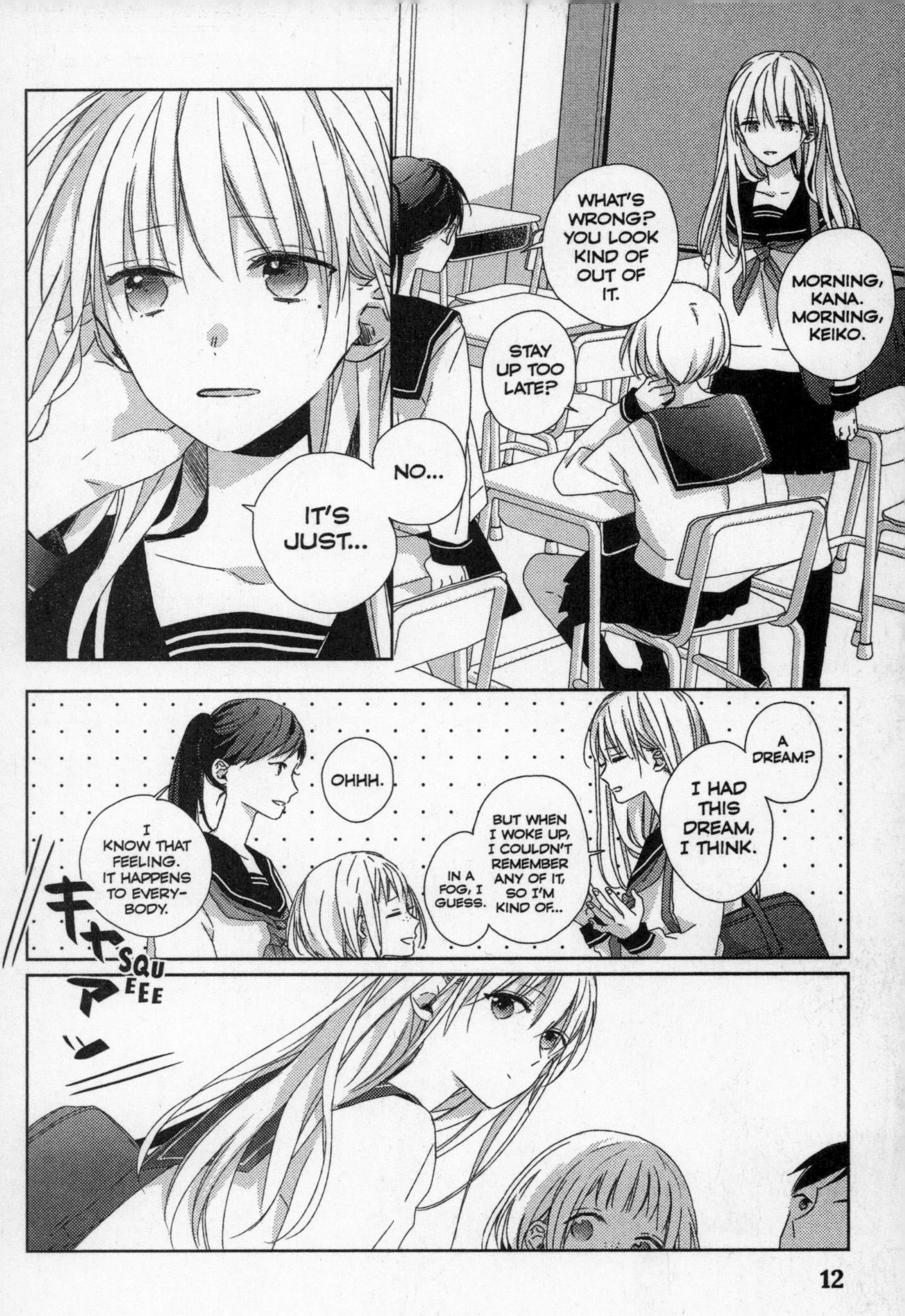
MORNING, KANA. MORNING, KEIKO.
WHAT'S WRONG? YOU LOOK KIND OF OUT OF IT.
STAY UP TOO LATE?
NO...
IT'S JUST...
A DREAM?
I HAD THIS DREAM, I THINK.
BUT WHEN I WOKE UP, I COULDN'T REMEMBER ANY OF IT, SO I'M KIND OF...
IN A FOG, I GUESS.
OHHH.
I KNOW THAT FEELING. IT HAPPENS TO EVERY-BODY.
キャア
SQUEEE

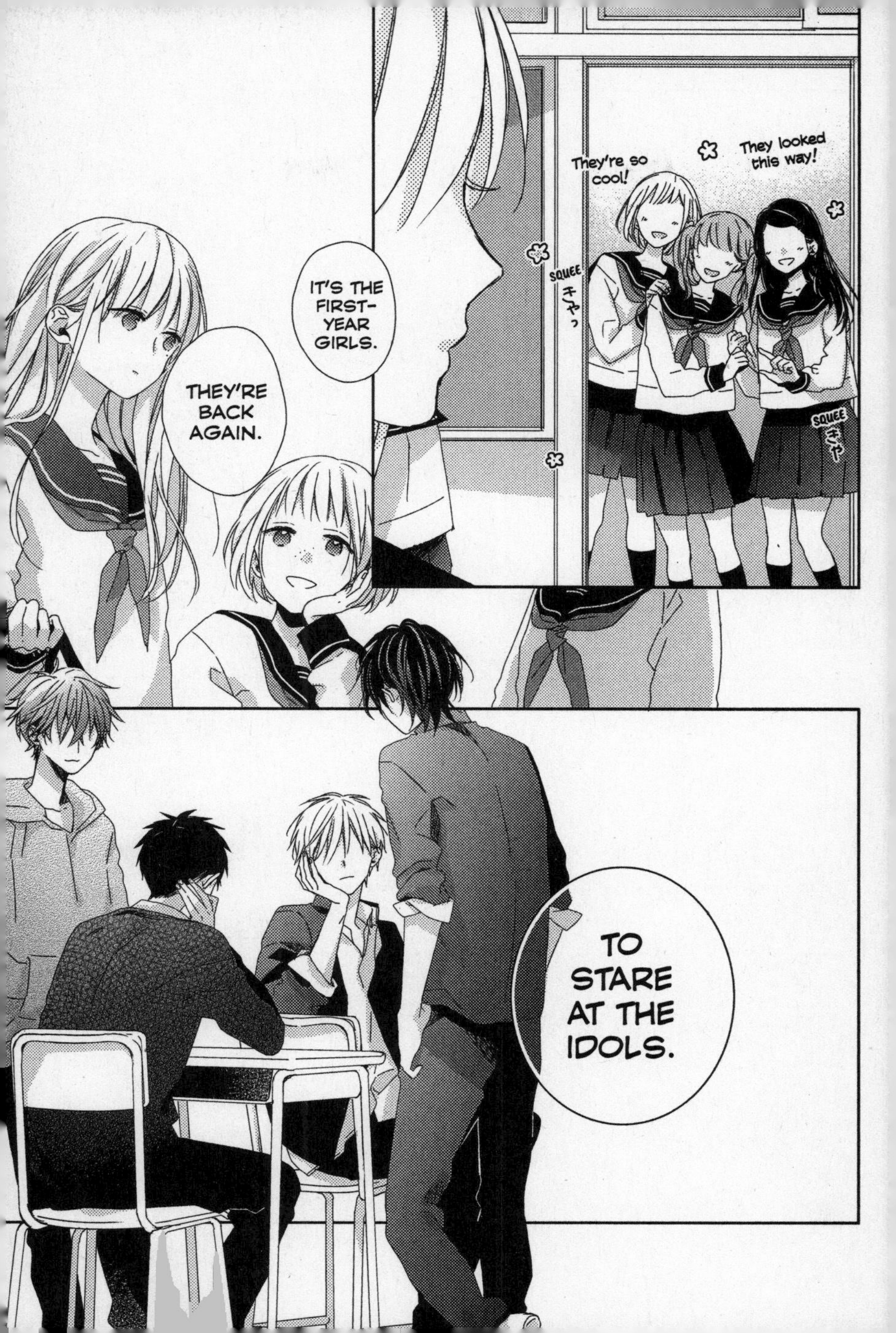
They looked this way!
They're so cool!
SQUEE キャ
SQUEE キャっ
IT'S THE FIRST-YEAR GIRLS.
THEY'RE BACK AGAIN.
TO STARE AT THE IDOLS.

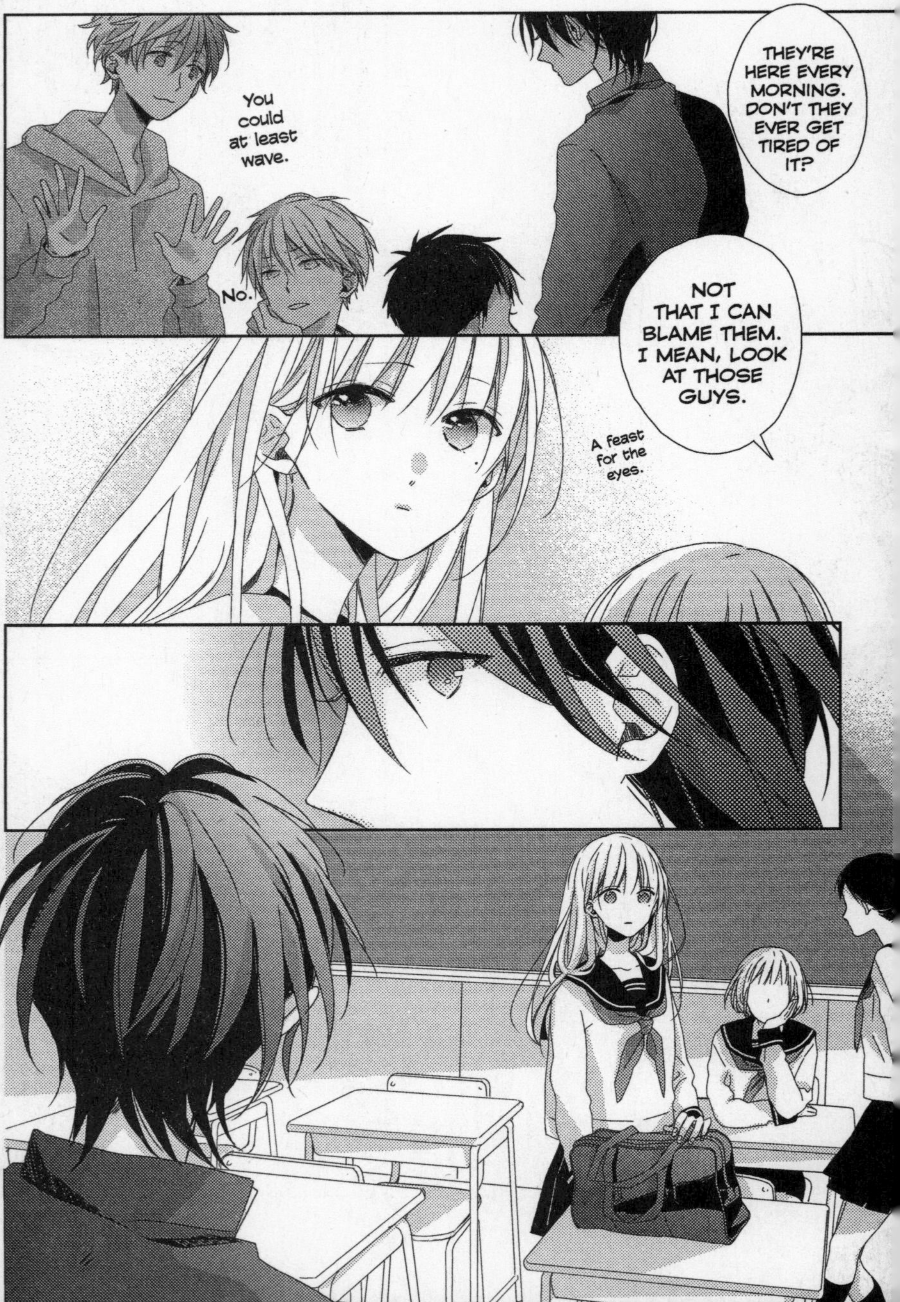
THEY'RE HERE EVERY MORNING. DON'T THEY EVER GET TIRED OF IT?
You could at least wave.
No.
NOT THAT I CAN BLAME THEM. I MEAN, LOOK AT THOSE GUYS.
A feast for the eyes.

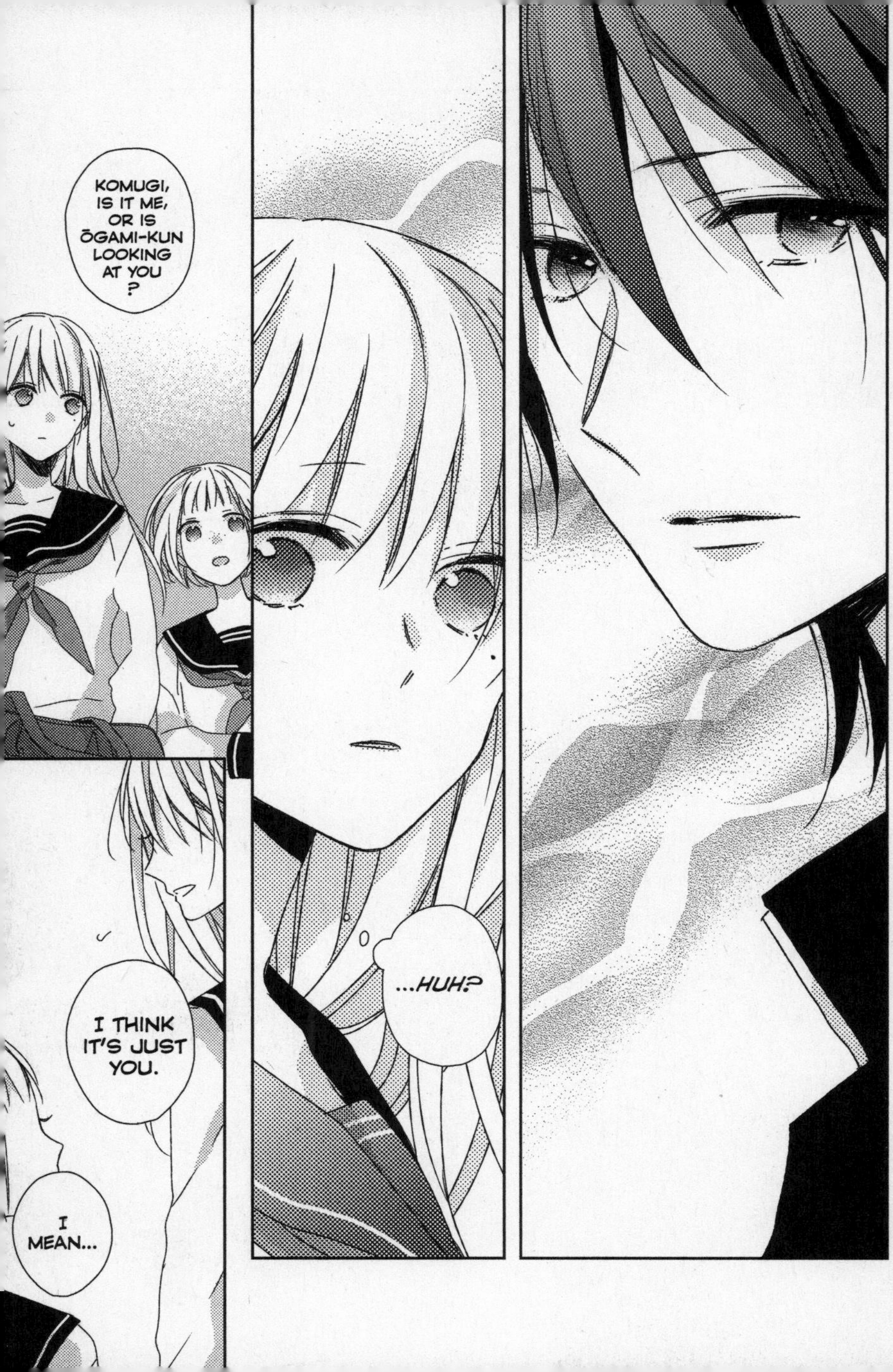
...HUH?
KOMUGI, IS IT ME, OR IS ŌGAMI-KUN LOOKING AT YOU?
I THINK IT'S JUST YOU.
I MEAN...

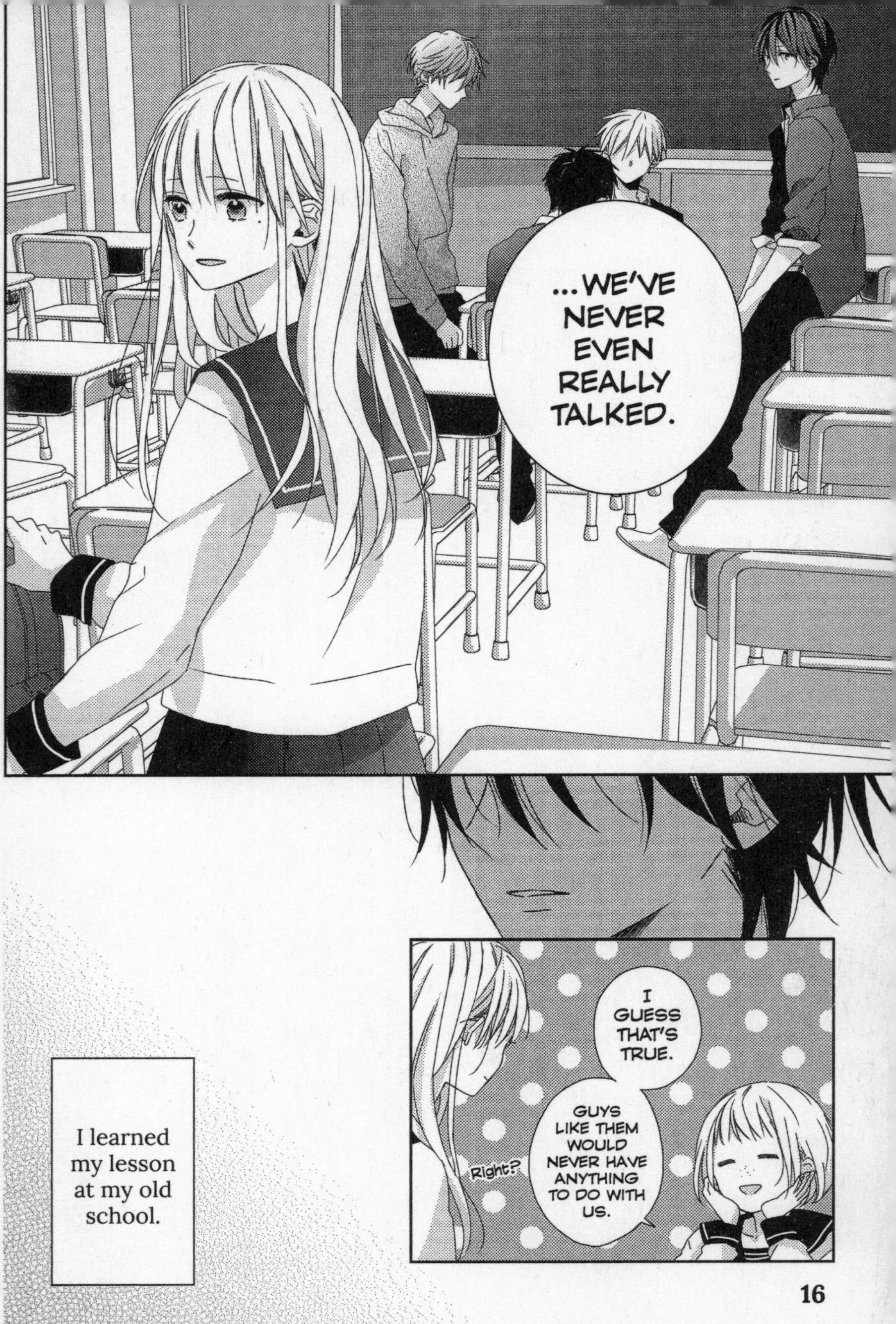
...WE'VE NEVER EVEN REALLY TALKED.
I GUESS THAT'S TRUE.
GUYS LIKE THEM WOULD NEVER HAVE ANYTHING TO DO WITH US.
Right?
I learned my lesson at my old school.

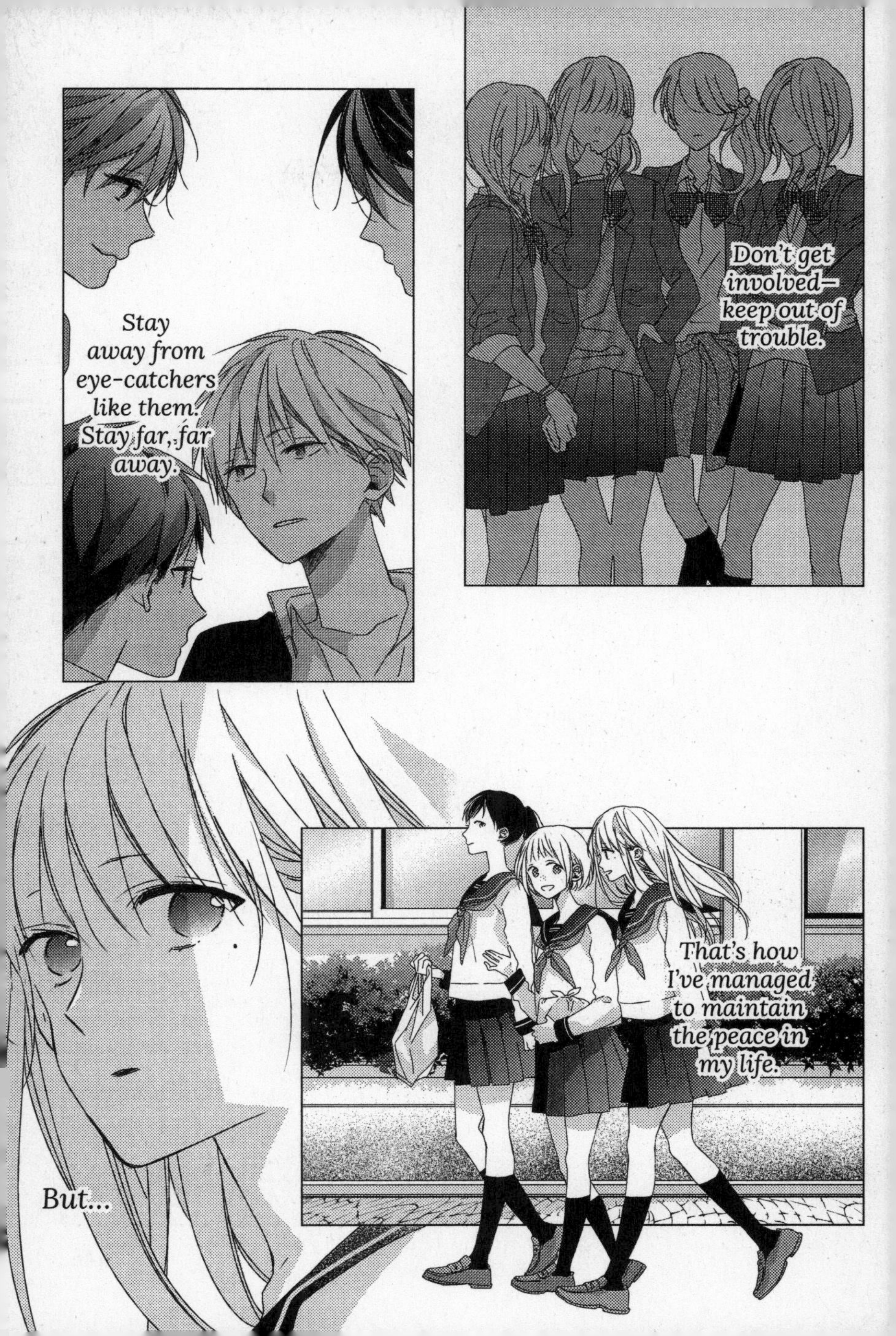
Don't get involved—keep out of trouble.
Stay away from eye-catchers like them. Stay far, far away.
That's how I've managed to maintain the peace in my life.
But...

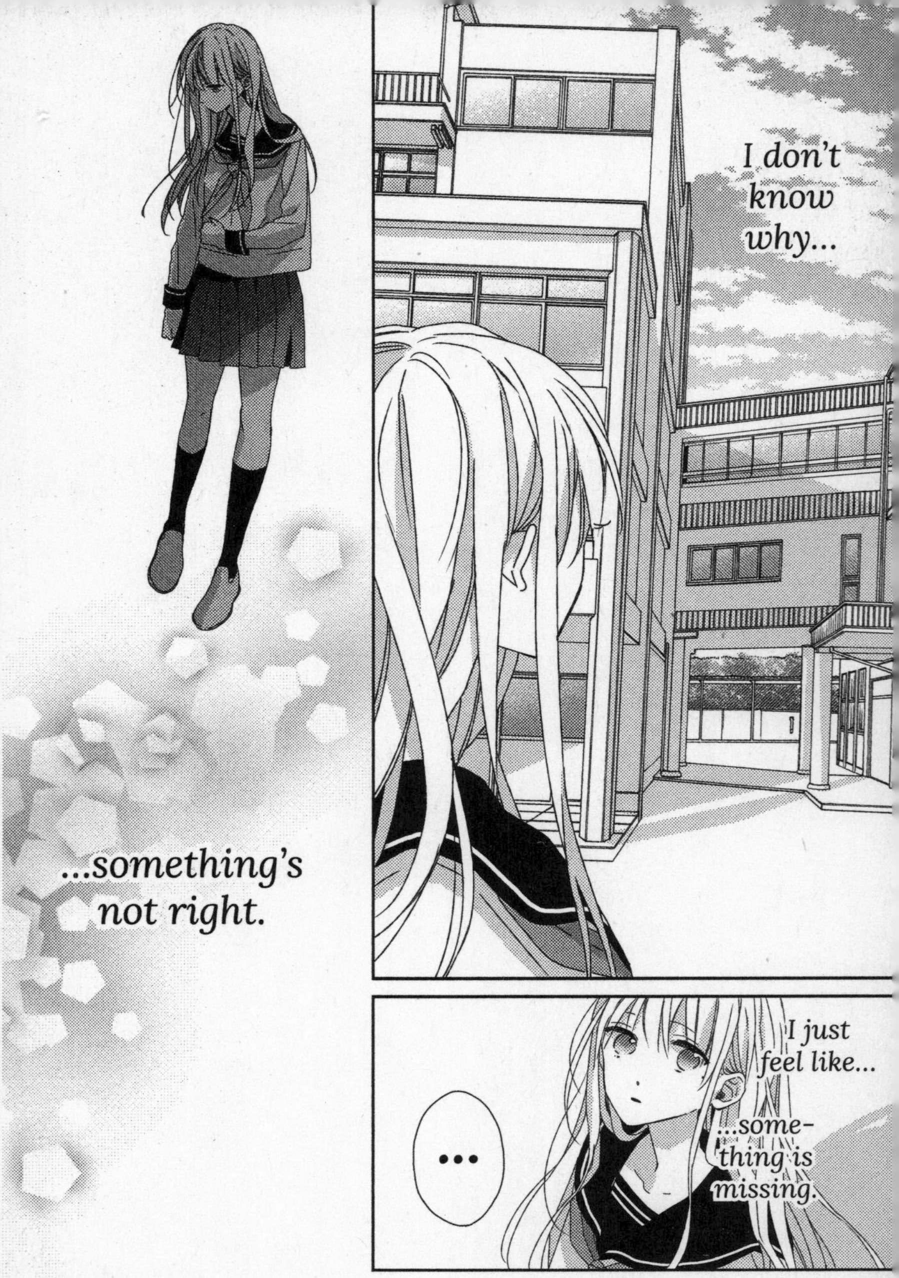
I don't know why...
I just feel like...
...something is missing.
...
...something's not right.

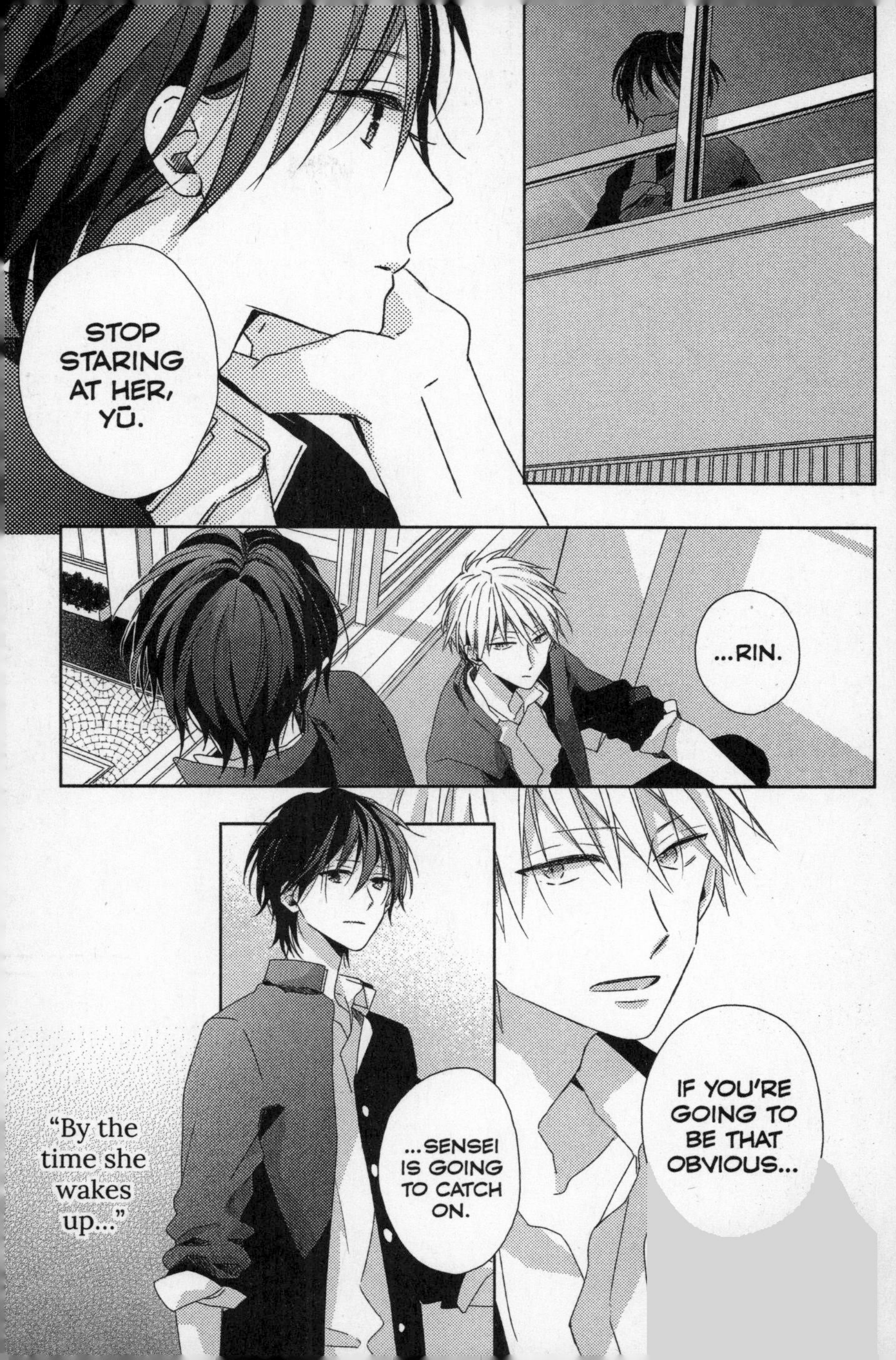
STOP STARING AT HER, YŪ.
...RIN.
IF YOU'RE GOING TO BE THAT OBVIOUS...
...SENSEI IS GOING TO CATCH ON.
"By the time she wakes up..."

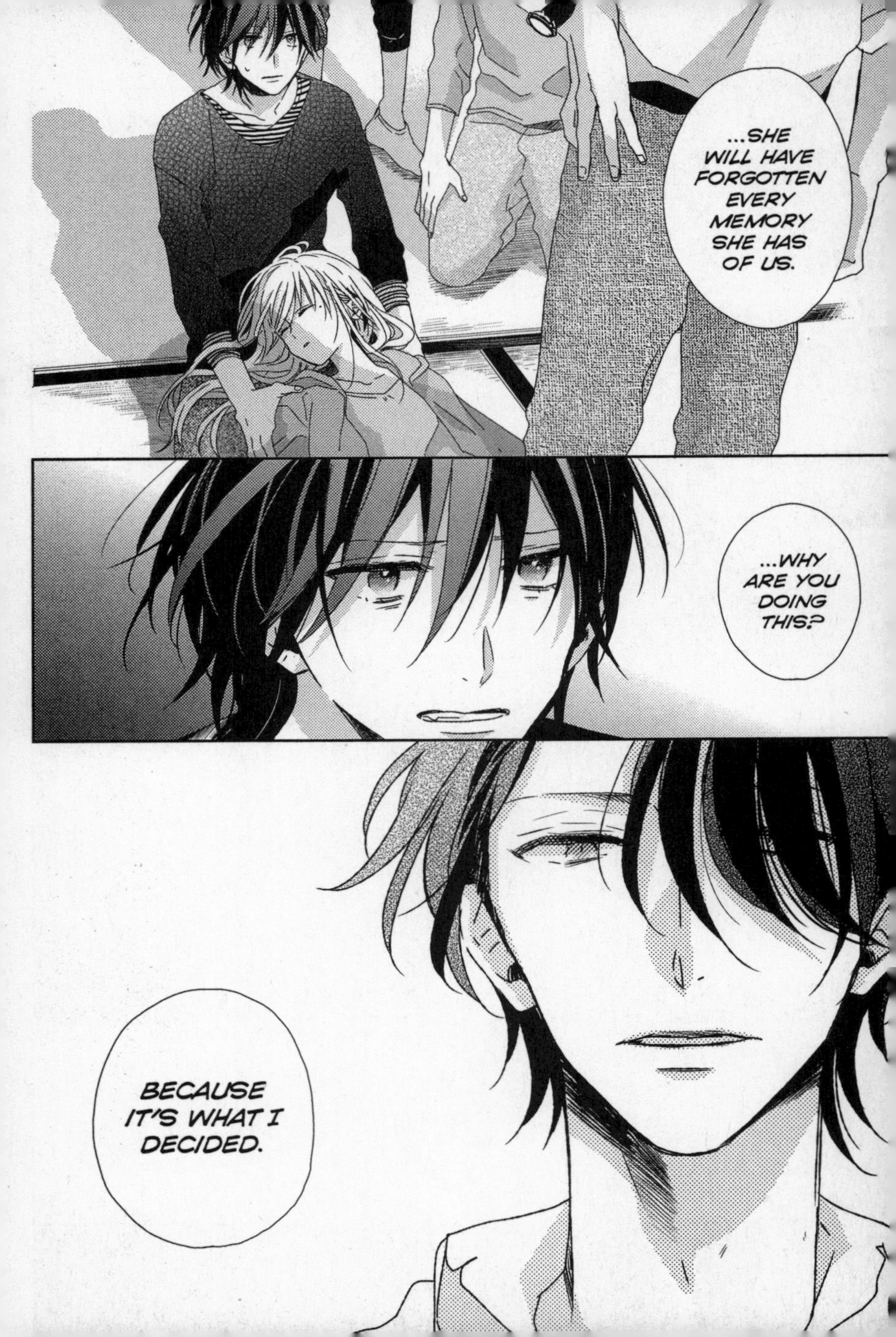
...SHE WILL HAVE FORGOTTEN EVERY MEMORY SHE HAS OF US.
...WHY ARE YOU DOING THIS?
BECAUSE IT'S WHAT I DECIDED.

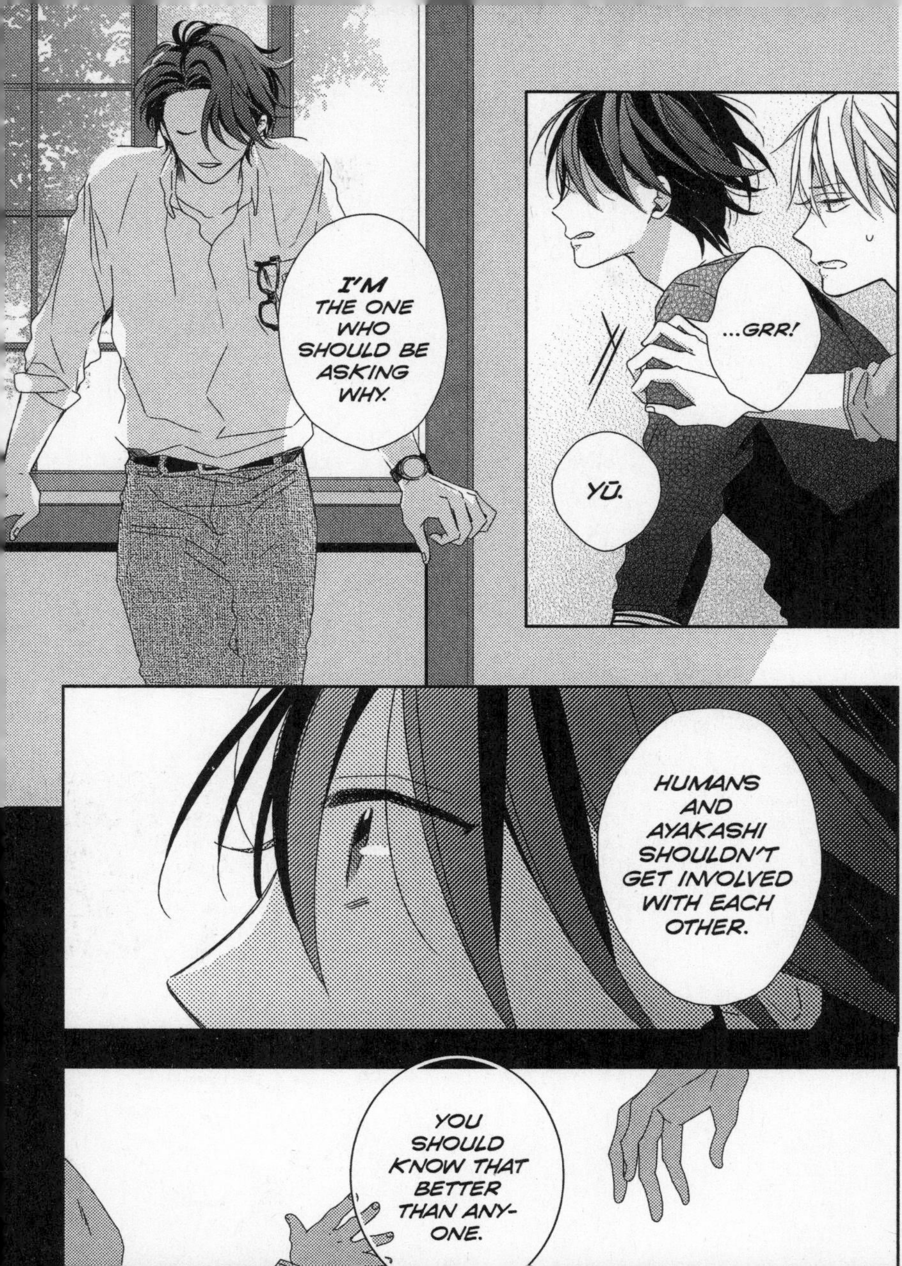
...GRR!
YŪ.
I'M THE ONE WHO SHOULD BE ASKING WHY.
HUMANS AND AYAKASHI SHOULDN'T GET INVOLVED WITH EACH OTHER.
YOU SHOULD KNOW THAT BETTER THAN ANY-ONE.

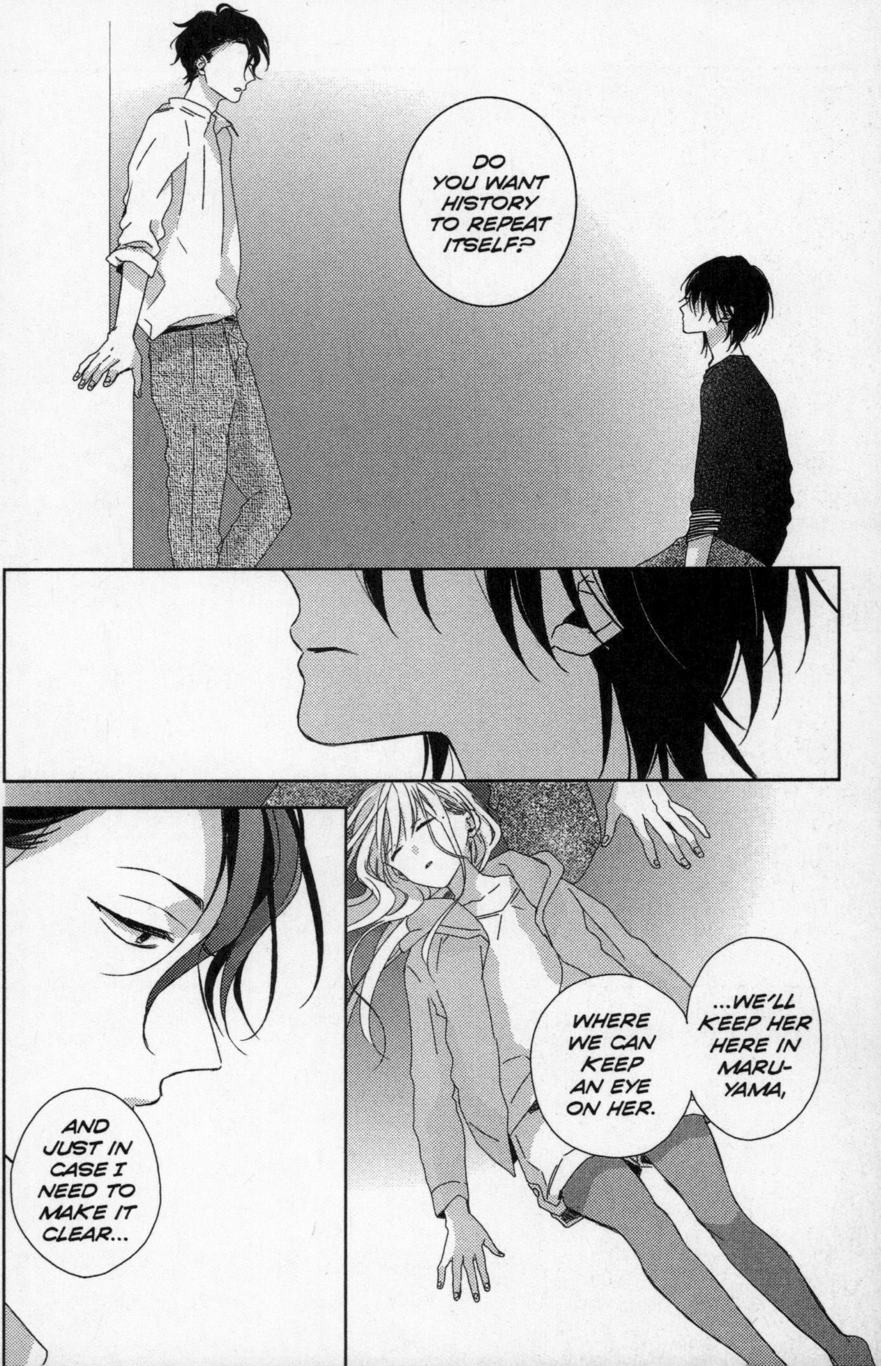
DO YOU WANT HISTORY TO REPEAT ITSELF?
...WE'LL KEEP HER HERE IN MARU-YAMA,
WHERE WE CAN KEEP AN EYE ON HER.
AND JUST IN CASE I NEED TO MAKE IT CLEAR...

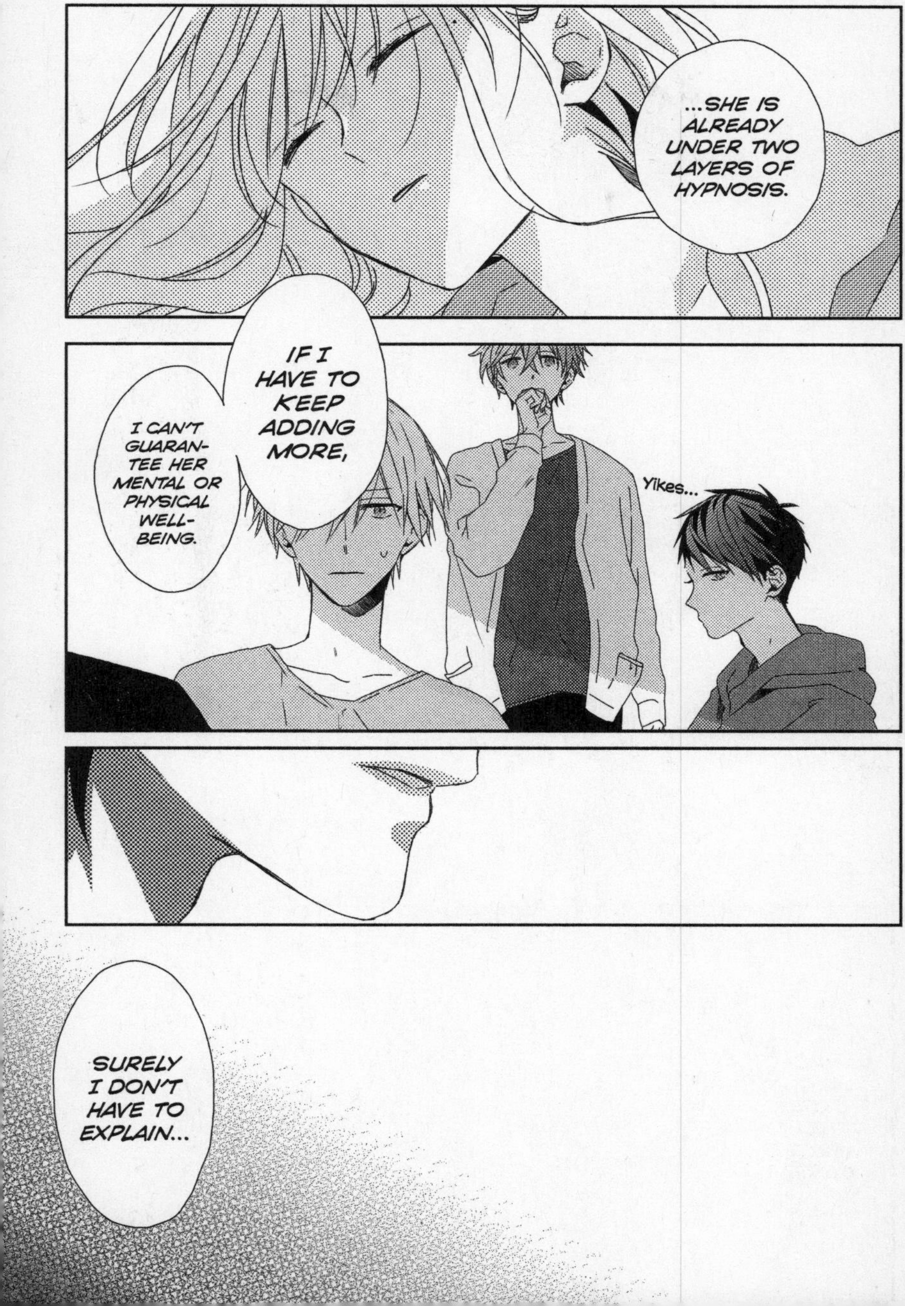
...SHE IS ALREADY UNDER TWO LAYERS OF HYPNOSIS.
IF I HAVE TO KEEP ADDING MORE,
I CAN'T GUARAN-TEE HER MENTAL OR PHYSICAL WELL-BEING.
Yikes...
SURELY I DON'T HAVE TO EXPLAIN...

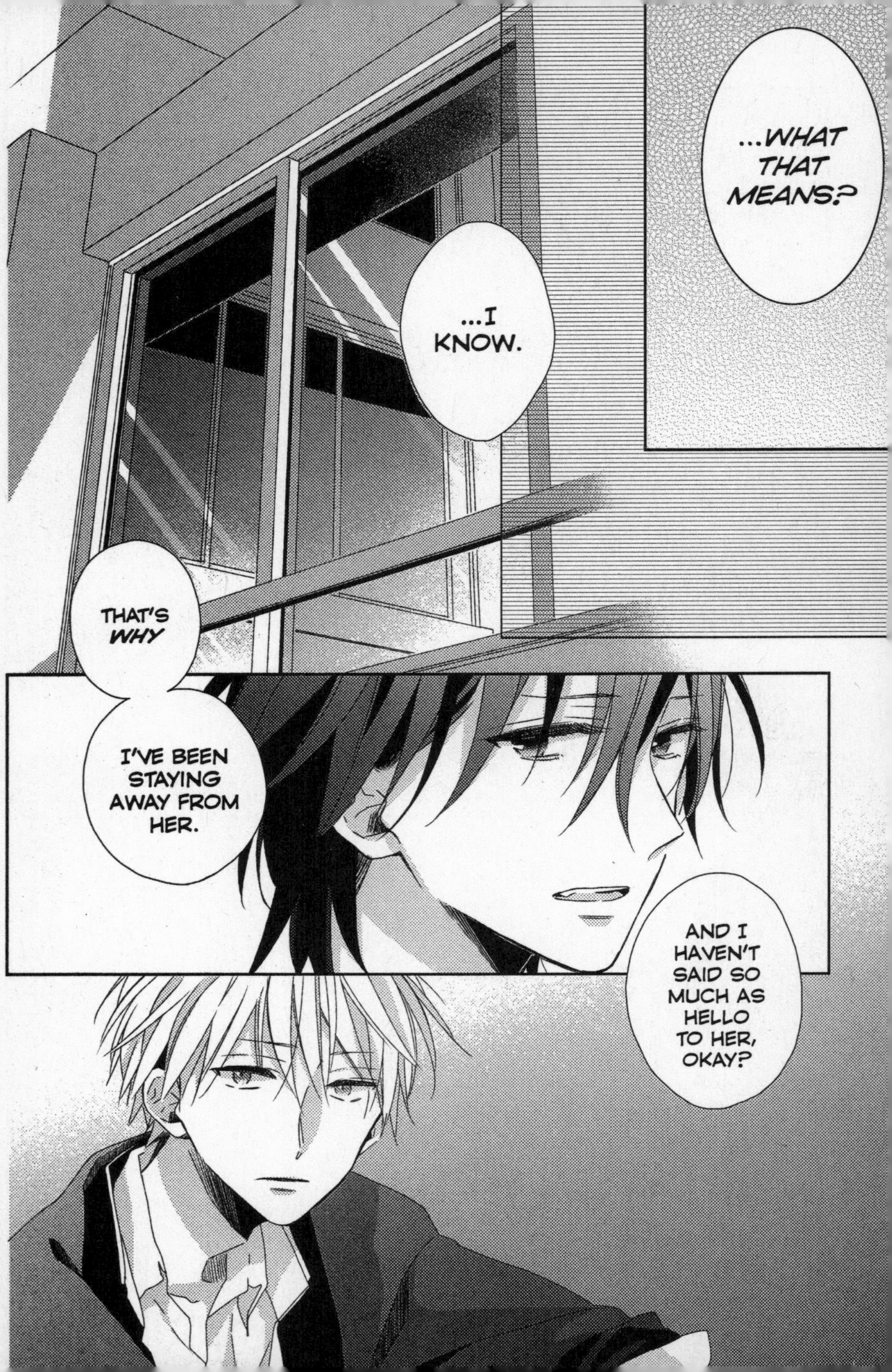
...WHAT THAT MEANS?
...I KNOW.
THAT'S *WHY*
I'VE BEEN STAYING AWAY FROM HER.
AND I HAVEN'T SAID SO MUCH AS HELLO TO HER, OKAY?

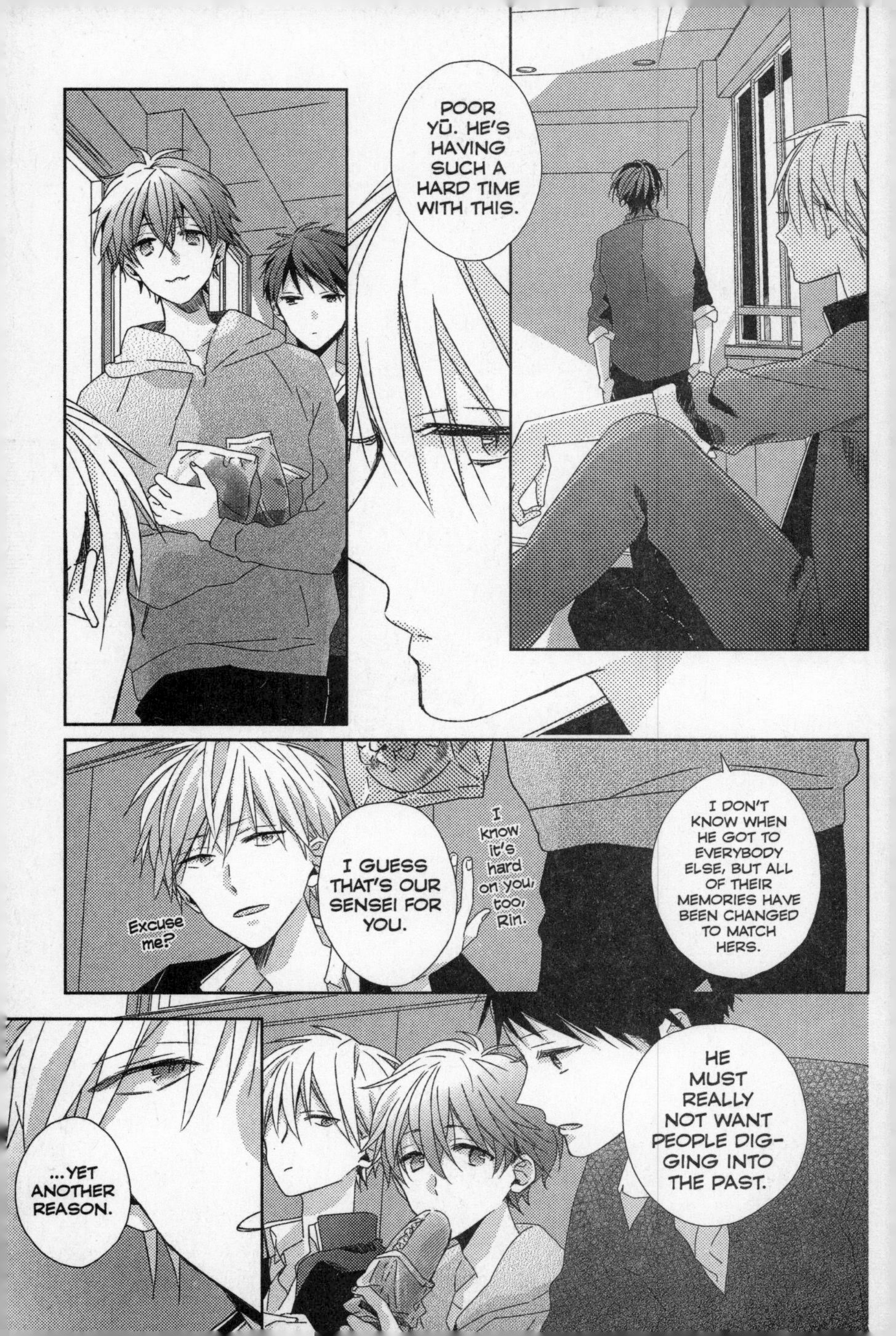
POOR YŪ. HE'S HAVING SUCH A HARD TIME WITH THIS.
I DON'T KNOW WHEN HE GOT TO EVERYBODY ELSE, BUT ALL OF THEIR MEMORIES HAVE BEEN CHANGED TO MATCH HERS.
I know it's hard on you, too, Rin.
I GUESS THAT'S OUR SENSEI FOR YOU.
Excuse me?
HE MUST REALLY NOT WANT PEOPLE DIG-GING INTO THE PAST.
...YET ANOTHER REASON.

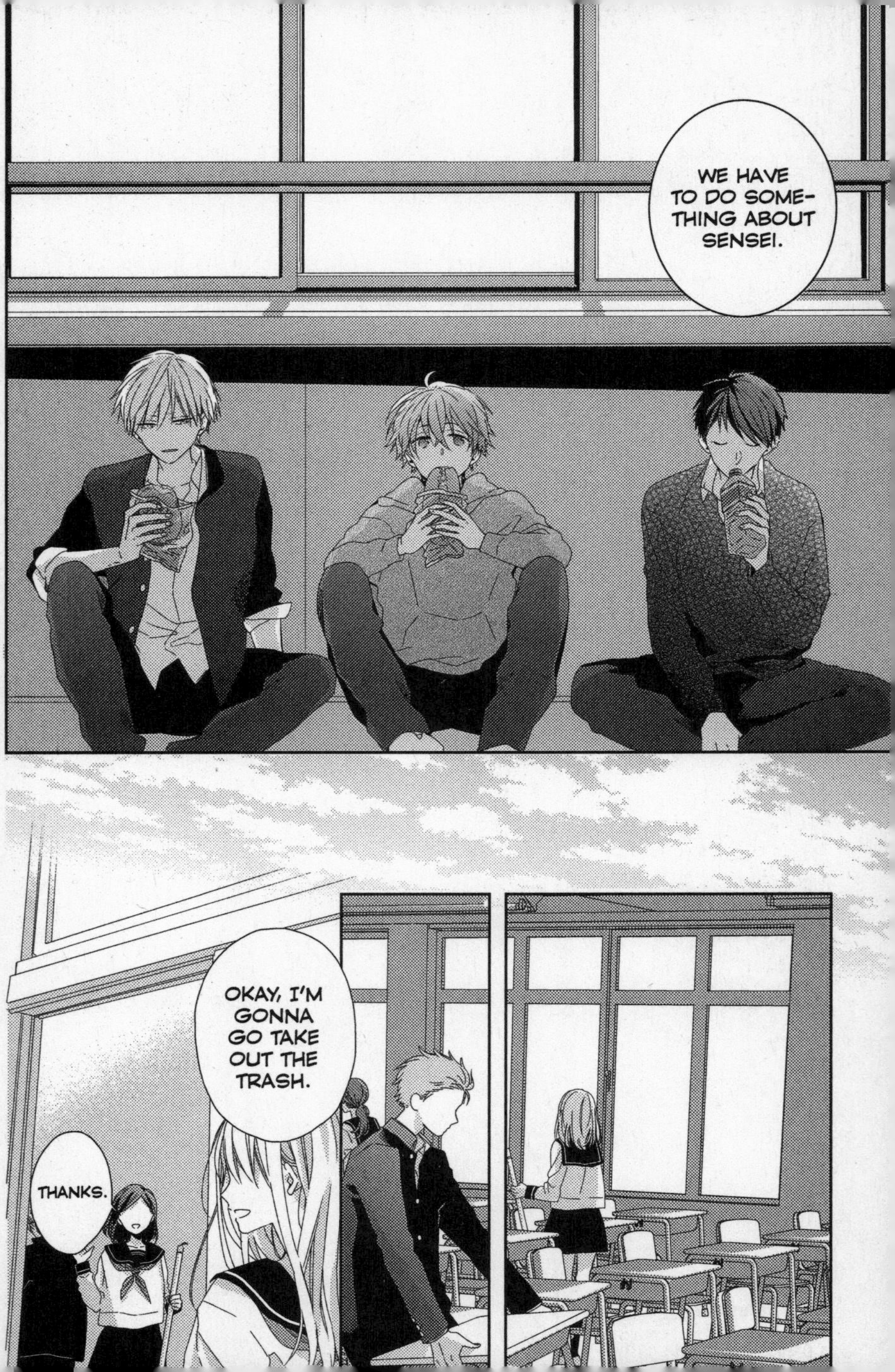
WE HAVE TO DO SOME-THING ABOUT SENSEI.
OKAY, I'M GONNA GO TAKE OUT THE TRASH.
THANKS.

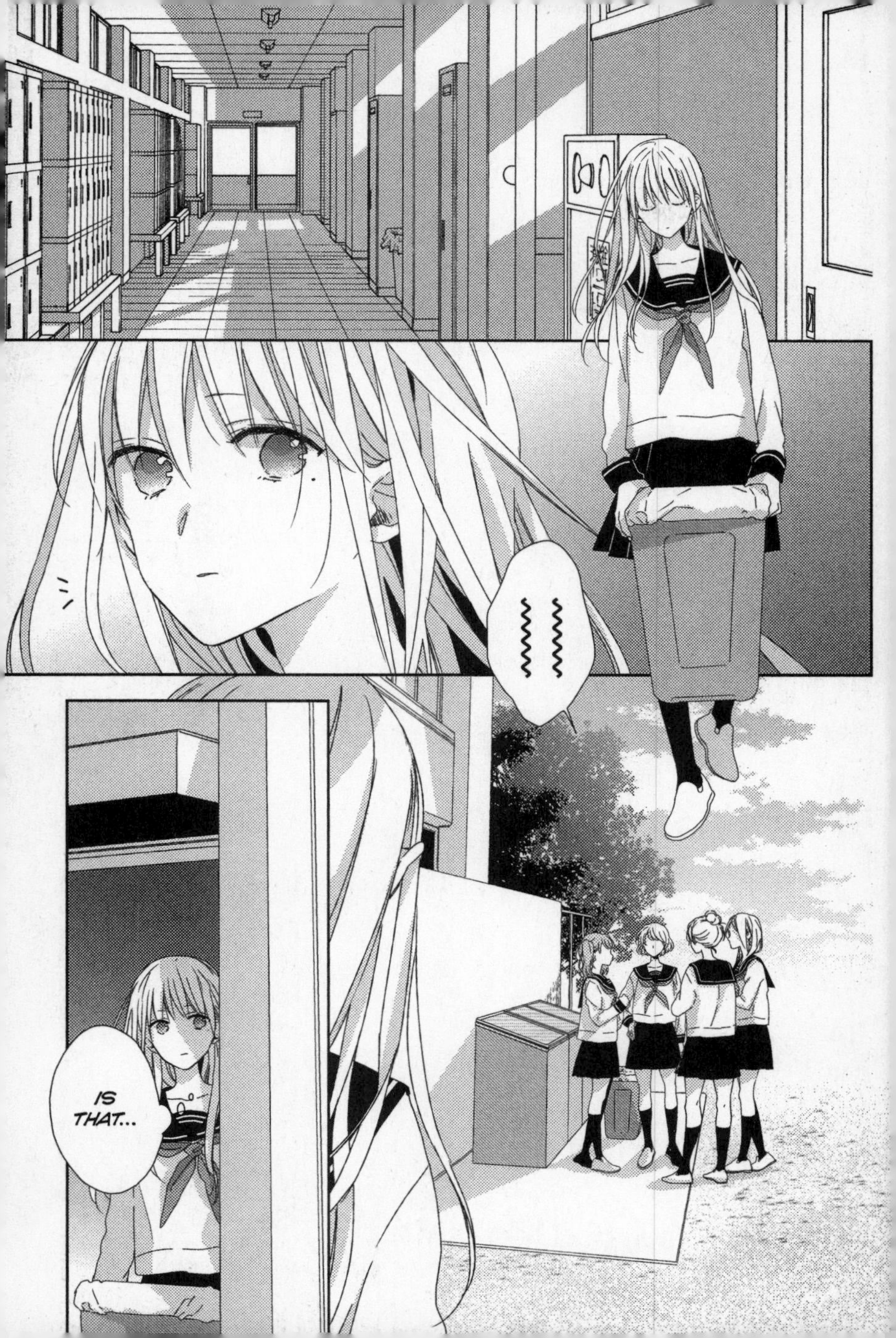
IS THAT...

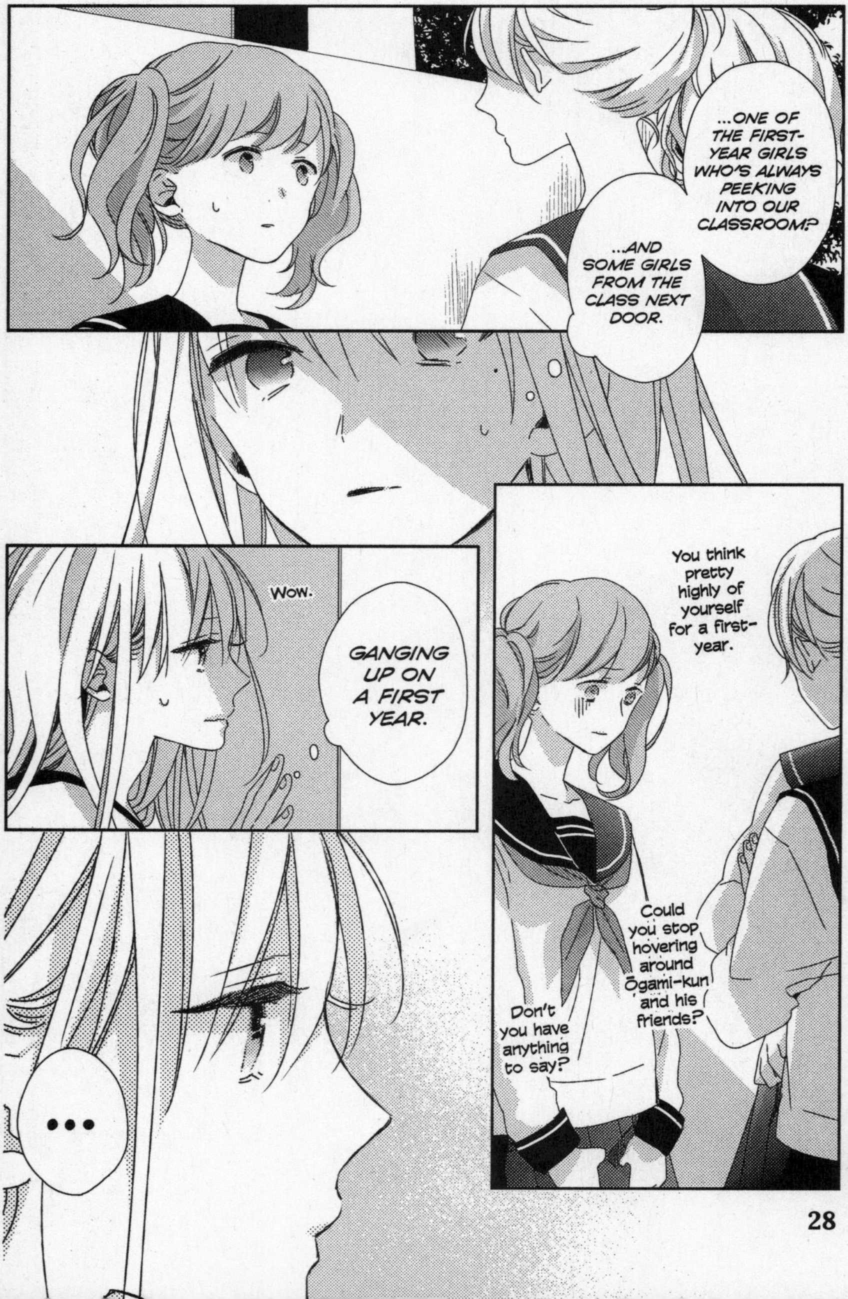
...ONE OF THE FIRST-YEAR GIRLS WHO'S ALWAYS PEEKING INTO OUR CLASSROOM?
...AND SOME GIRLS FROM THE CLASS NEXT DOOR.
You think pretty highly of yourself for a first-year.
Could you stop hovering around Ōgami-kun and his friends?
Don't you have anything to say?
Wow.
GANGING UP ON A FIRST YEAR.
...

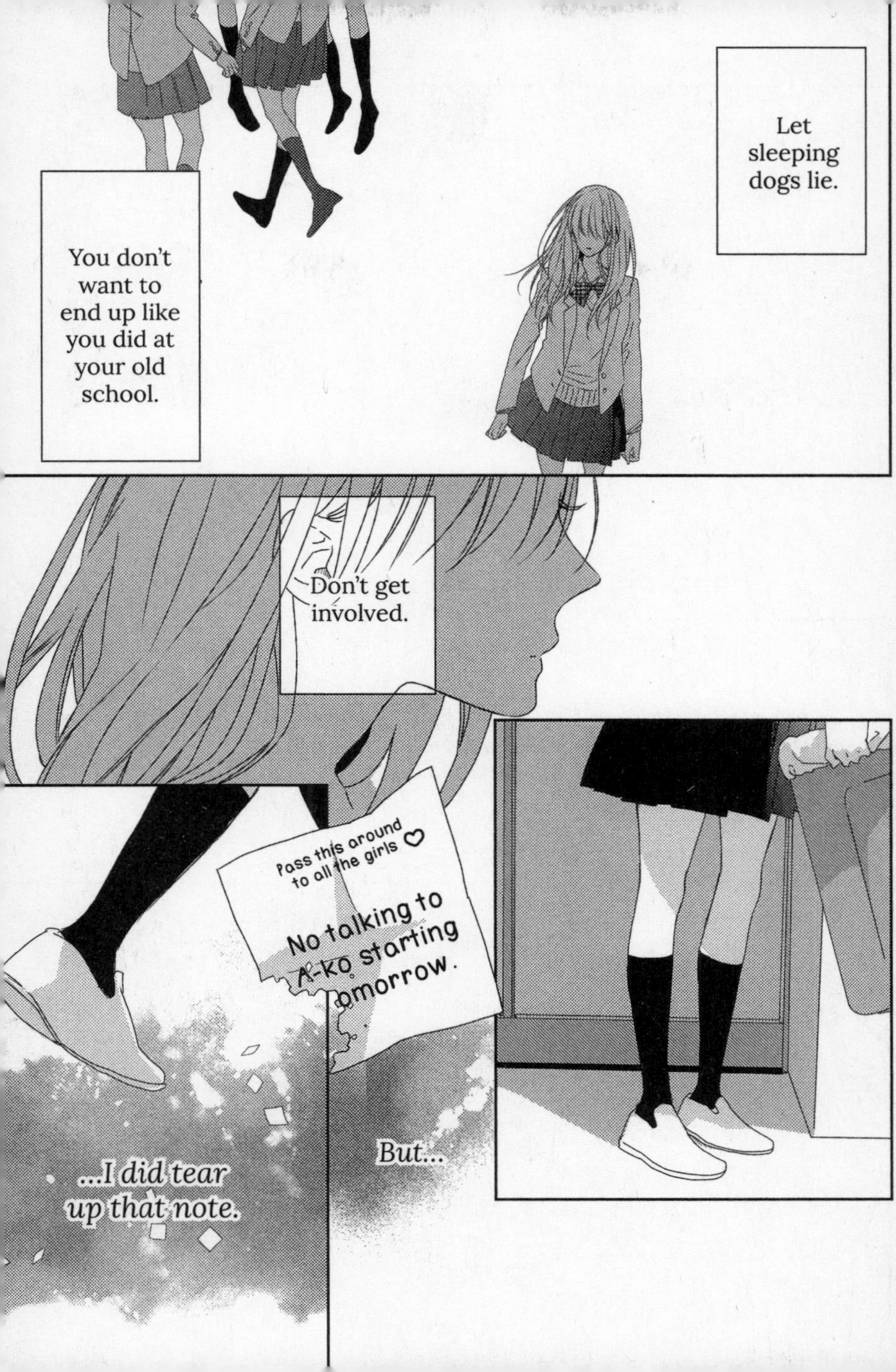
Let sleeping dogs lie.
You don't want to end up like you did at your old school.
Don't get involved.
Pass this around to all the girls ♡
No talking to A-ko starting omorrow.
But...
...I did tear up that note.

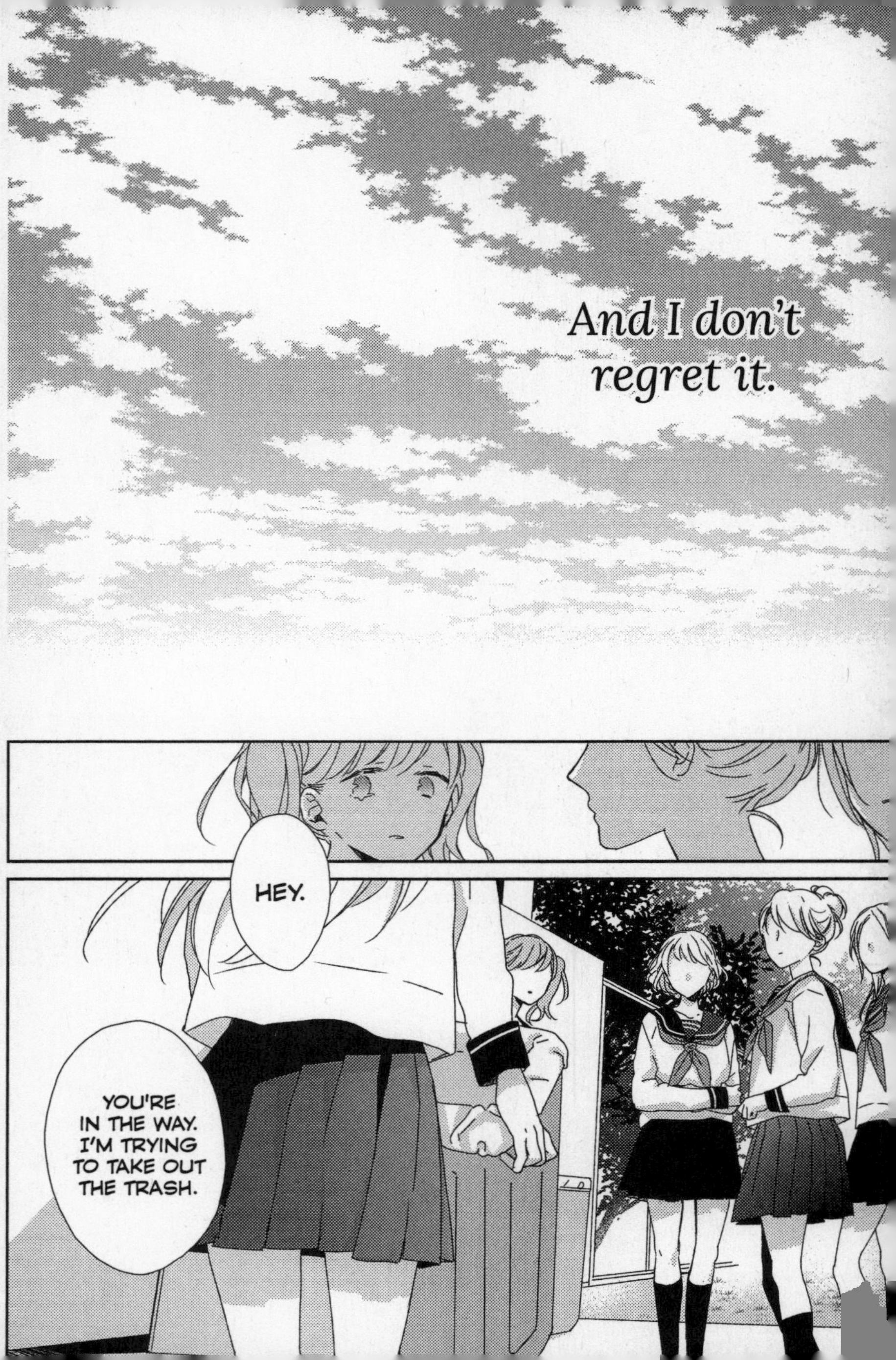
And I don't regret it.
HEY.
YOU'RE IN THE WAY. I'M TRYING TO TAKE OUT THE TRASH.

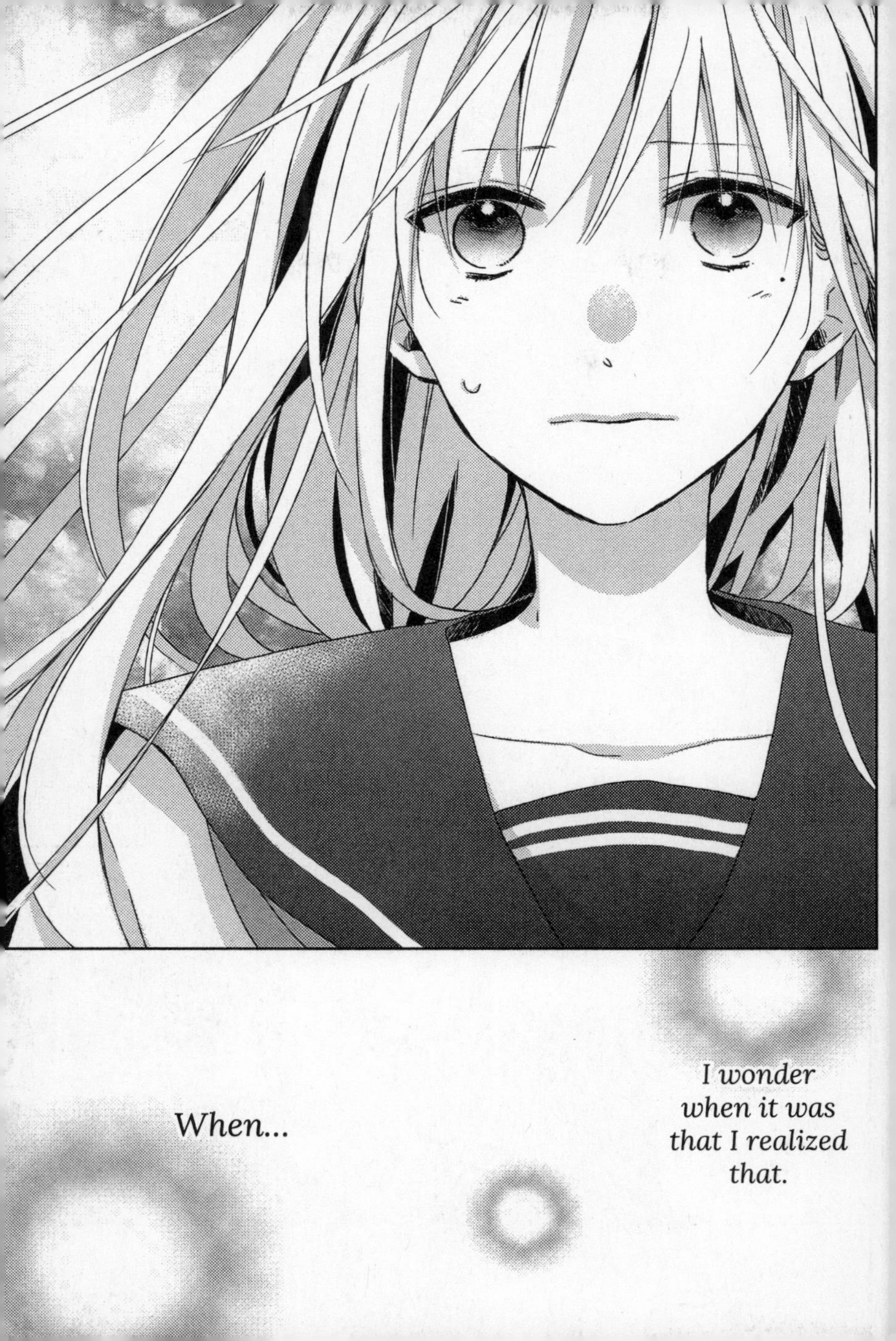
I wonder when it was that I realized that.
When...

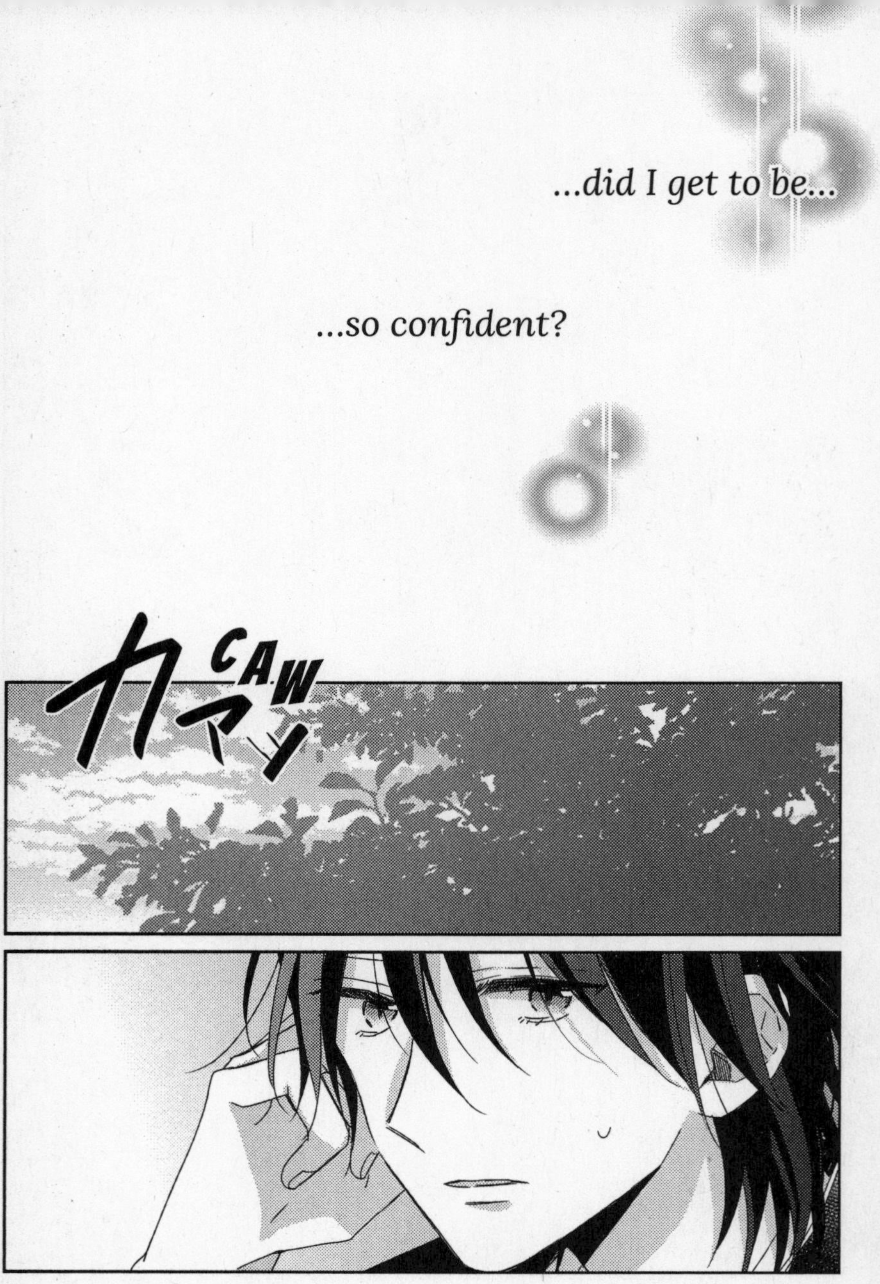
...did I get to be...
...so confident?
CAW

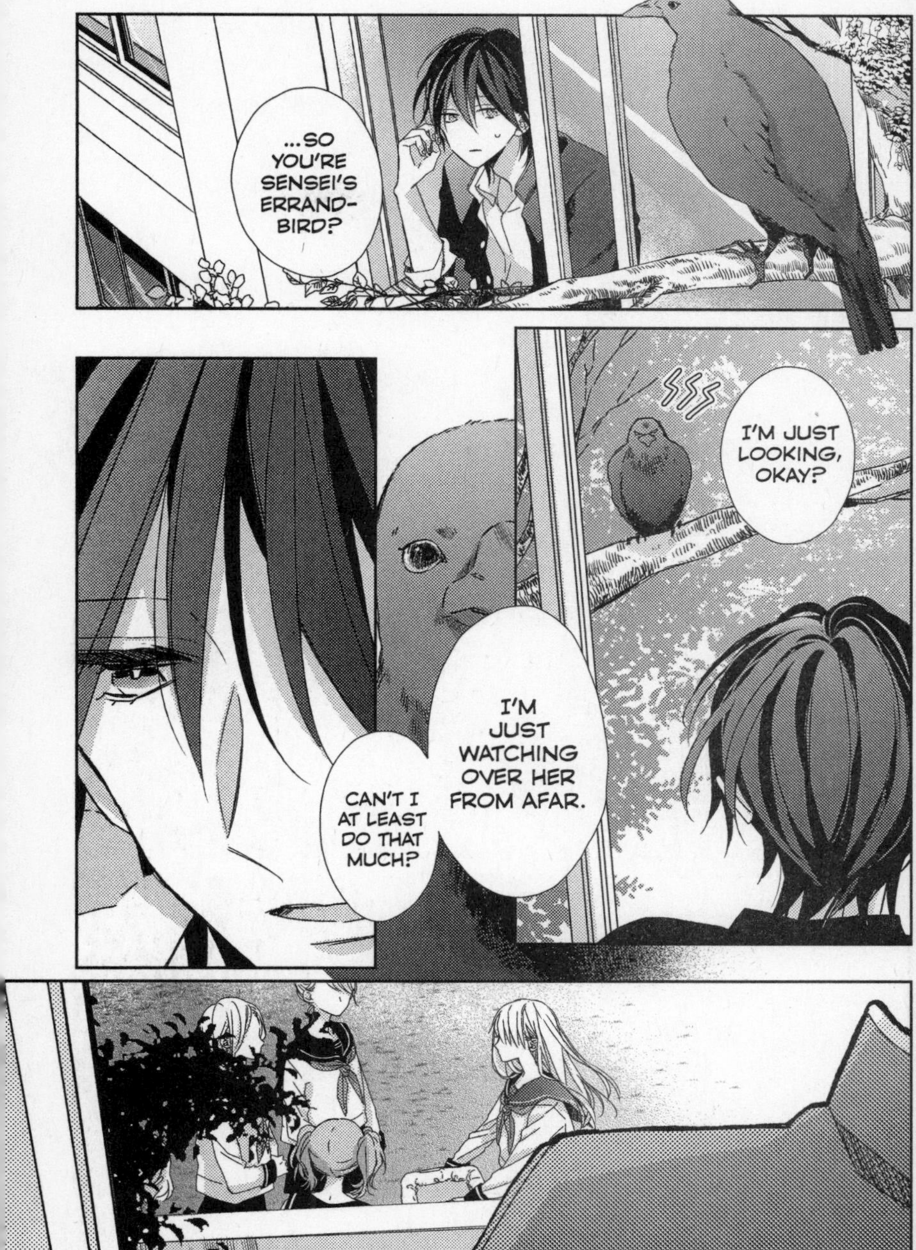
...SO YOU'RE SENSEI'S ERRAND-BIRD?
I'M JUST LOOKING, OKAY?
I'M JUST WATCHING OVER HER FROM AFAR.
CAN'T I AT LEAST DO THAT MUCH?

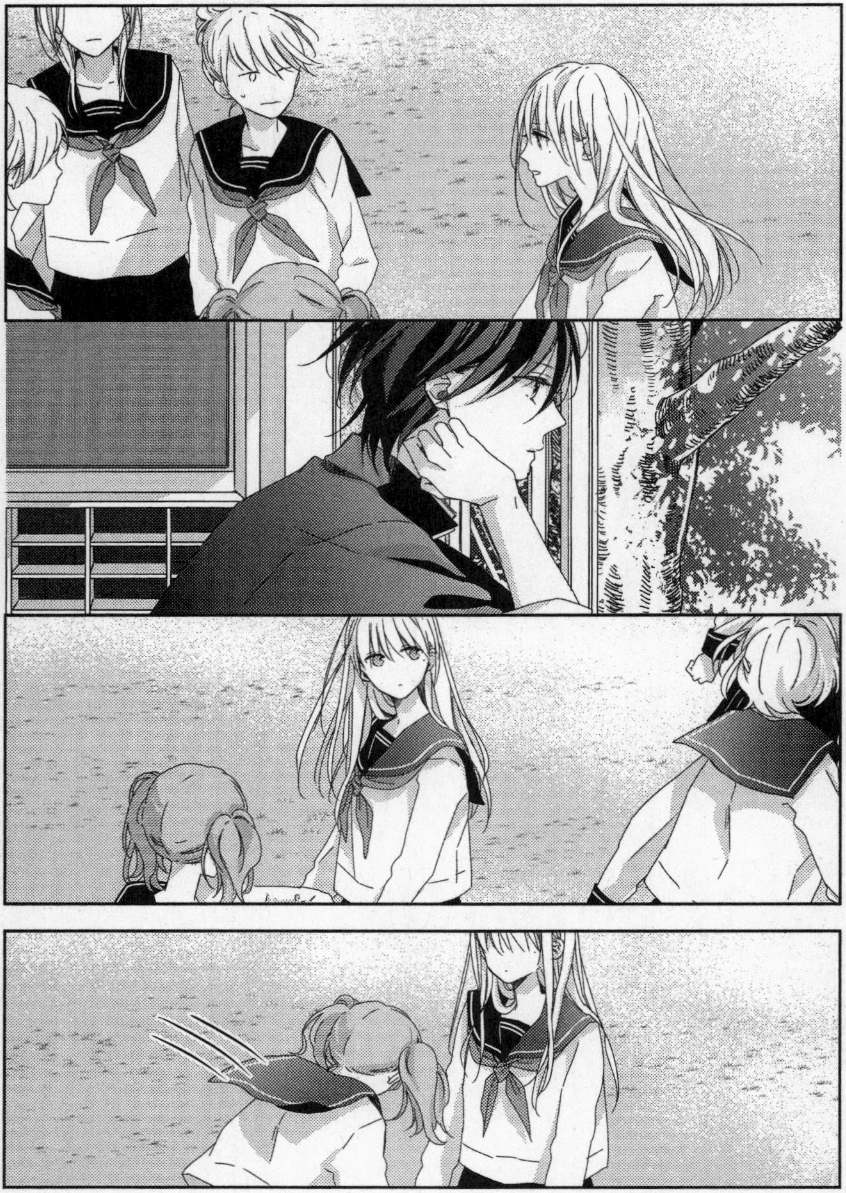

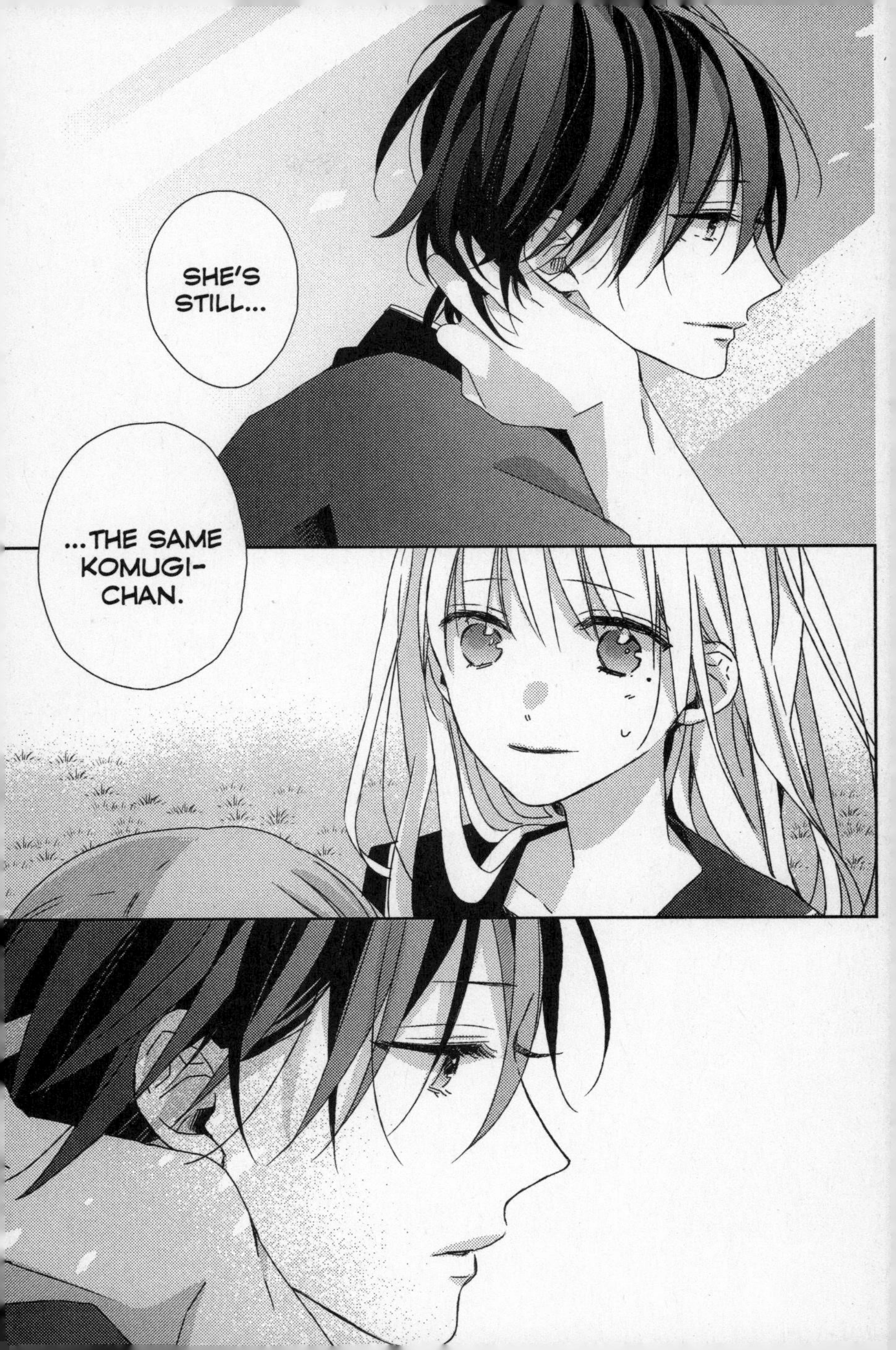
SHE'S STILL...
...THE SAME KOMUGI-CHAN.

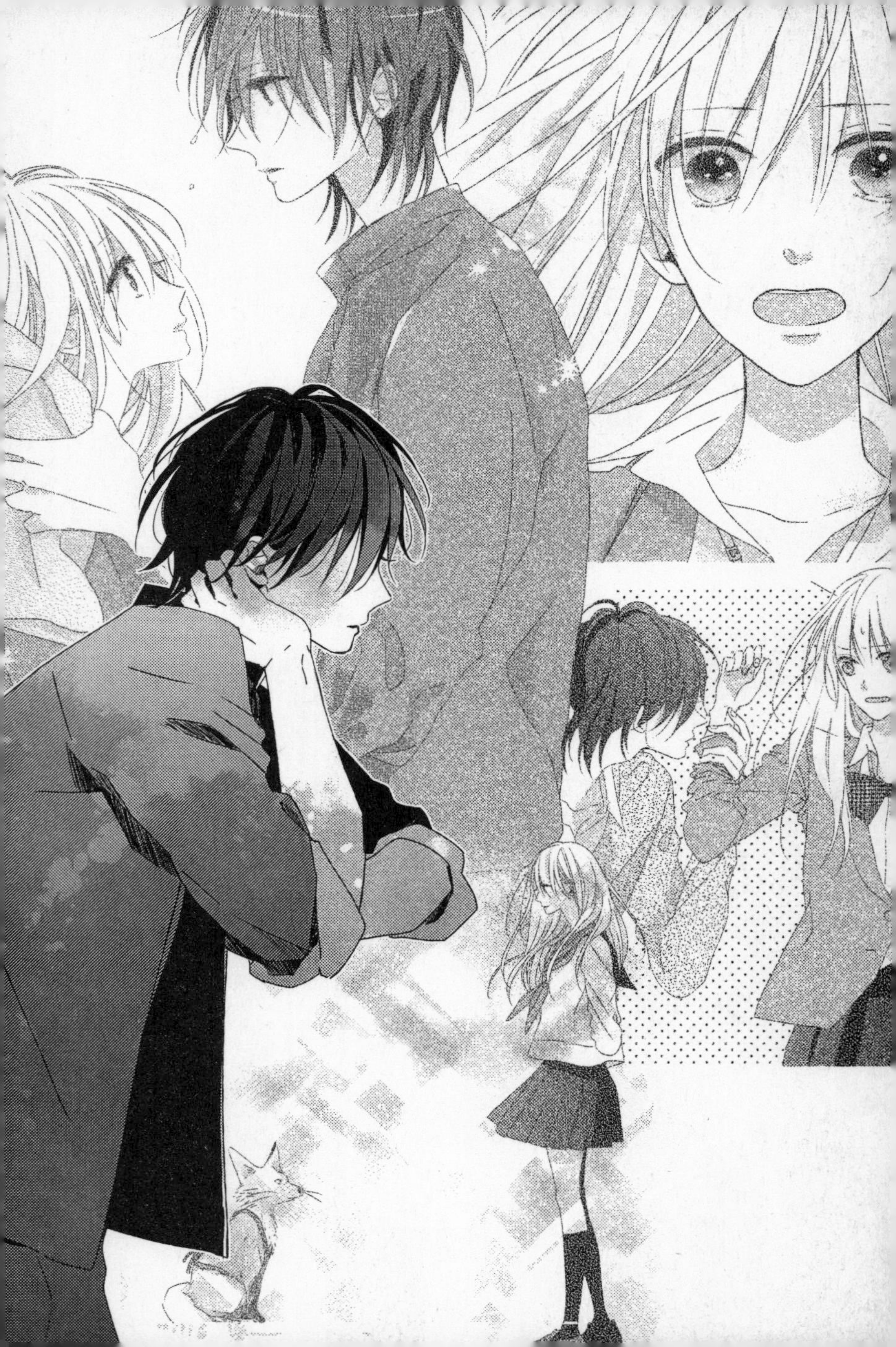

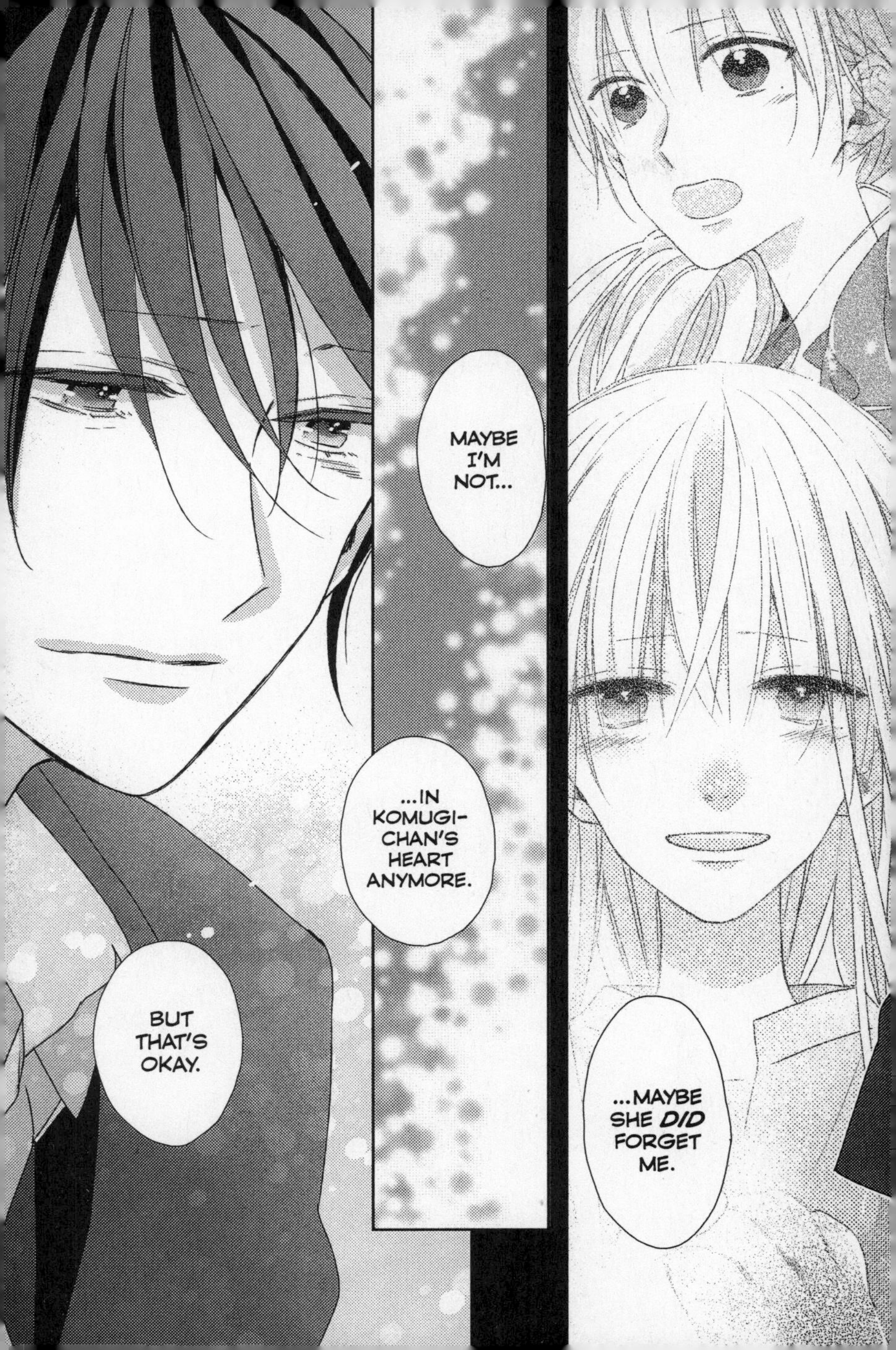
...MAYBE SHE *DID* FORGET ME.
MAYBE I'M NOT...
...IN KOMUGI-CHAN'S HEART ANYMORE.
BUT THAT'S OKAY.

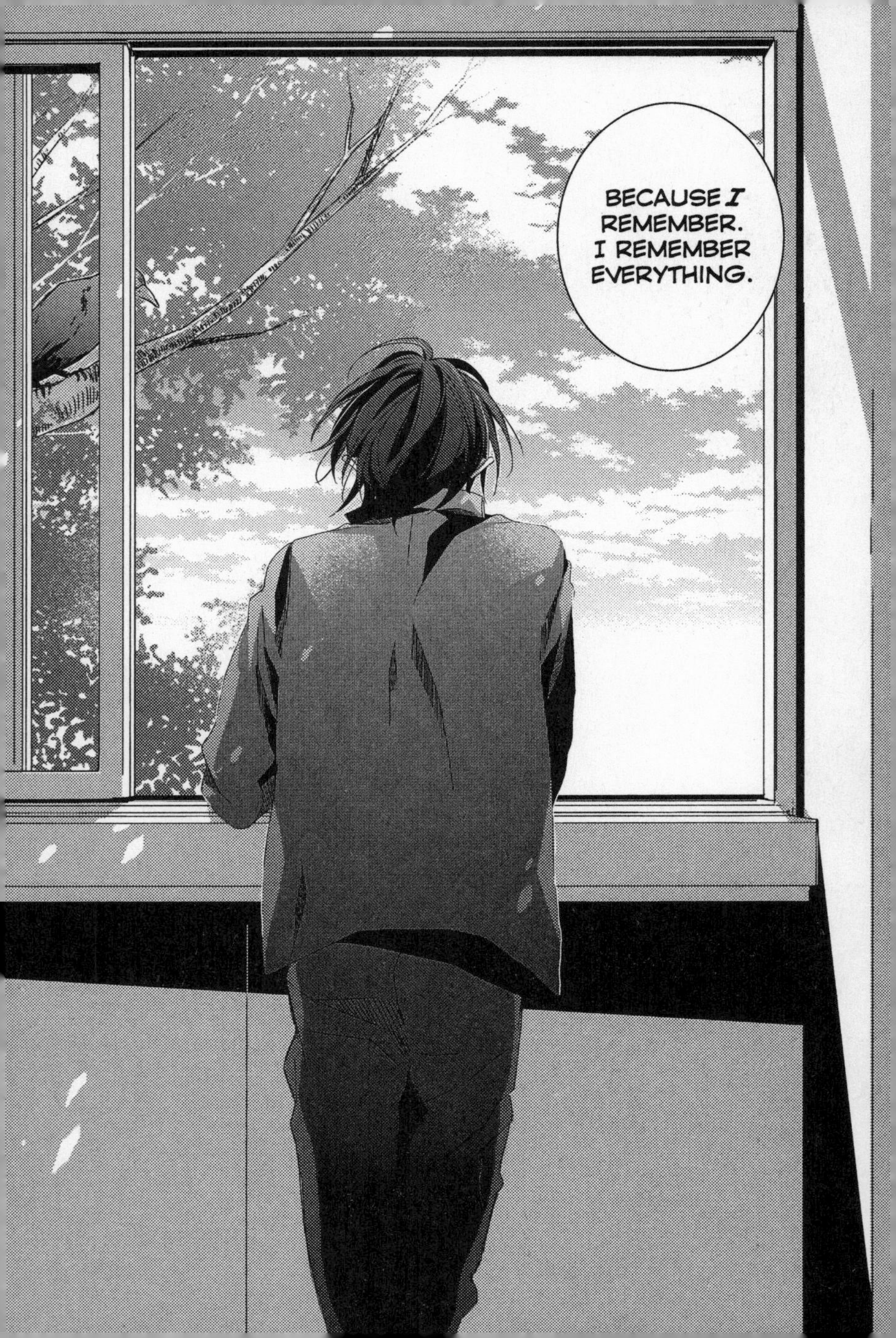
BECAUSE *I* REMEMBER. I REMEMBER EVERYTHING.

Chapter 15

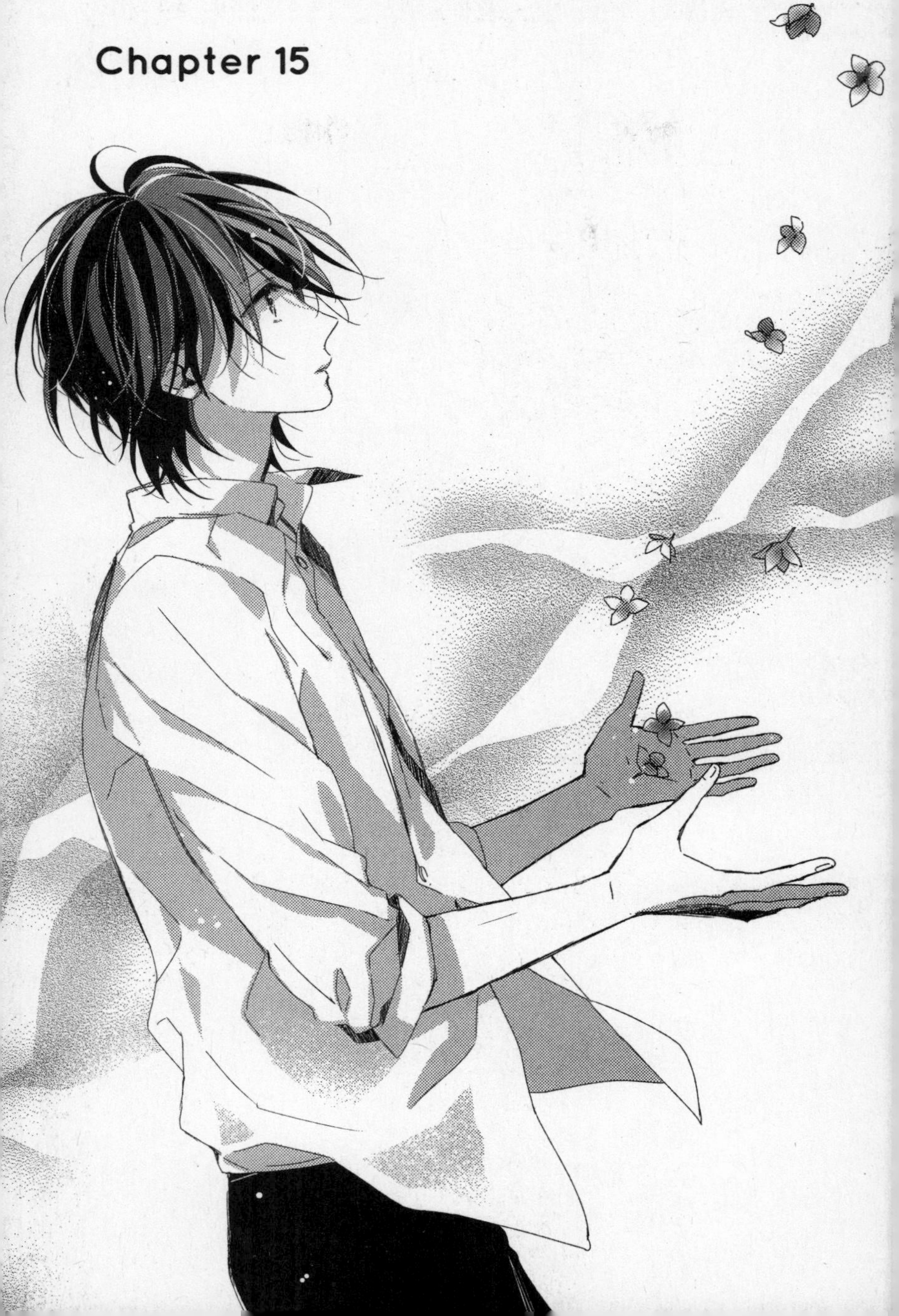

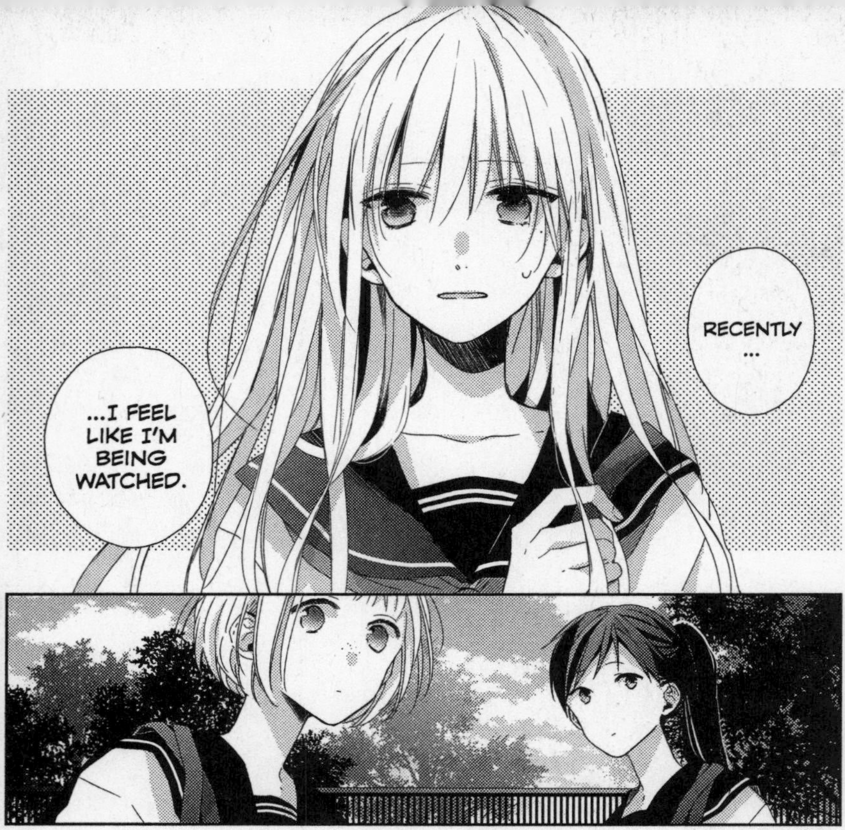
RECENTLY ...
...I FEEL LIKE I'M BEING WATCHED.

That Wolf-Boy is Mine!

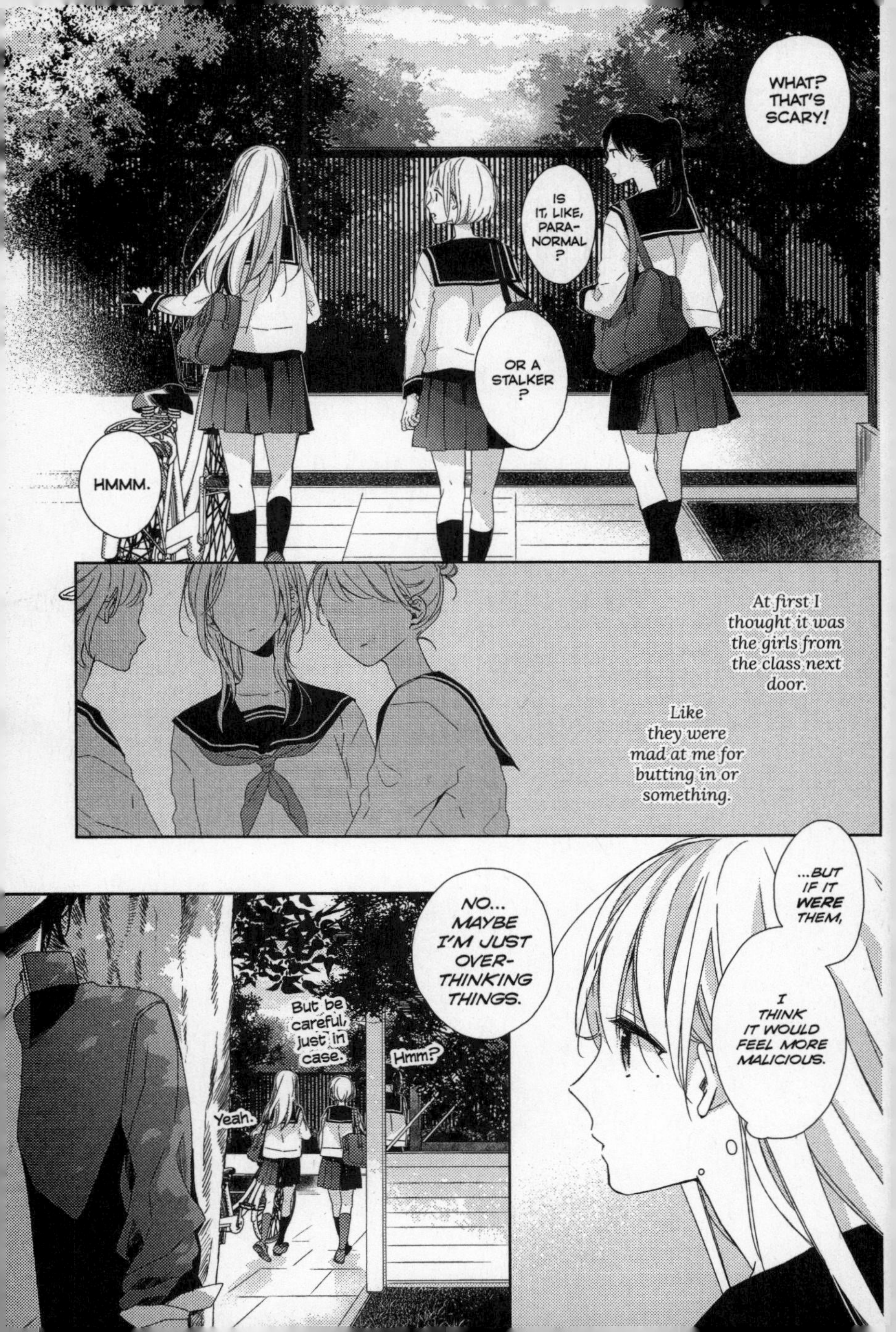
WHAT? THAT'S SCARY!
IS IT, LIKE, PARA-NORMAL?
OR A STALKER?
HMMM.
At first I thought it was the girls from the class next door.
Like they were mad at me for butting in or something.
...BUT IF IT WERE THEM,
I THINK IT WOULD FEEL MORE MALICIOUS.
NO... MAYBE I'M JUST OVER-THINKING THINGS.
Hmm?
But be careful, just in case.
Yeah.

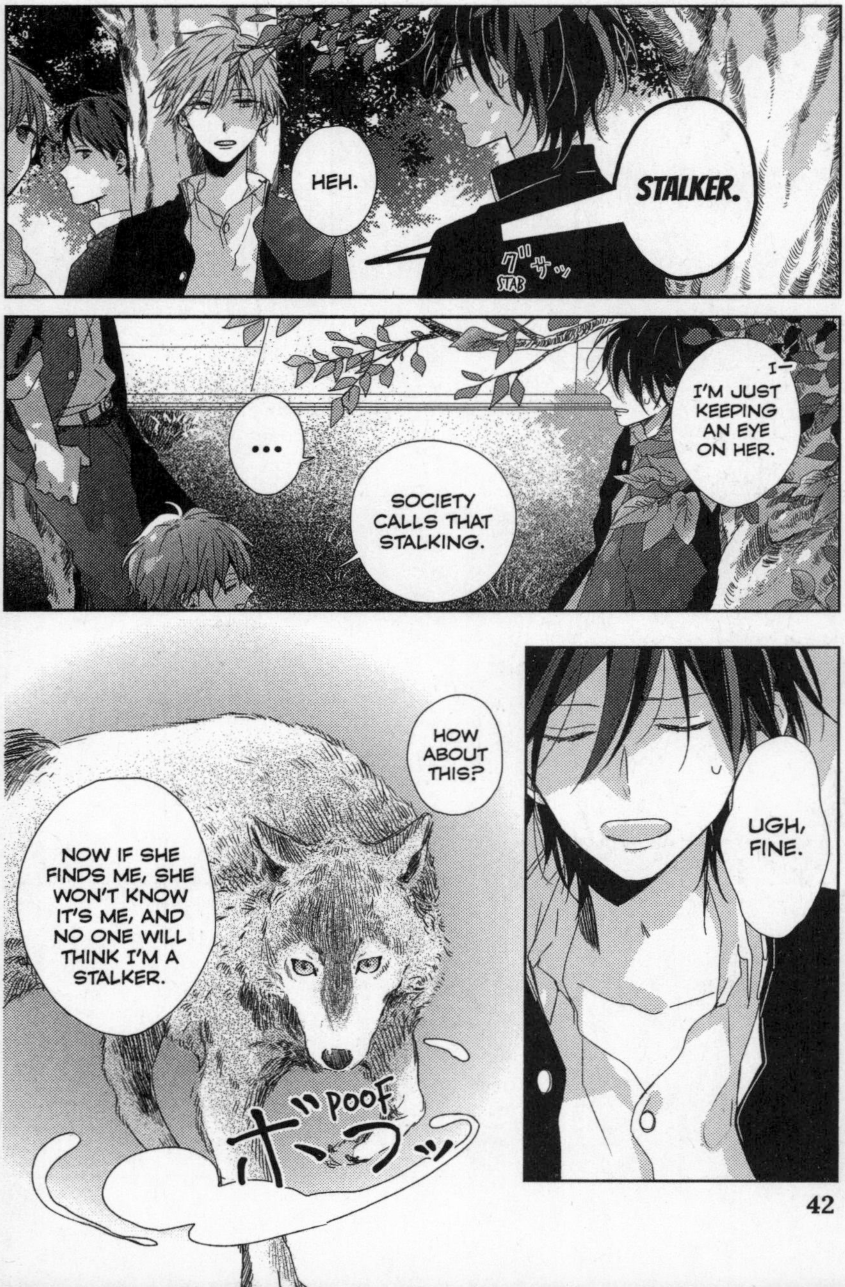
STALKER.
グサッ STAB
HEH.
I— I'M JUST KEEPING AN EYE ON HER.
SOCIETY CALLS THAT STALKING.
...
UGH, FINE.
HOW ABOUT THIS?
NOW IF SHE FINDS ME, SHE WON'T KNOW IT'S ME, AND NO ONE WILL THINK I'M A STALKER.
ボンッ POOF

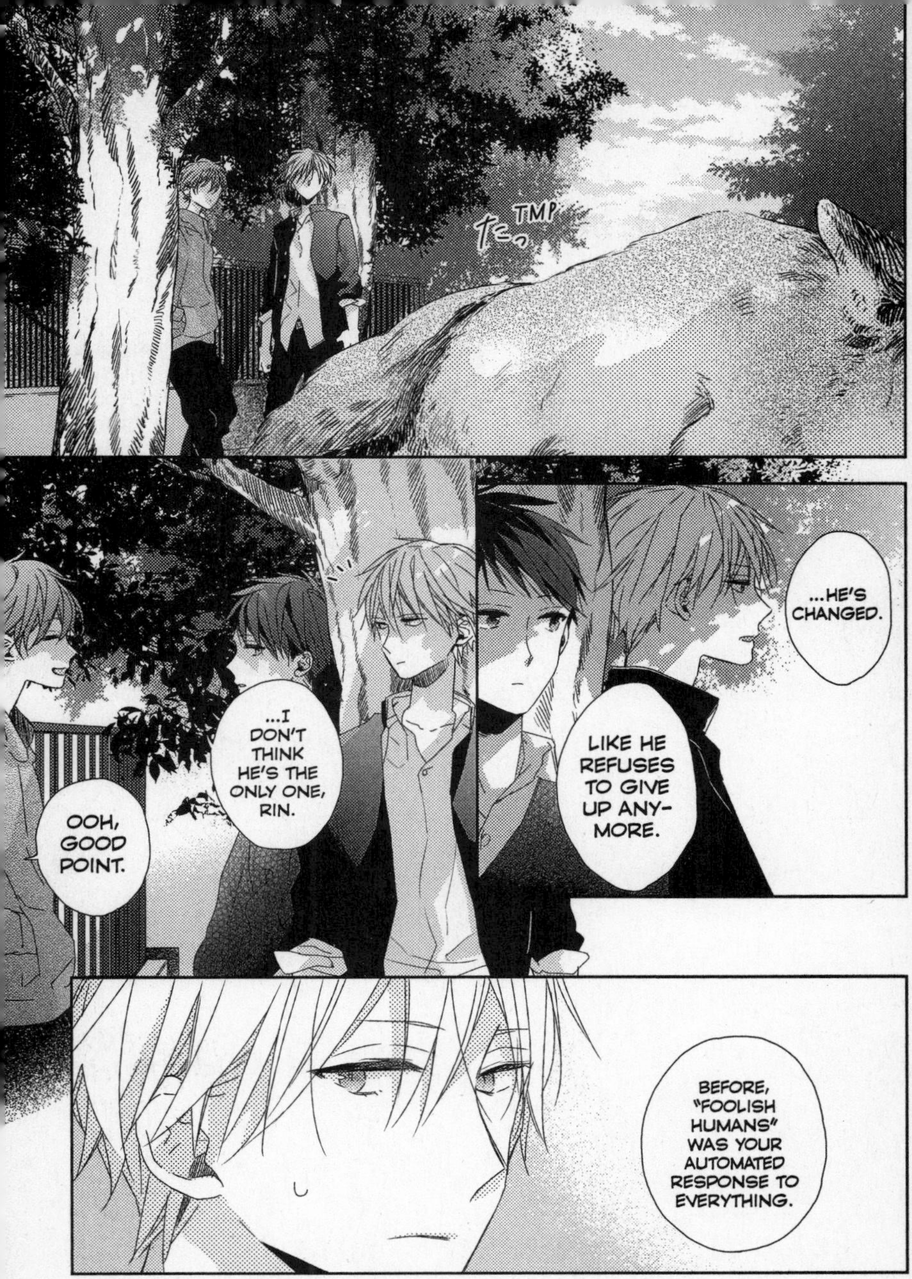
TMP
...HE'S CHANGED.
LIKE HE REFUSES TO GIVE UP ANY-MORE.
...I DON'T THINK HE'S THE ONLY ONE, RIN.
OOH, GOOD POINT.
BEFORE, "FOOLISH HUMANS" WAS YOUR AUTOMATED RESPONSE TO EVERYTHING.

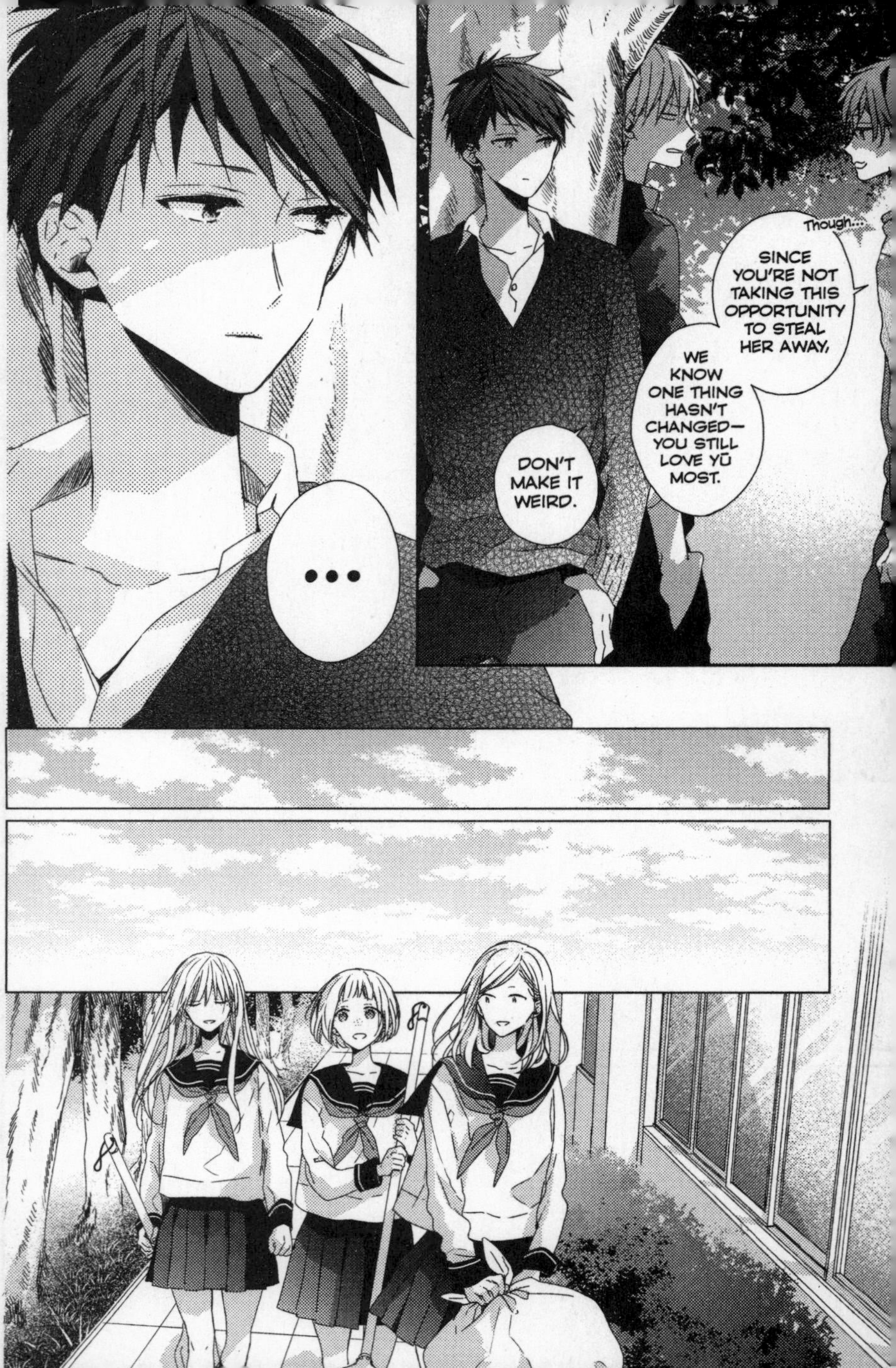
Though...
SINCE YOU'RE NOT TAKING THIS OPPORTUNITY TO STEAL HER AWAY,
WE KNOW ONE THING HASN'T CHANGED— YOU STILL LOVE YŪ MOST.
DON'T MAKE IT WEIRD.
...

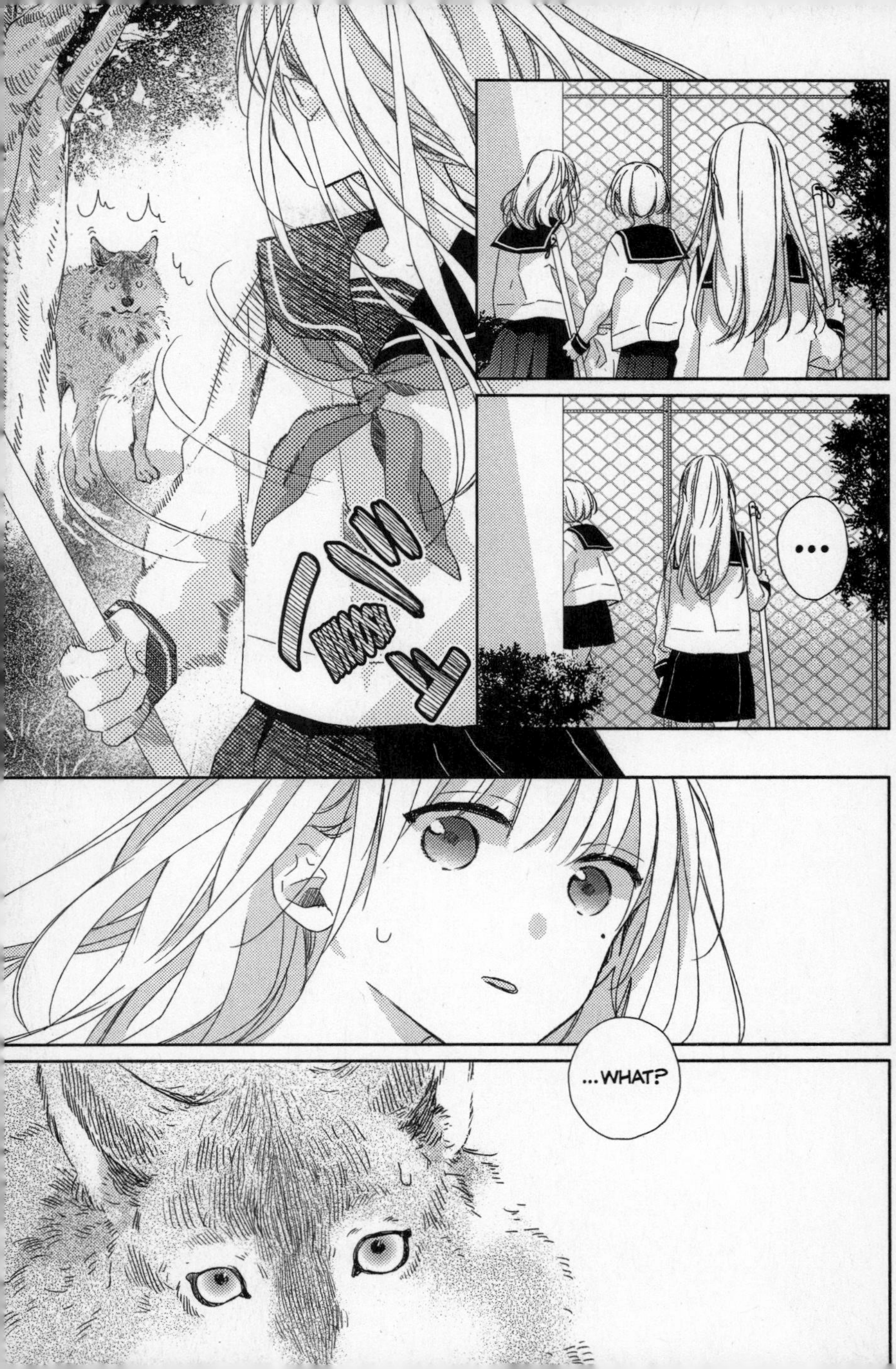
...
...WHAT?

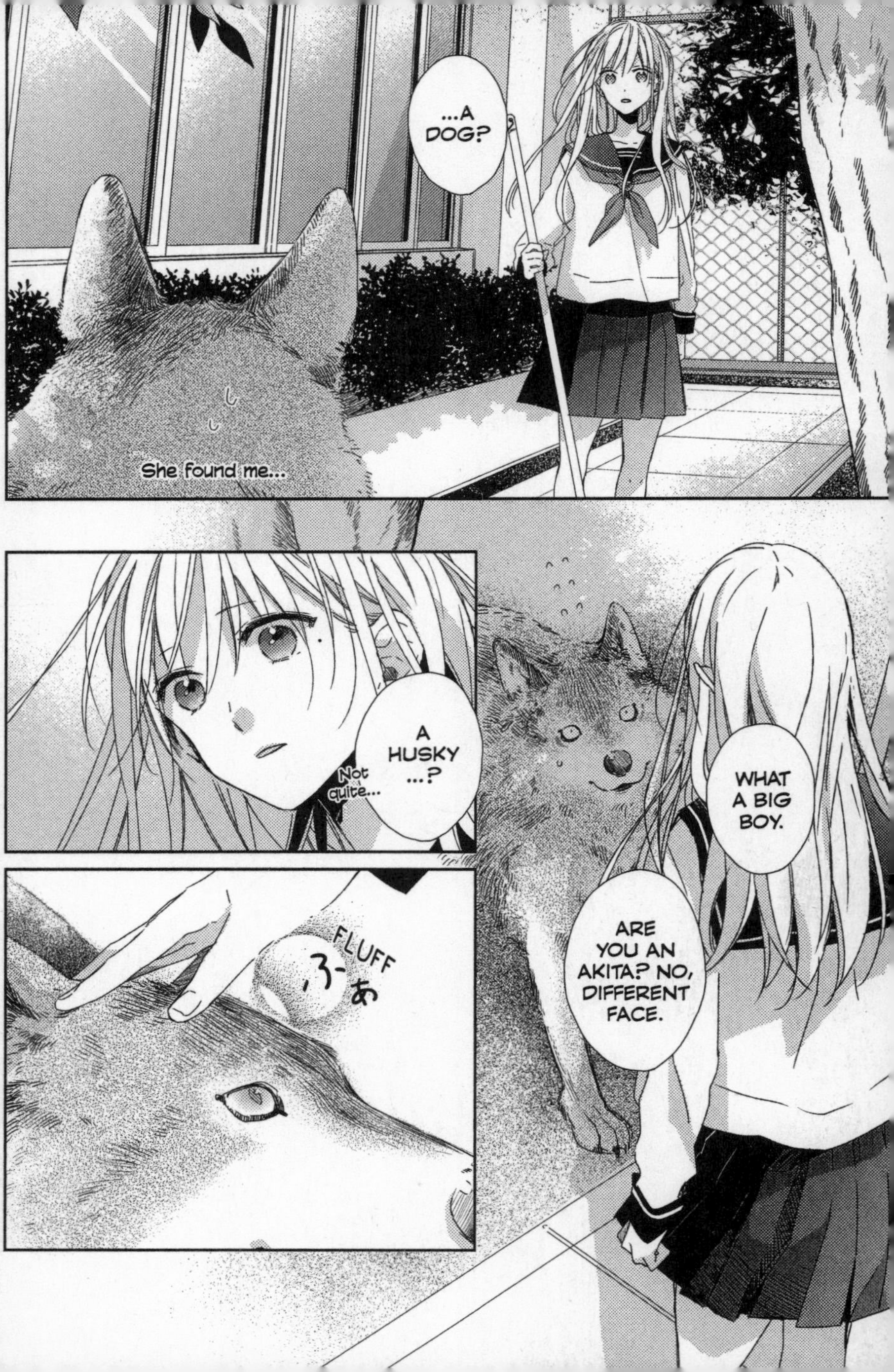

...A DOG?
She found me...
WHAT A BIG BOY.
ARE YOU AN AKITA? NO, DIFFERENT FACE.
A HUSKY ...?
Not quite...
FLUFF
ふーあ

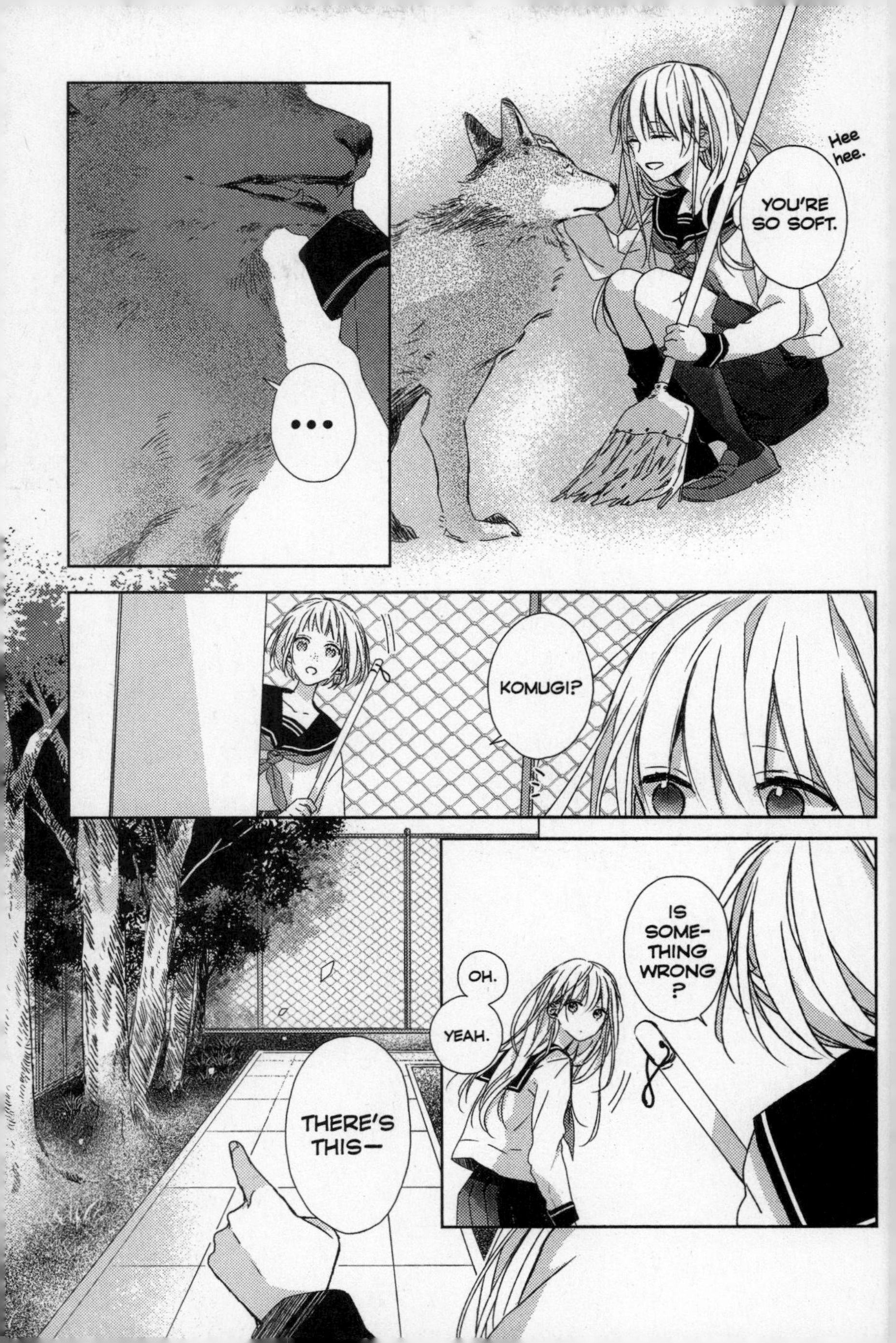
YOU'RE SO SOFT.
Hee hee.
...
KOMUGI?
IS SOME-THING WRONG?
OH.
YEAH.
THERE'S THIS—

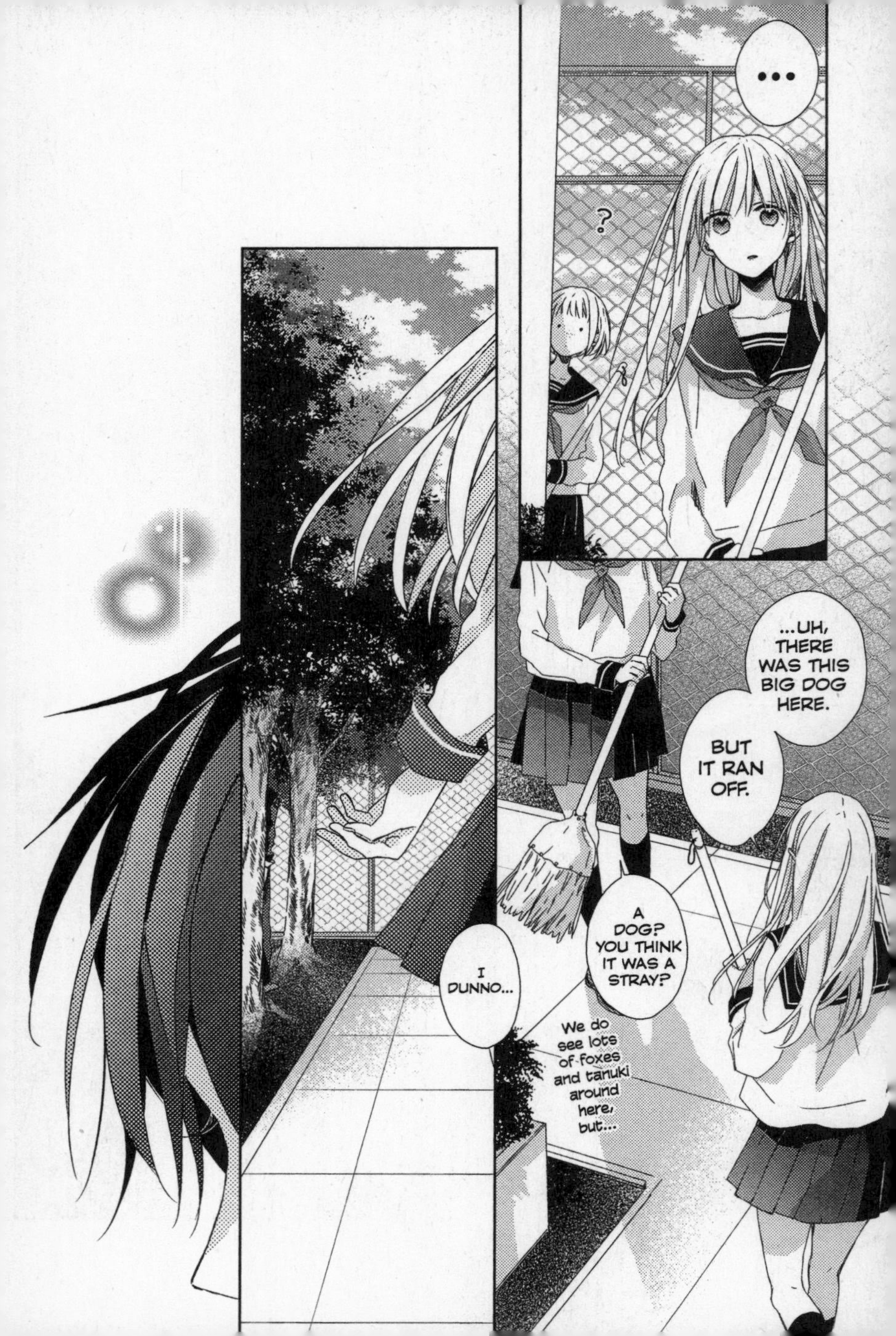

...
?
...UH, THERE WAS THIS BIG DOG HERE.
BUT IT RAN OFF.
A DOG? YOU THINK IT WAS A STRAY?
We do see lots of foxes and tanuki around here, but...
I DUNNO...

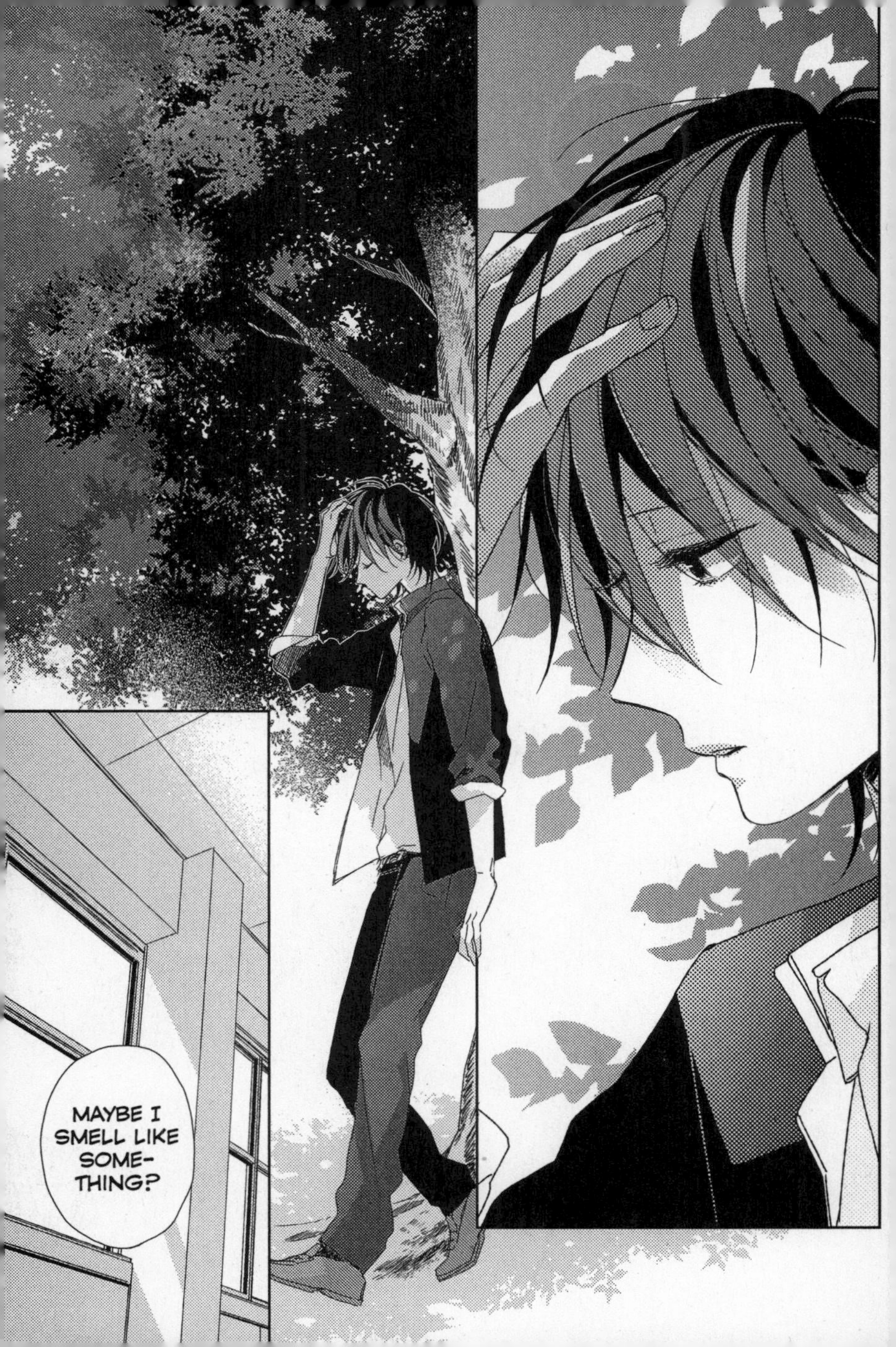
MAYBE I SMELL LIKE SOME-THING?

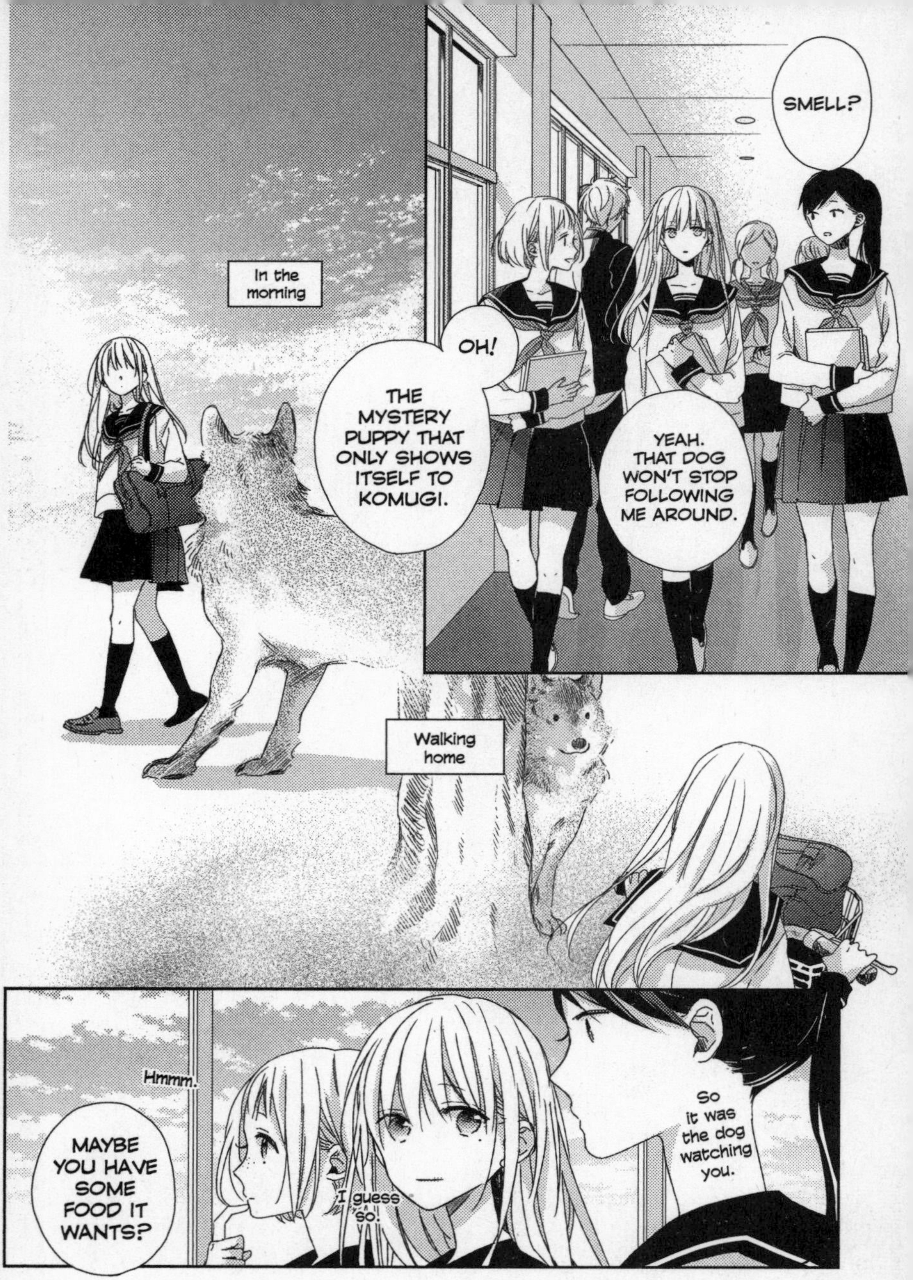
SMELL?
OH!
THE MYSTERY PUPPY THAT ONLY SHOWS ITSELF TO KOMUGI.
YEAH. THAT DOG WON'T STOP FOLLOWING ME AROUND.
In the morning
Walking home
So it was the dog watching you.
I guess so.
Hmmm.
MAYBE YOU HAVE SOME FOOD IT WANTS?

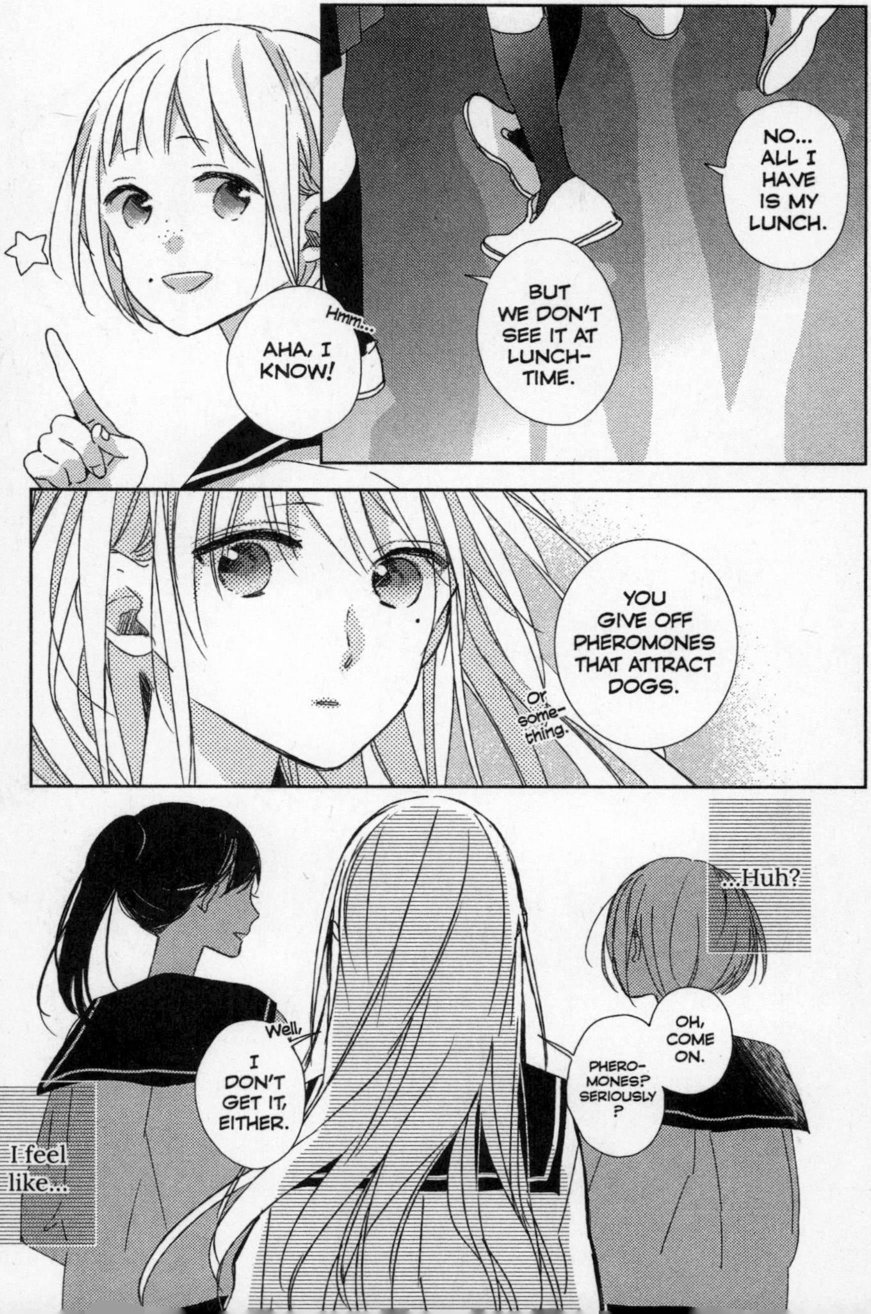
NO... ALL I HAVE IS MY LUNCH.
BUT WE DON'T SEE IT AT LUNCH-TIME.
Hmm...
AHA, I KNOW!
YOU GIVE OFF PHEROMONES THAT ATTRACT DOGS.
Or some-thing.
...Huh?
OH, COME ON.
PHERO-MONES? SERIOUSLY?
Well,
I DON'T GET IT, EITHER.
I feel like...

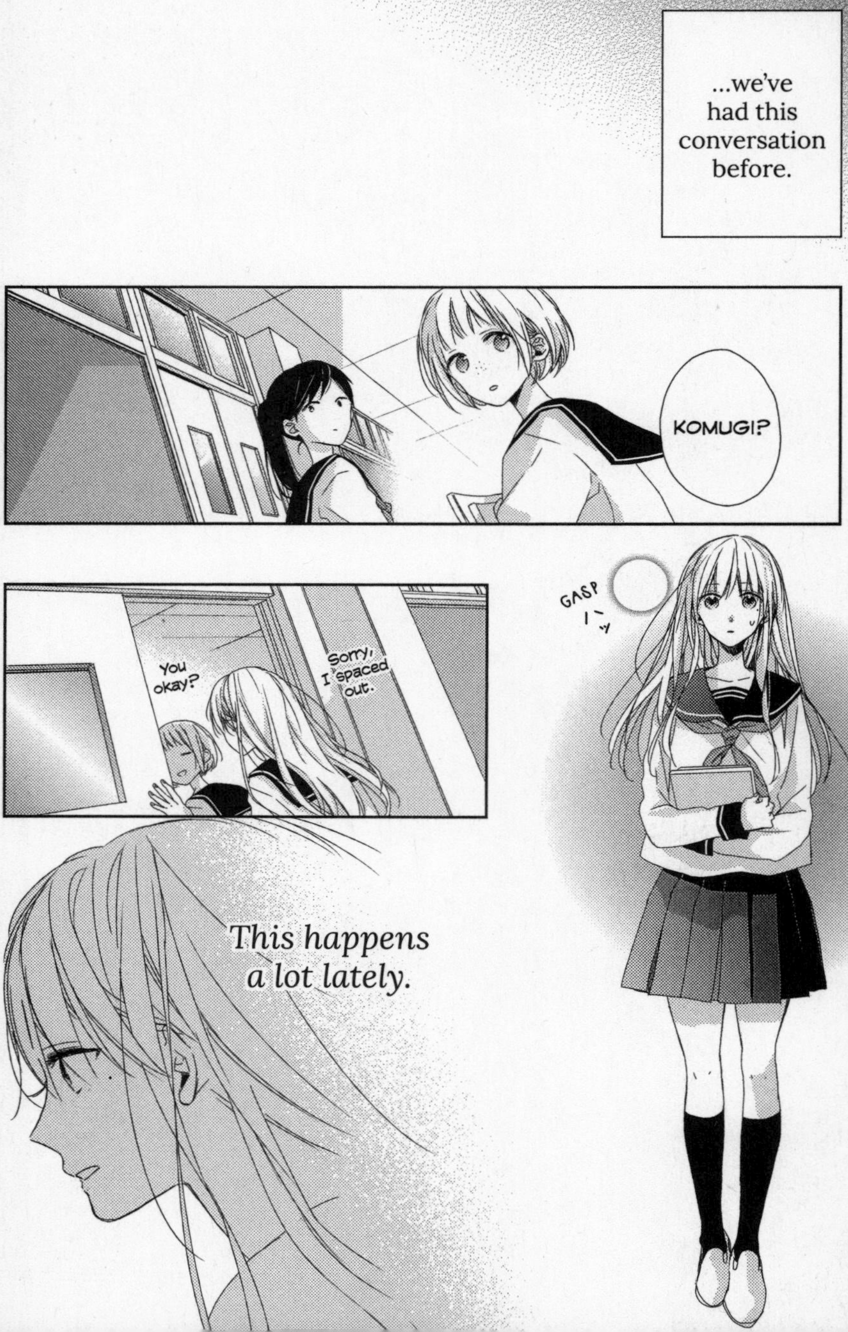
...we've had this conversation before.
KOMUGI?
GASP
Sorry, I spaced out.
You okay?
This happens a lot lately.

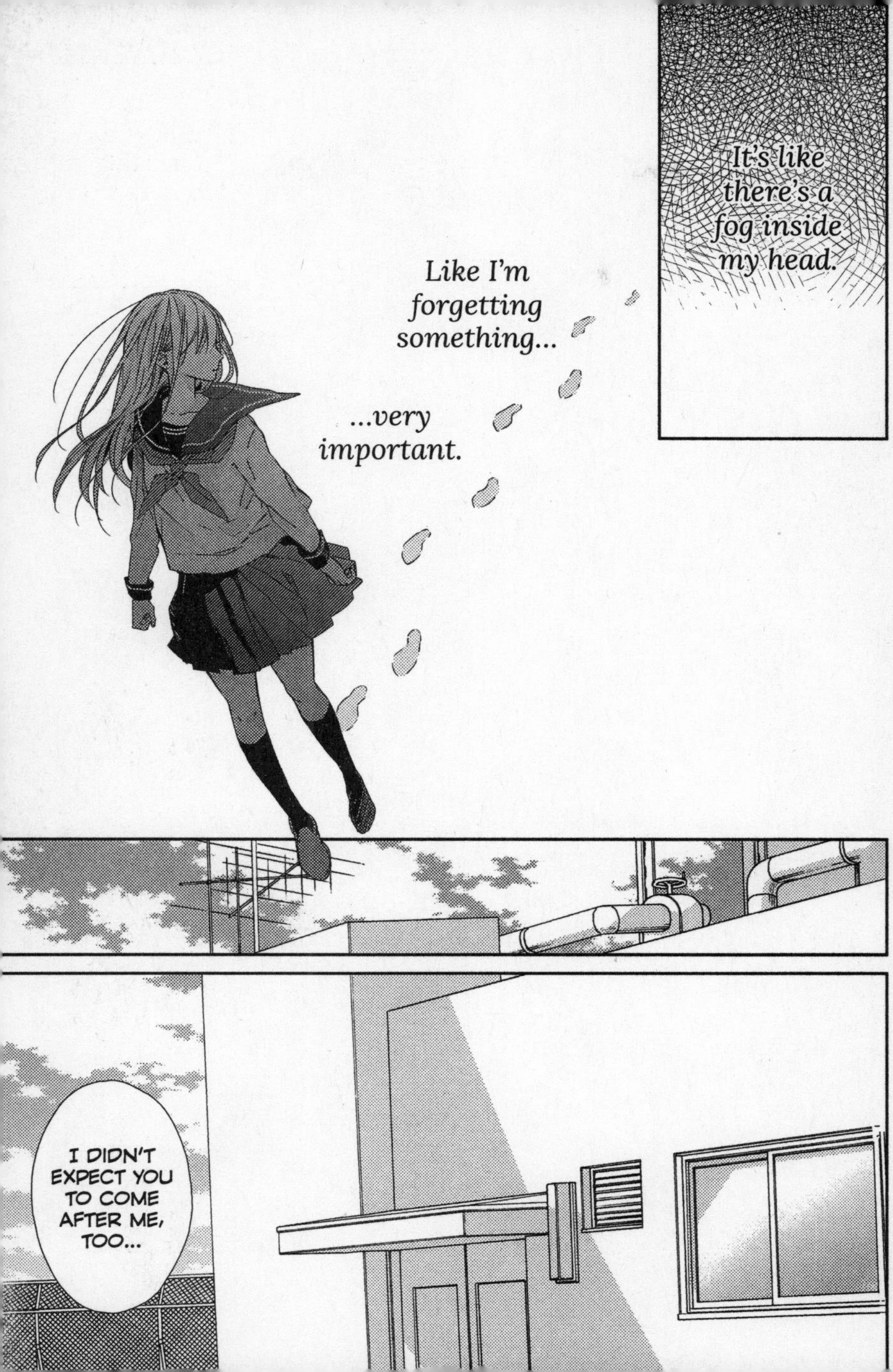
It's like there's a fog inside my head.
Like I'm forgetting something...
...very important.
I DIDN'T EXPECT YOU TO COME AFTER ME, TOO...

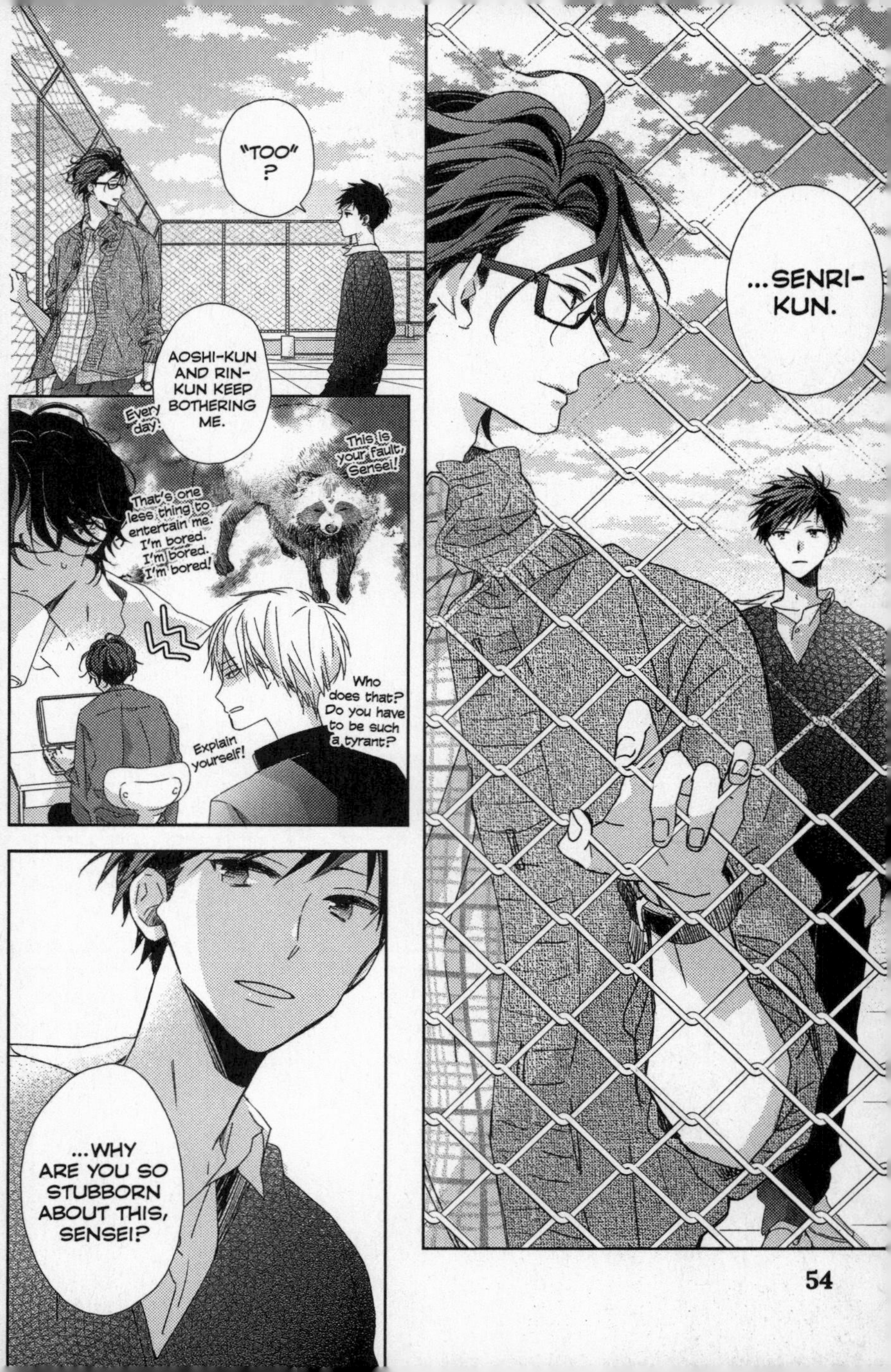
...SENRI-KUN.
"TOO" ?
AOSHI-KUN AND RIN-KUN KEEP BOTHERING ME.
Every day!
This is your fault, Sensei!
That's one less thing to entertain me. I'm bored. I'm bored. I'm bored!
Who does that? Do you have to be such a tyrant?
Explain yourself!
...WHY ARE YOU SO STUBBORN ABOUT THIS, SENSEI?

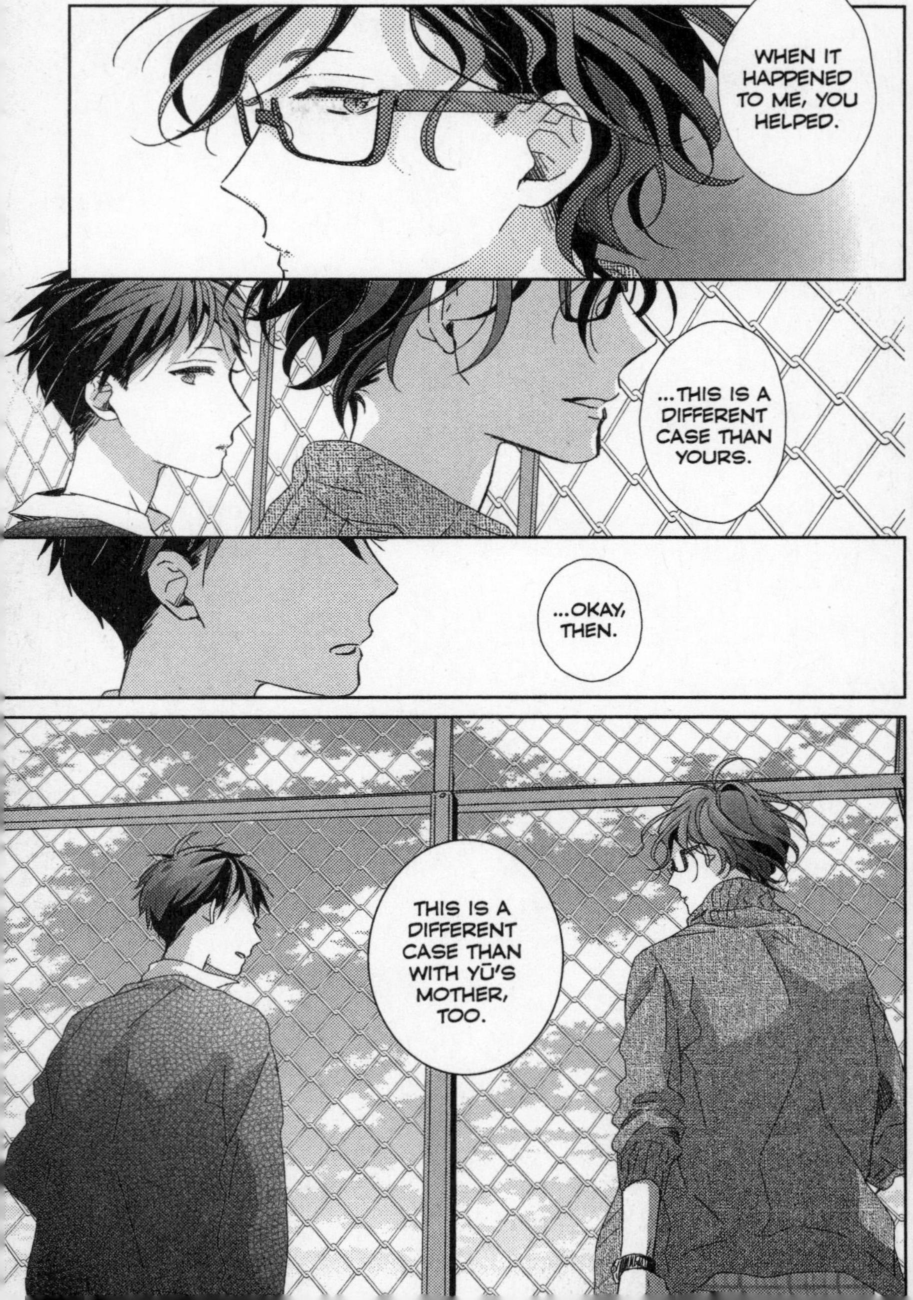
WHEN IT HAPPENED TO ME, YOU HELPED.
...THIS IS A DIFFERENT CASE THAN YOURS.
...OKAY, THEN.
THIS IS A DIFFERENT CASE THAN WITH YŪ'S MOTHER, TOO.

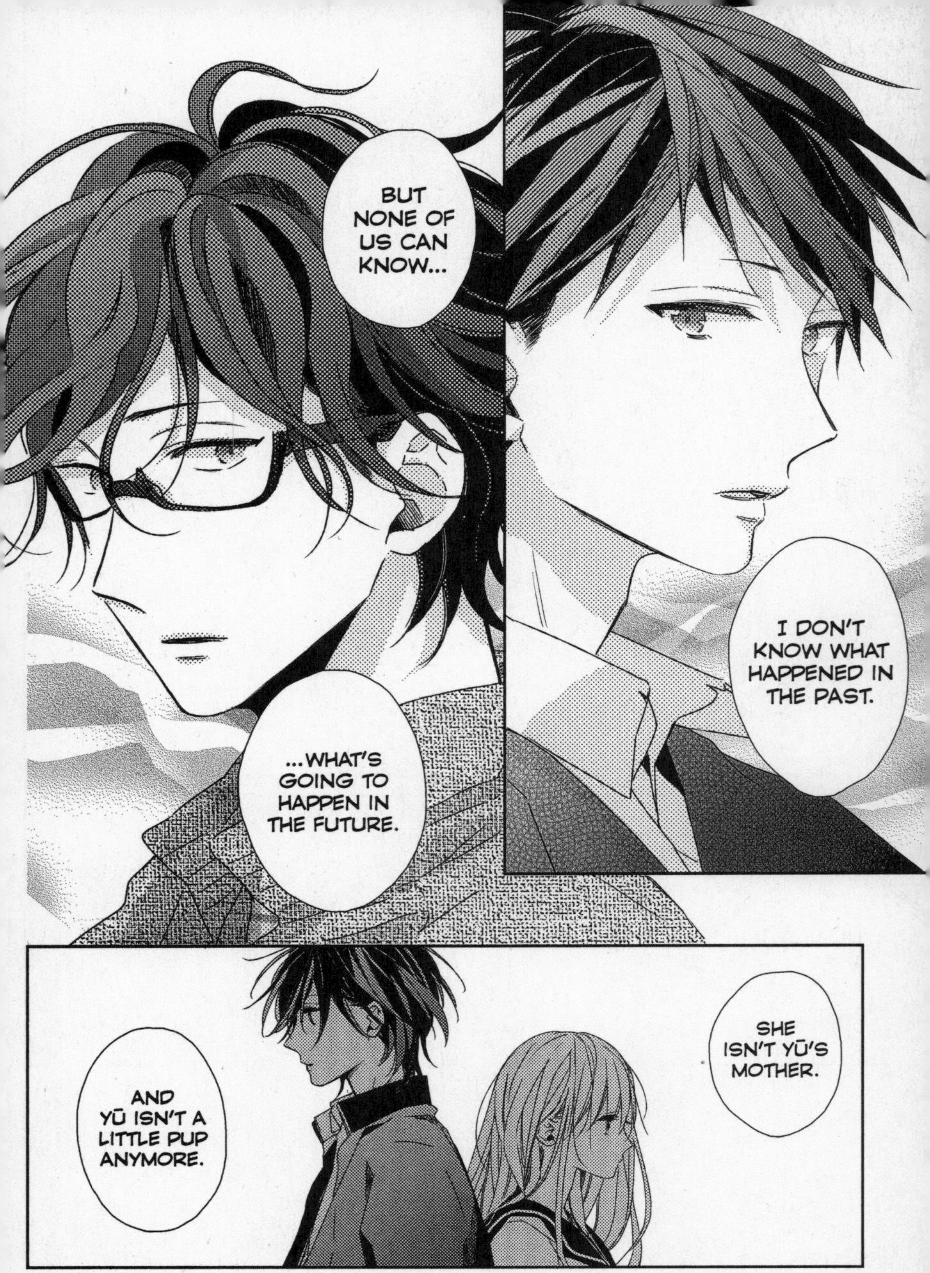
I DON'T KNOW WHAT HAPPENED IN THE PAST.
BUT NONE OF US CAN KNOW...
...WHAT'S GOING TO HAPPEN IN THE FUTURE.
SHE ISN'T YŪ'S MOTHER.
AND YŪ ISN'T A LITTLE PUP ANYMORE.

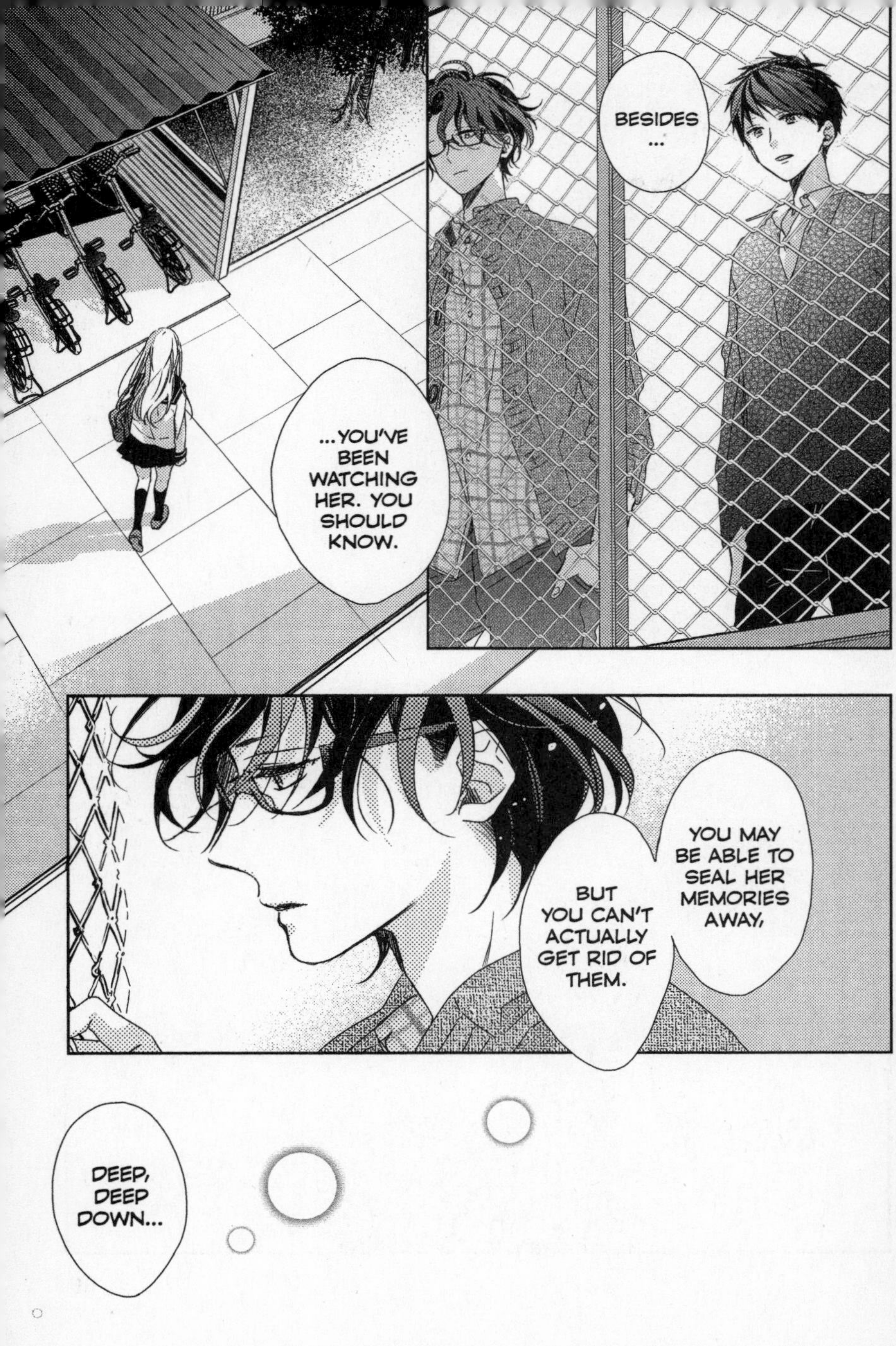
BESIDES ...
...YOU'VE BEEN WATCHING HER. YOU SHOULD KNOW.
YOU MAY BE ABLE TO SEAL HER MEMORIES AWAY,
BUT YOU CAN'T ACTUALLY GET RID OF THEM.
DEEP, DEEP DOWN...

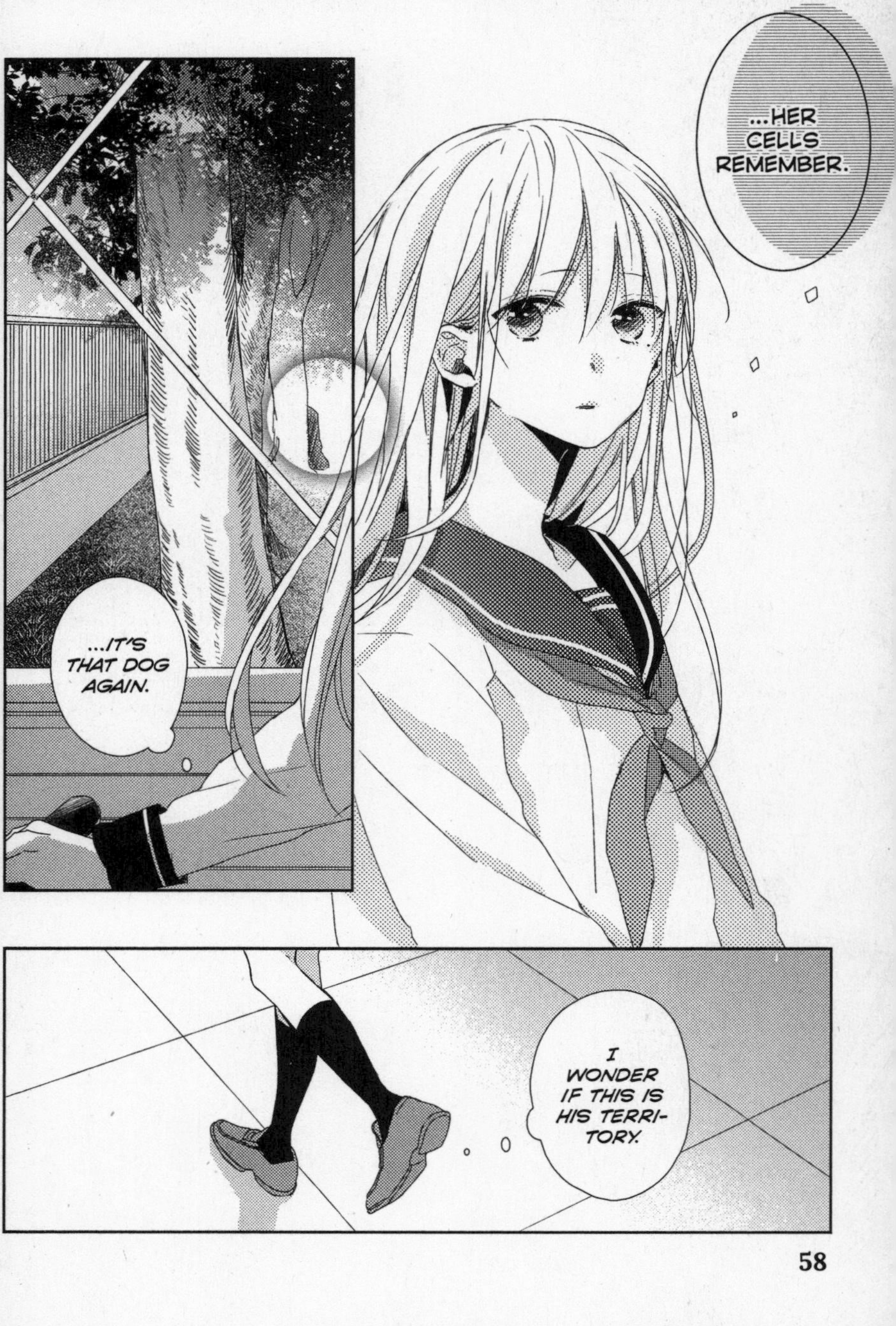
...HER CELLS REMEMBER.
...IT'S THAT DOG AGAIN.
I WONDER IF THIS IS HIS TERRI-TORY.

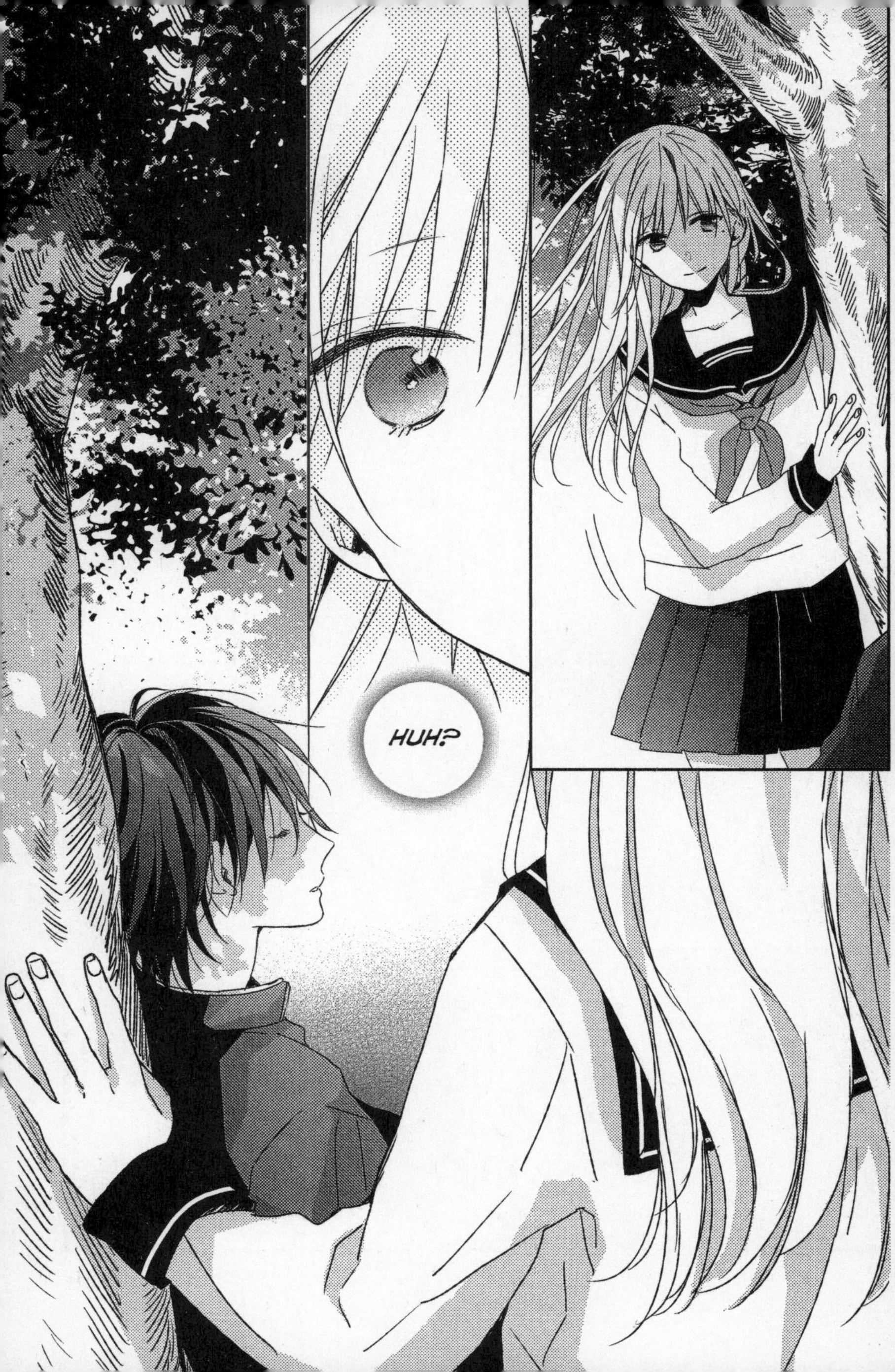
HUH?

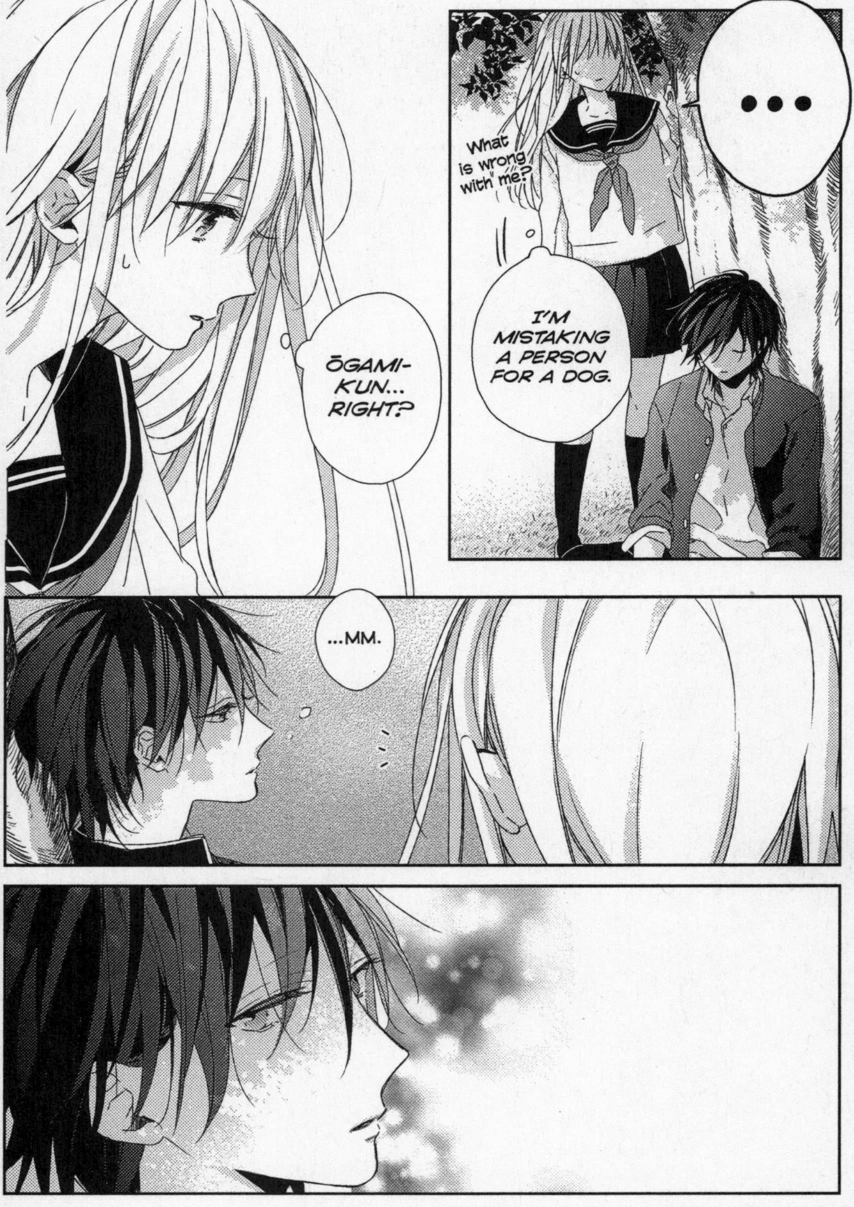

...
What is wrong with me?
I'M MISTAKING A PERSON FOR A DOG.
ŌGAMI-KUN... RIGHT?
...MM.

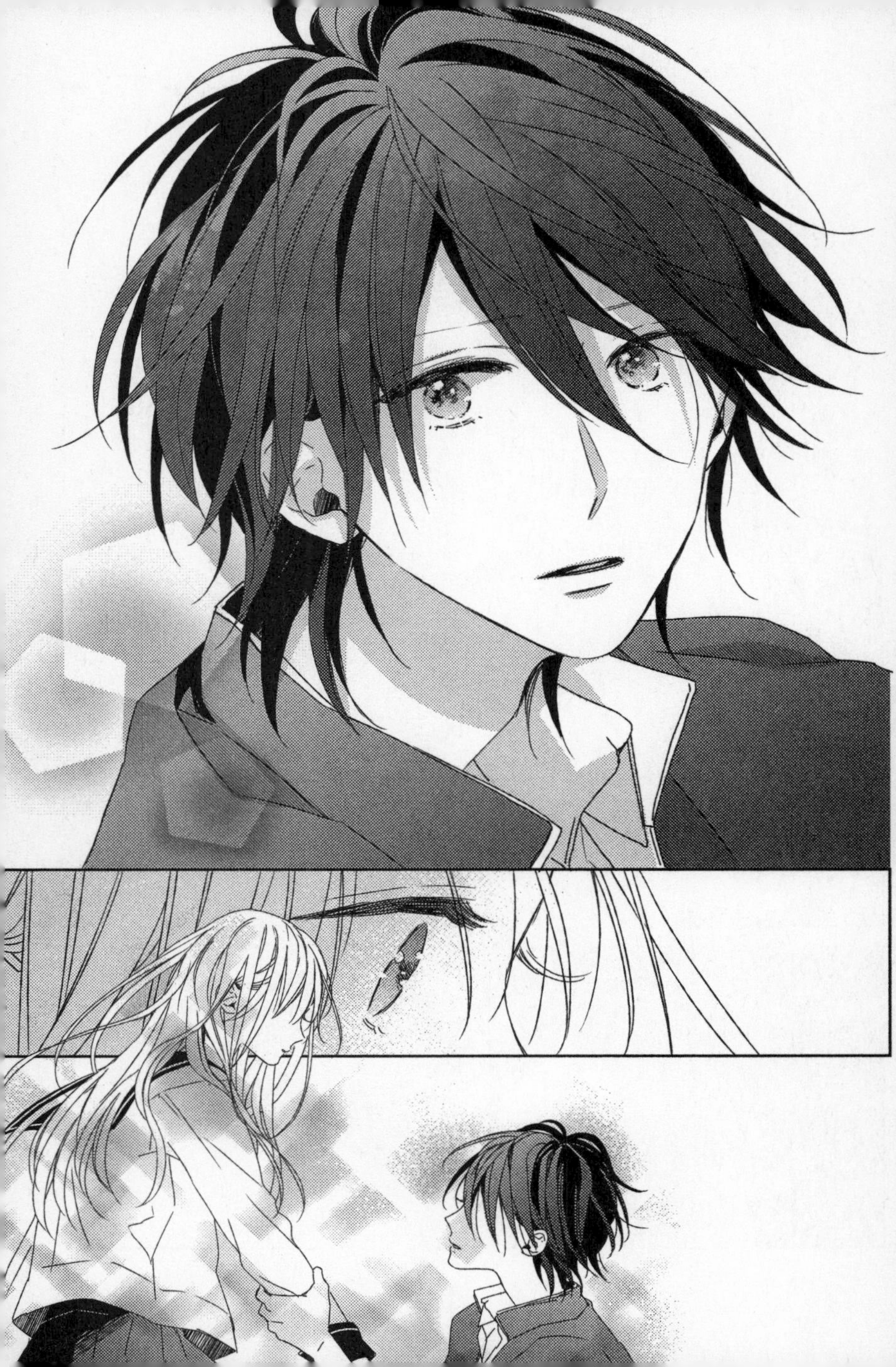

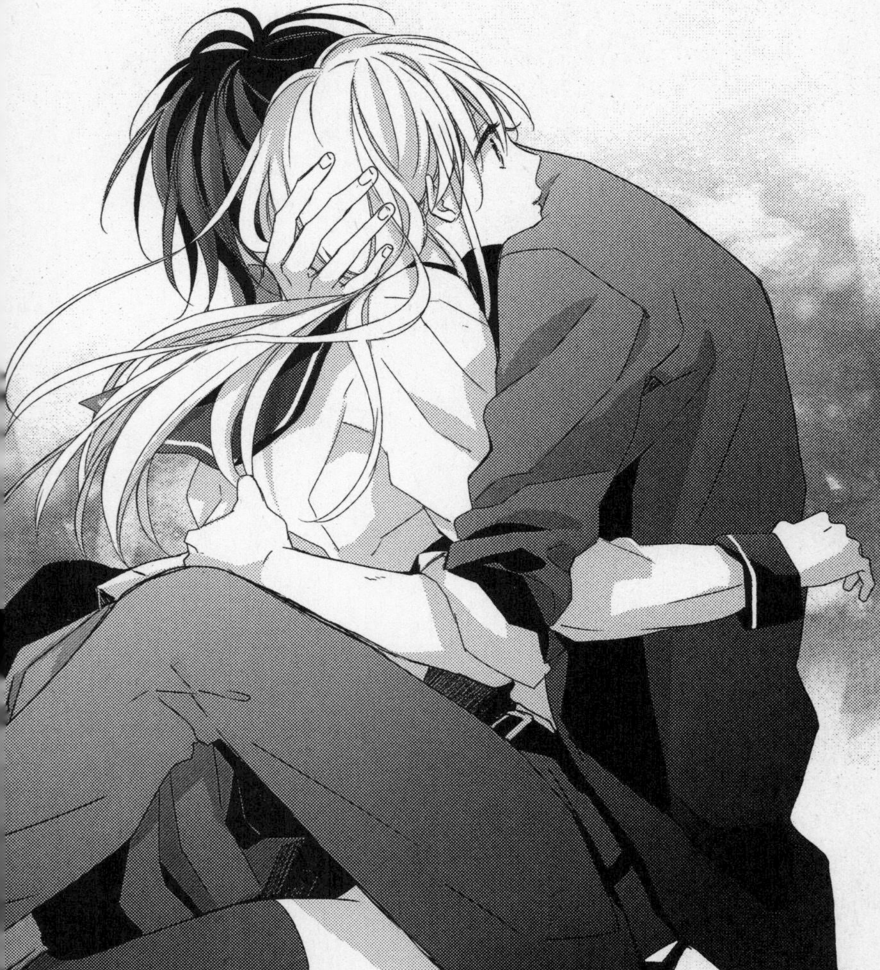

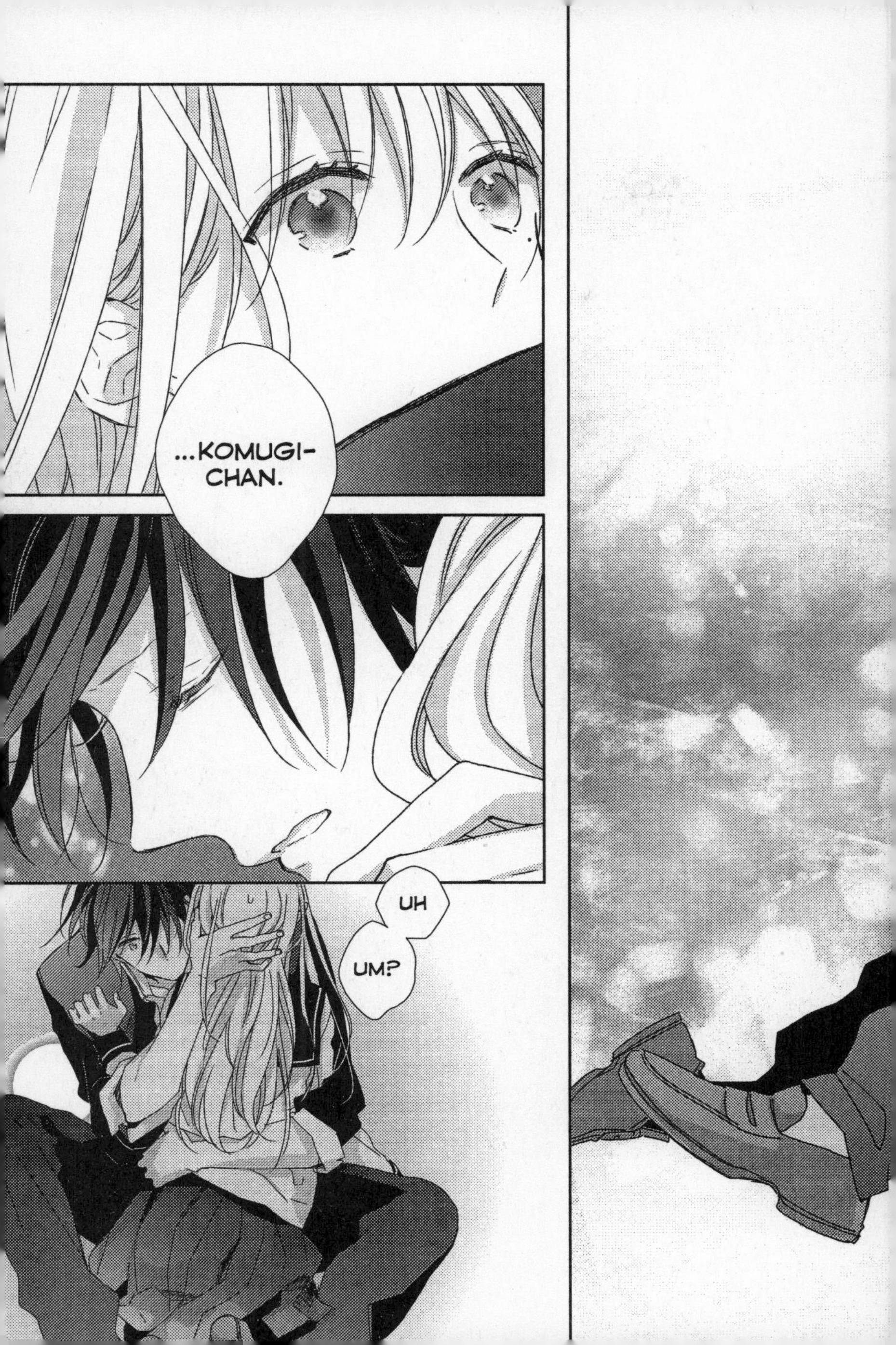
...KOMUGI-CHAN.
UH
UM?

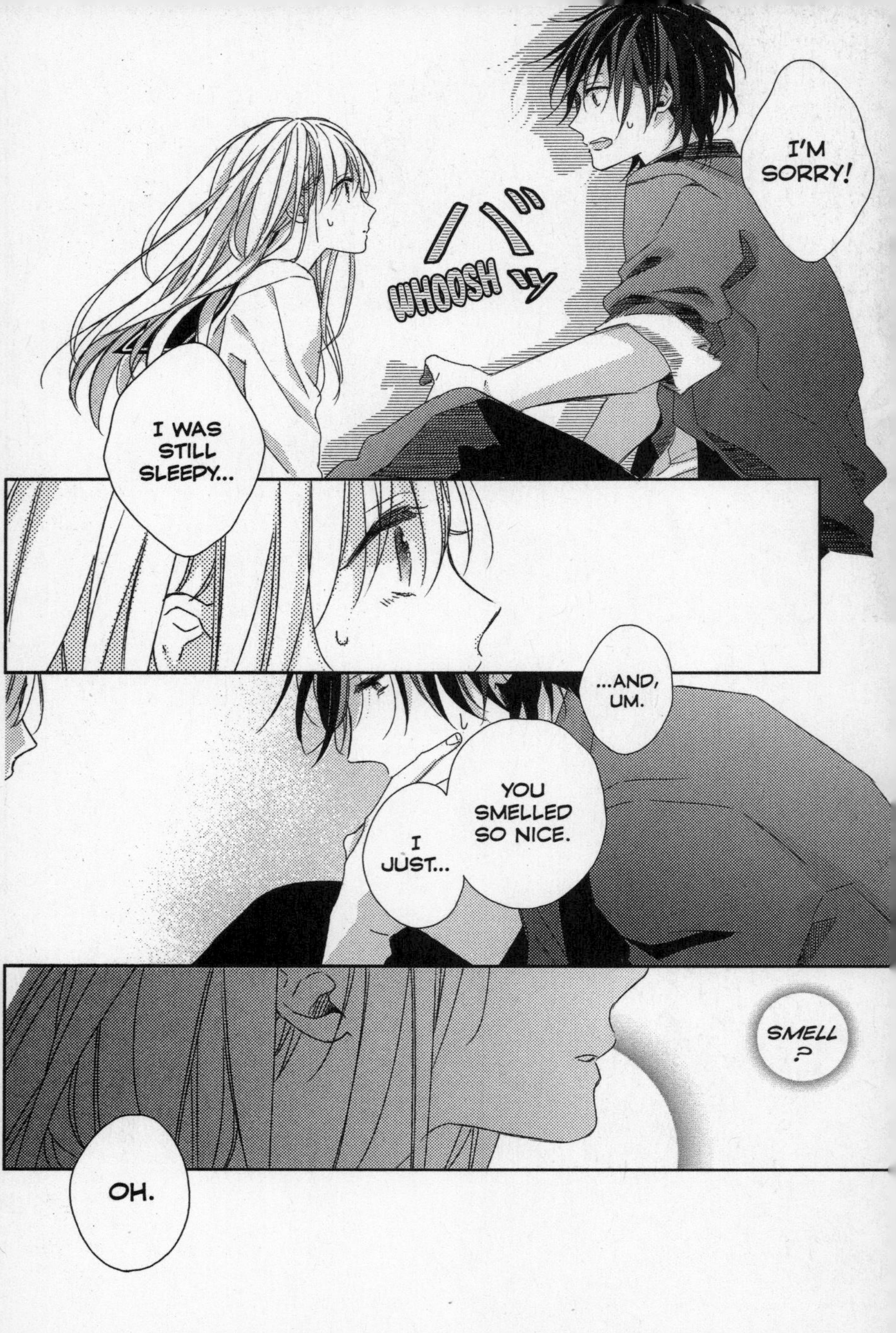
I'M SORRY!
WHOOSH
I WAS STILL SLEEPY...
...AND, UM.
I JUST...
YOU SMELLED SO NICE.
SMELL?
OH.

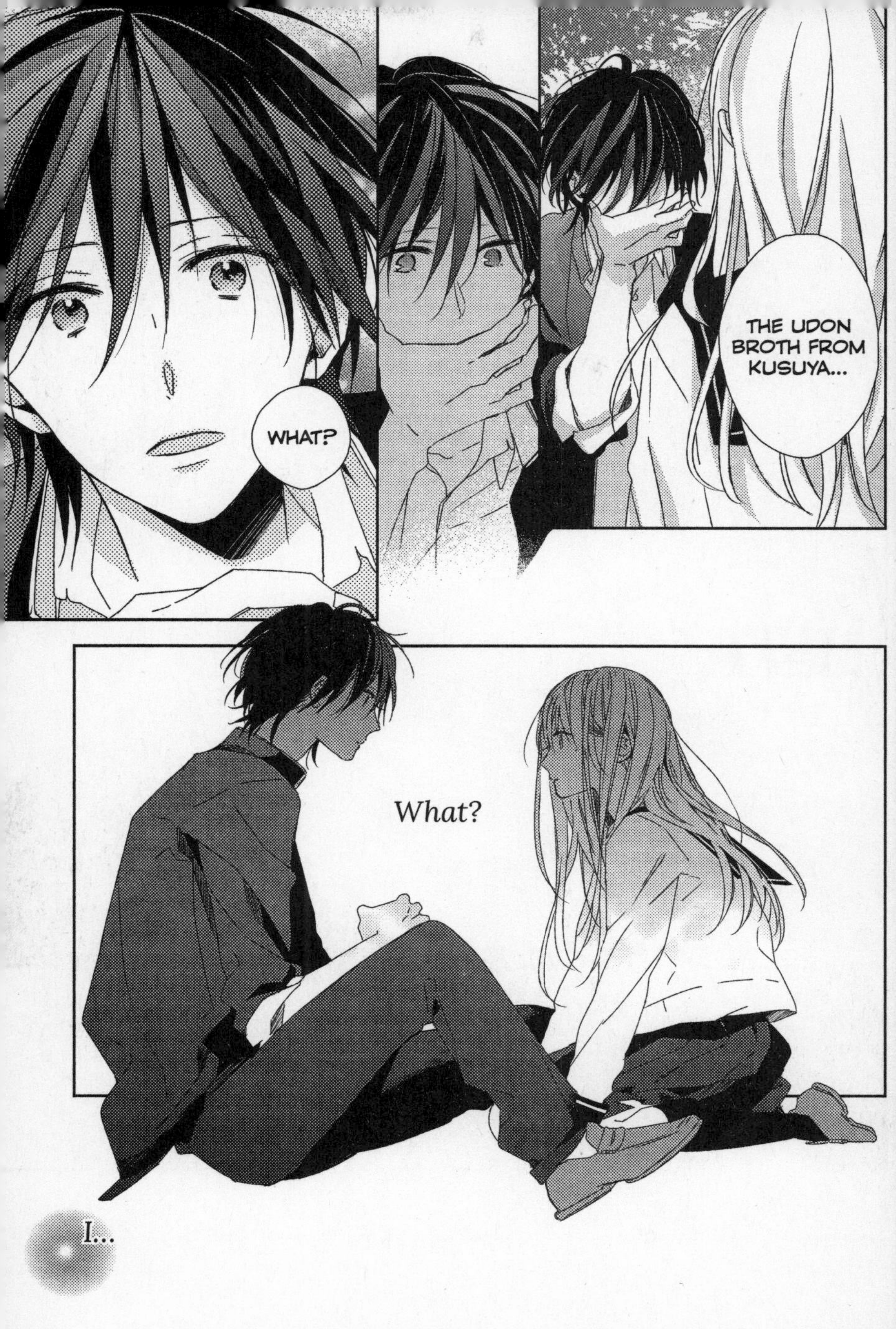
THE UDON BROTH FROM KUSUYA...
WHAT?
What?
I...

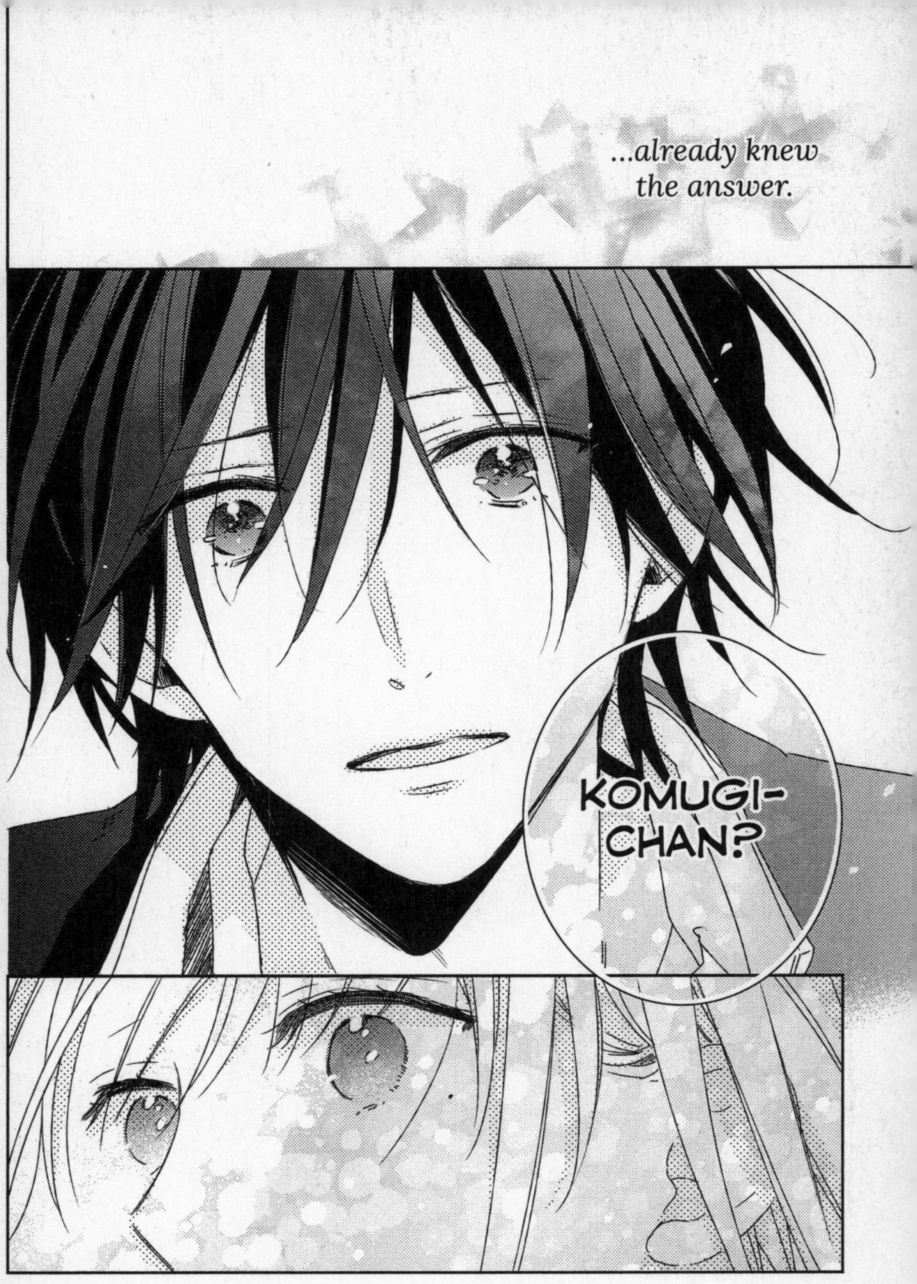
...already knew
the answer.
KOMUGI-
CHAN?

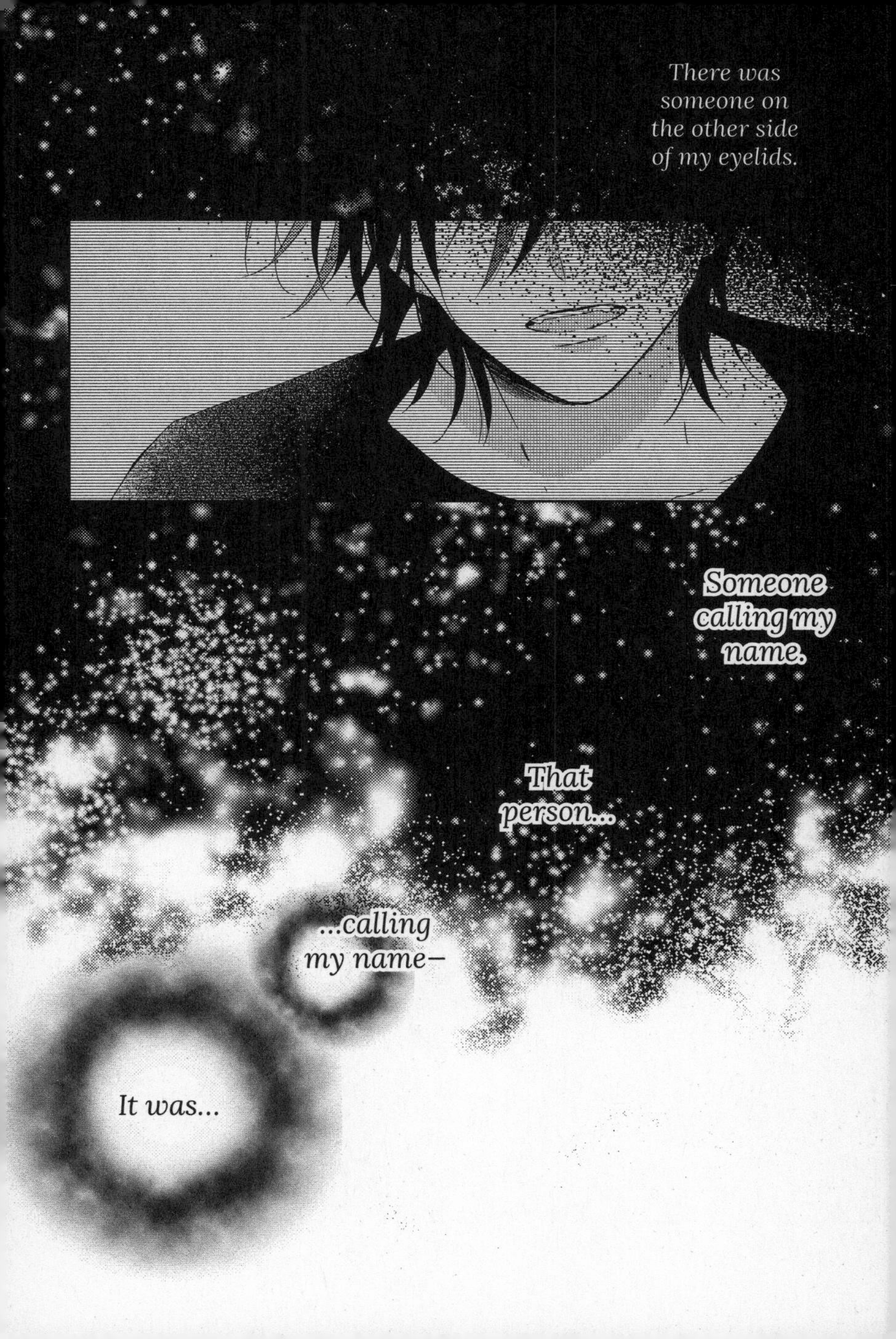
There was someone on the other side of my eyelids.
Someone calling my name.
That person...
...calling my name—
It was...

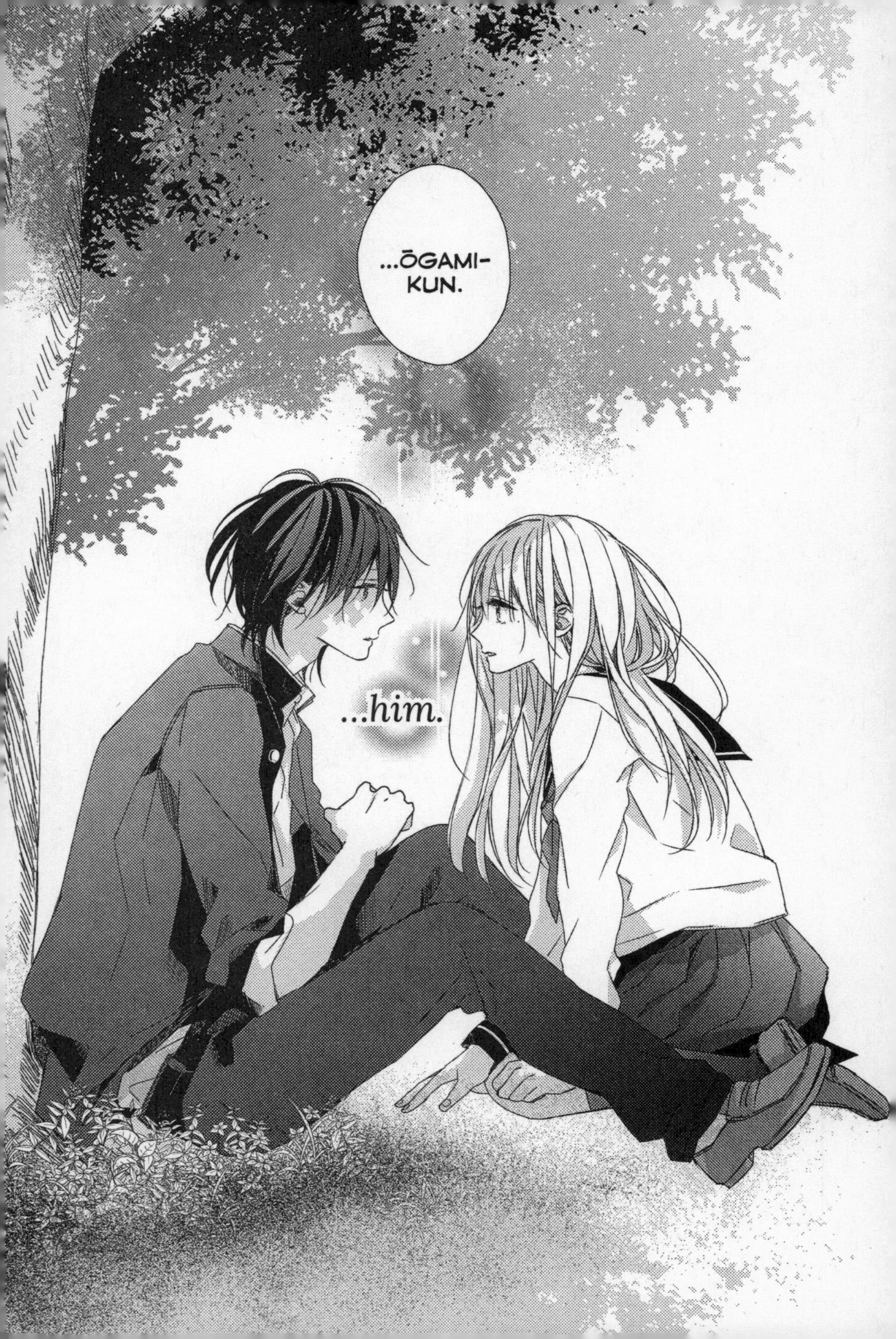
...ŌGAMI-KUN.
...him.

Chapter 16

"Ōgami-kun."

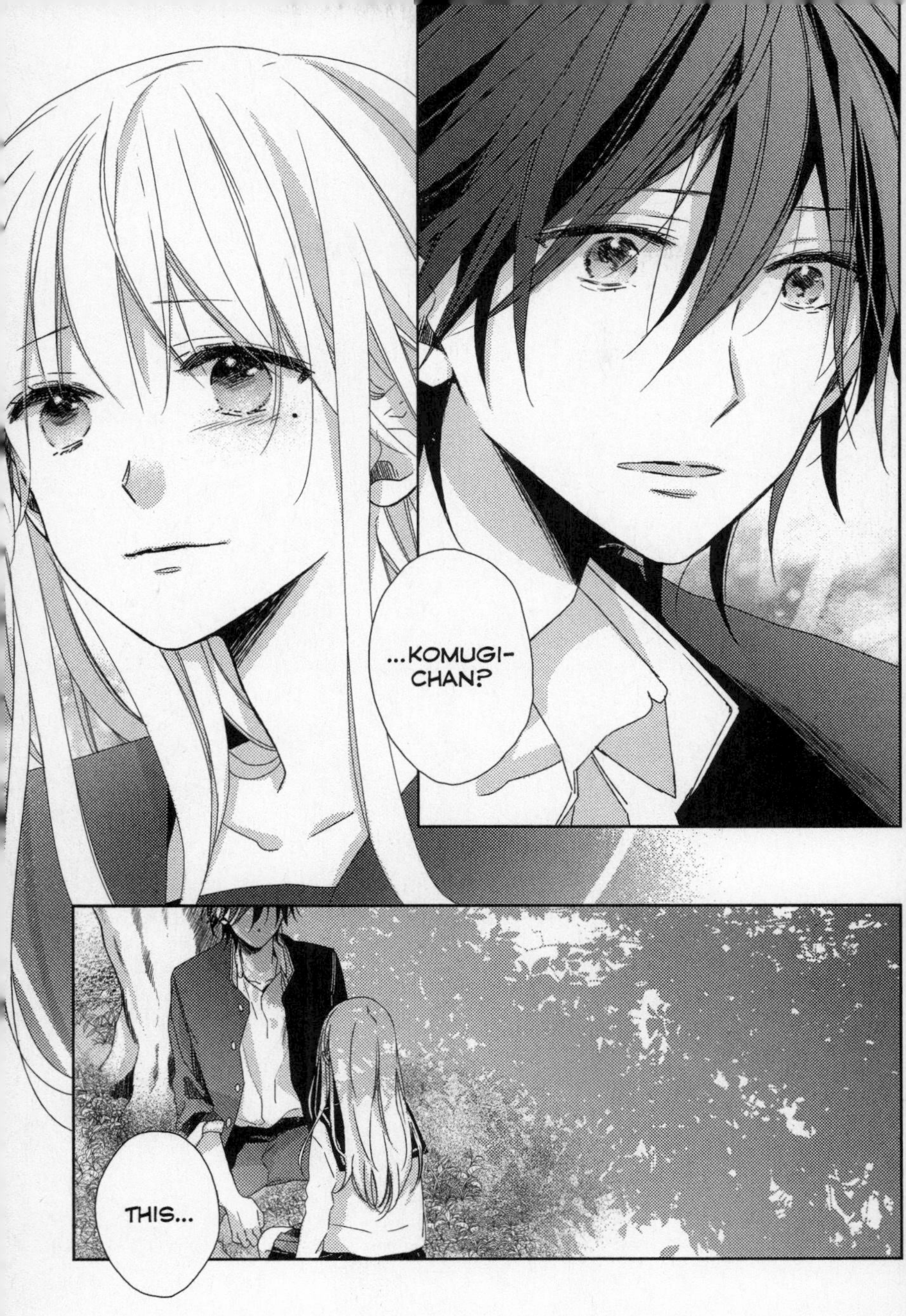
...KOMUGI-CHAN?
THIS...

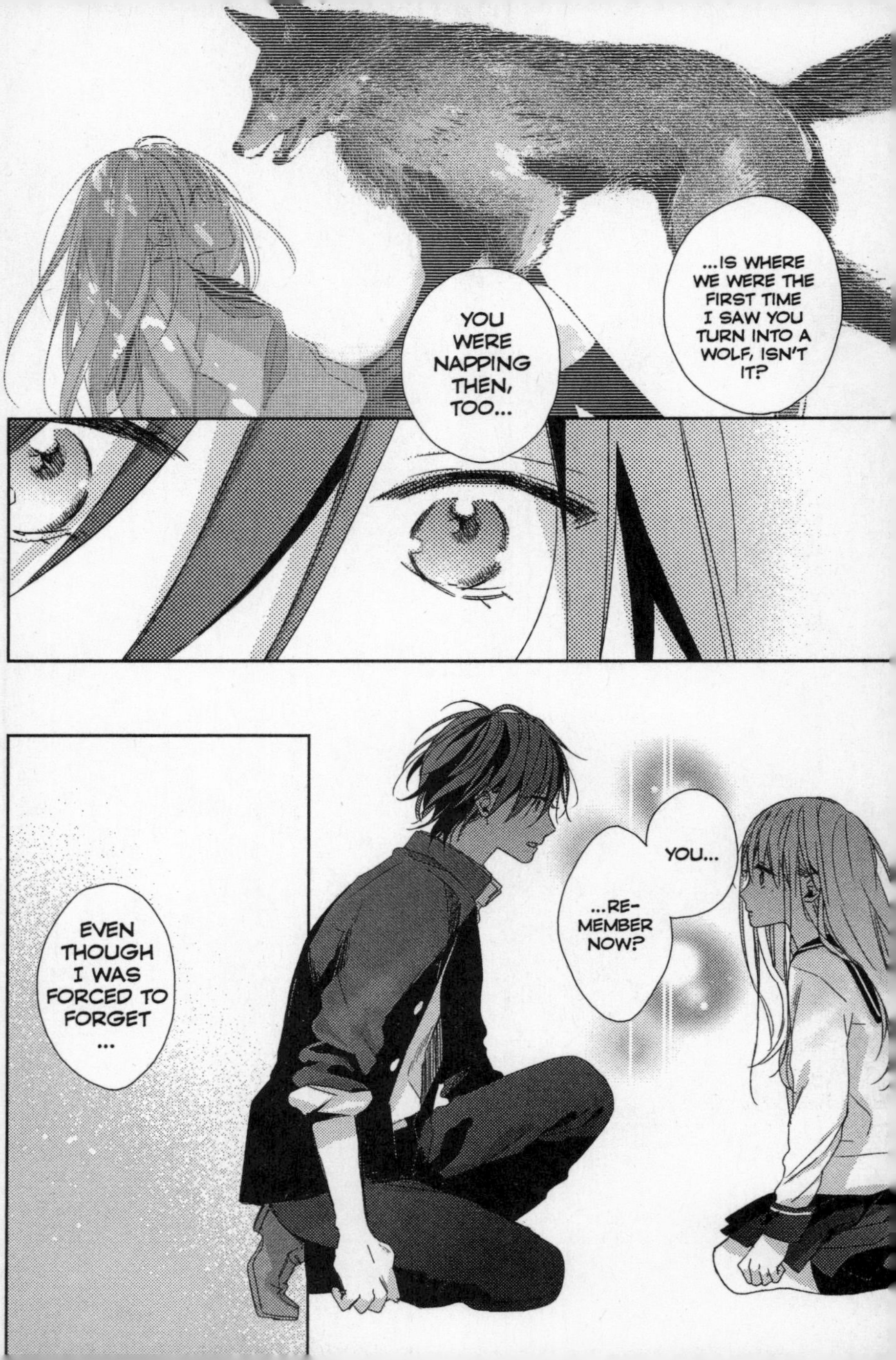
...IS WHERE WE WERE THE FIRST TIME I SAW YOU TURN INTO A WOLF, ISN'T IT?
YOU WERE NAPPING THEN, TOO...
YOU...
...RE-MEMBER NOW?
EVEN THOUGH I WAS FORCED TO FORGET ...

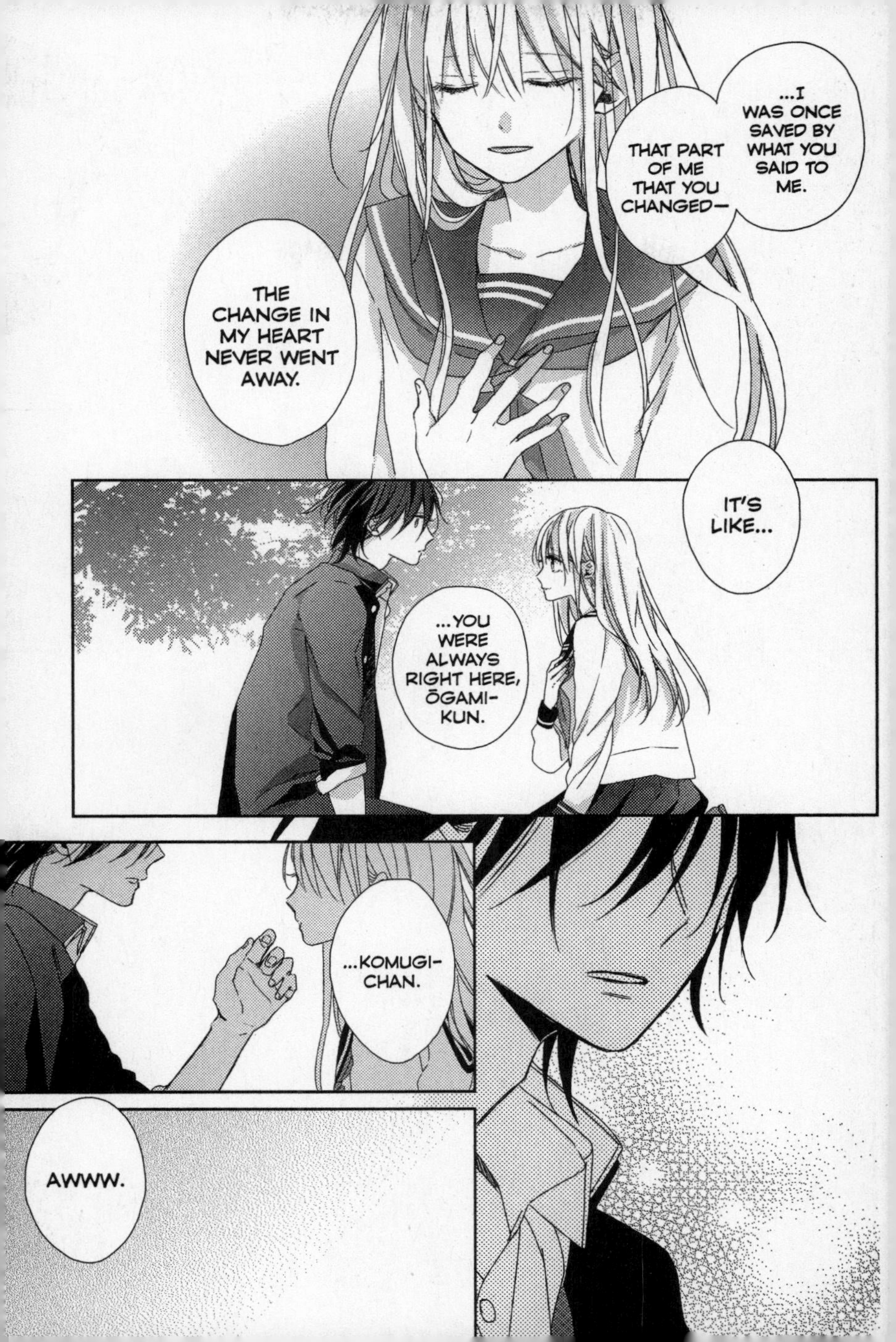
...I WAS ONCE SAVED BY WHAT YOU SAID TO ME.
THAT PART OF ME THAT YOU CHANGED—
THE CHANGE IN MY HEART NEVER WENT AWAY.
IT'S LIKE...
...YOU WERE ALWAYS RIGHT HERE, ŌGAMI-KUN.
...KOMUGI-CHAN.
AWWW.

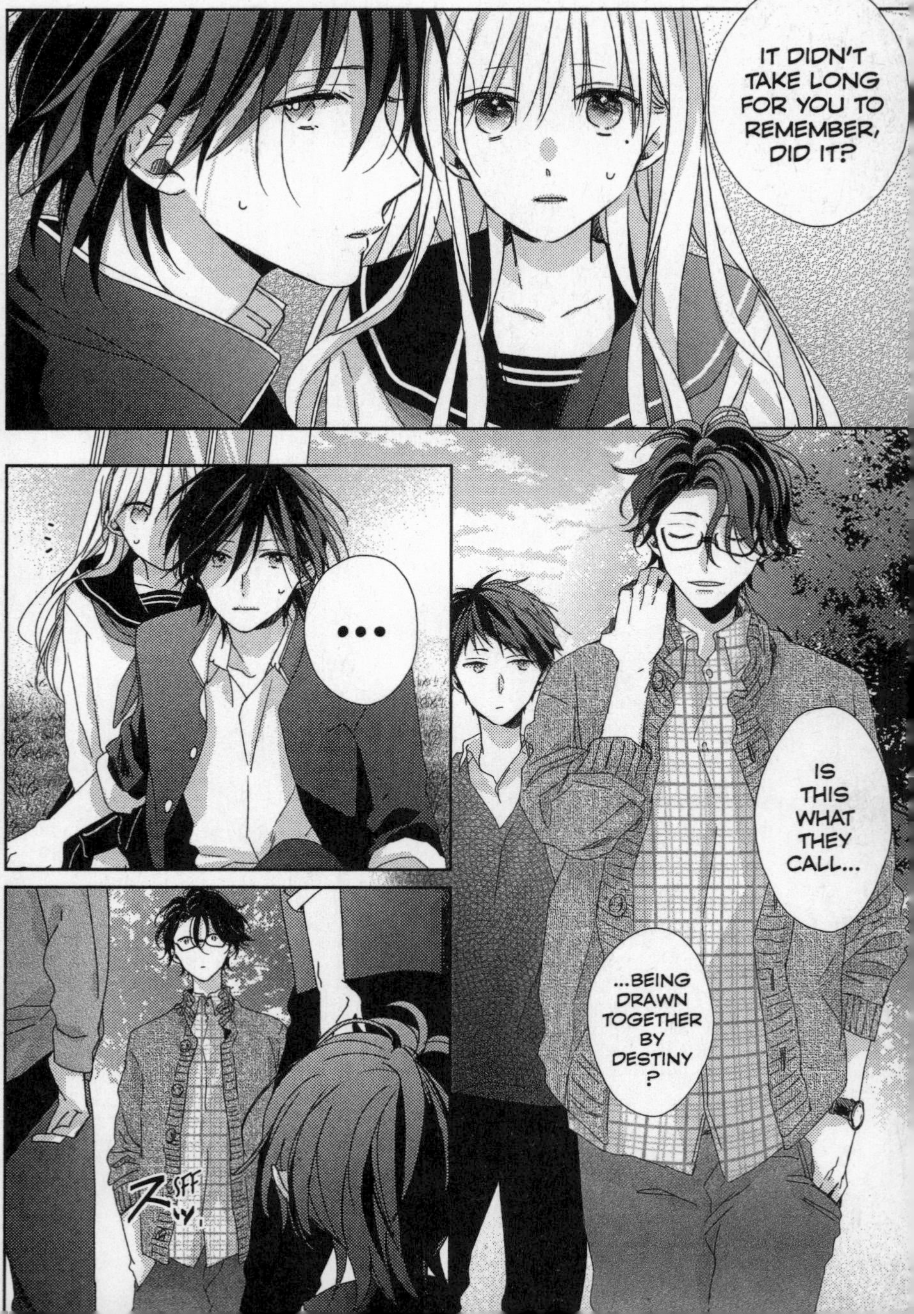
IT DIDN'T TAKE LONG FOR YOU TO REMEMBER, DID IT?
IS THIS WHAT THEY CALL...
...BEING DRAWN TOGETHER BY DESTINY?
...
SFF

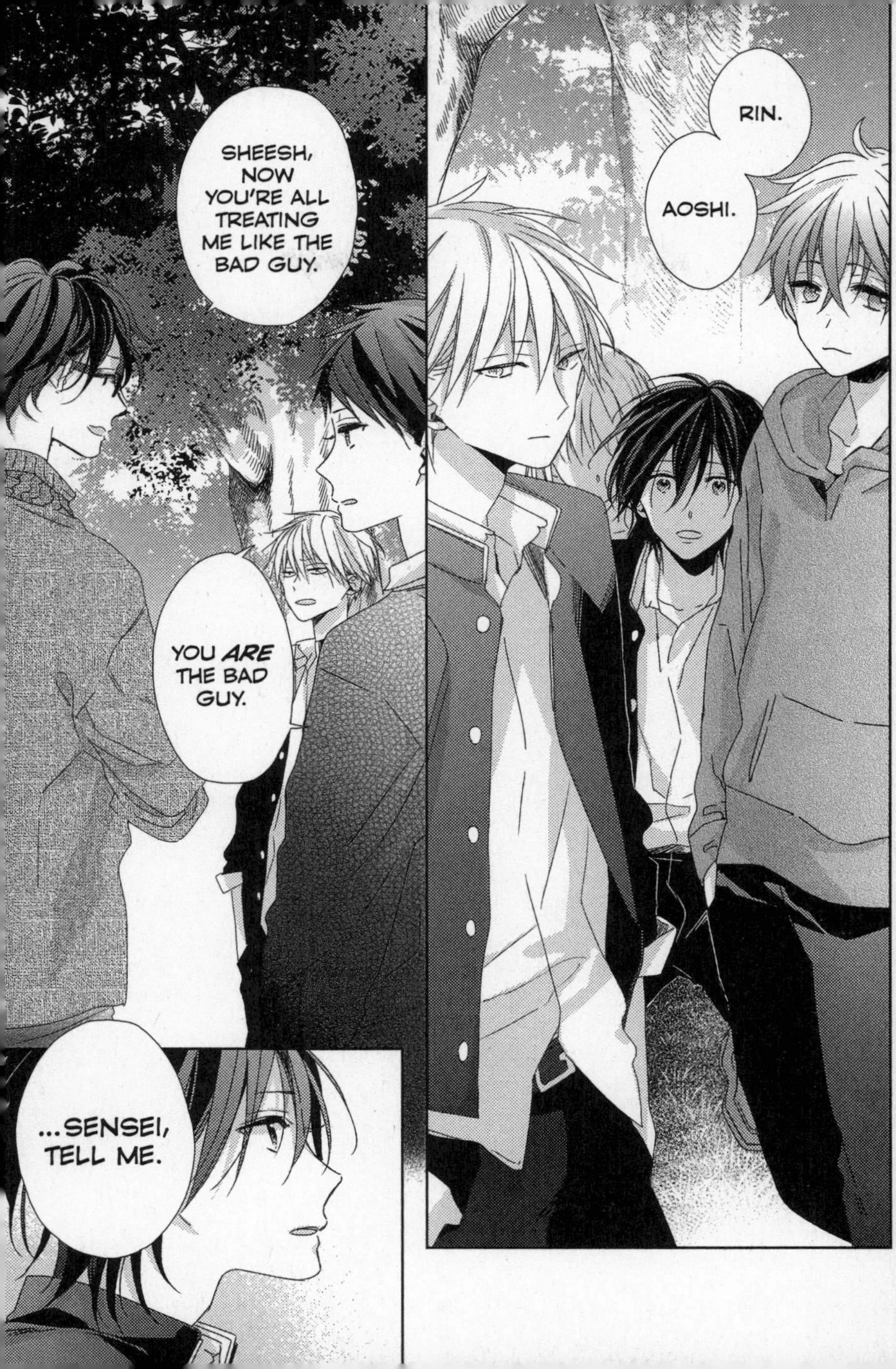
RIN.
AOSHI.
SHEESH, NOW YOU'RE ALL TREATING ME LIKE THE BAD GUY.
YOU *ARE* THE BAD GUY.
...SENSEI, TELL ME.

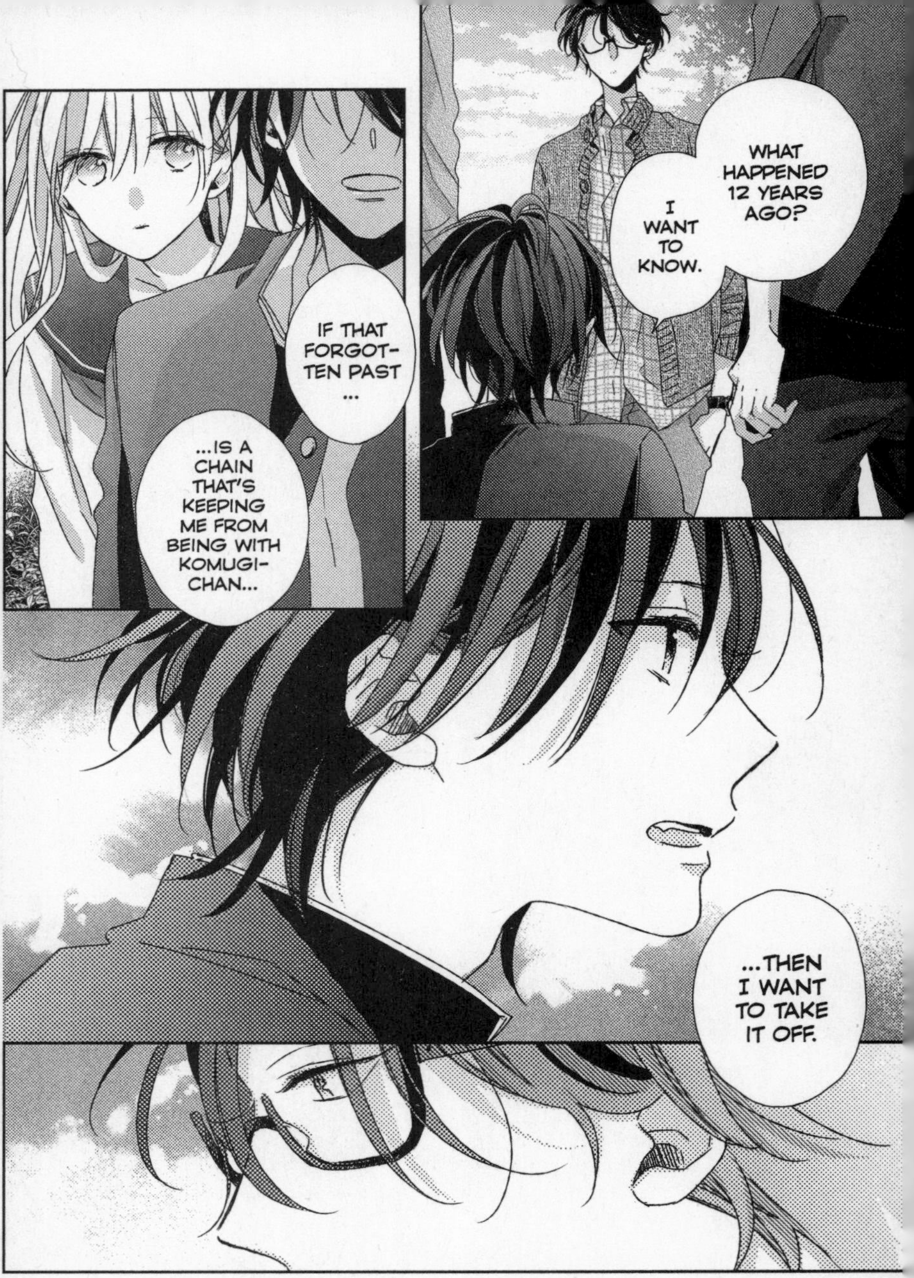
WHAT HAPPENED 12 YEARS AGO?
I WANT TO KNOW.
IF THAT FORGOT-TEN PAST ...
...IS A CHAIN THAT'S KEEPING ME FROM BEING WITH KOMUGI-CHAN...
...THEN I WANT TO TAKE IT OFF.

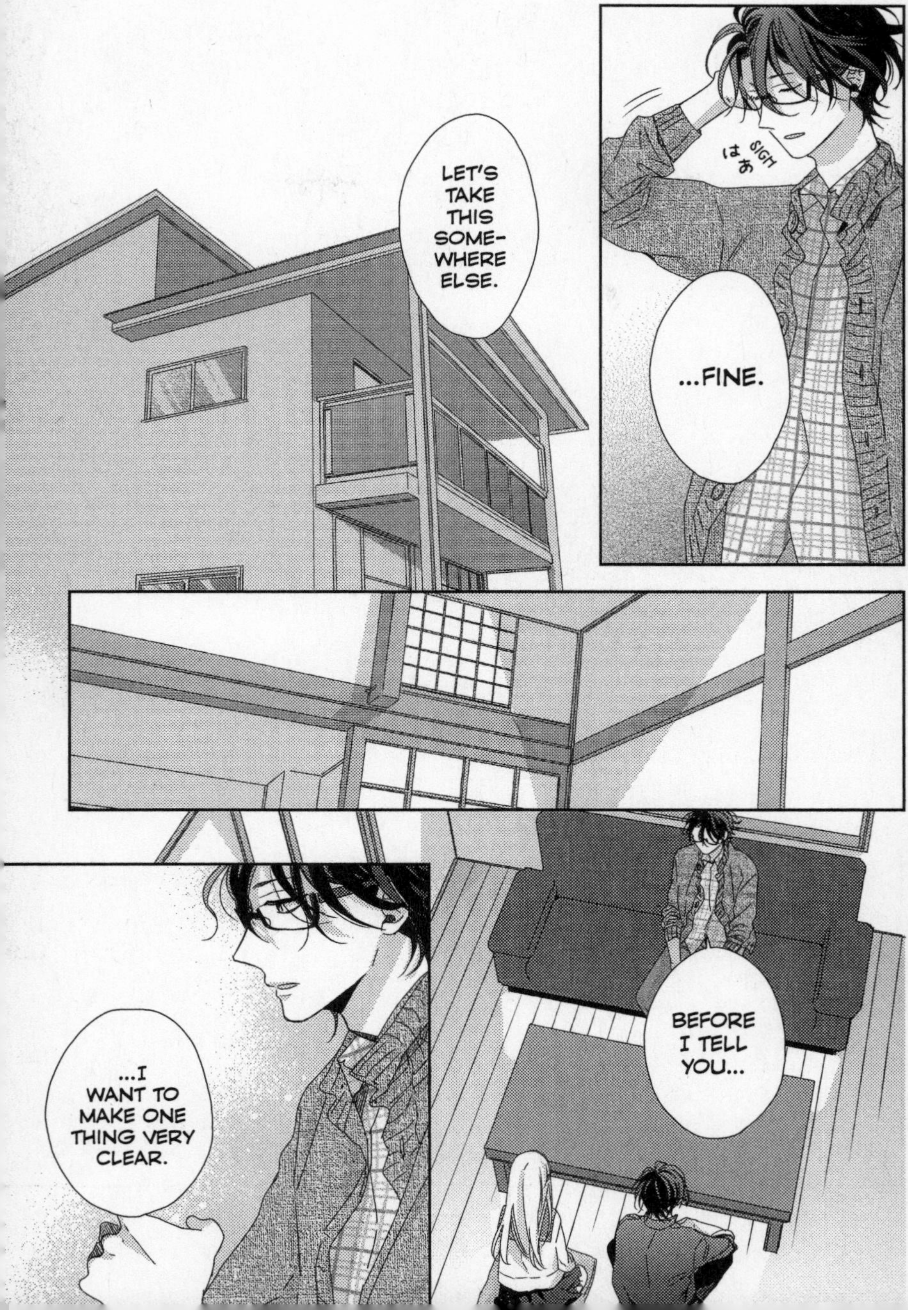
SIGH
はあ
...FINE.
LET'S TAKE THIS SOME-WHERE ELSE.
BEFORE I TELL YOU...
...I WANT TO MAKE ONE THING VERY CLEAR.

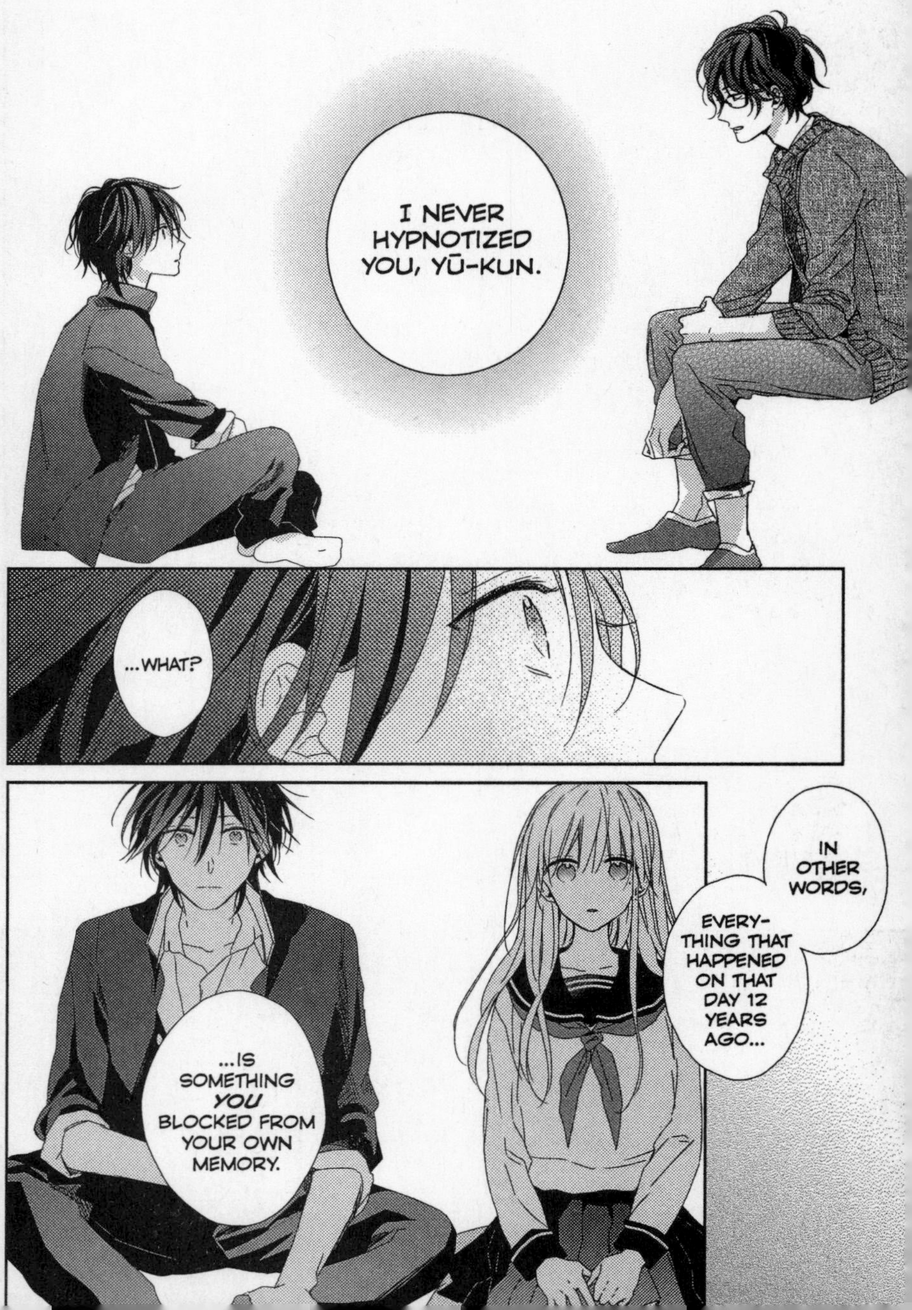
I NEVER HYPNOTIZED YOU, YŪ-KUN.
...WHAT?
IN OTHER WORDS,
EVERY-THING THAT HAPPENED ON THAT DAY 12 YEARS AGO...
...IS SOMETHING *YOU* BLOCKED FROM YOUR OWN MEMORY.

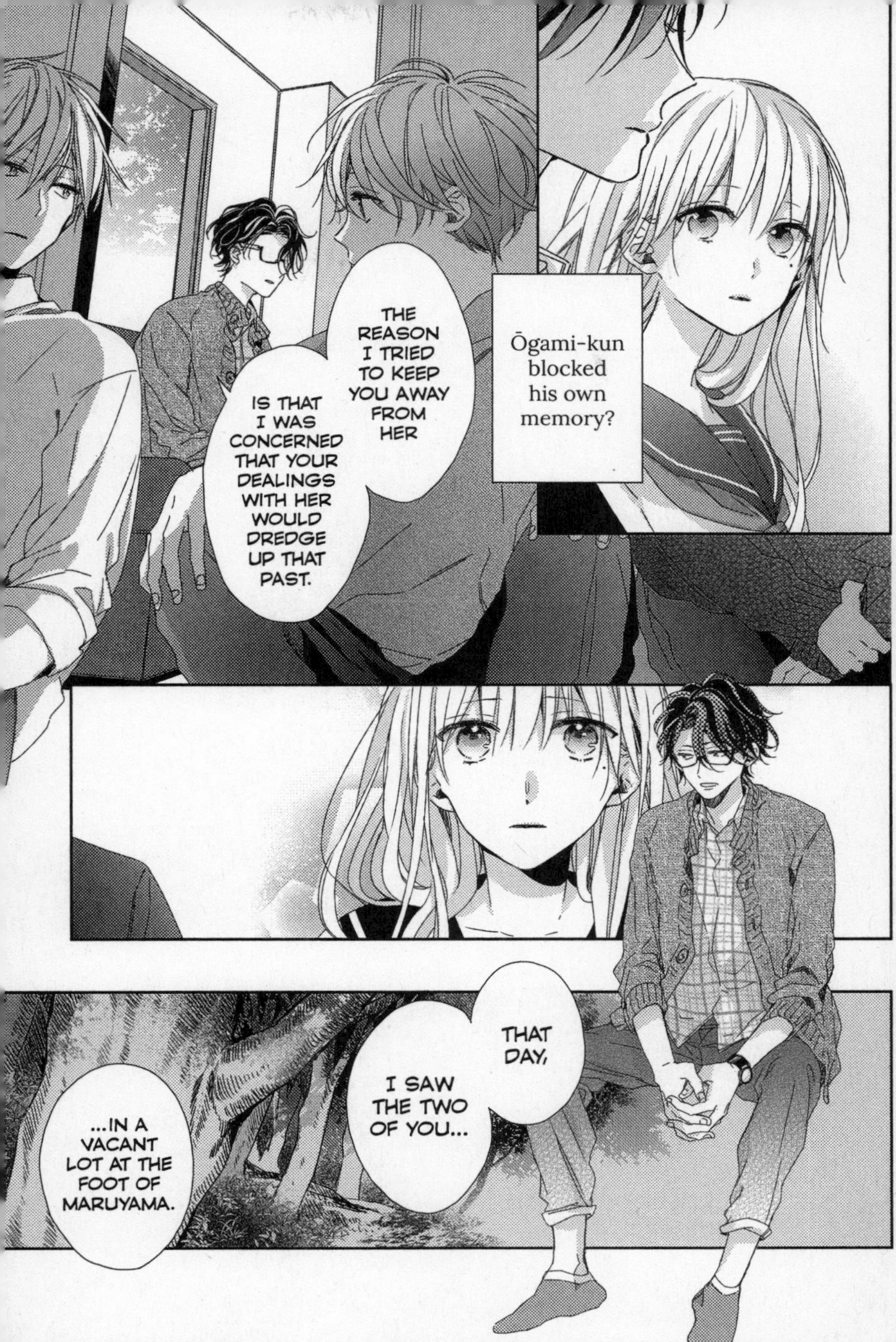
Ōgami-kun blocked his own memory?
THE REASON I TRIED TO KEEP YOU AWAY FROM HER
IS THAT I WAS CONCERNED THAT YOUR DEALINGS WITH HER WOULD DREDGE UP THAT PAST.
THAT DAY,
I SAW THE TWO OF YOU...
...IN A VACANT LOT AT THE FOOT OF MARUYAMA.

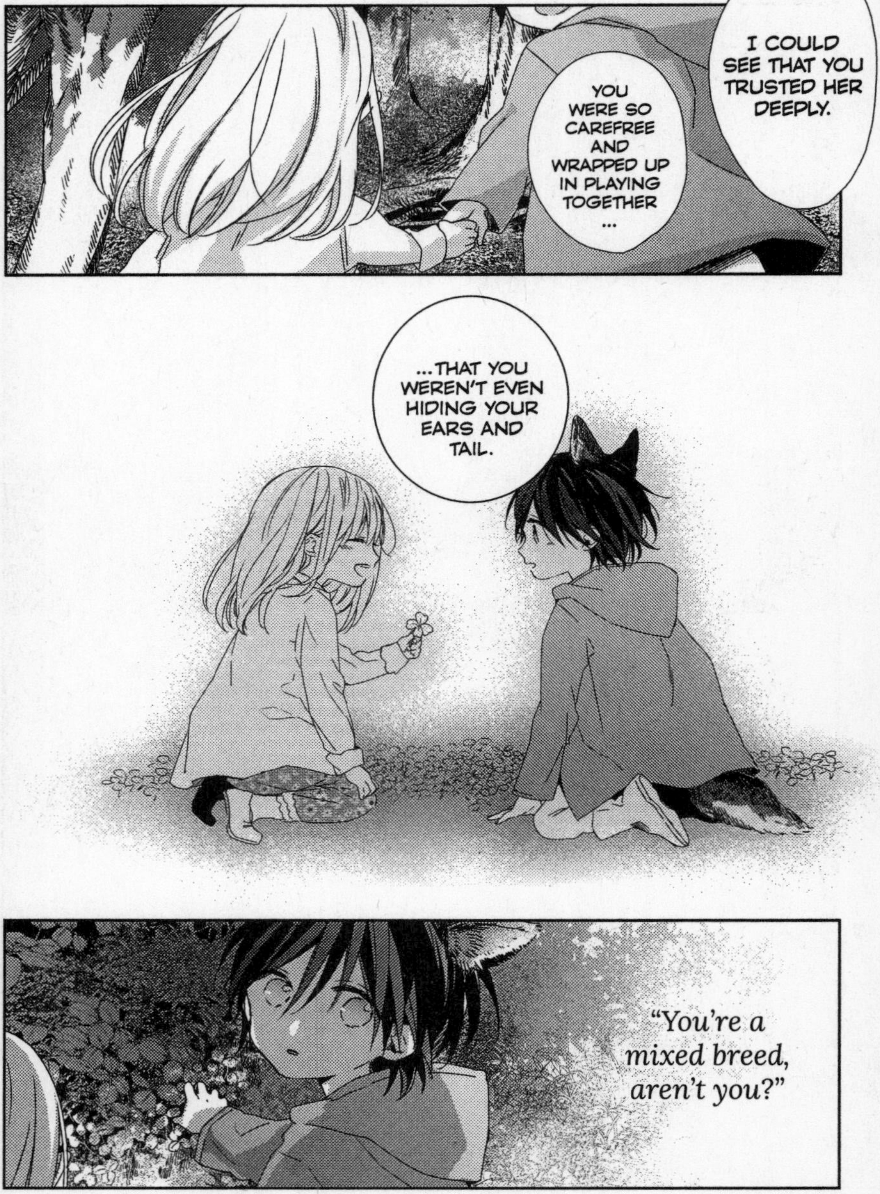
I COULD SEE THAT YOU TRUSTED HER DEEPLY.
YOU WERE SO CAREFREE AND WRAPPED UP IN PLAYING TOGETHER ...
...THAT YOU WEREN'T EVEN HIDING YOUR EARS AND TAIL.
"You're a mixed breed, aren't you?"

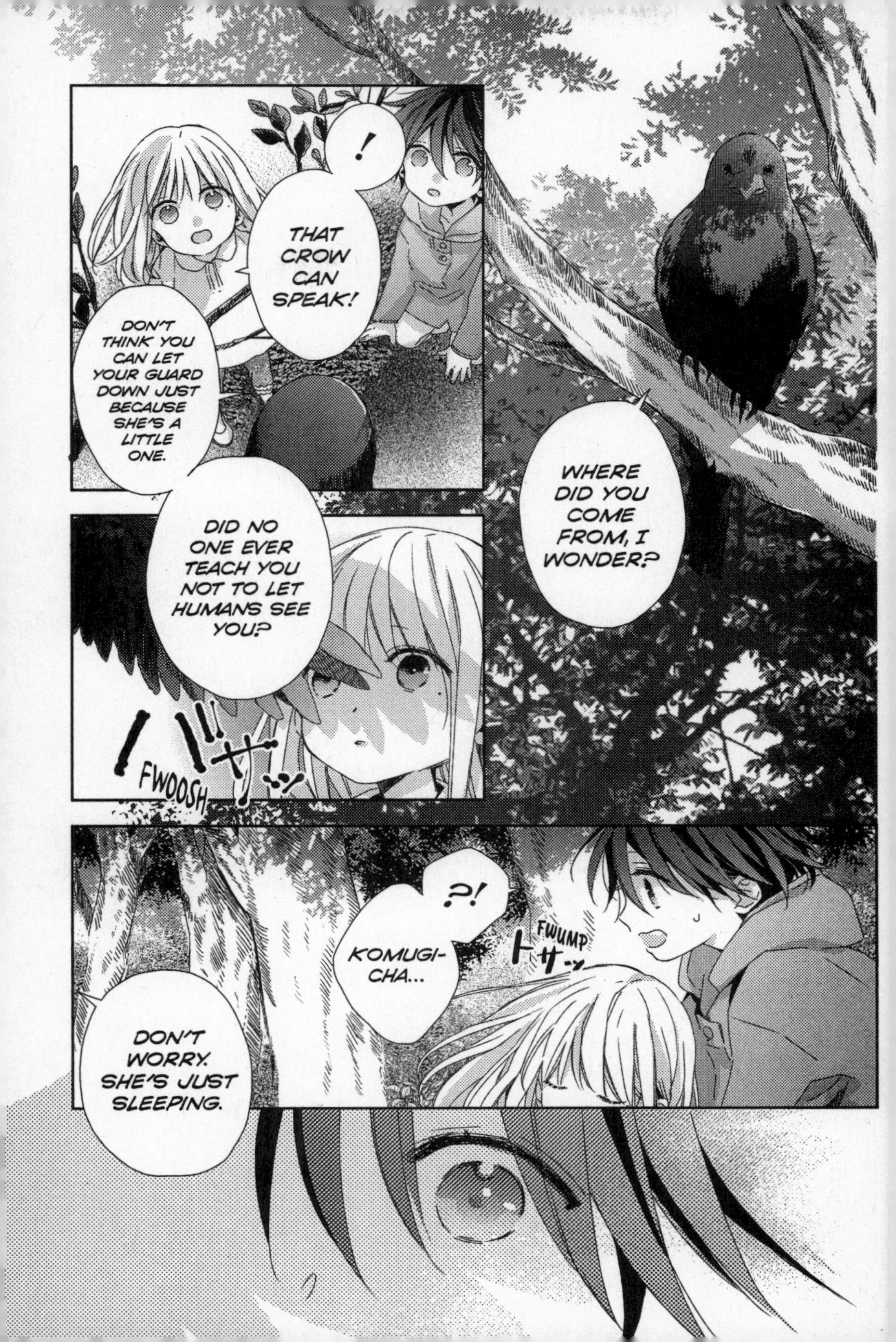
WHERE DID YOU COME FROM, I WONDER?
!
THAT CROW CAN SPEAK!
DON'T THINK YOU CAN LET YOUR GUARD DOWN JUST BECAUSE SHE'S A LITTLE ONE.
DID NO ONE EVER TEACH YOU NOT TO LET HUMANS SEE YOU?
FWOOSH
?!
FWUMP
KOMUGI-CHA...
DON'T WORRY. SHE'S JUST SLEEPING.

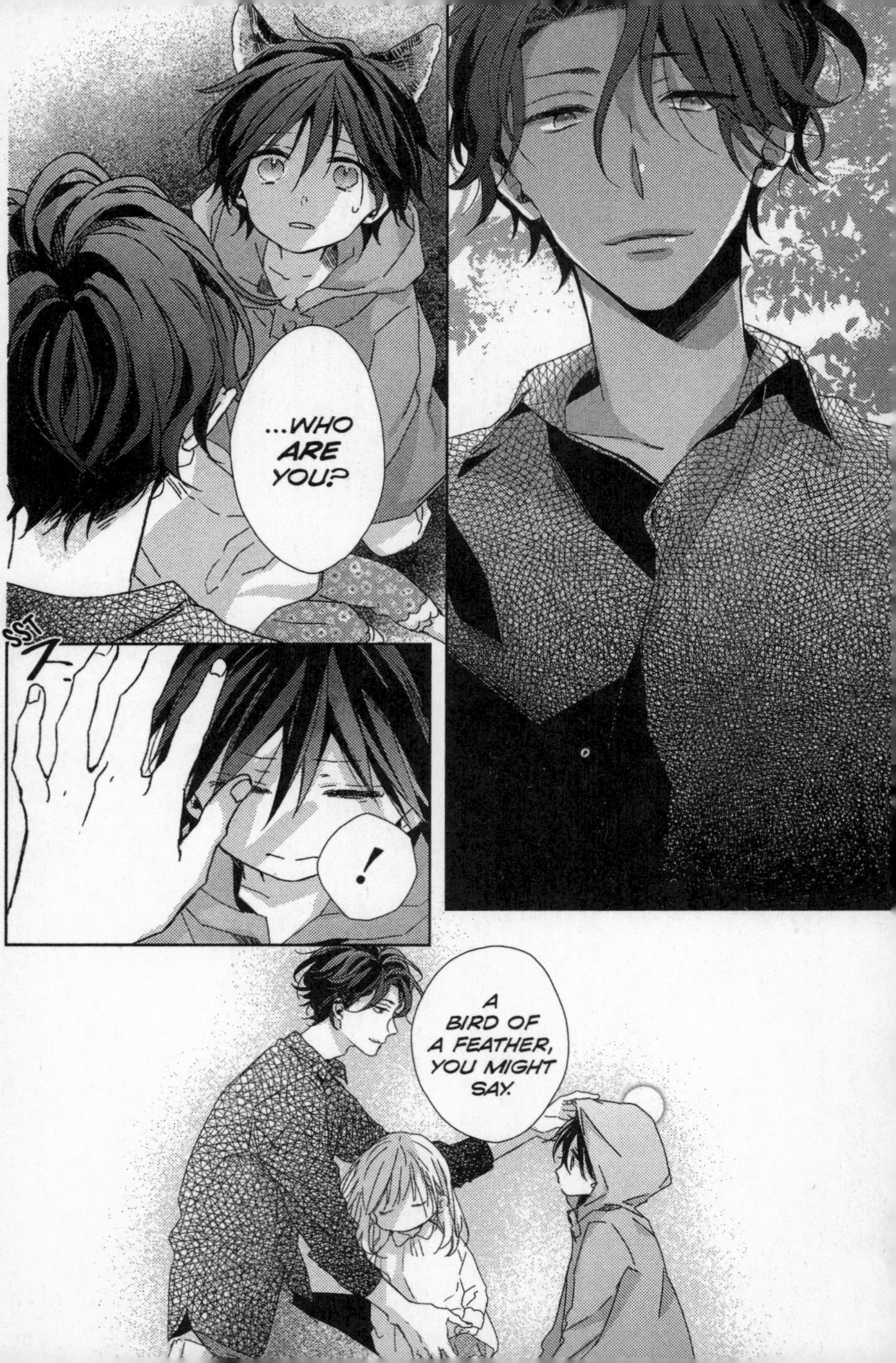
...WHO ARE YOU?
SST
!
A BIRD OF A FEATHER, YOU MIGHT SAY.

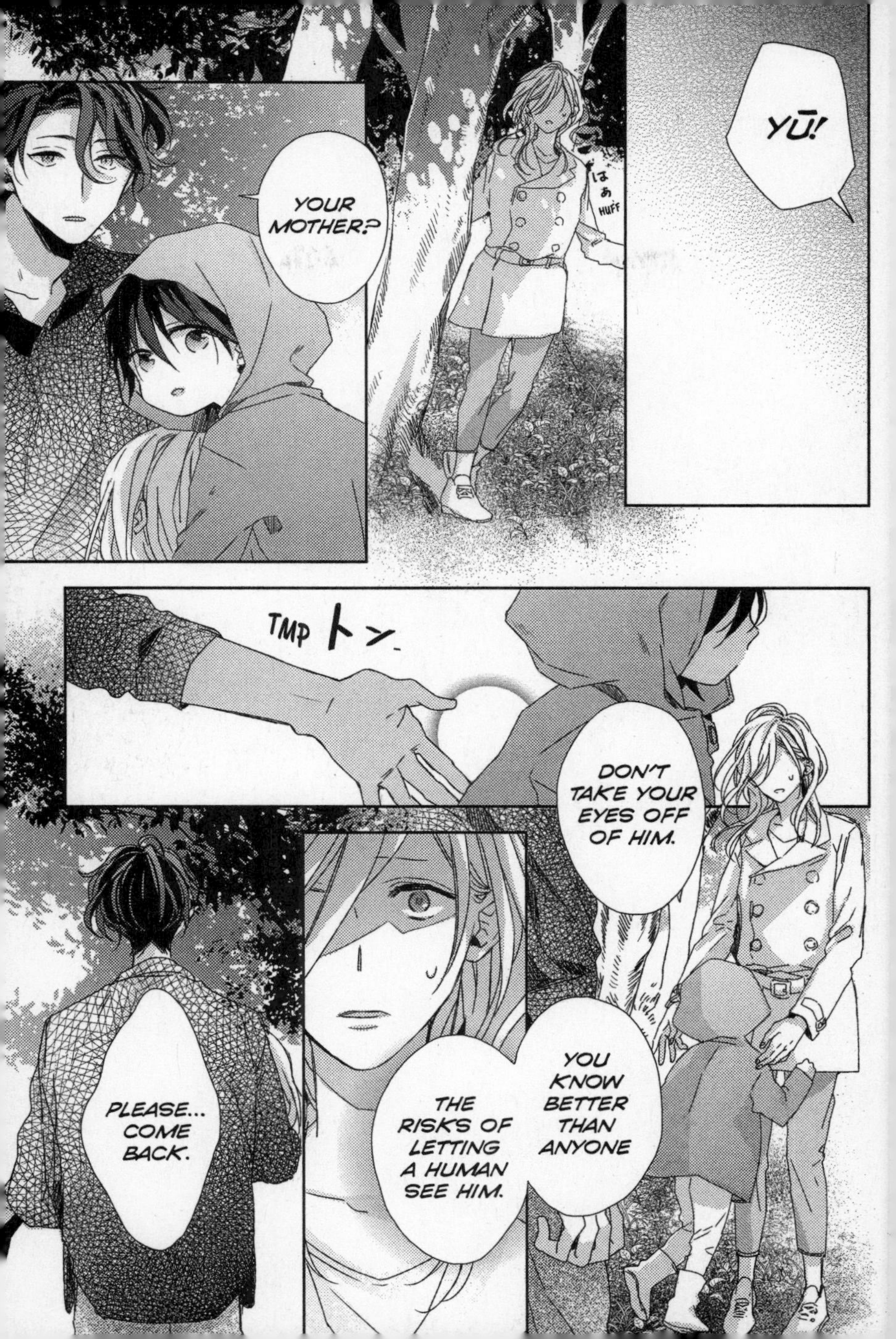
YŪ!
はぁ HUFF
YOUR MOTHER?
TMP トン
DON'T TAKE YOUR EYES OFF OF HIM.
YOU KNOW BETTER THAN ANYONE
THE RISKS OF LETTING A HUMAN SEE HIM.
PLEASE... COME BACK.

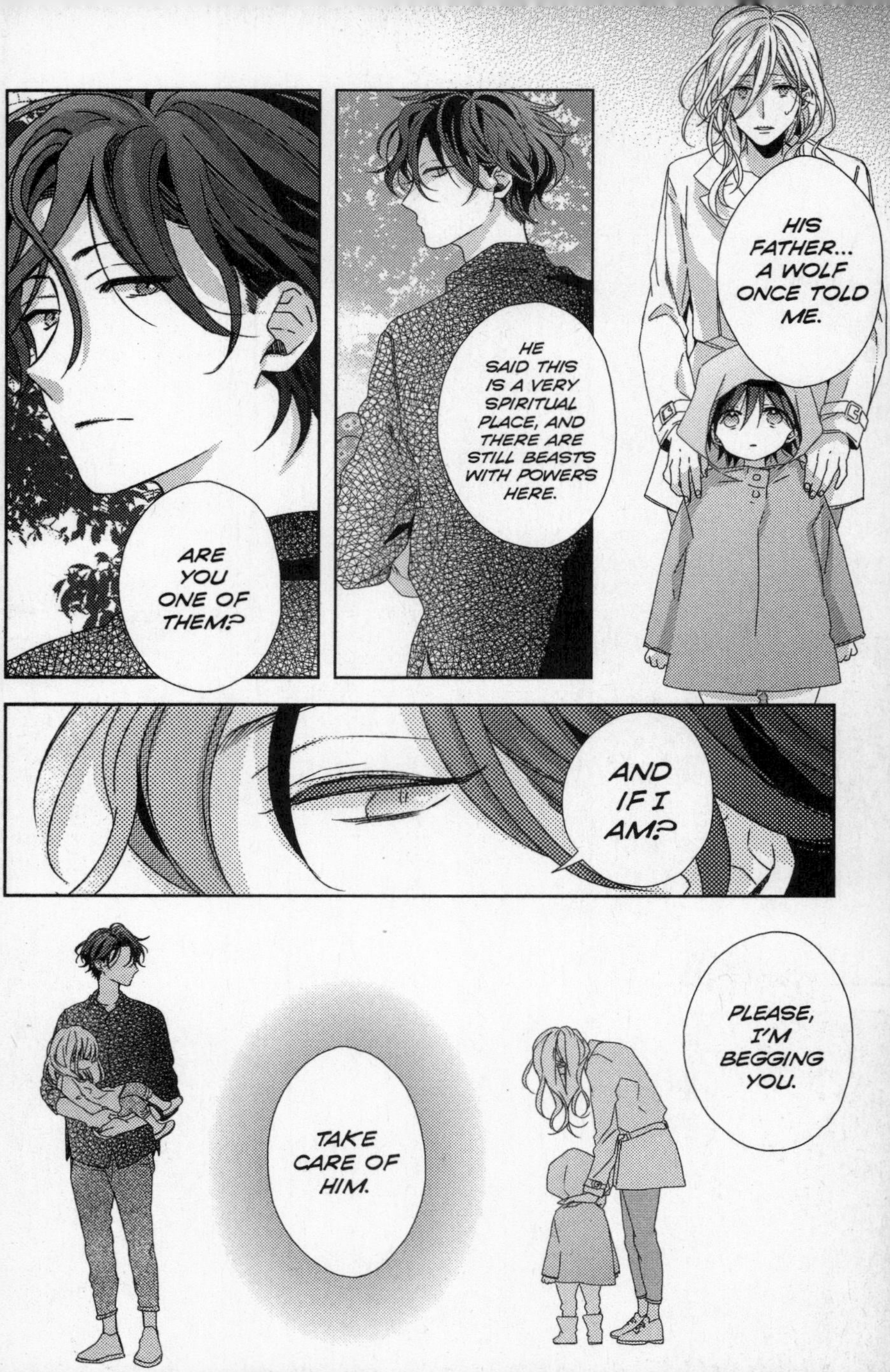
HIS FATHER... A WOLF ONCE TOLD ME.
HE SAID THIS IS A VERY SPIRITUAL PLACE, AND THERE ARE STILL BEASTS WITH POWERS HERE.
ARE YOU ONE OF THEM?
AND IF I AM?
PLEASE, I'M BEGGING YOU.
TAKE CARE OF HIM.

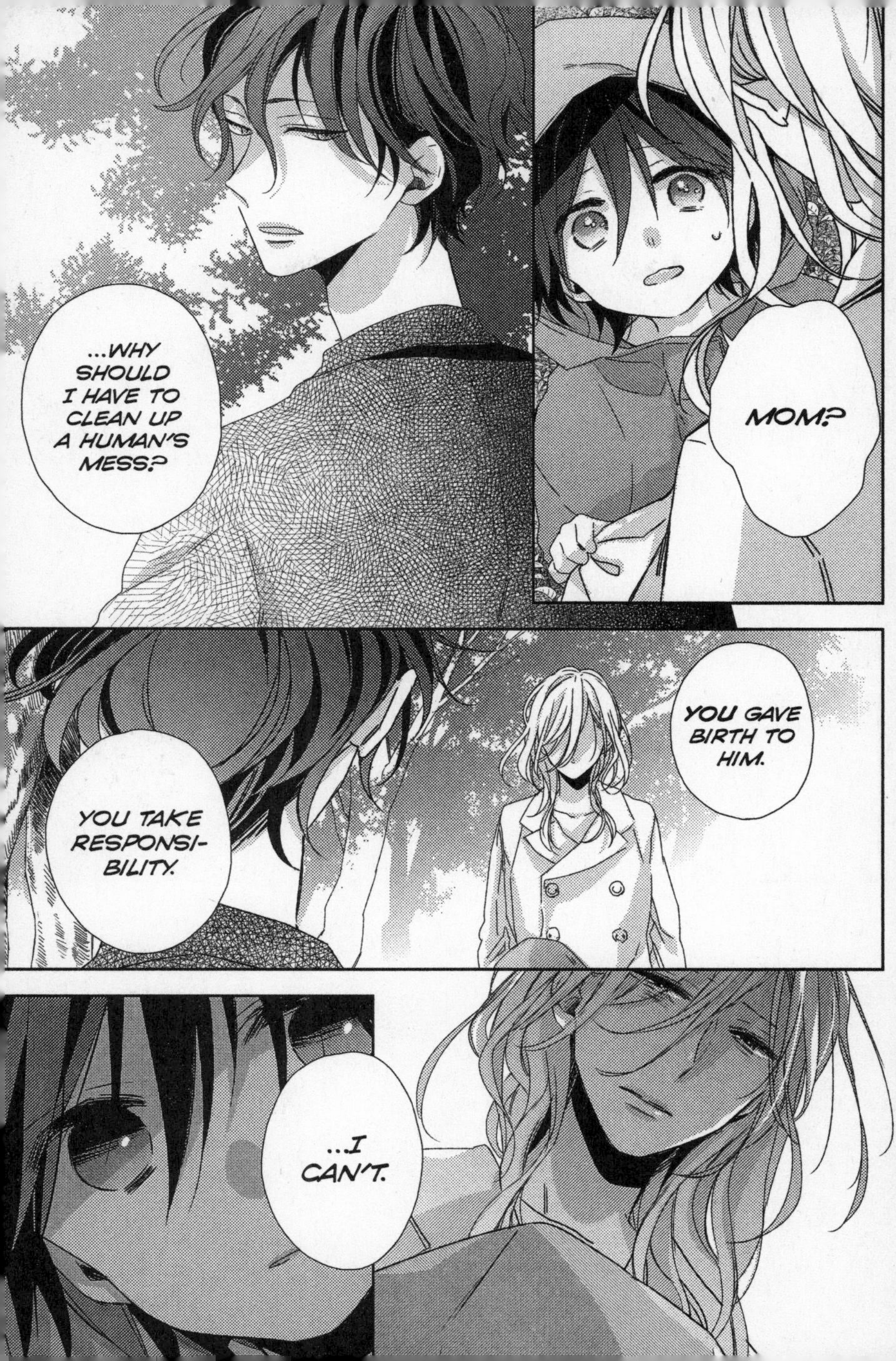
MOM?
...WHY SHOULD I HAVE TO CLEAN UP A HUMAN'S MESS?
YOU GAVE BIRTH TO HIM.
YOU TAKE RESPONSI-BILITY.
...I CAN'T.

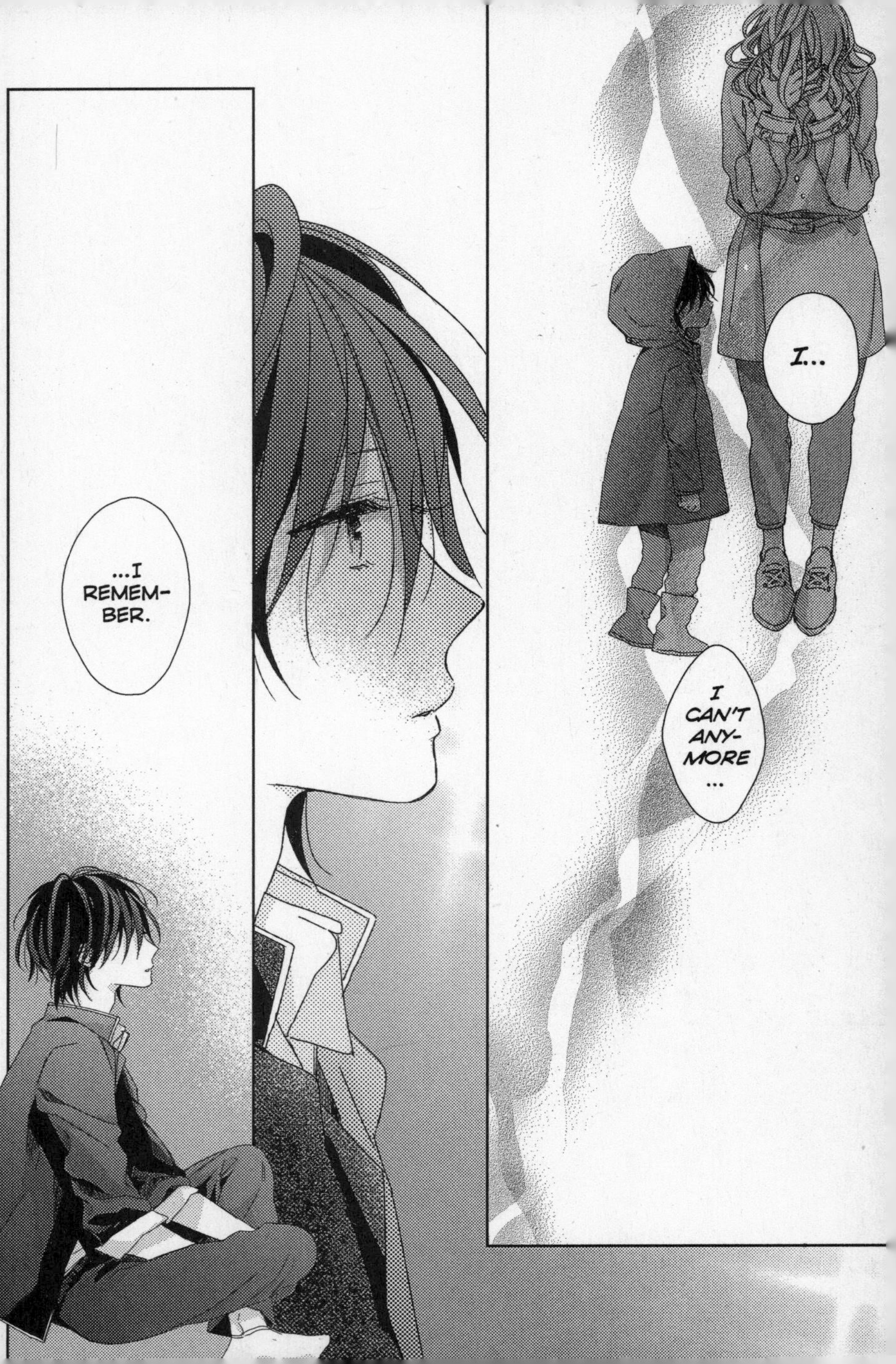
I...
I CAN'T ANY-MORE ...
...I REMEM-BER.

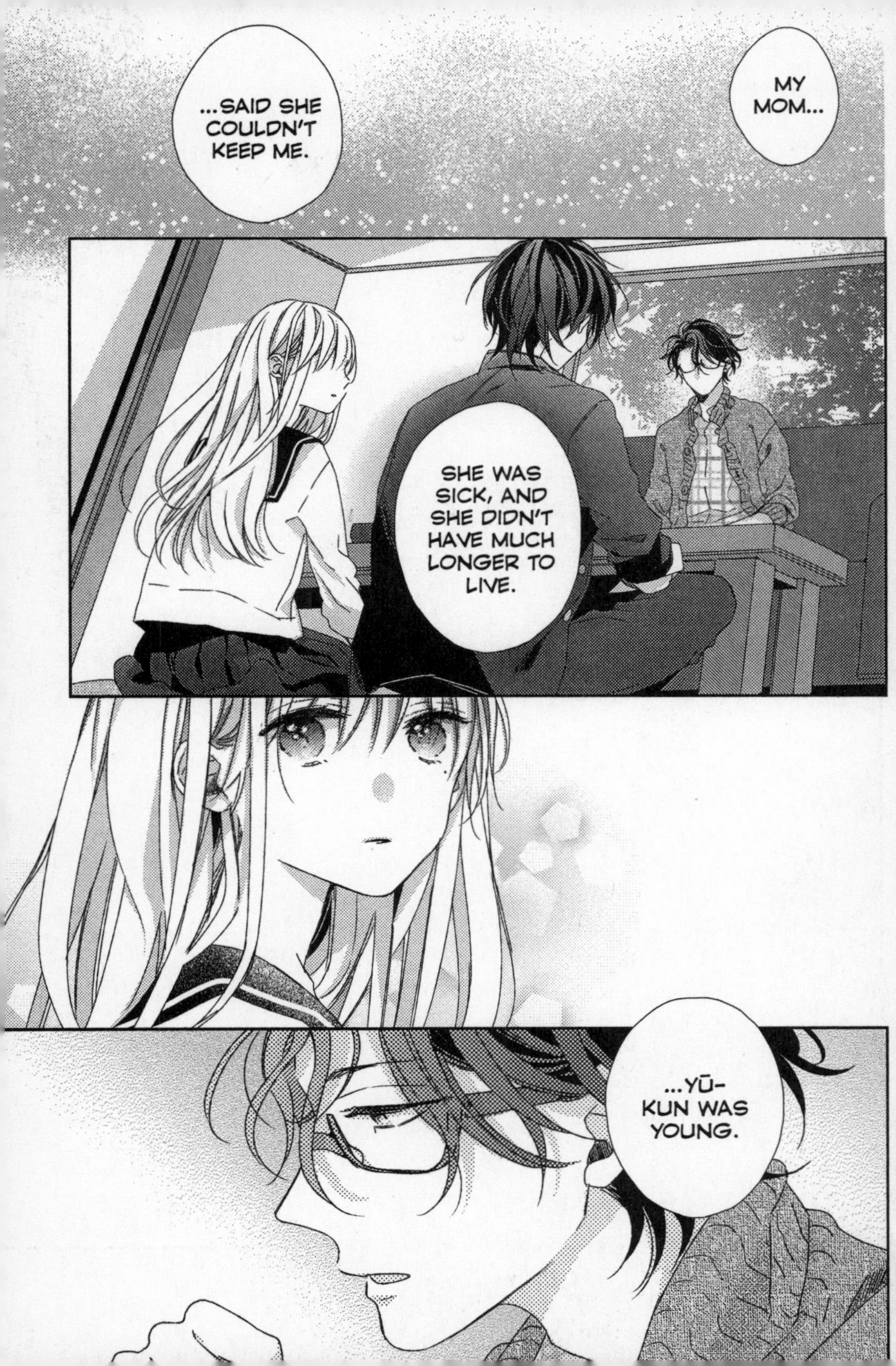
MY MOM...
...SAID SHE COULDN'T KEEP ME.
SHE WAS SICK, AND SHE DIDN'T HAVE MUCH LONGER TO LIVE.
...YŪ-KUN WAS YOUNG.

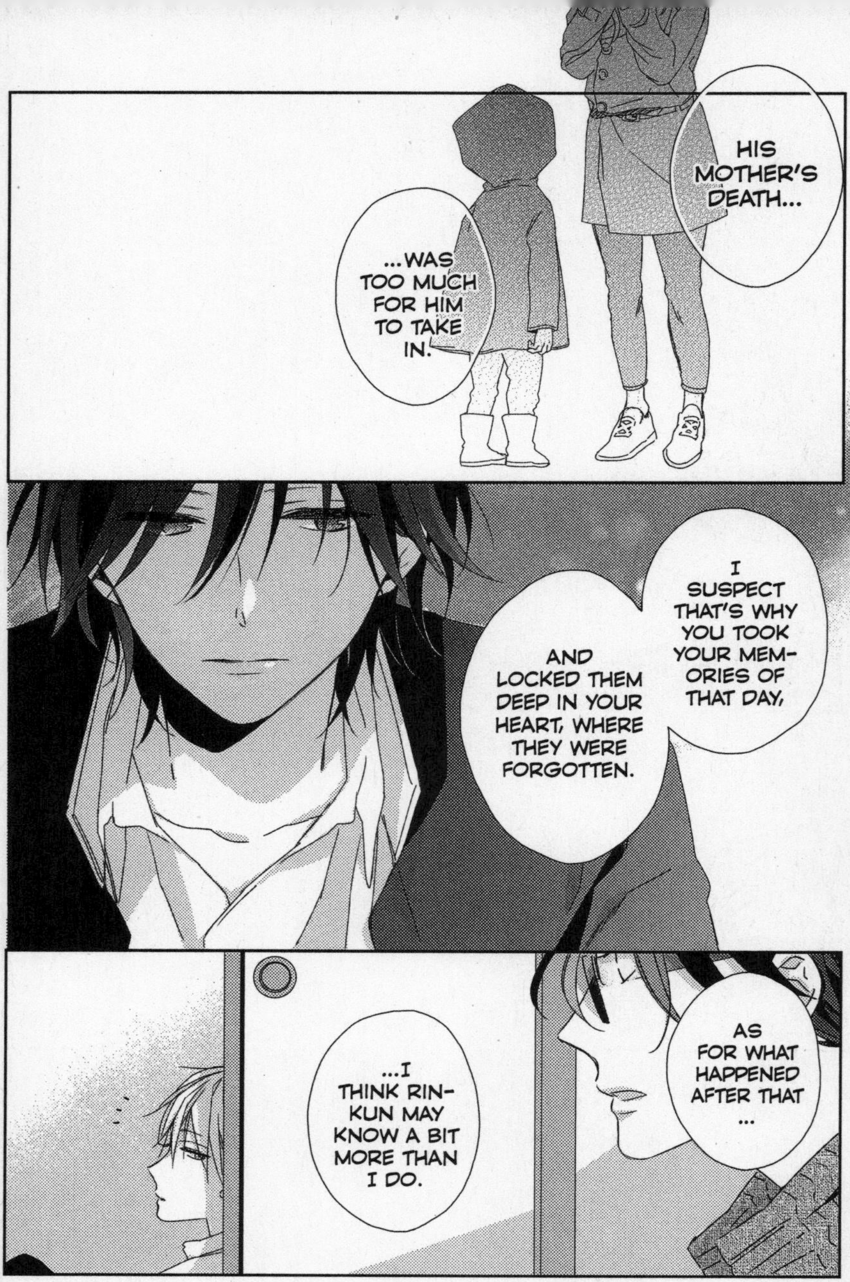
HIS MOTHER'S DEATH...
...WAS TOO MUCH FOR HIM TO TAKE IN.
I SUSPECT THAT'S WHY YOU TOOK YOUR MEM-ORIES OF THAT DAY,
AND LOCKED THEM DEEP IN YOUR HEART, WHERE THEY WERE FORGOTTEN.
AS FOR WHAT HAPPENED AFTER THAT ...
...I THINK RIN-KUN MAY KNOW A BIT MORE THAN I DO.

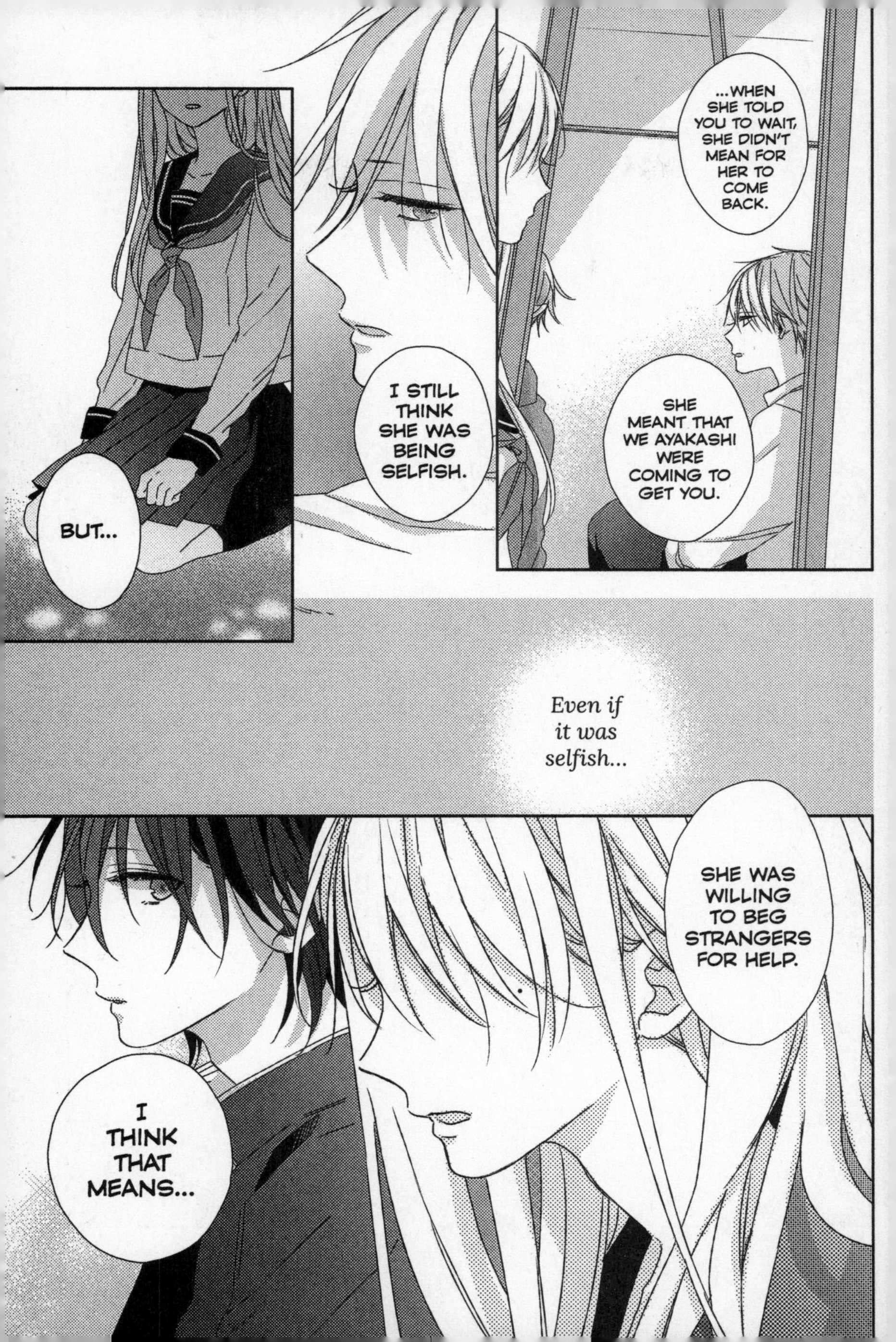
...WHEN SHE TOLD YOU TO WAIT, SHE DIDN'T MEAN FOR HER TO COME BACK.
SHE MEANT THAT WE AYAKASHI WERE COMING TO GET YOU.
I STILL THINK SHE WAS BEING SELFISH.
BUT...
Even if it was selfish...
SHE WAS WILLING TO BEG STRANGERS FOR HELP.
I THINK THAT MEANS...

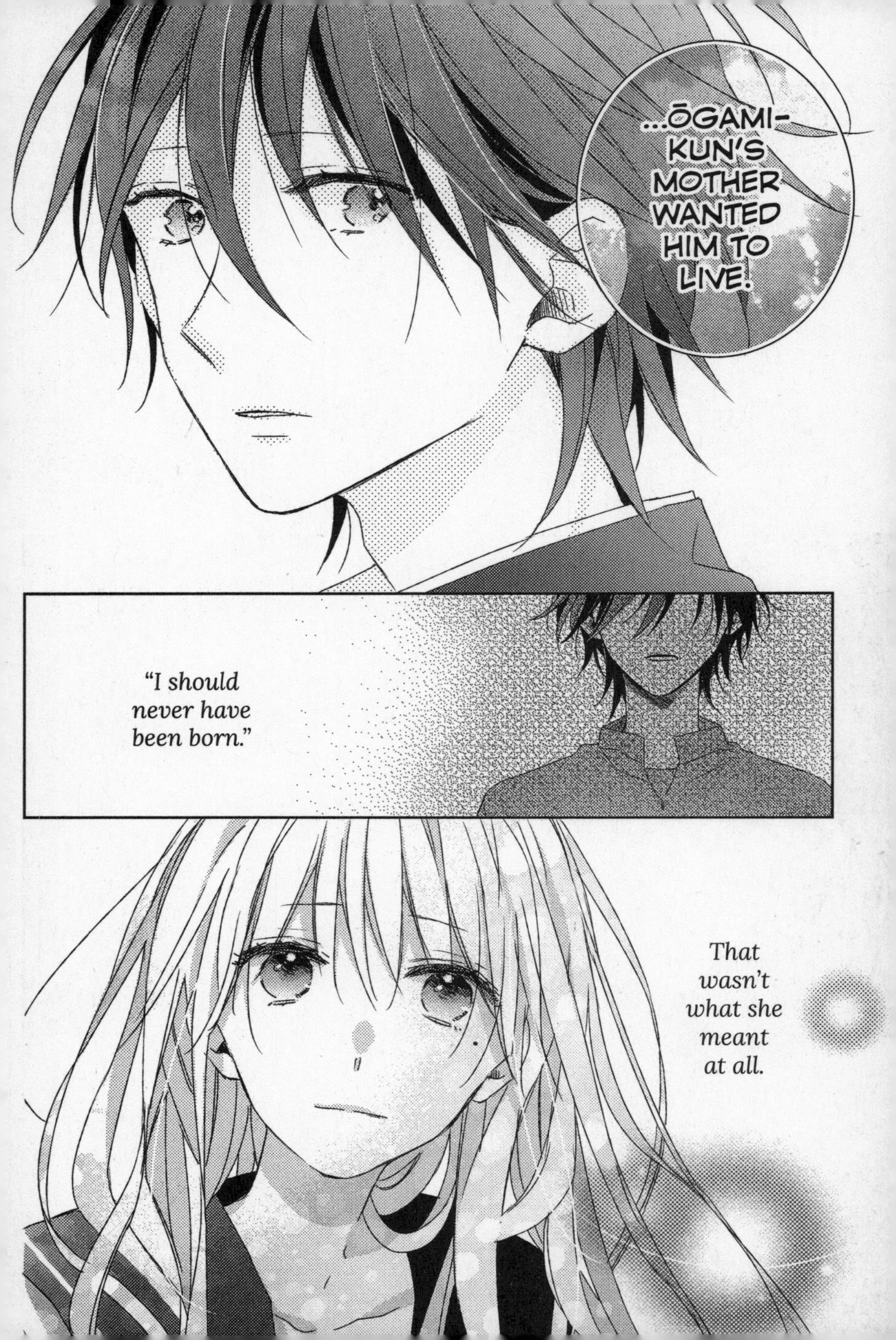

...ŌGAMI-KUN'S MOTHER WANTED HIM TO LIVE.
"I should never have been born."
That wasn't what she meant at all.

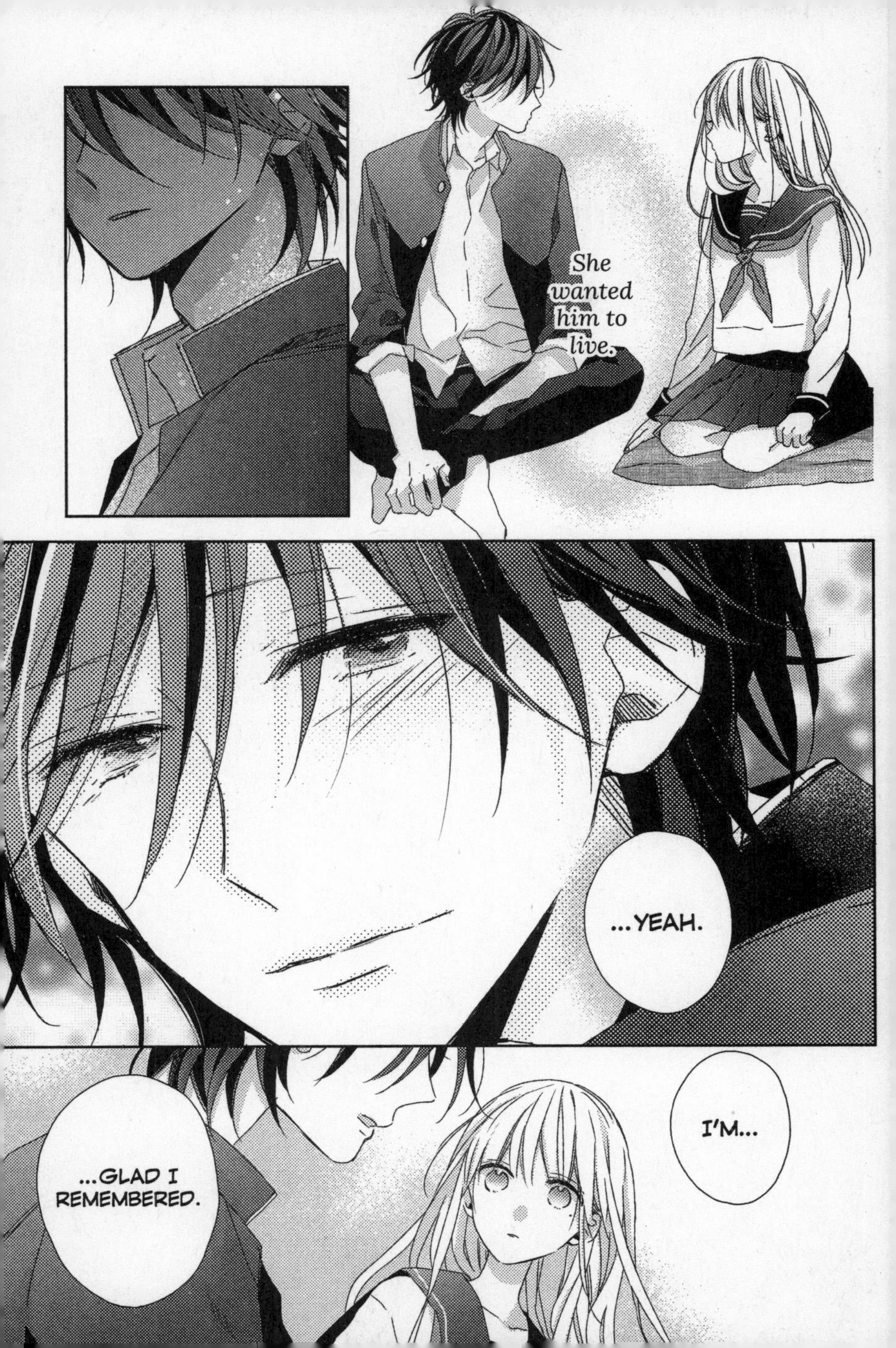
She wanted him to live.
...YEAH.
I'M...
...GLAD I REMEMBERED.

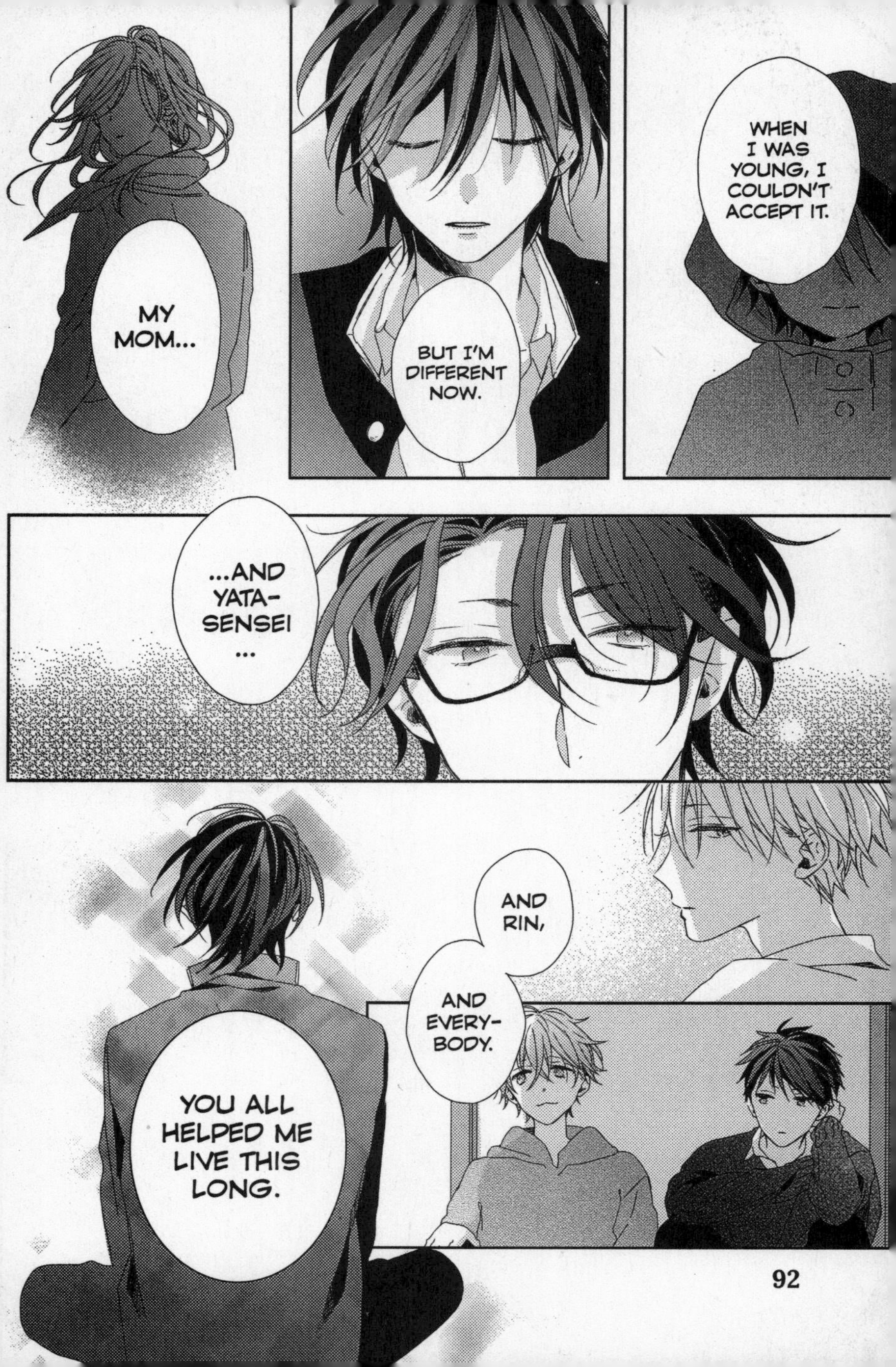
WHEN I WAS YOUNG, I COULDN'T ACCEPT IT.
BUT I'M DIFFERENT NOW.
MY MOM...
...AND YATA-SENSEI ...
AND RIN,
AND EVERY-BODY.
YOU ALL HELPED ME LIVE THIS LONG.

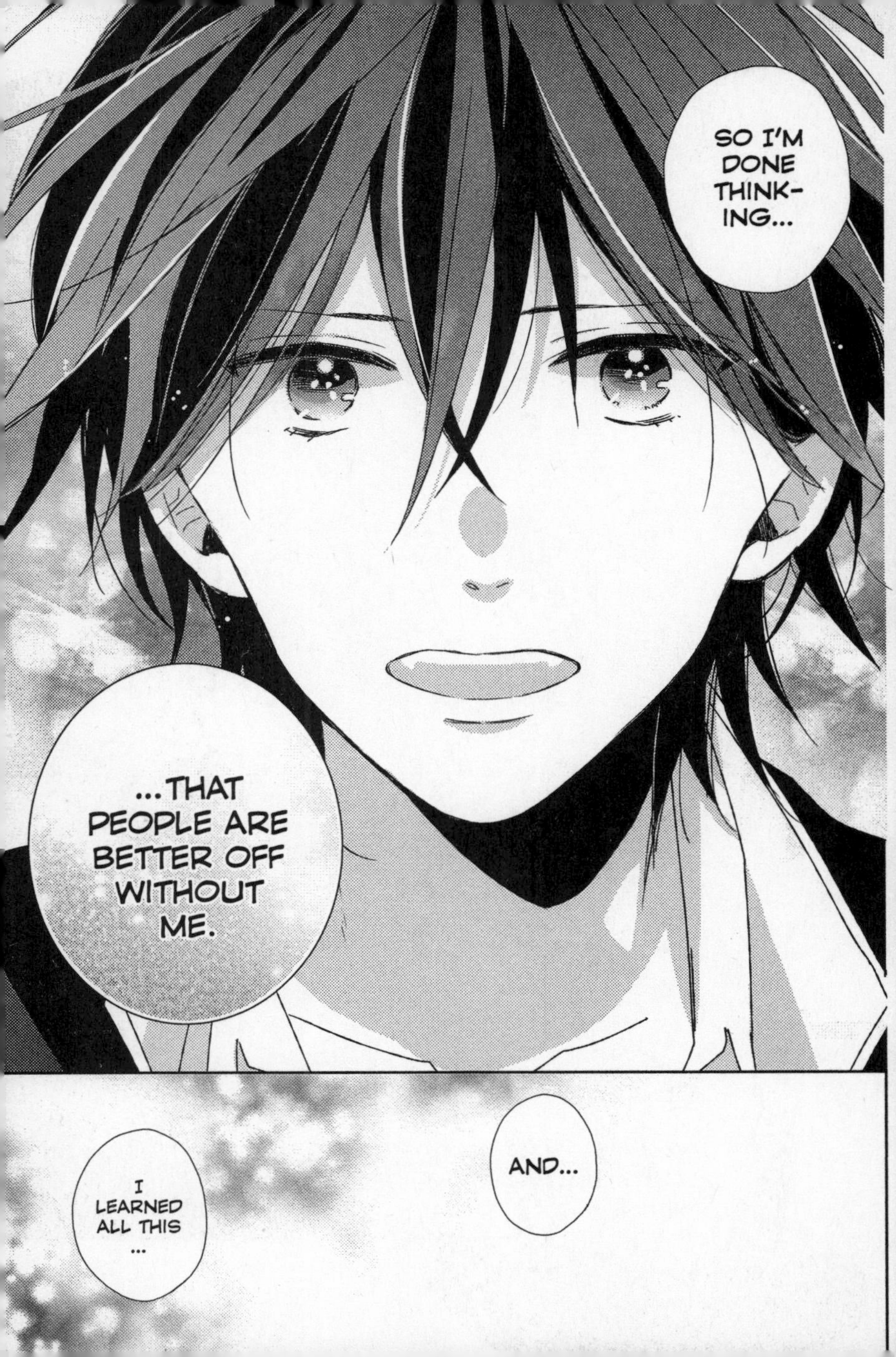
SO I'M DONE THINKING...
...THAT PEOPLE ARE BETTER OFF WITHOUT ME.
AND...
I LEARNED ALL THIS ...

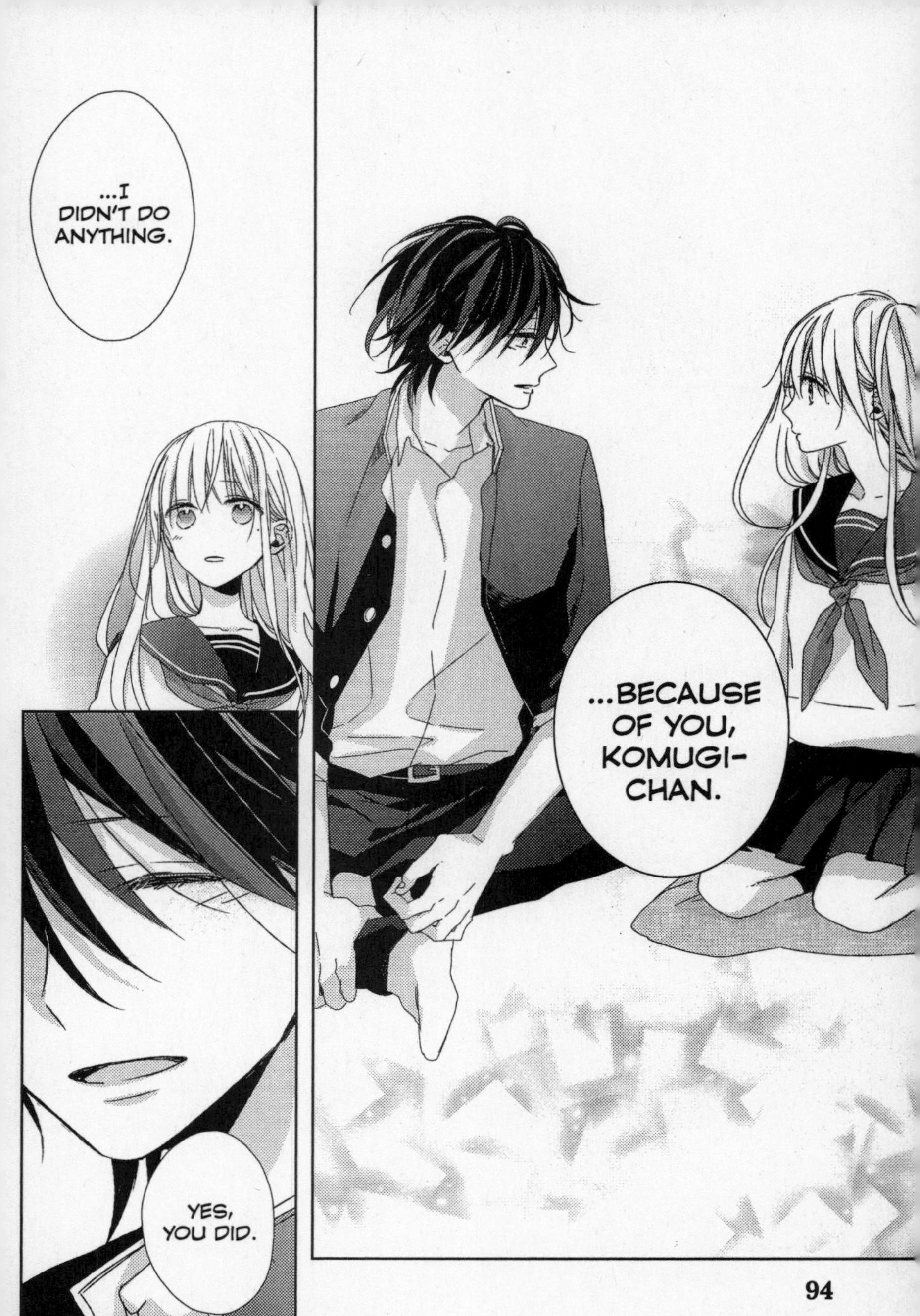
...BECAUSE OF YOU, KOMUGI-CHAN.
...I DIDN'T DO ANYTHING.
YES, YOU DID.

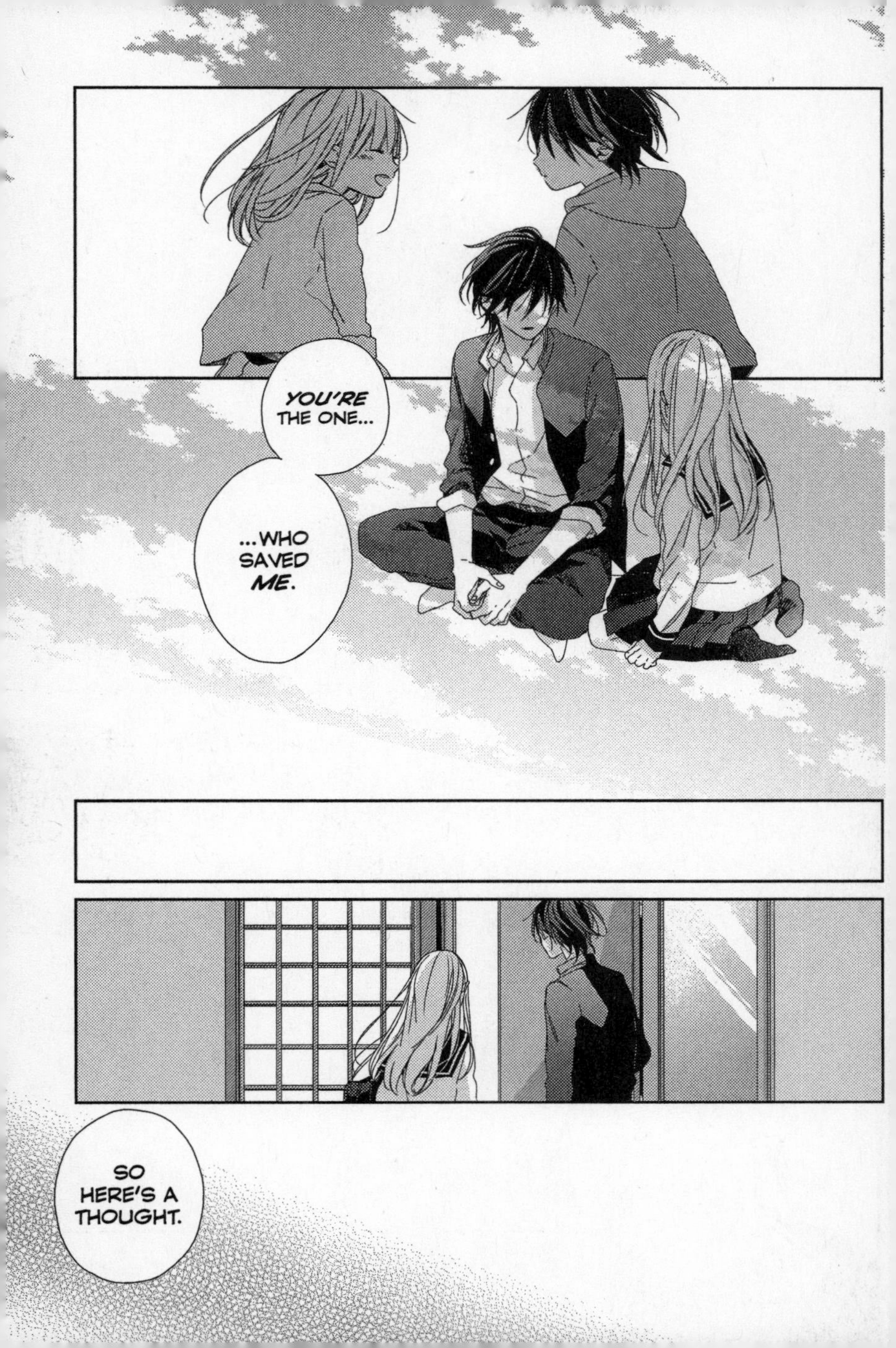

YOU'RE THE ONE...
...WHO SAVED ME.
SO HERE'S A THOUGHT.

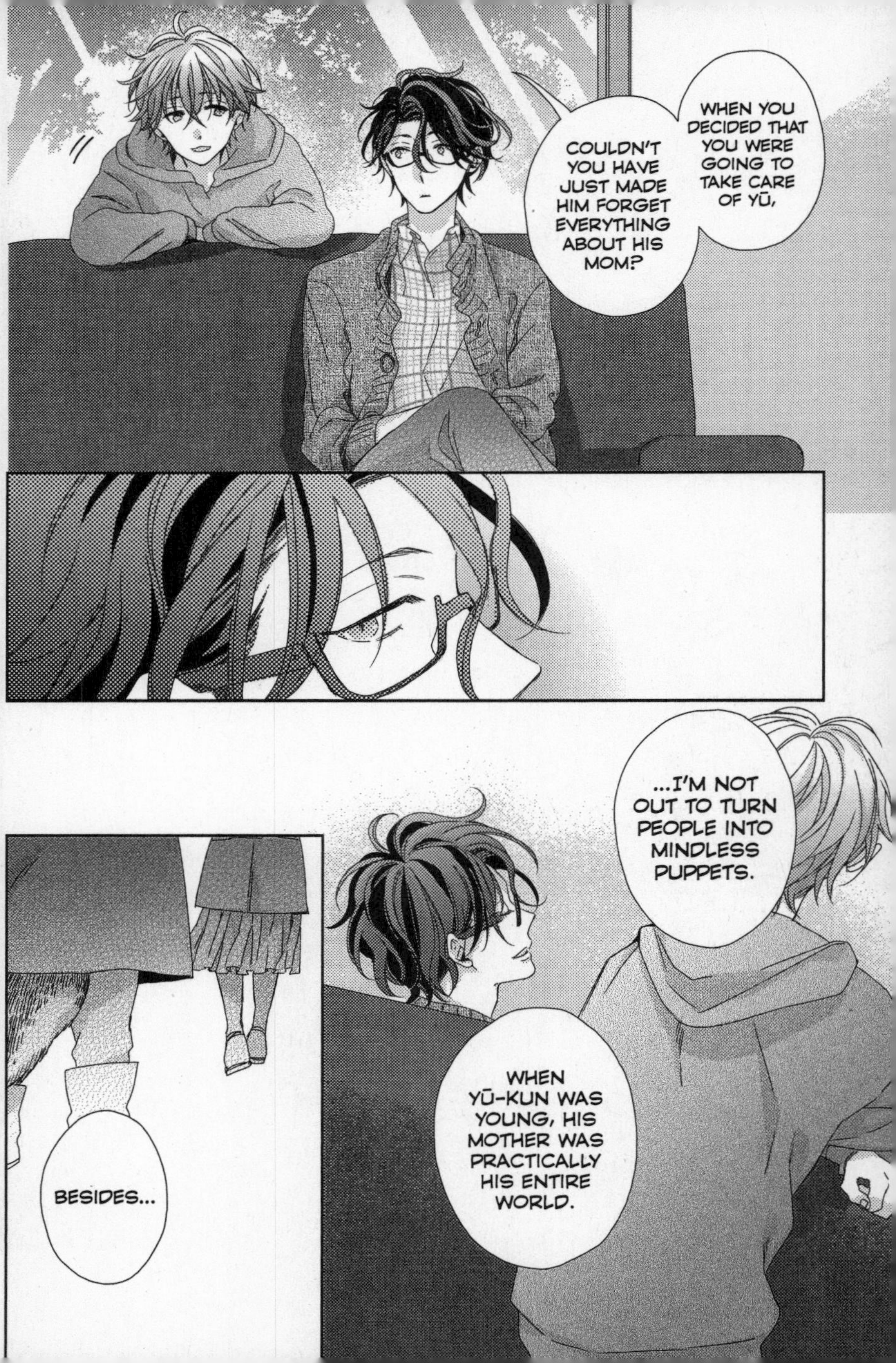
WHEN YOU DECIDED THAT YOU WERE GOING TO TAKE CARE OF YŪ,
COULDN'T YOU HAVE JUST MADE HIM FORGET EVERYTHING ABOUT HIS MOM?
...I'M NOT OUT TO TURN PEOPLE INTO MINDLESS PUPPETS.
WHEN YŪ-KUN WAS YOUNG, HIS MOTHER WAS PRACTICALLY HIS ENTIRE WORLD.
BESIDES...

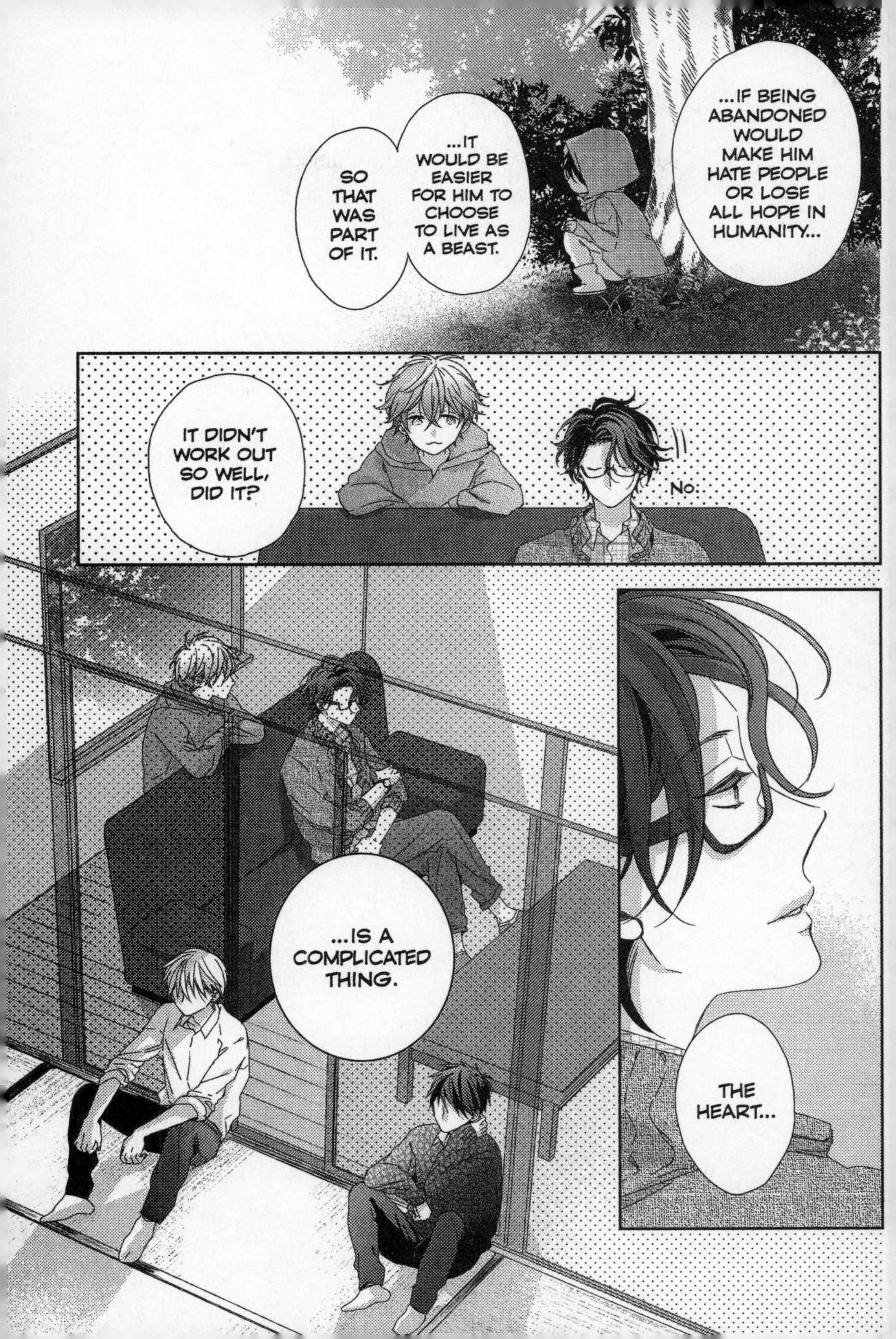
...IF BEING ABANDONED WOULD MAKE HIM HATE PEOPLE OR LOSE ALL HOPE IN HUMANITY...
...IT WOULD BE EASIER FOR HIM TO CHOOSE TO LIVE AS A BEAST.
SO THAT WAS PART OF IT.
IT DIDN'T WORK OUT SO WELL, DID IT?
No.
THE HEART...
...IS A COMPLICATED THING.

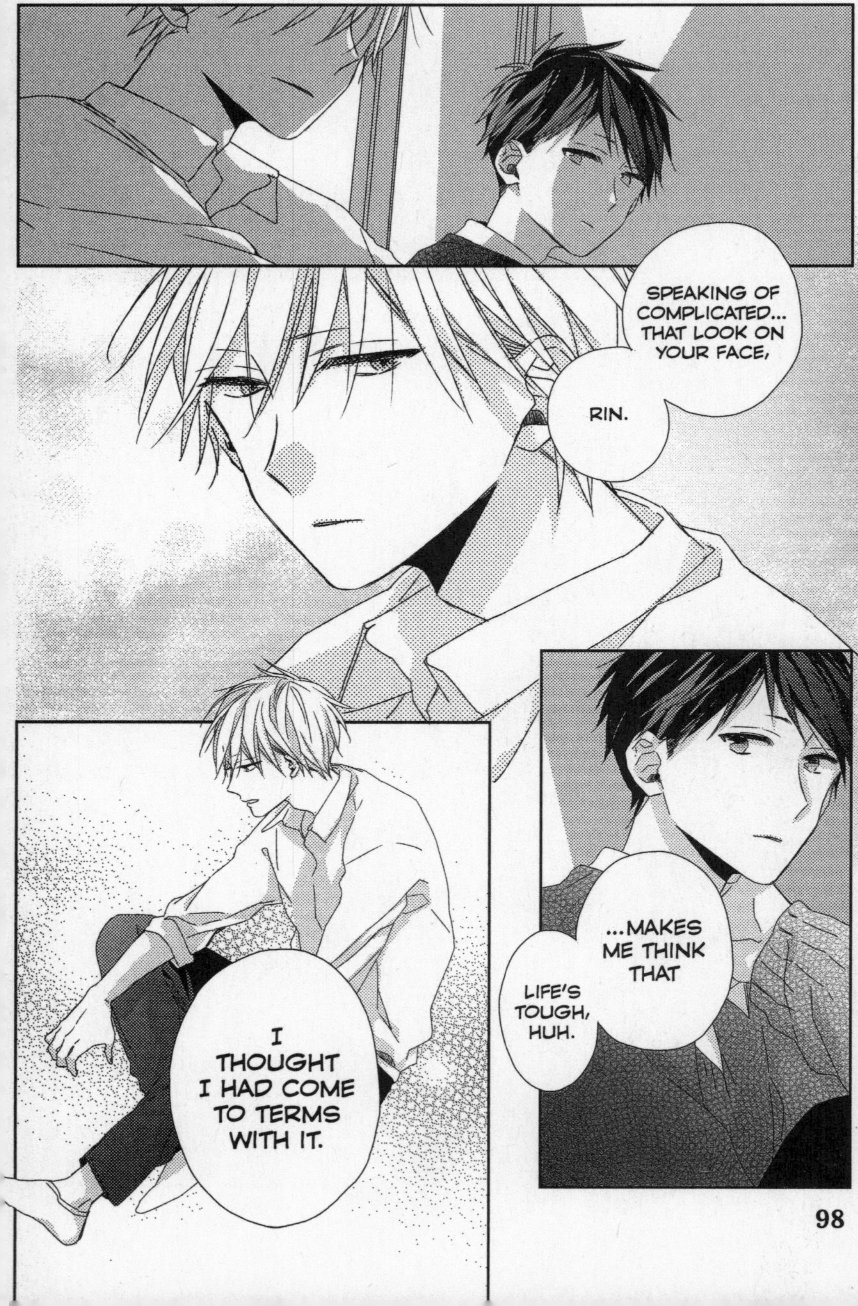
SPEAKING OF COMPLICATED... THAT LOOK ON YOUR FACE,
RIN.
...MAKES ME THINK THAT
LIFE'S TOUGH, HUH.
I THOUGHT I HAD COME TO TERMS WITH IT.

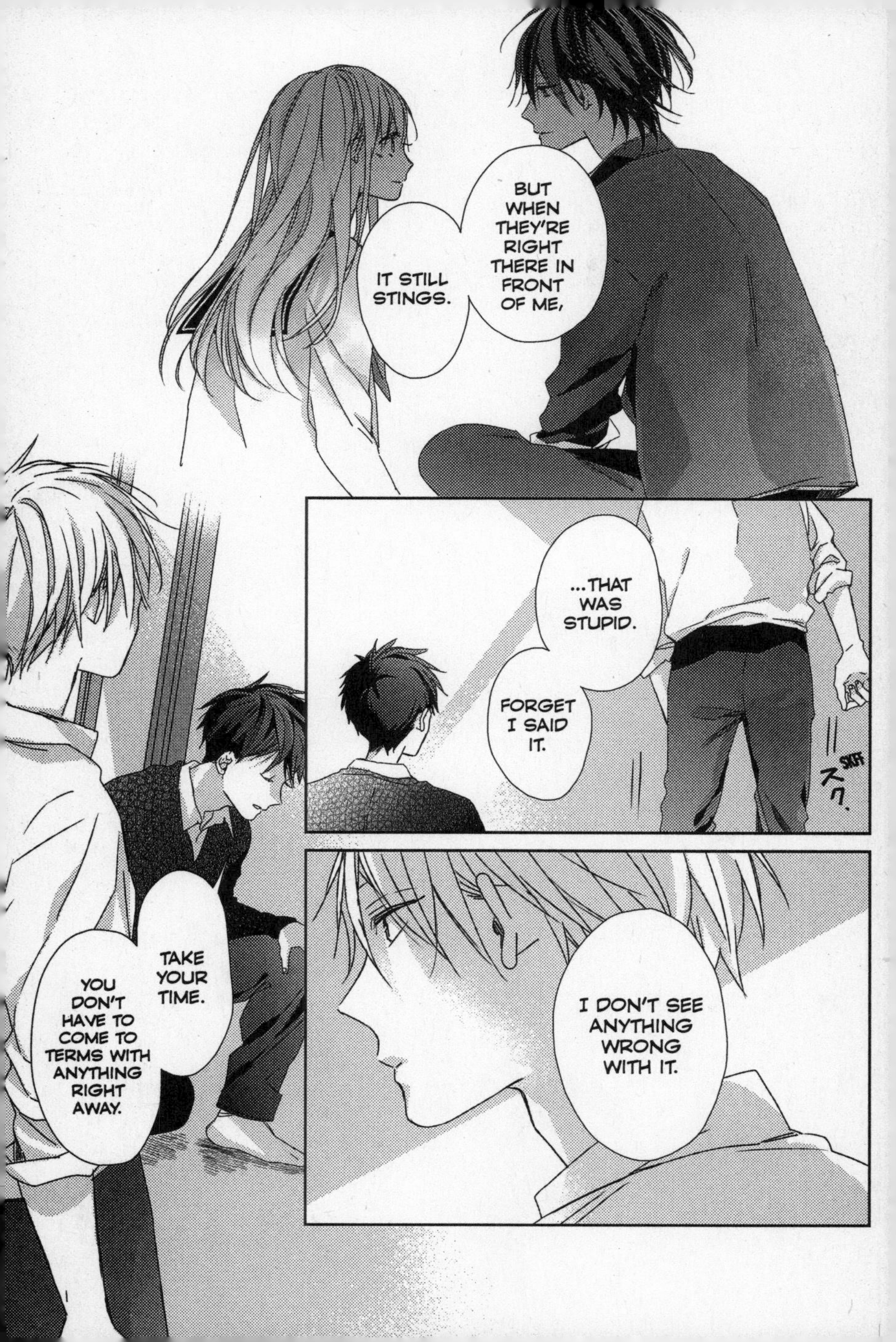
BUT WHEN THEY'RE RIGHT THERE IN FRONT OF ME,
IT STILL STINGS.
...THAT WAS STUPID.
FORGET I SAID IT.
SKFF
I DON'T SEE ANYTHING WRONG WITH IT.
TAKE YOUR TIME.
YOU DON'T HAVE TO COME TO TERMS WITH ANYTHING RIGHT AWAY.

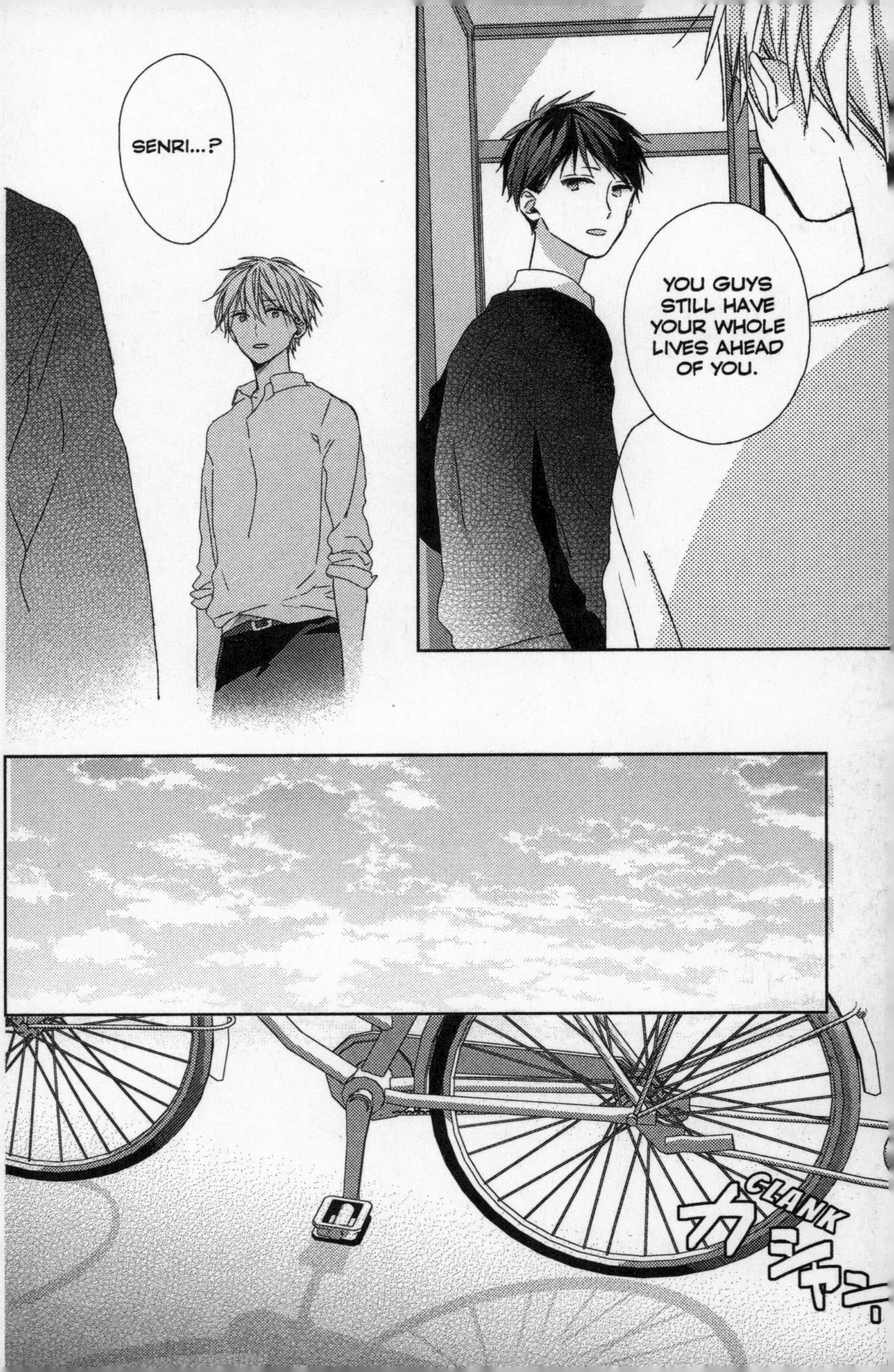
YOU GUYS STILL HAVE YOUR WHOLE LIVES AHEAD OF YOU.
SENRI...?
CLANK
ガシャン!

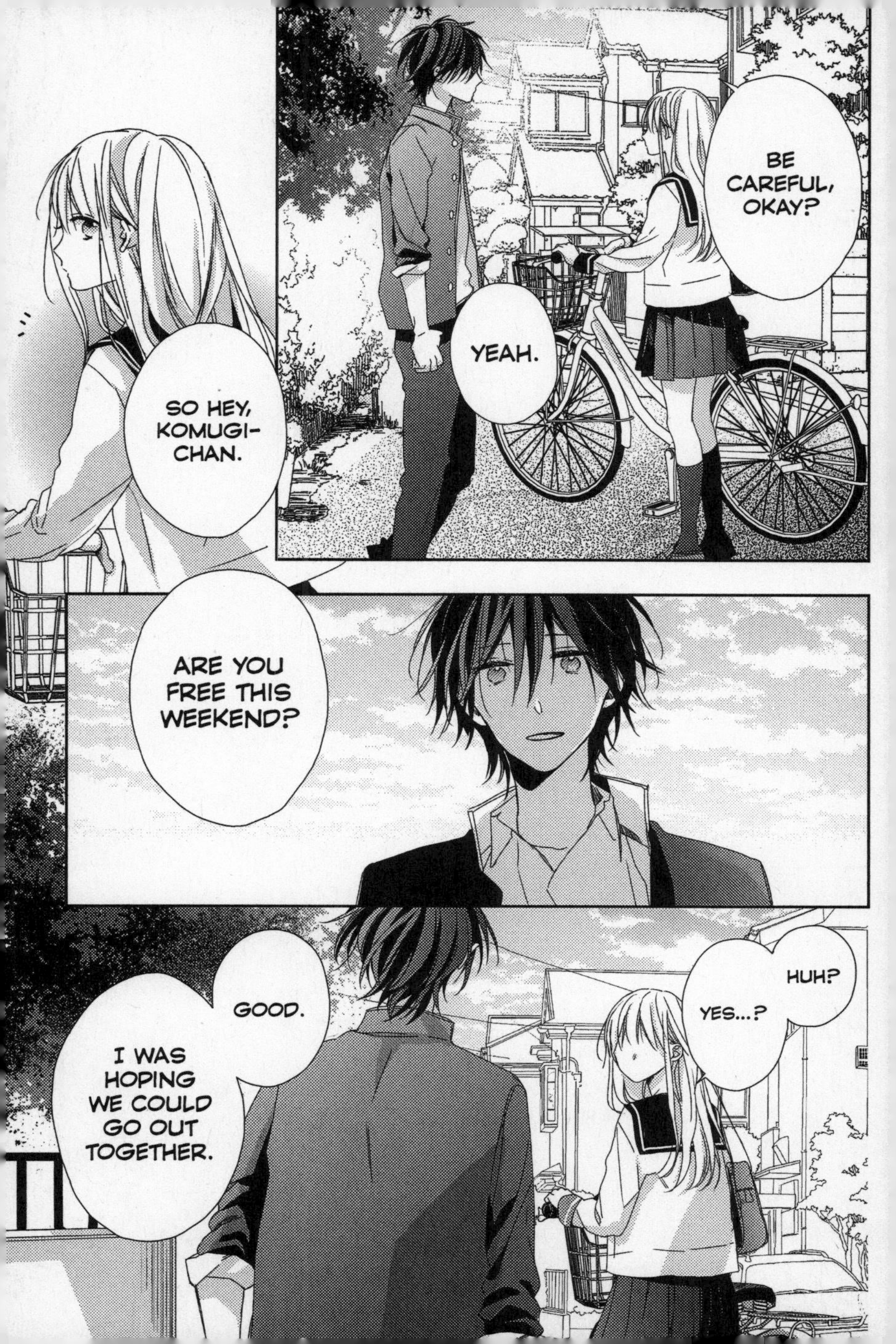
BE CAREFUL, OKAY?
YEAH.
SO HEY, KOMUGI-CHAN.
ARE YOU FREE THIS WEEKEND?
HUH? YES...?
GOOD. I WAS HOPING WE COULD GO OUT TOGETHER.

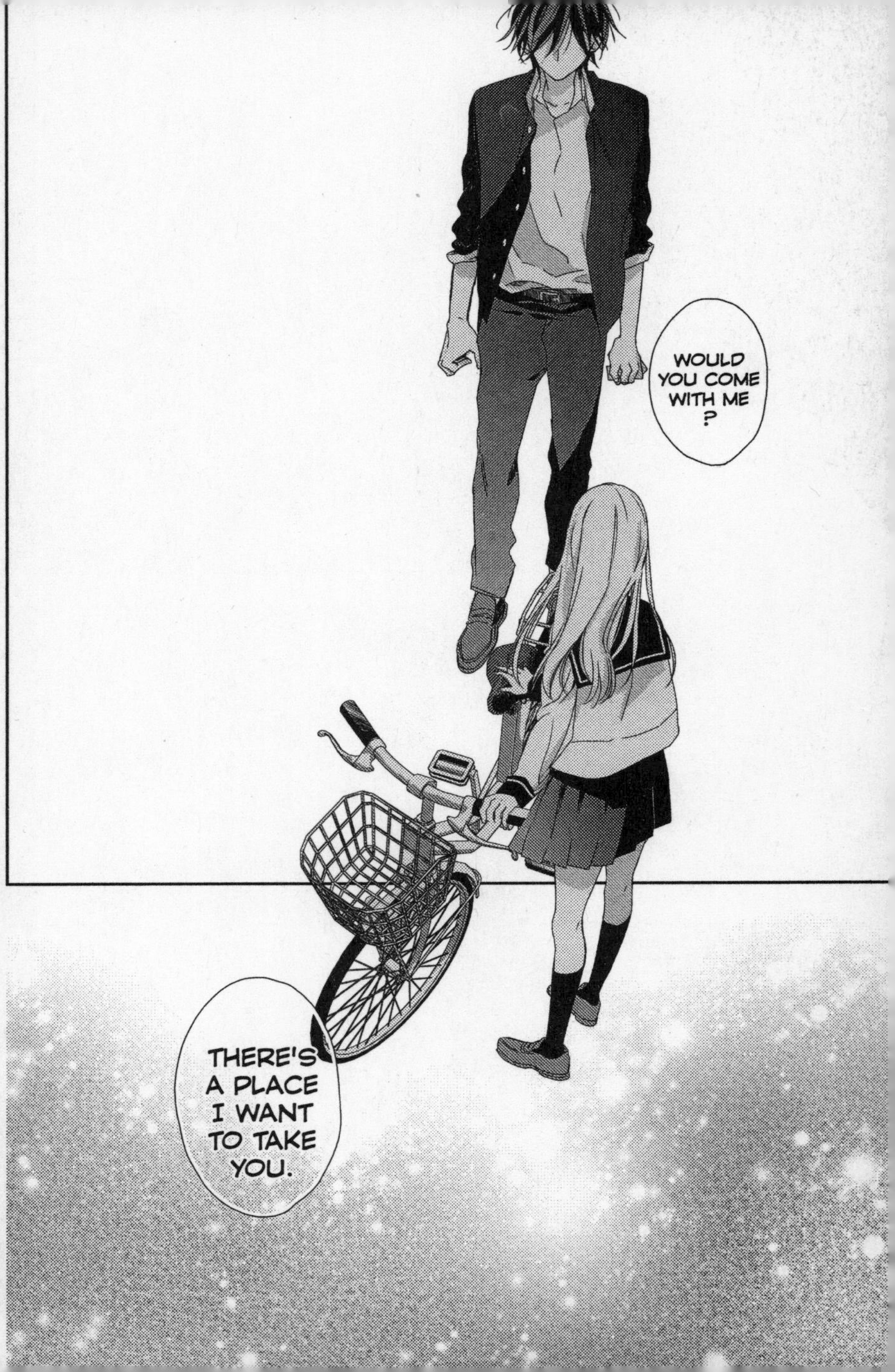
WOULD YOU COME WITH ME ?
THERE'S A PLACE I WANT TO TAKE YOU.

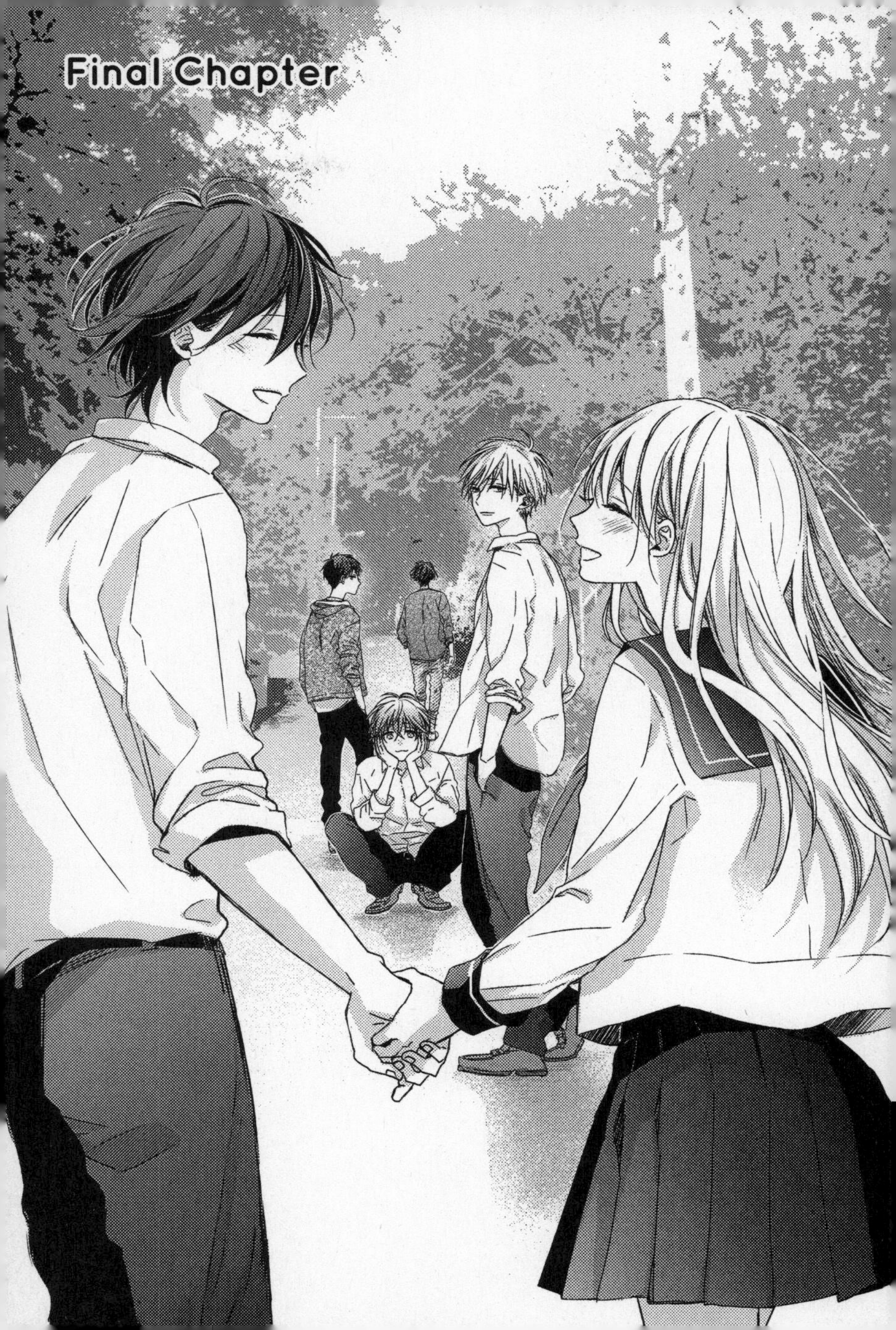
Final Chapter

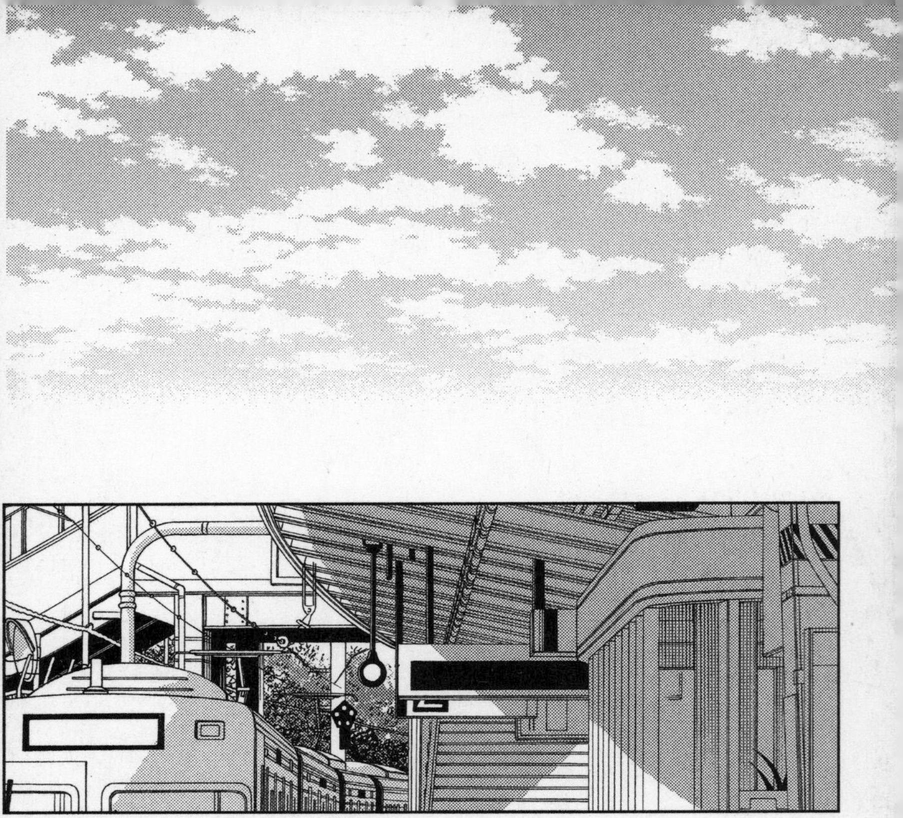

That Wolf-Boy is Mine!

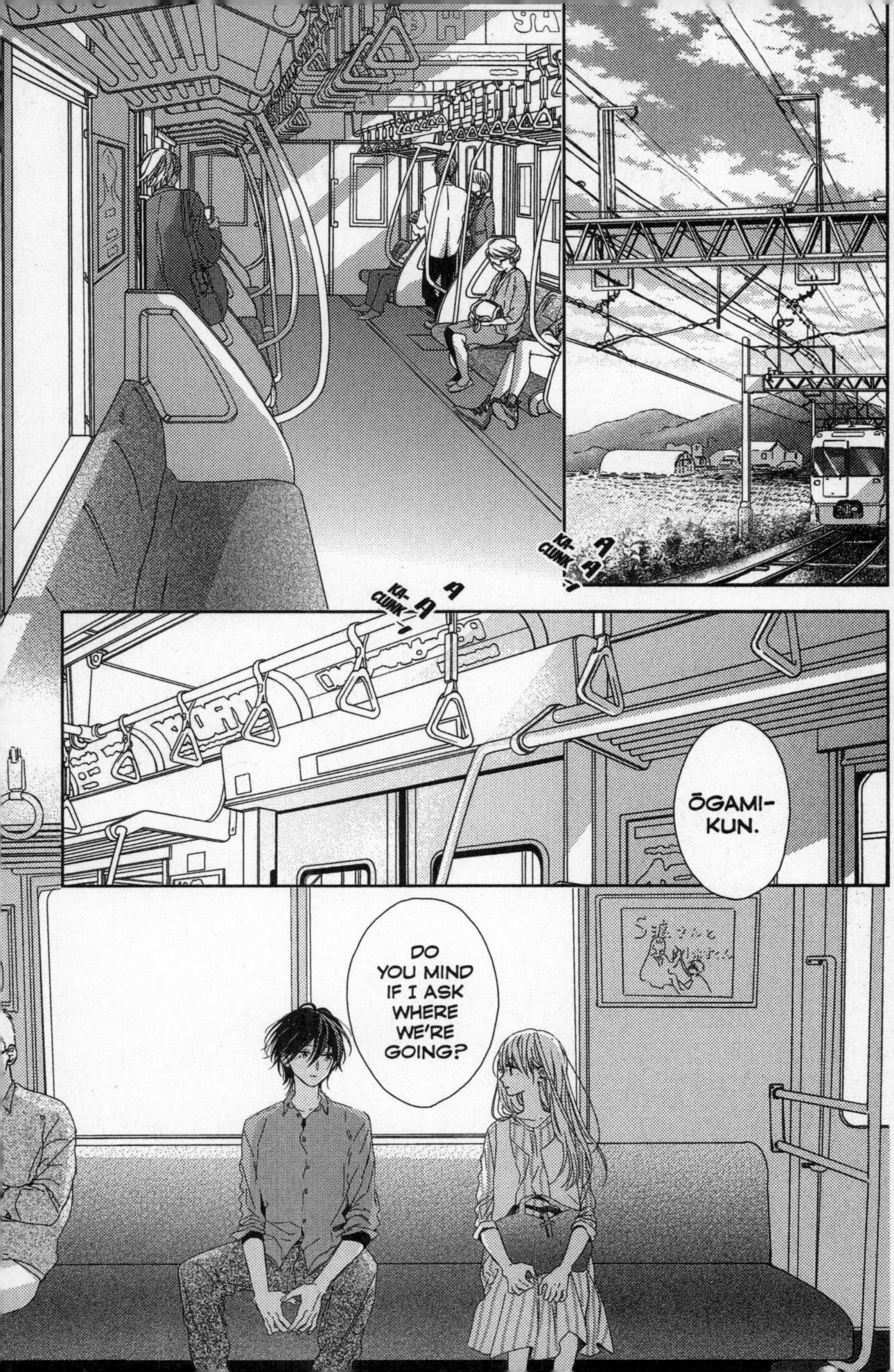
KA-CLUNK
KA-CLUNK
ŌGAMI-KUN.
DO YOU MIND IF I ASK WHERE WE'RE GOING?

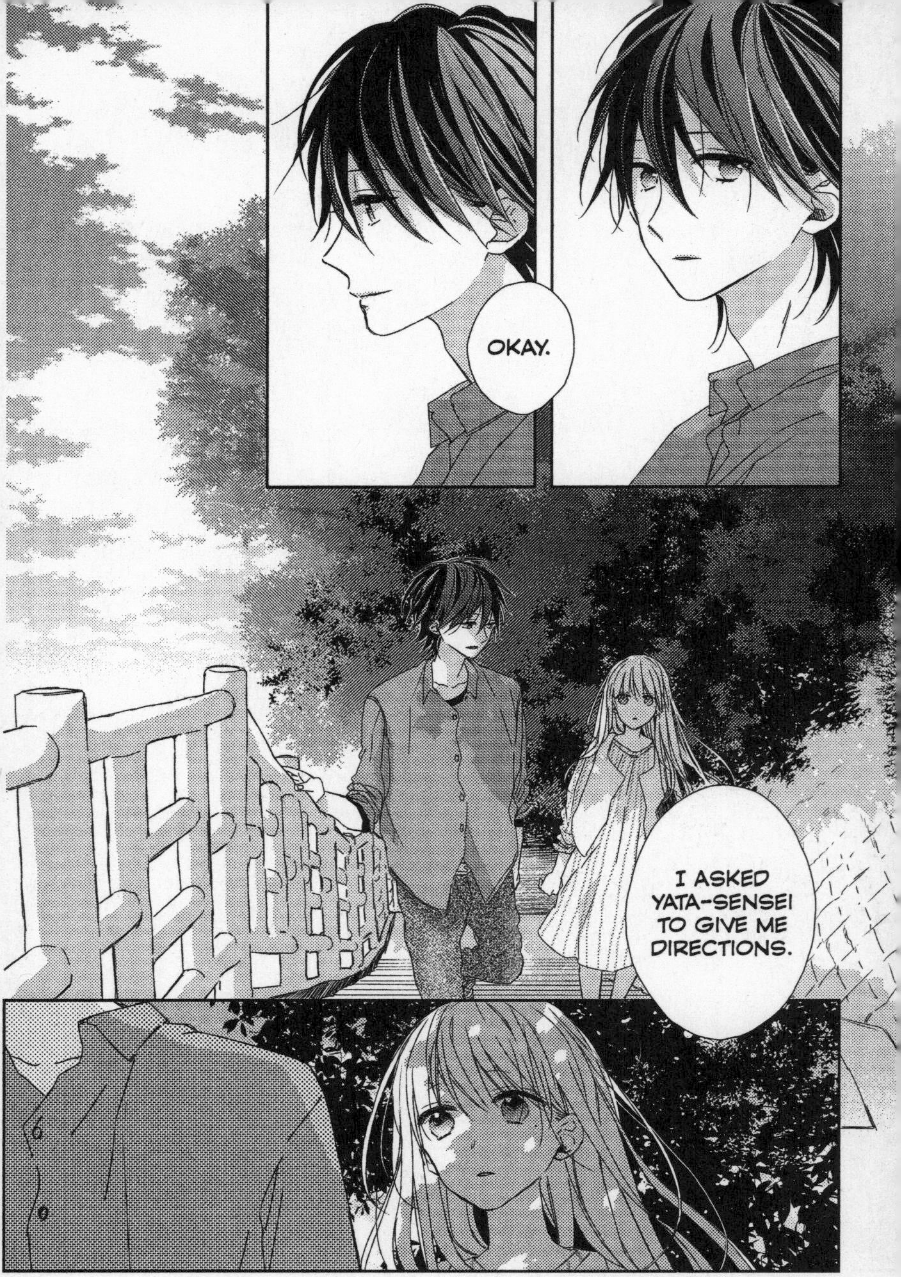
OKAY.
I ASKED YATA-SENSEI TO GIVE ME DIRECTIONS.

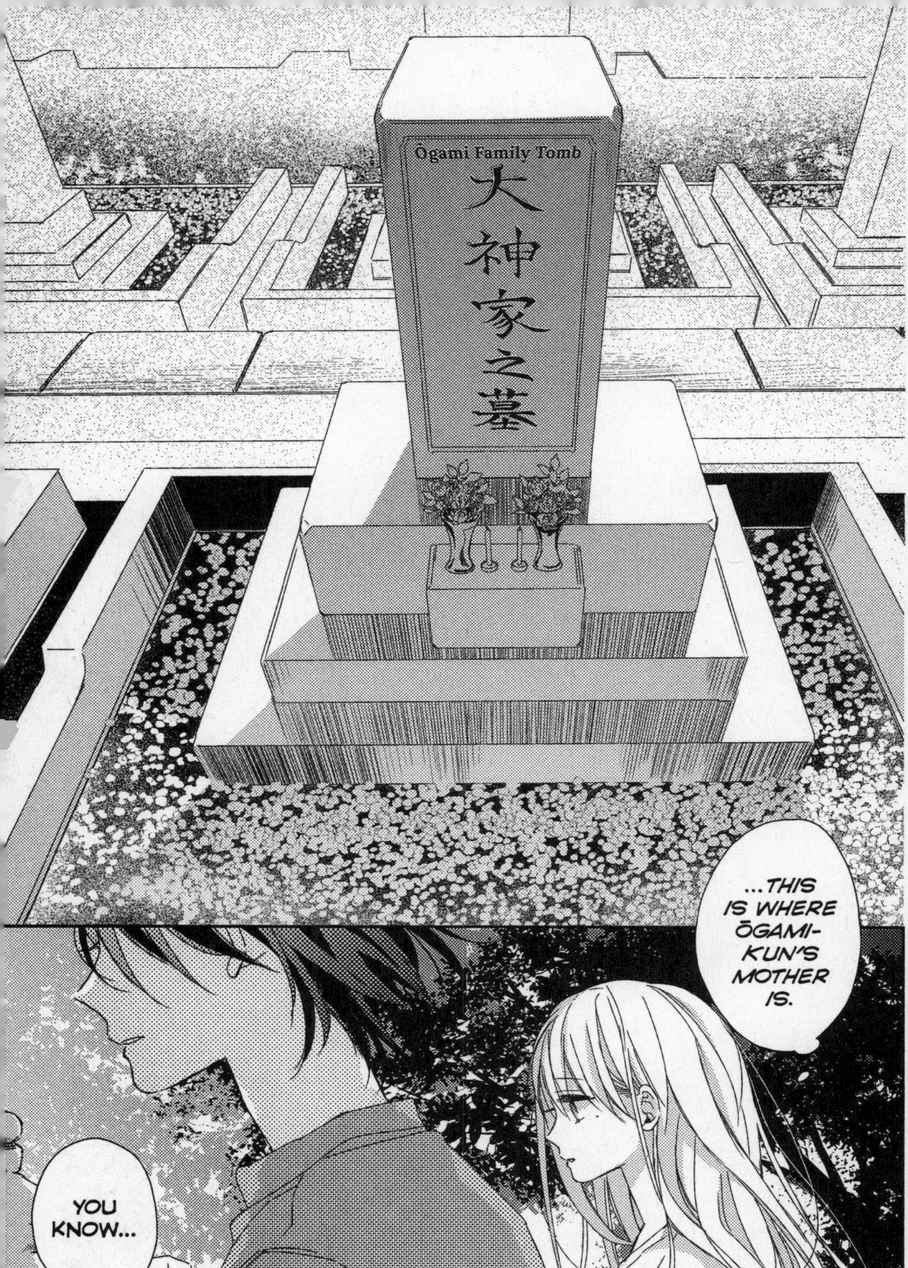
Ōgami Family Tomb
大神家之墓
...THIS IS WHERE ŌGAMI-KUN'S MOTHER IS.
YOU KNOW...

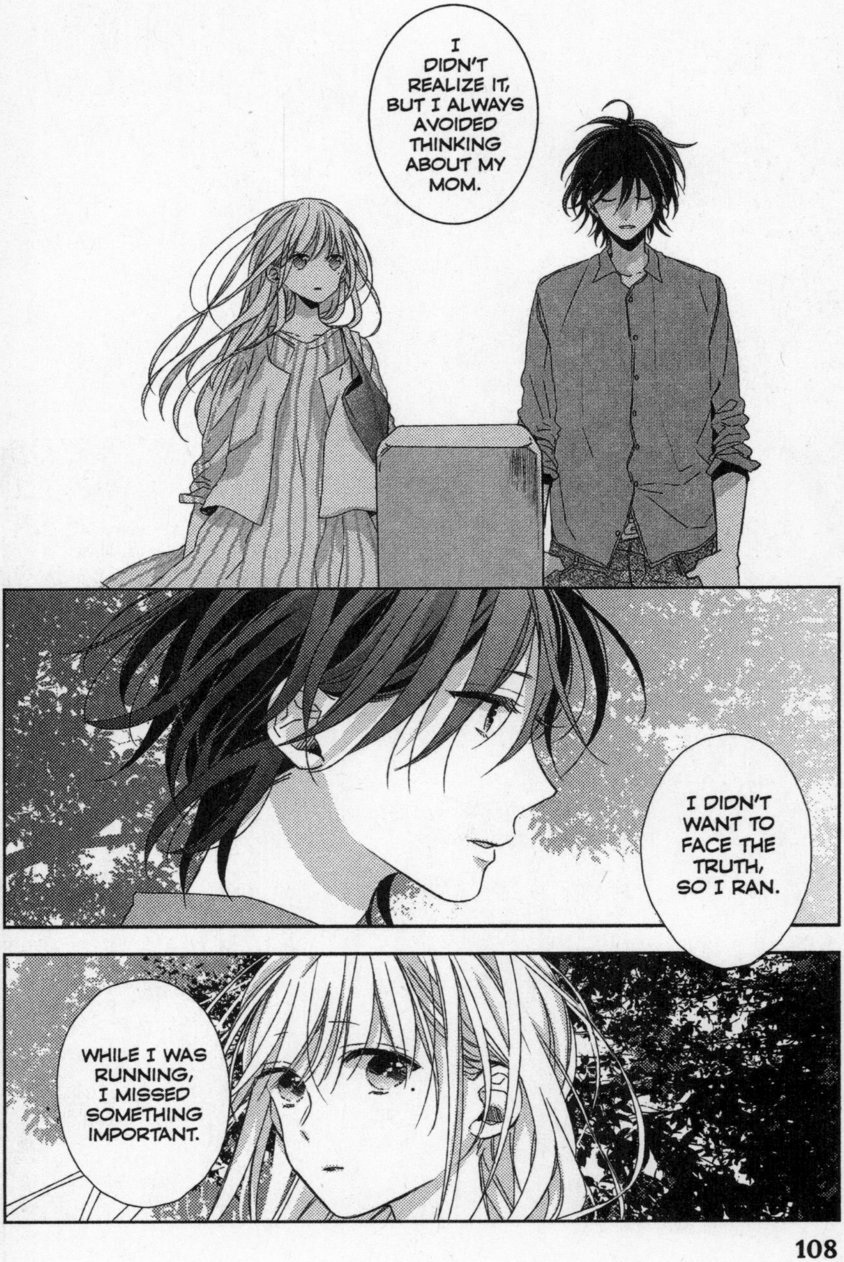
I DIDN'T REALIZE IT, BUT I ALWAYS AVOIDED THINKING ABOUT MY MOM.
I DIDN'T WANT TO FACE THE TRUTH, SO I RAN.
WHILE I WAS RUNNING, I MISSED SOMETHING IMPORTANT.

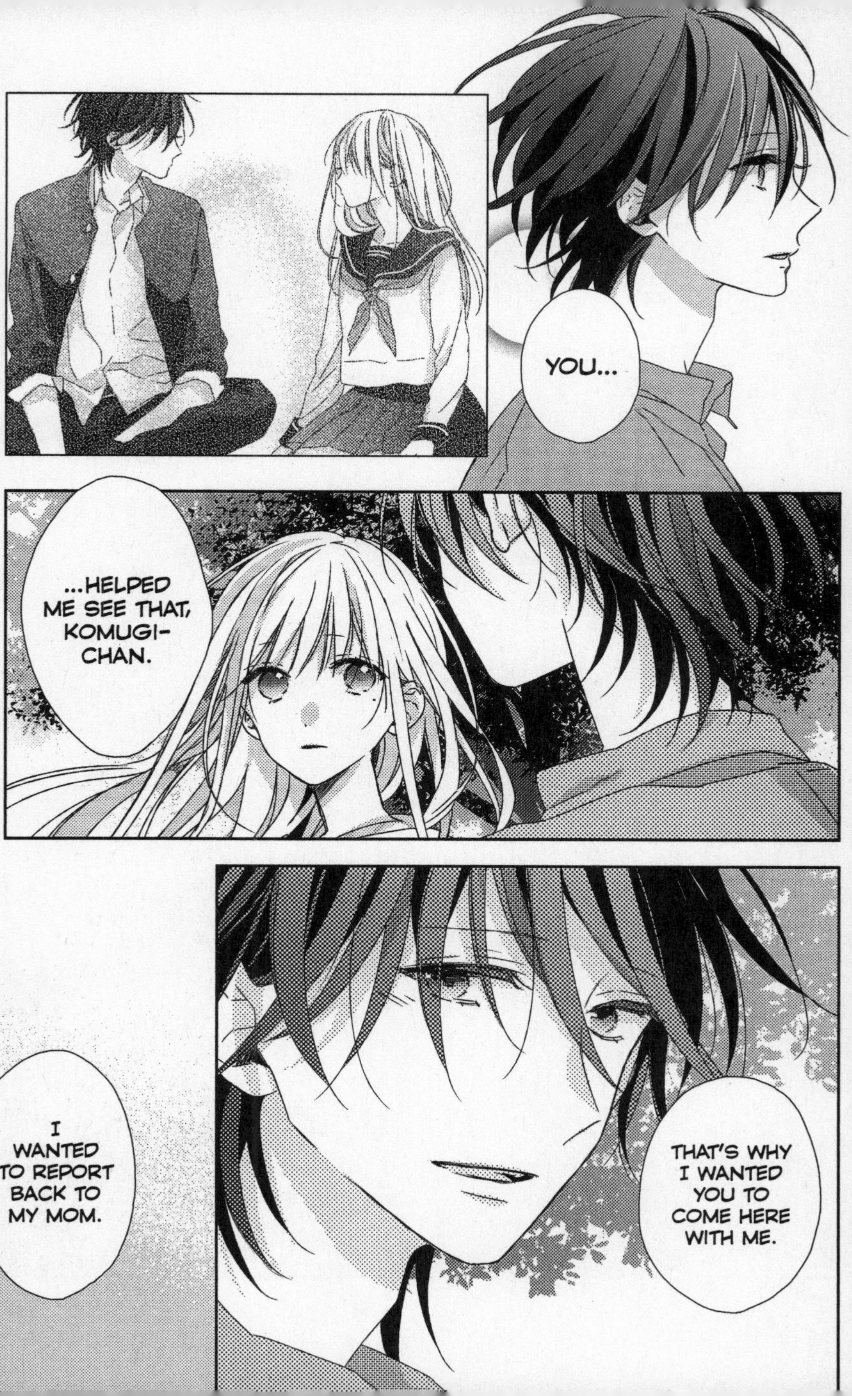
YOU...
...HELPED ME SEE THAT, KOMUGI-CHAN.
THAT'S WHY I WANTED YOU TO COME HERE WITH ME.
I WANTED TO REPORT BACK TO MY MOM.

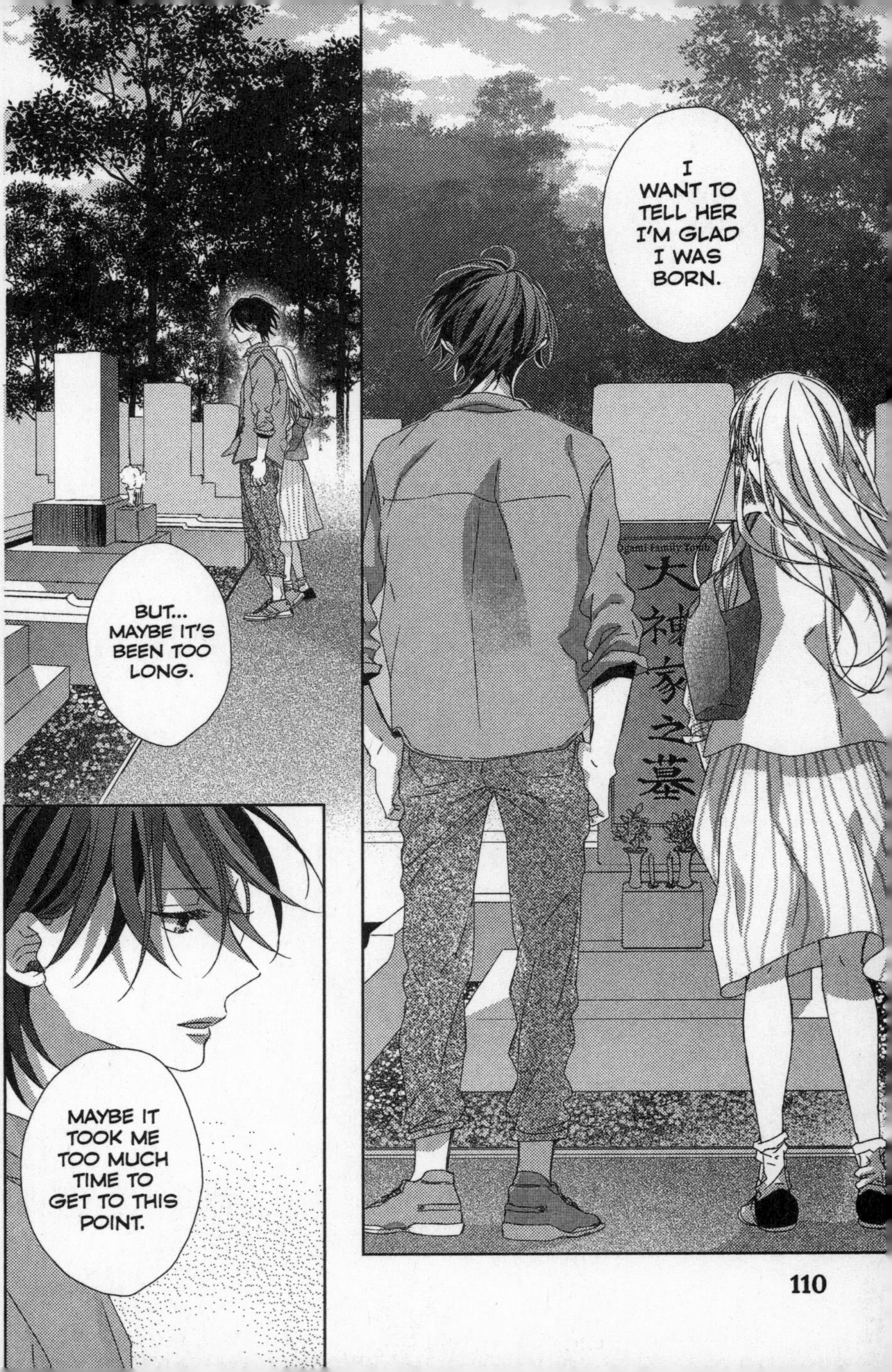
I WANT TO TELL HER I'M GLAD I WAS BORN.
BUT... MAYBE IT'S BEEN TOO LONG.
MAYBE IT TOOK ME TOO MUCH TIME TO GET TO THIS POINT.

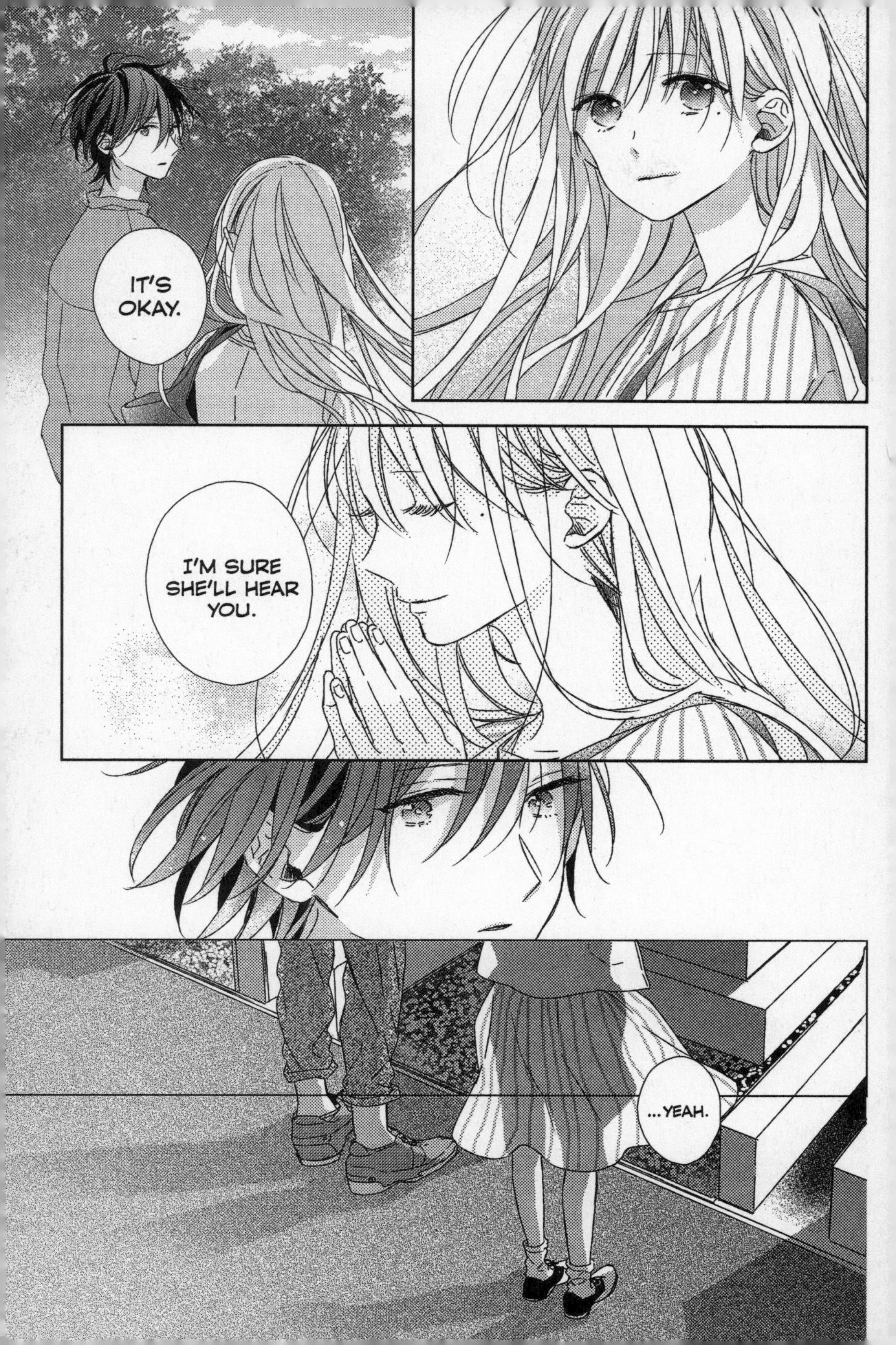
IT'S OKAY.
I'M SURE SHE'LL HEAR YOU.
...YEAH.

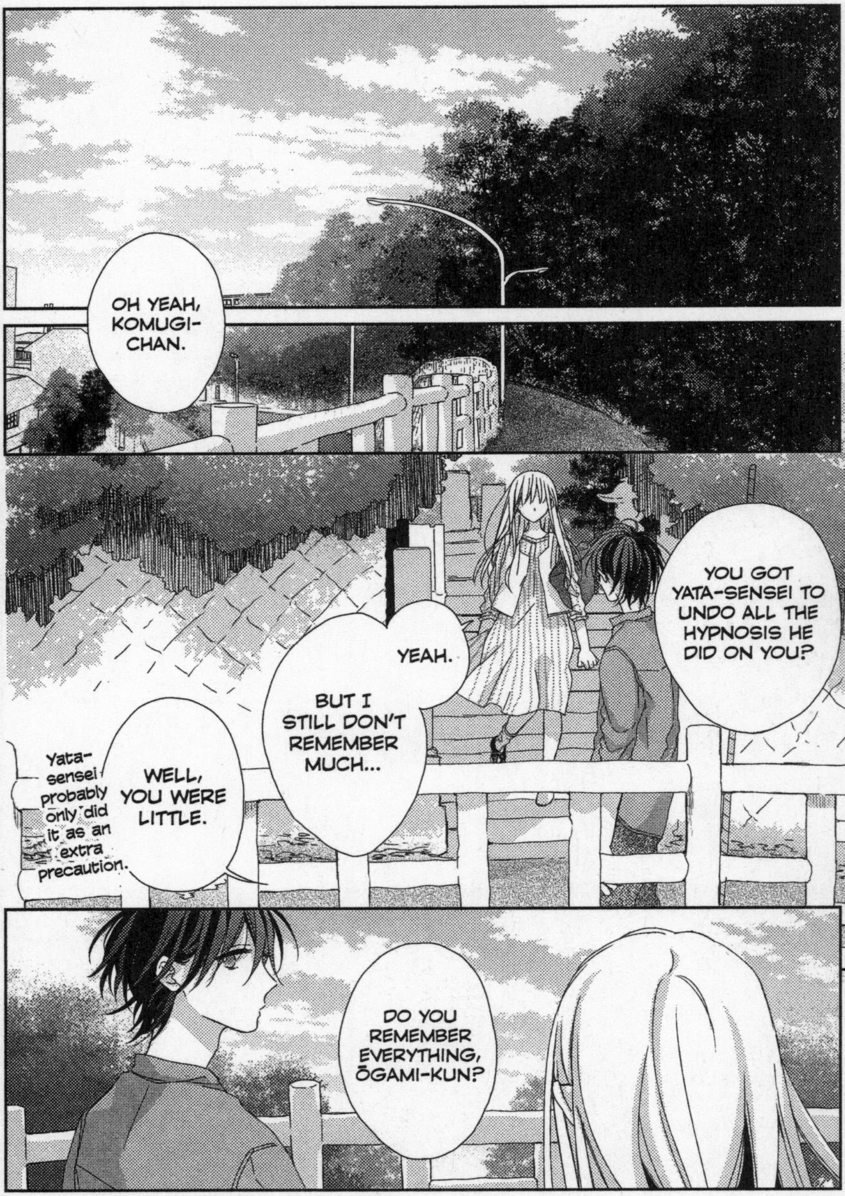
OH YEAH, KOMUGI-CHAN.
YOU GOT YATA-SENSEI TO UNDO ALL THE HYPNOSIS HE DID ON YOU?
YEAH.
BUT I STILL DON'T REMEMBER MUCH...
WELL, YOU WERE LITTLE.
Yata-sensei probably only did it as an extra precaution.
DO YOU REMEMBER EVERYTHING, ŌGAMI-KUN?

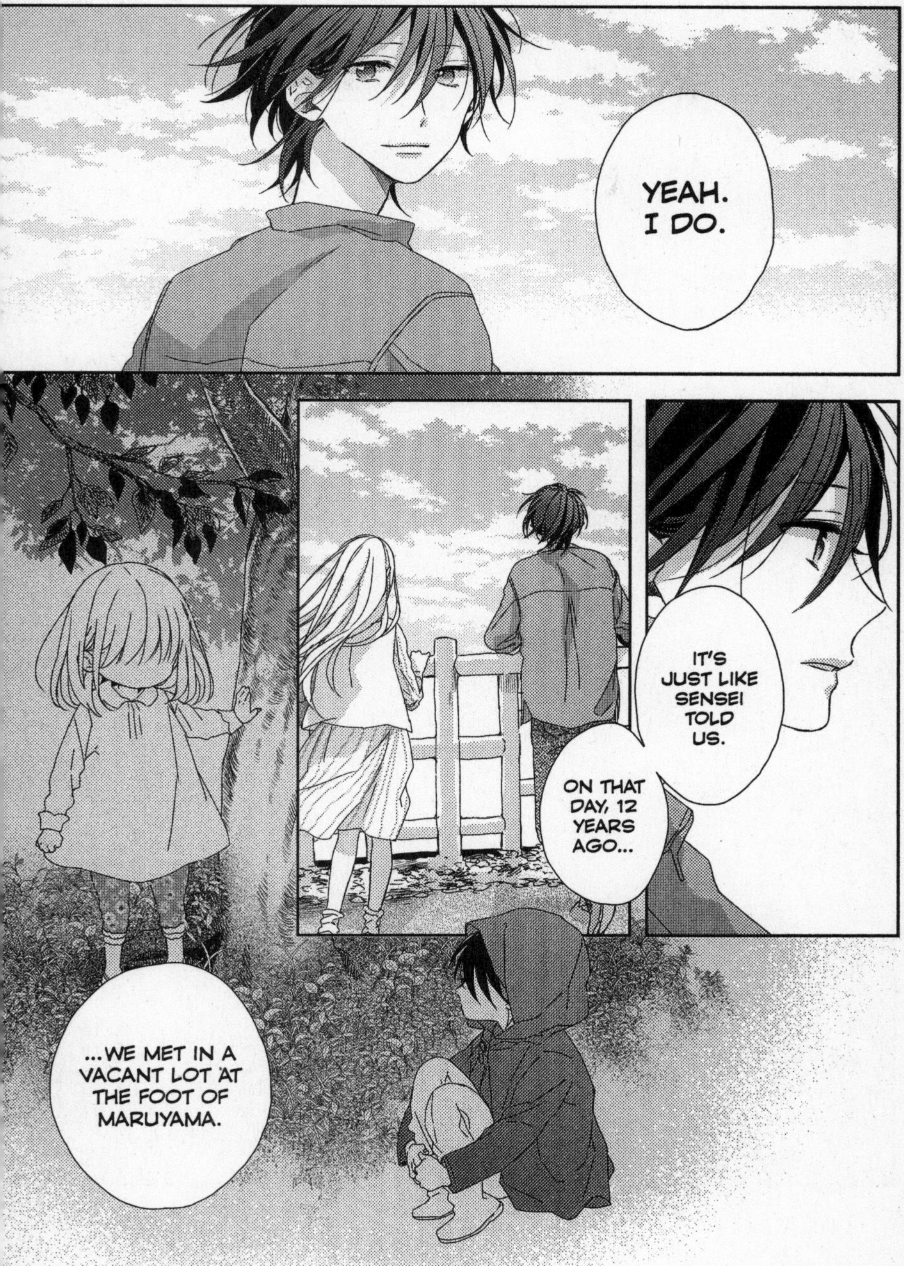
YEAH. I DO.
IT'S JUST LIKE SENSEI TOLD US.
ON THAT DAY, 12 YEARS AGO...
...WE MET IN A VACANT LOT AT THE FOOT OF MARUYAMA.

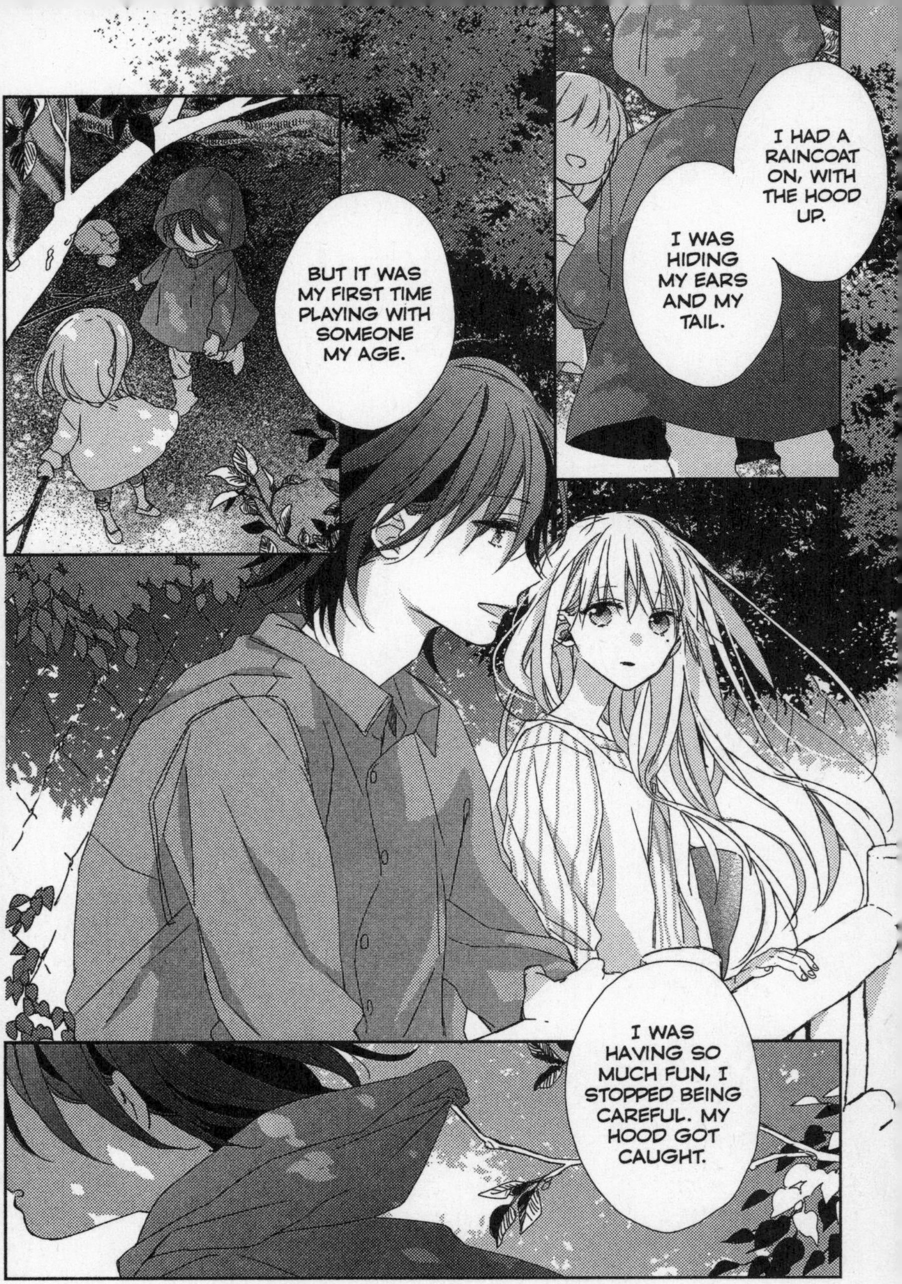
I HAD A RAINCOAT ON, WITH THE HOOD UP.
I WAS HIDING MY EARS AND MY TAIL.
BUT IT WAS MY FIRST TIME PLAYING WITH SOMEONE MY AGE.
I WAS HAVING SO MUCH FUN, I STOPPED BEING CAREFUL. MY HOOD GOT CAUGHT.

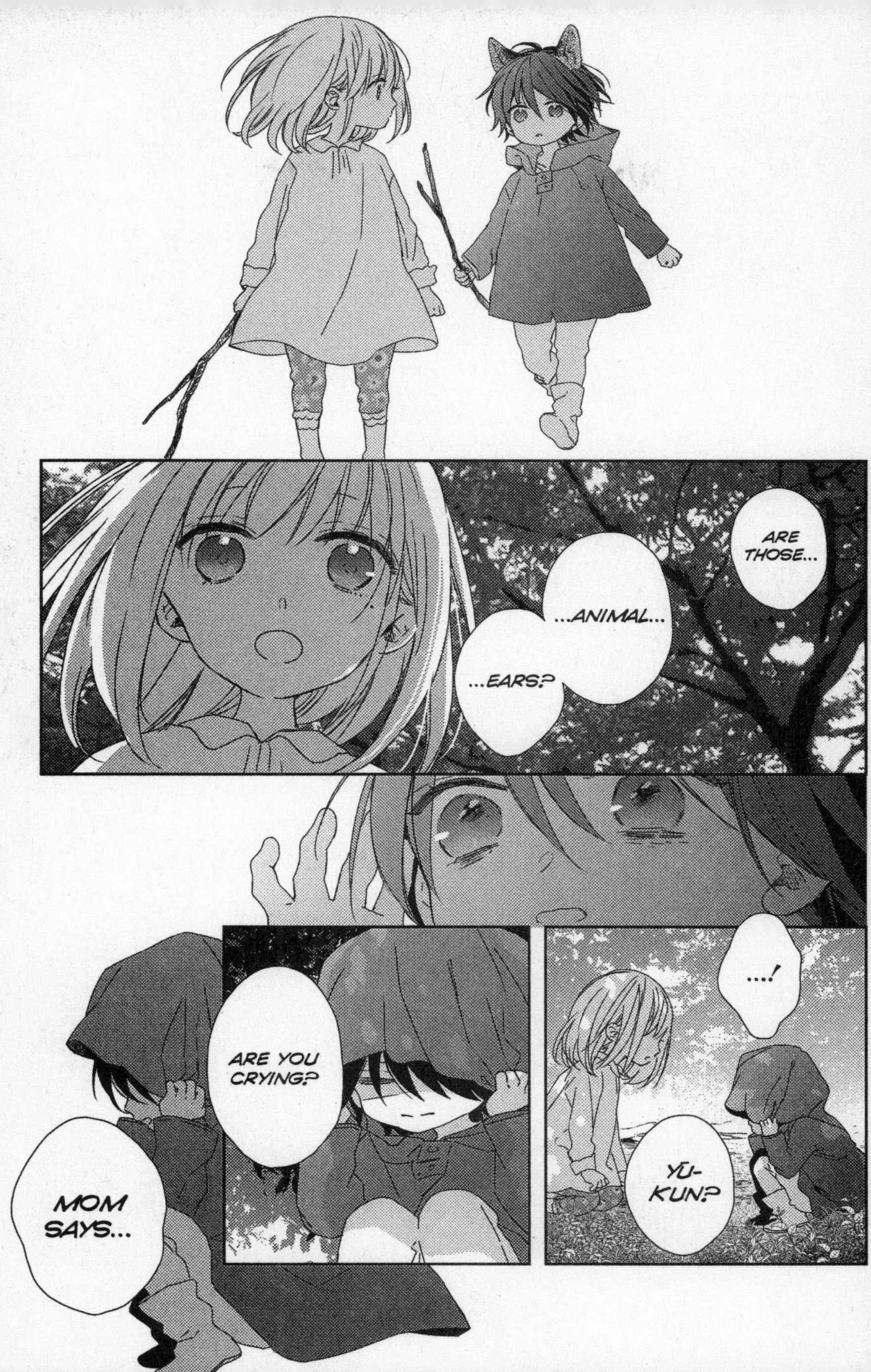
ARE THOSE...
...ANIMAL...
...EARS?
...!
YU-KUN?
ARE YOU CRYING?
MOM SAYS...

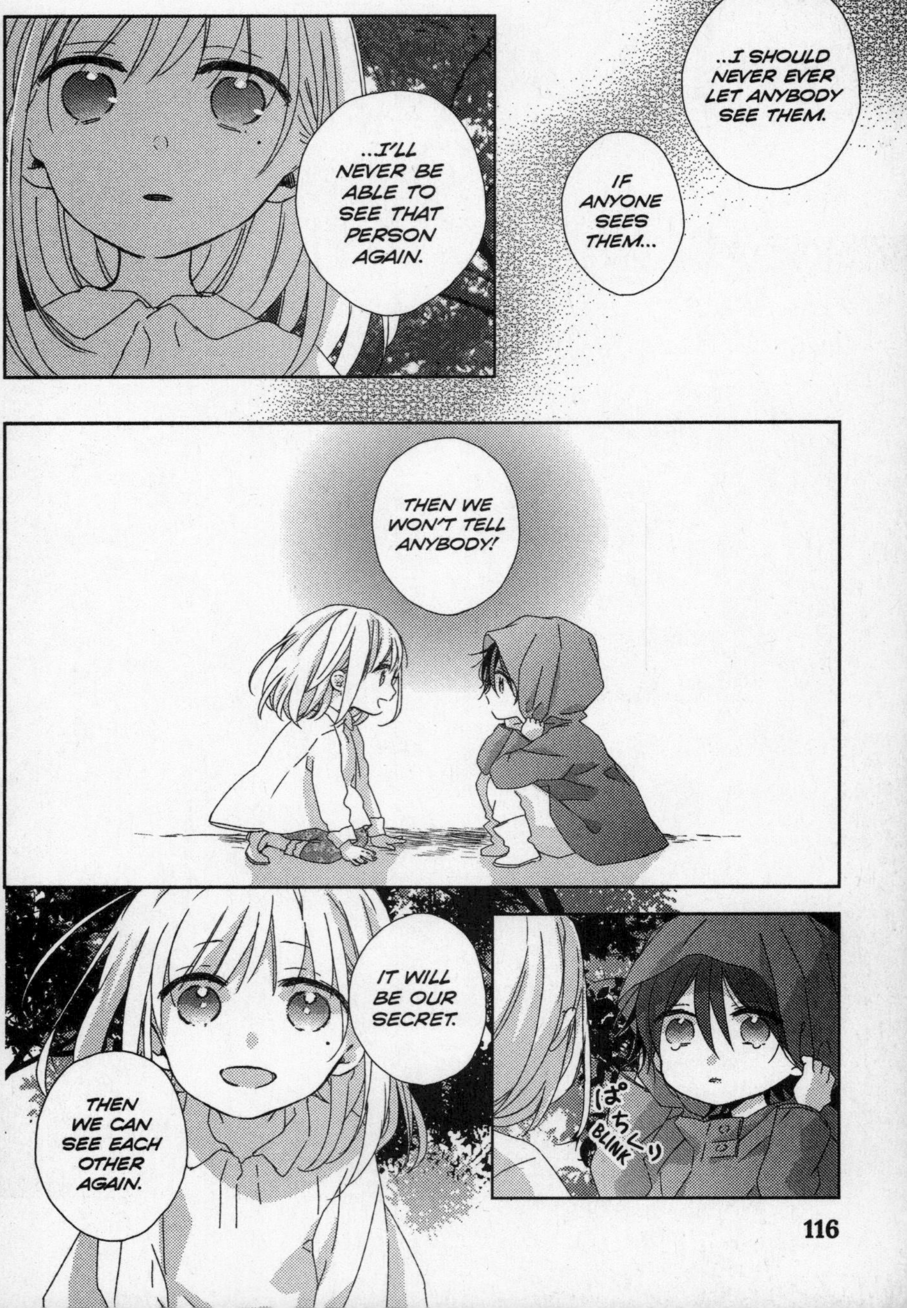
...I SHOULD NEVER EVER LET ANYBODY SEE THEM.
IF ANYONE SEES THEM...
...I'LL NEVER BE ABLE TO SEE THAT PERSON AGAIN.
THEN WE WON'T TELL ANYBODY!
ぱちくり
BLINK
IT WILL BE OUR SECRET.
THEN WE CAN SEE EACH OTHER AGAIN.

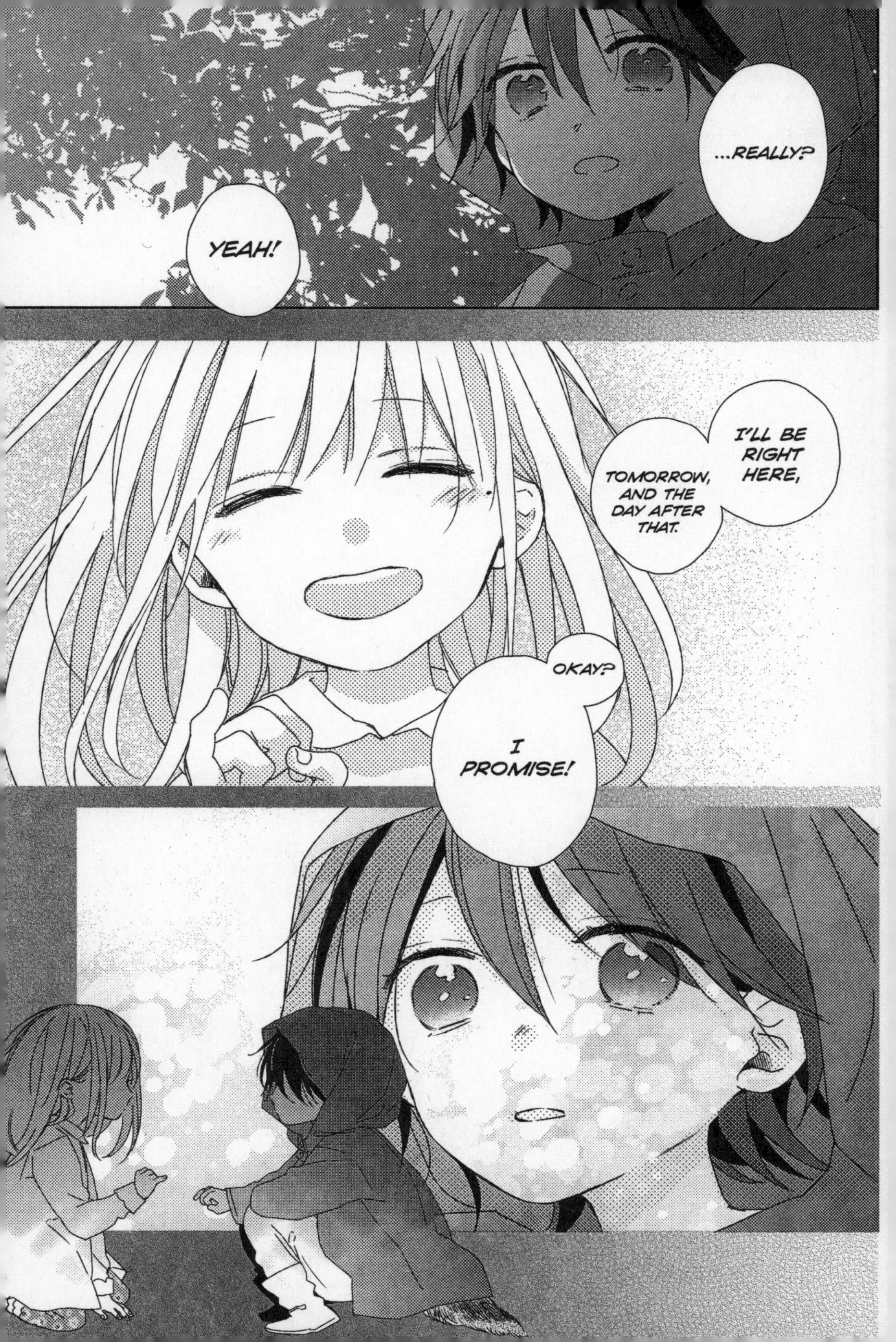
...REALLY?
YEAH!
I'LL BE RIGHT HERE,
TOMORROW, AND THE DAY AFTER THAT.
OKAY?
I PROMISE!

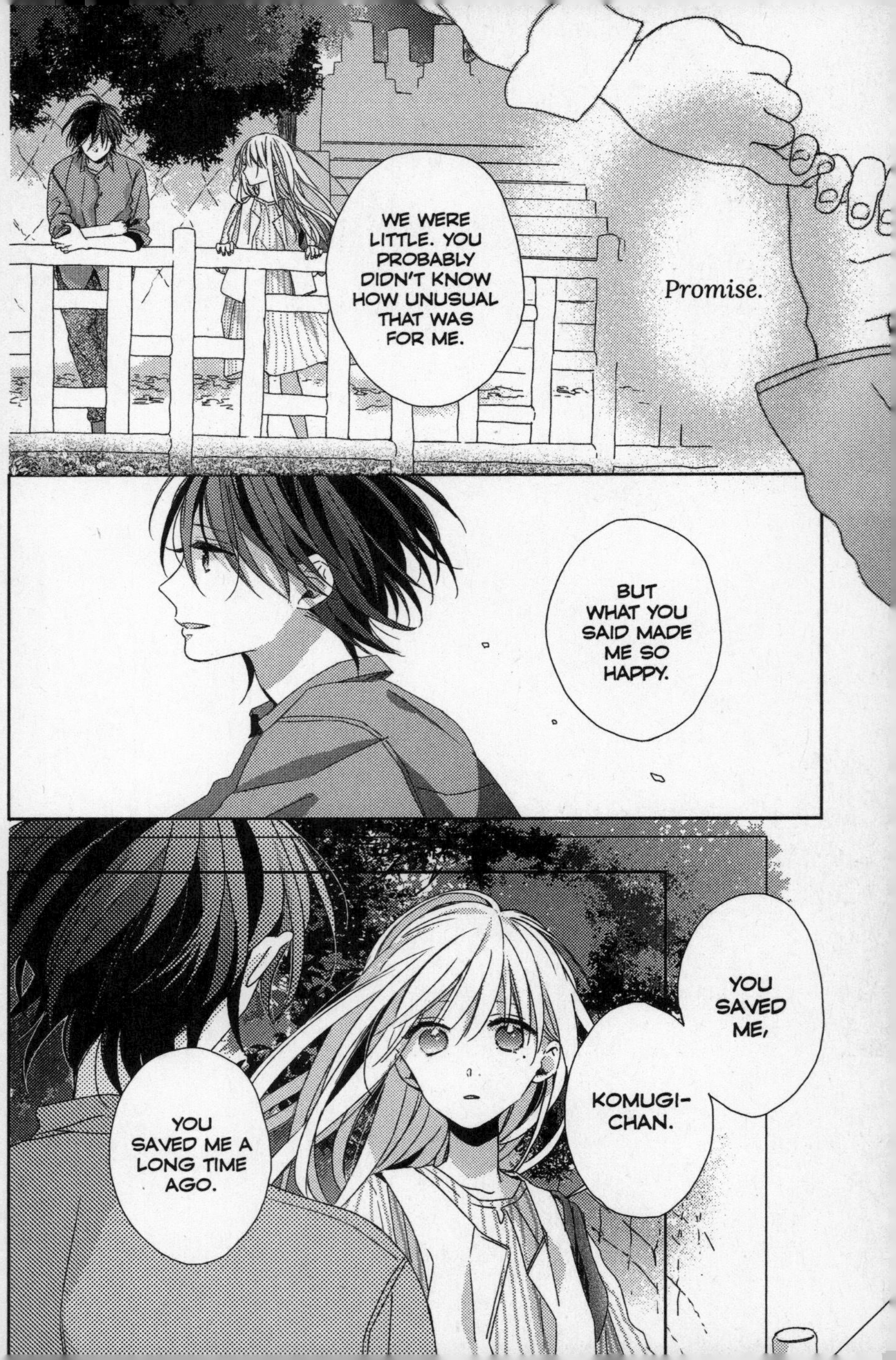
Promise.
WE WERE LITTLE. YOU PROBABLY DIDN'T KNOW HOW UNUSUAL THAT WAS FOR ME.
BUT WHAT YOU SAID MADE ME SO HAPPY.
YOU SAVED ME,
KOMUGI-CHAN.
YOU SAVED ME A LONG TIME AGO.

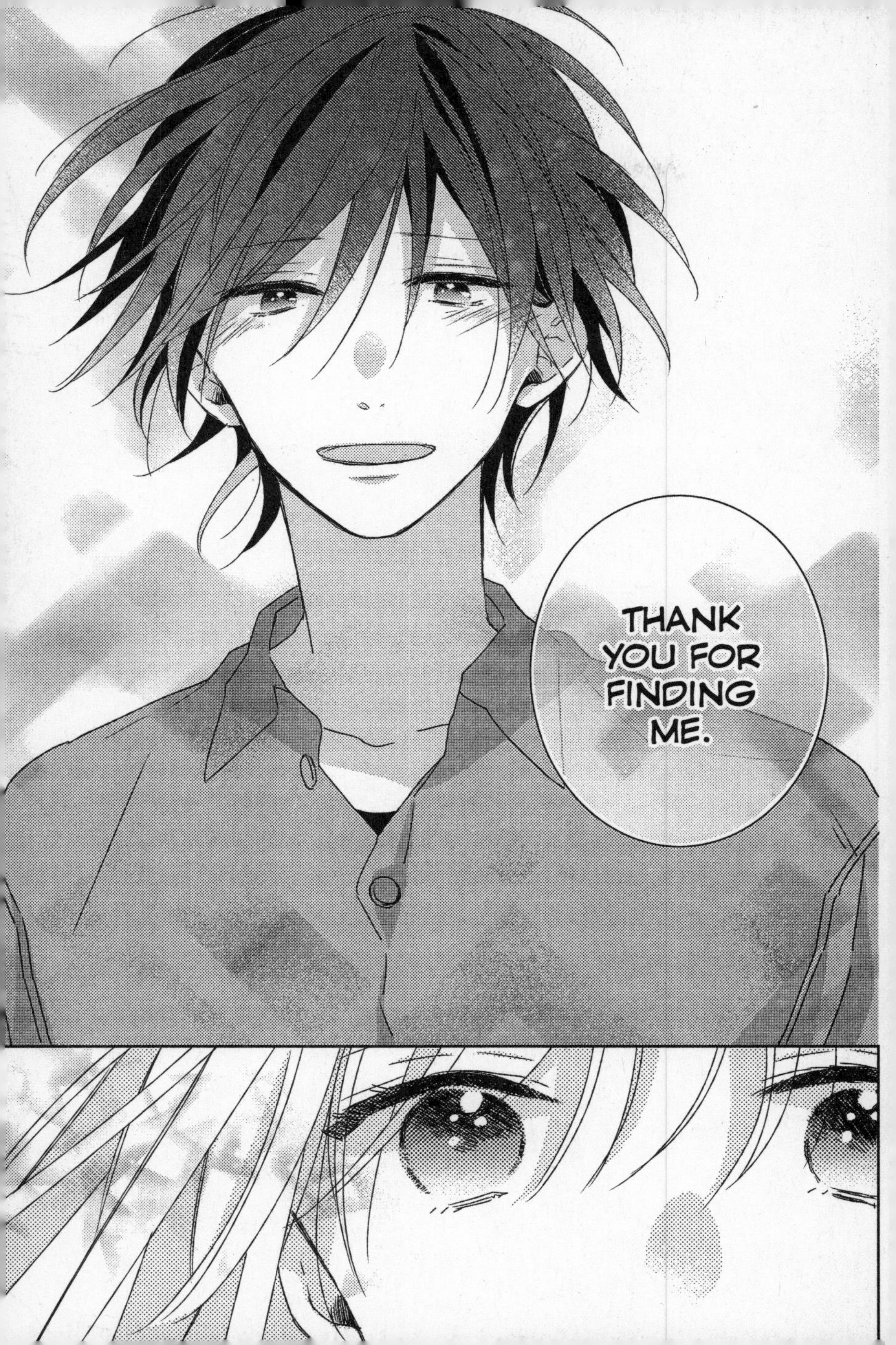
THANK YOU FOR FINDING ME.

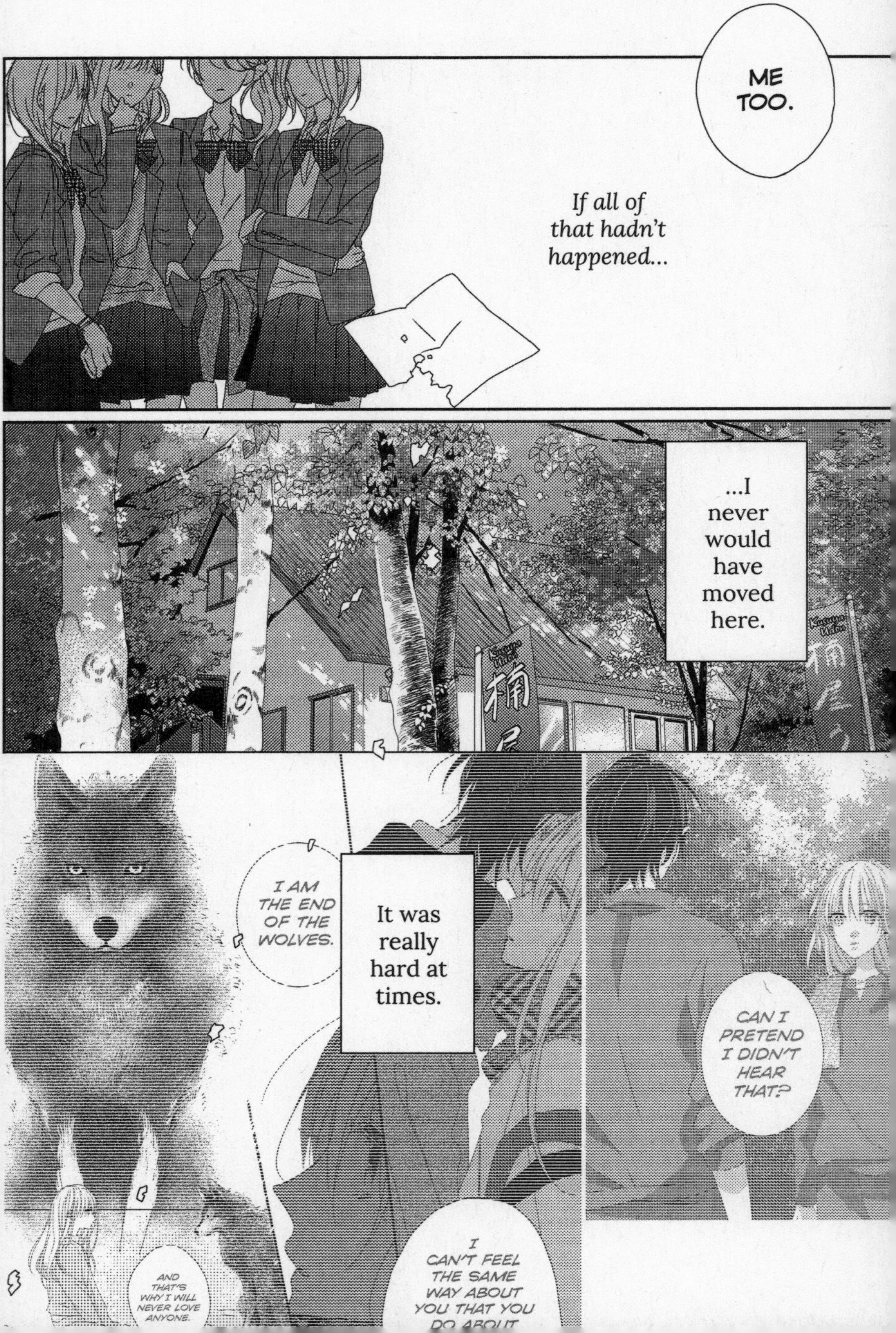
ME TOO.
If all of that hadn't happened...
...I never would have moved here.
CAN I PRETEND I DIDN'T HEAR THAT?
It was really hard at times.
I AM THE END OF THE WOLVES.
I CAN'T FEEL THE SAME WAY ABOUT YOU THAT YOU DO ABOUT
AND THAT'S WHY I WILL NEVER LOVE ANYONE.

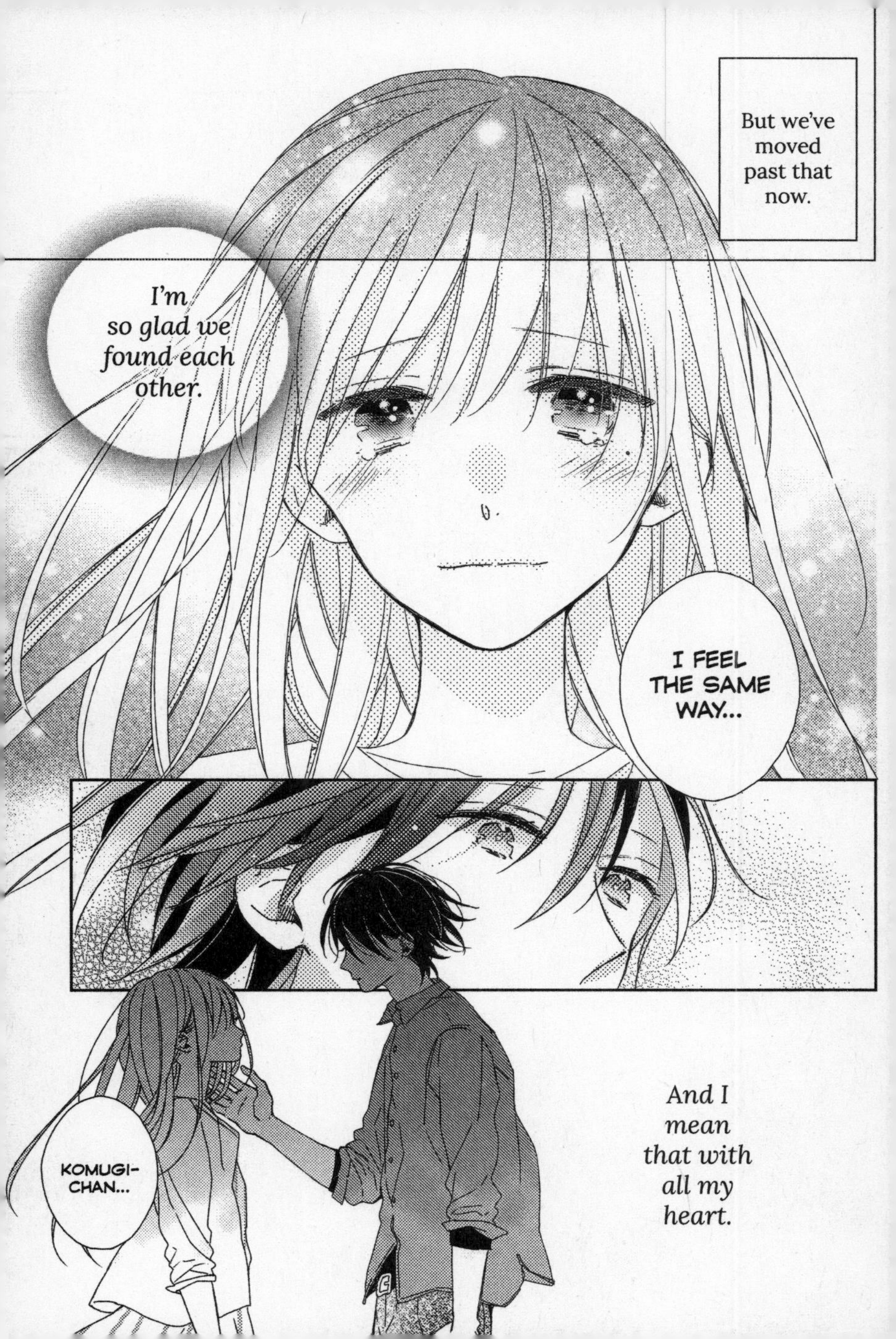
But we've moved past that now.
I'm so glad we found each other.
I FEEL THE SAME WAY...
And I mean that with all my heart.
KOMUGI-CHAN...

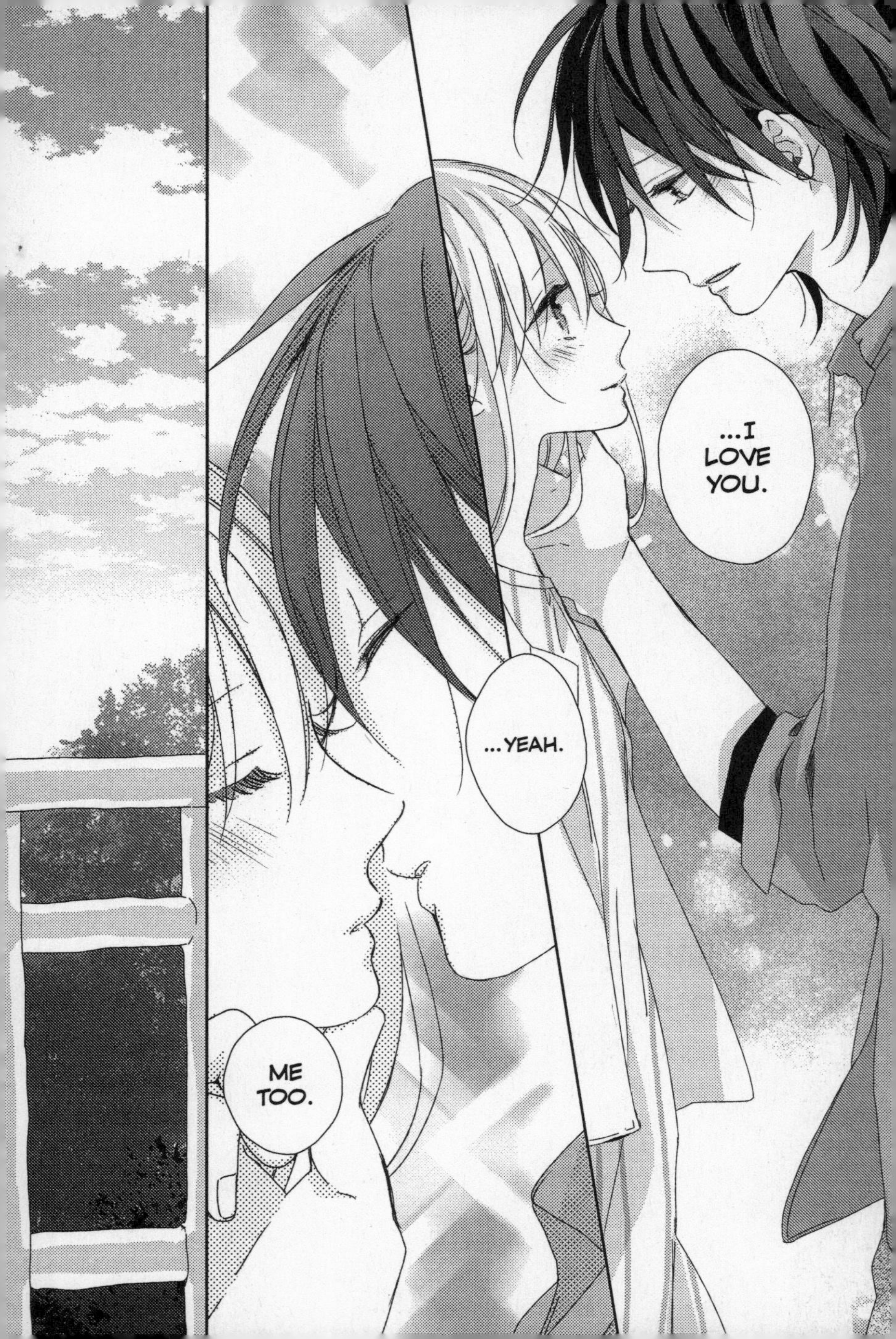
...I LOVE YOU.
...YEAH.
ME TOO.

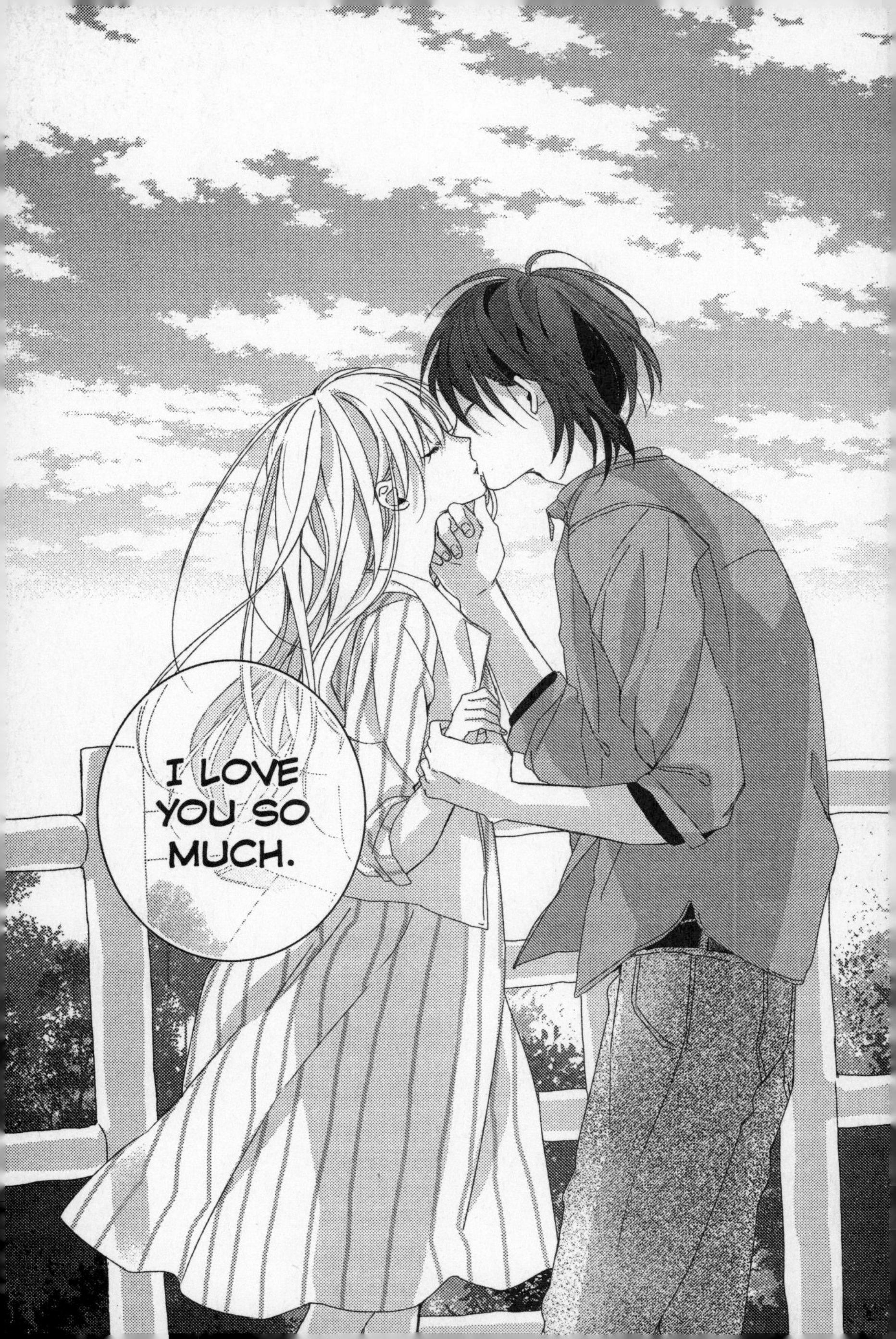
I LOVE YOU SO MUCH.

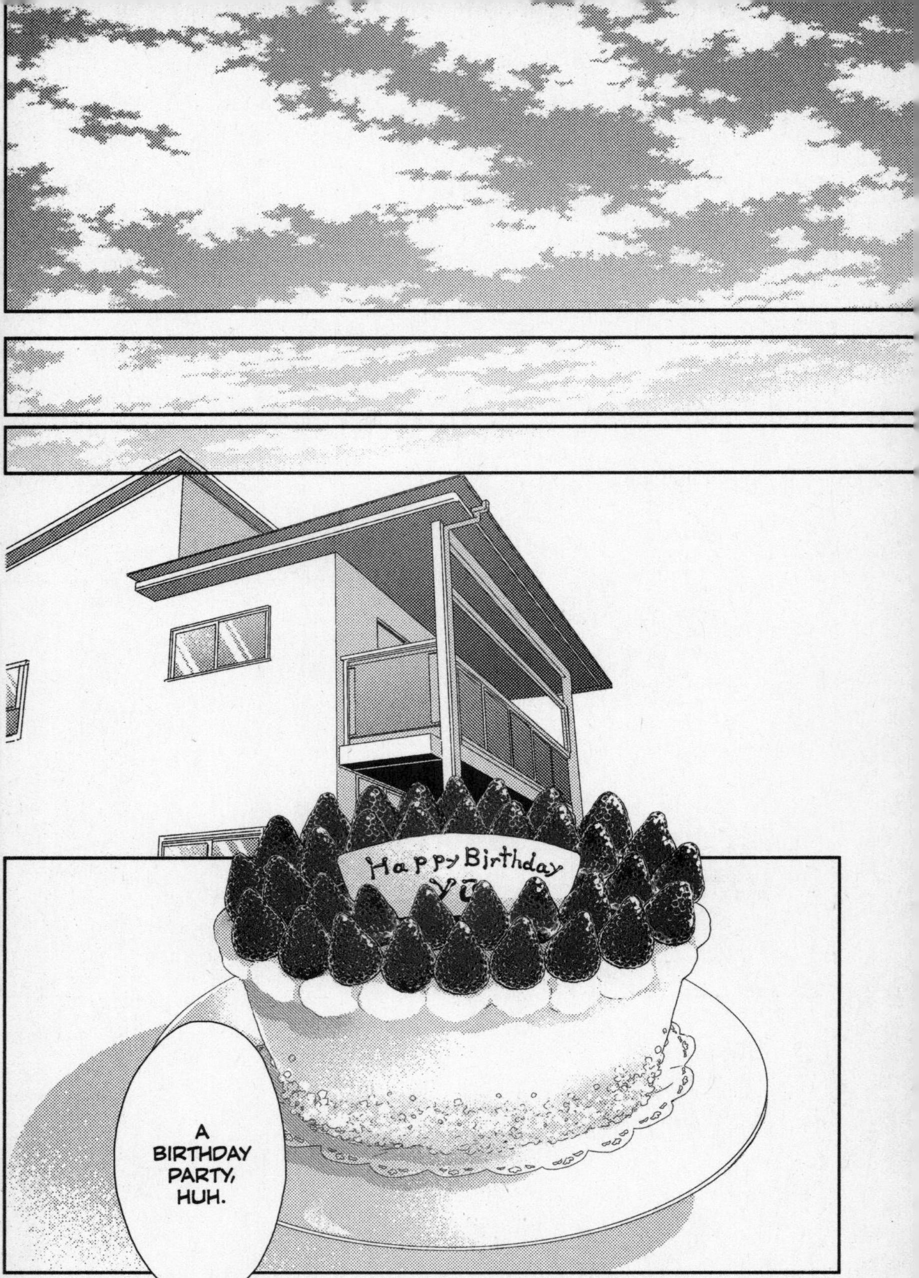
Happy Birthday
A BIRTHDAY PARTY, HUH.

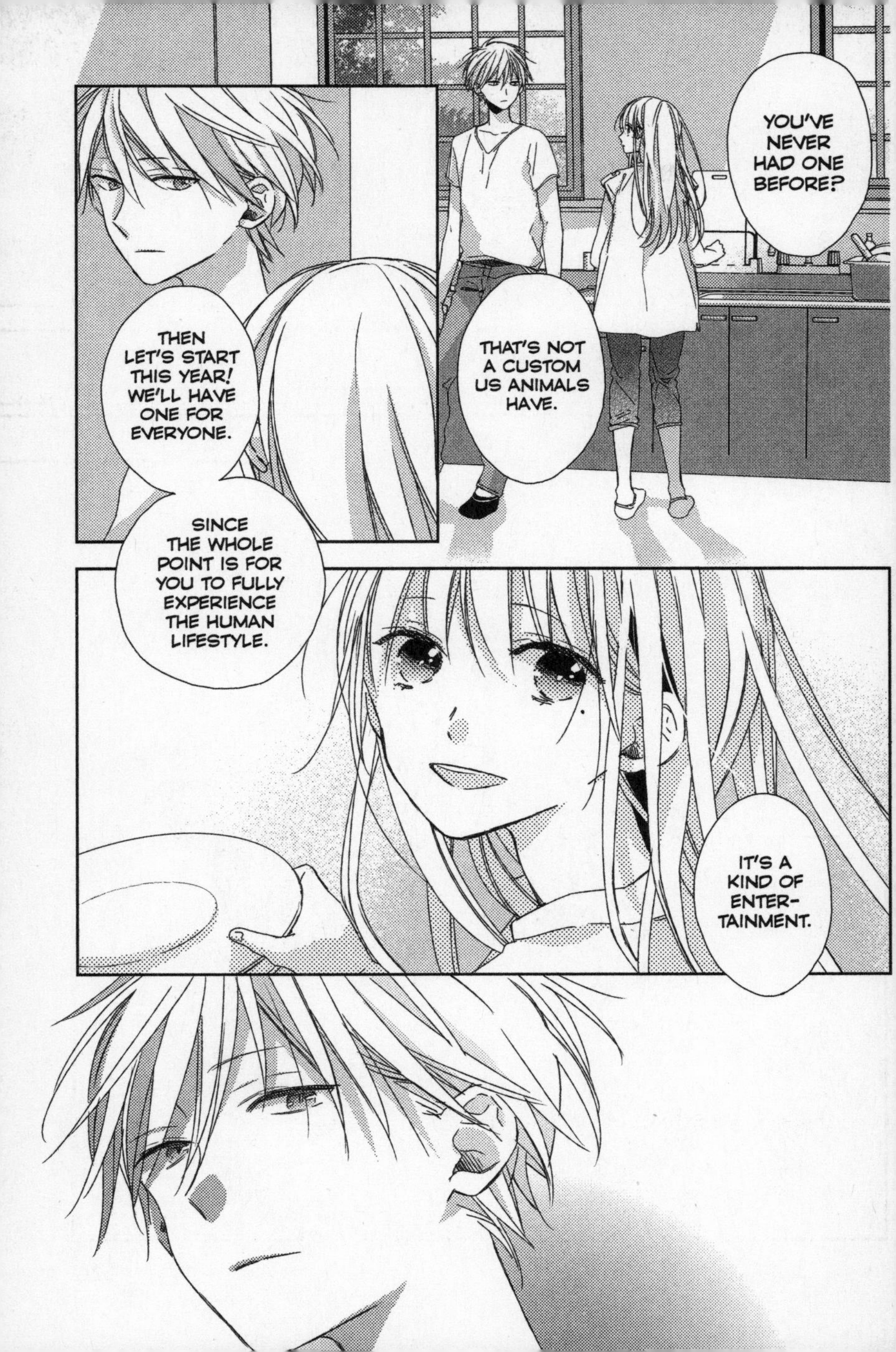
YOU'VE NEVER HAD ONE BEFORE?
THAT'S NOT A CUSTOM US ANIMALS HAVE.
THEN LET'S START THIS YEAR! WE'LL HAVE ONE FOR EVERYONE.
SINCE THE WHOLE POINT IS FOR YOU TO FULLY EXPERIENCE THE HUMAN LIFESTYLE.
IT'S A KIND OF ENTER-TAINMENT.

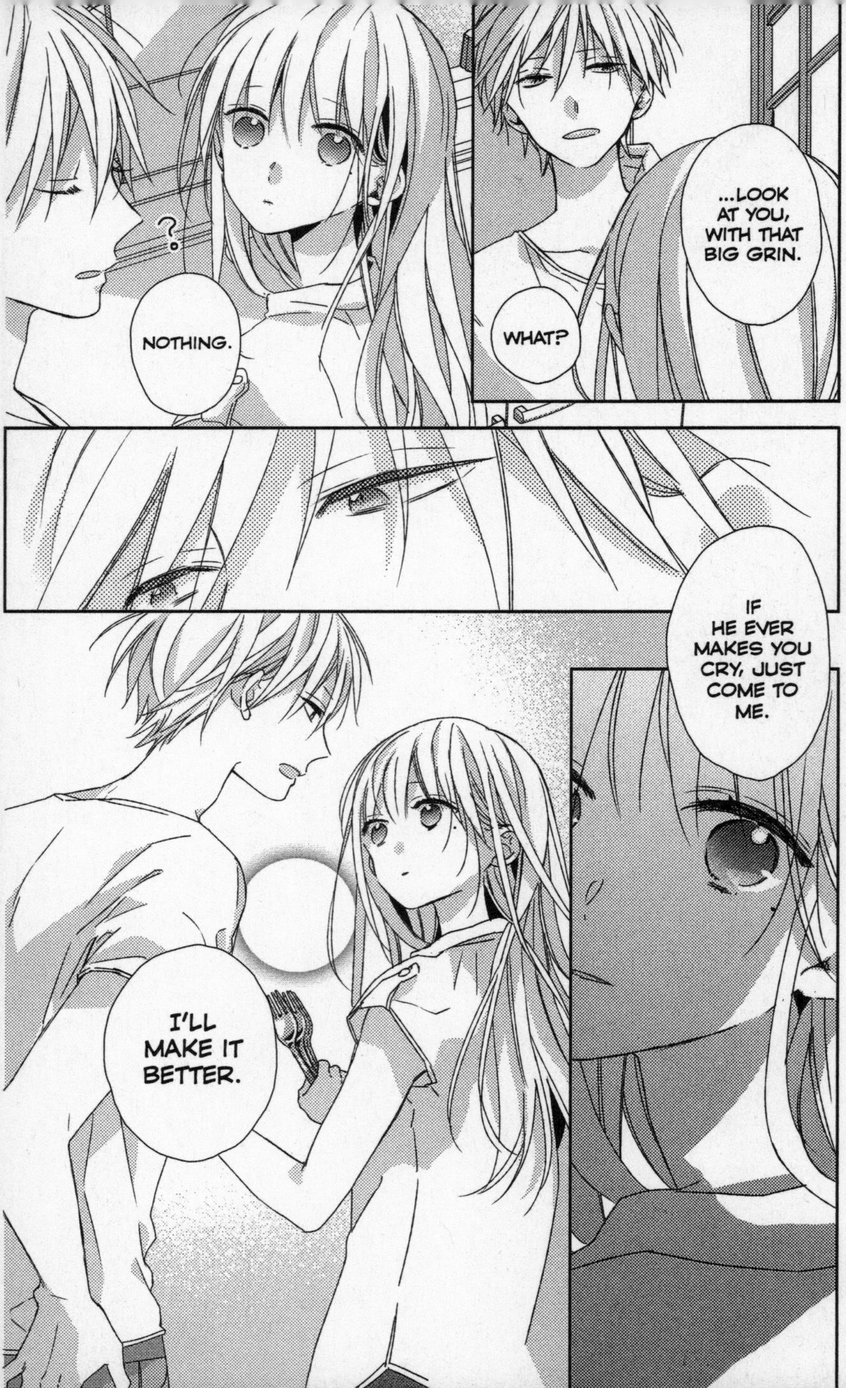
...LOOK AT YOU, WITH THAT BIG GRIN.
WHAT?
?
NOTHING.
IF HE EVER MAKES YOU CRY, JUST COME TO ME.
I'LL MAKE IT BETTER.

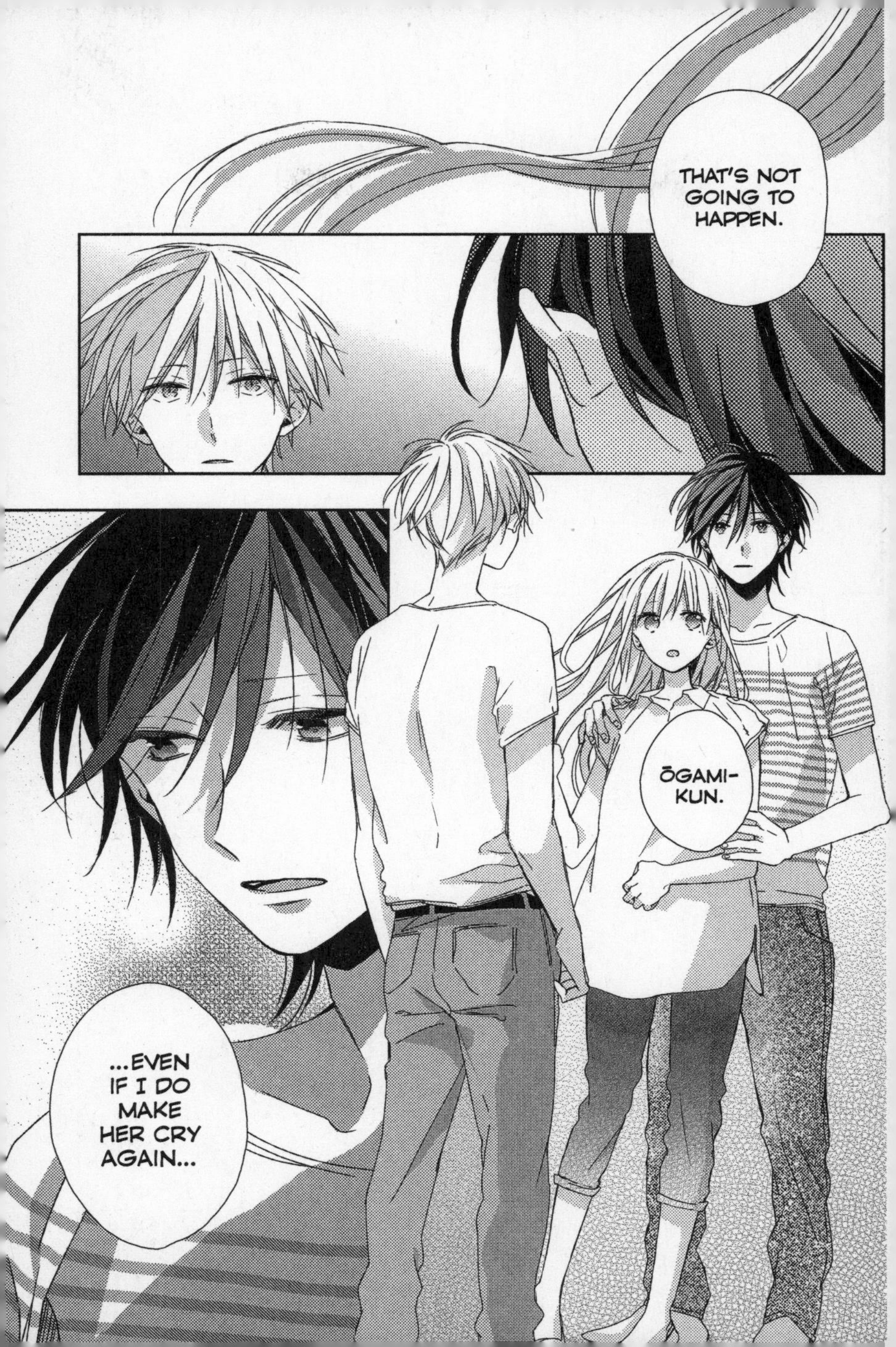
THAT'S NOT GOING TO HAPPEN.
ŌGAMI-KUN.
...EVEN IF I DO MAKE HER CRY AGAIN...

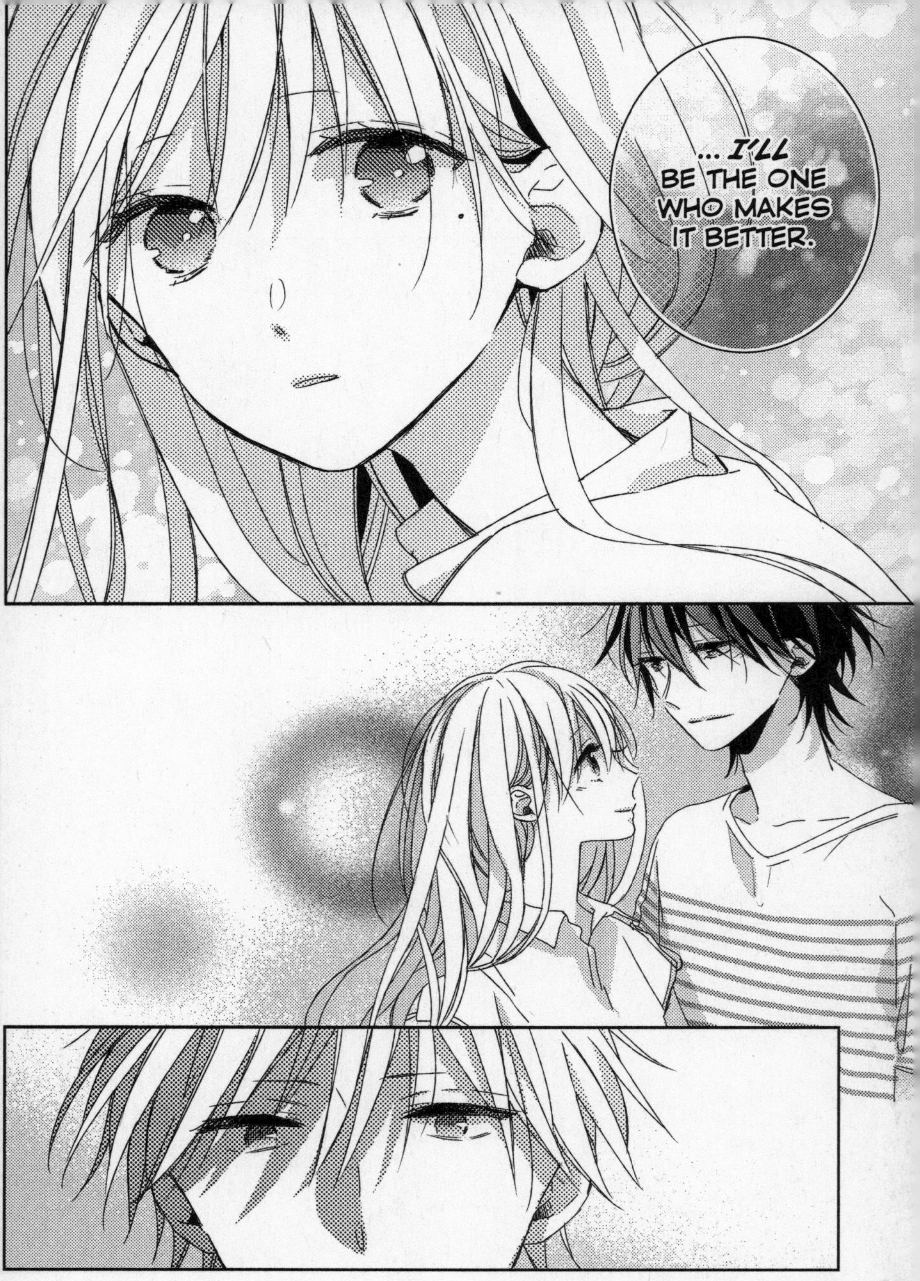
...I'LL BE THE ONE WHO MAKES IT BETTER.

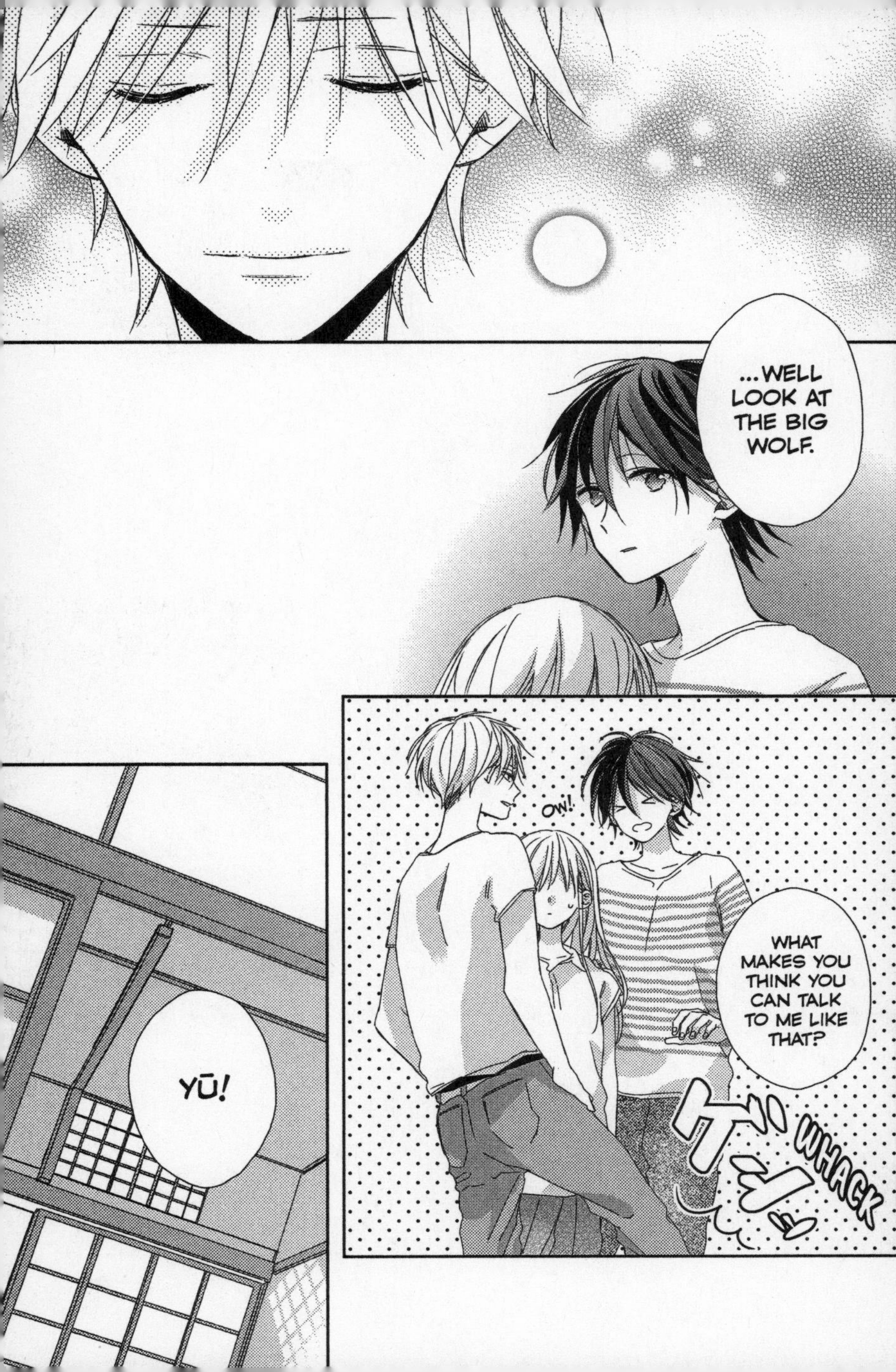
...WELL LOOK AT THE BIG WOLF.
OW!
WHAT MAKES YOU THINK YOU CAN TALK TO ME LIKE THAT?
WHACK
YŪ!

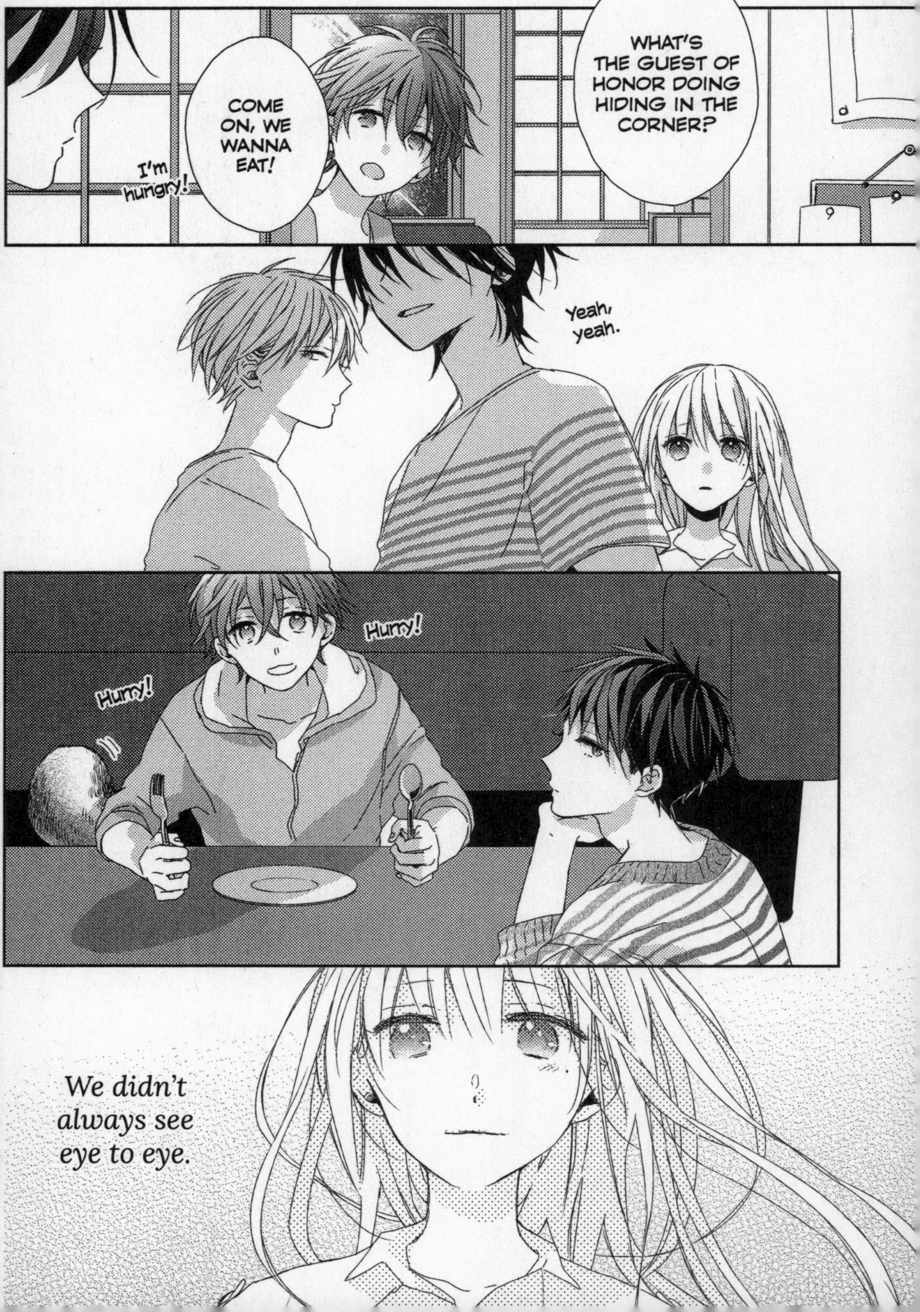
WHAT'S THE GUEST OF HONOR DOING HIDING IN THE CORNER?
COME ON, WE WANNA EAT!
I'm hungry!
Yeah, yeah.
Hurry!
Hurry!
We didn't always see eye to eye.

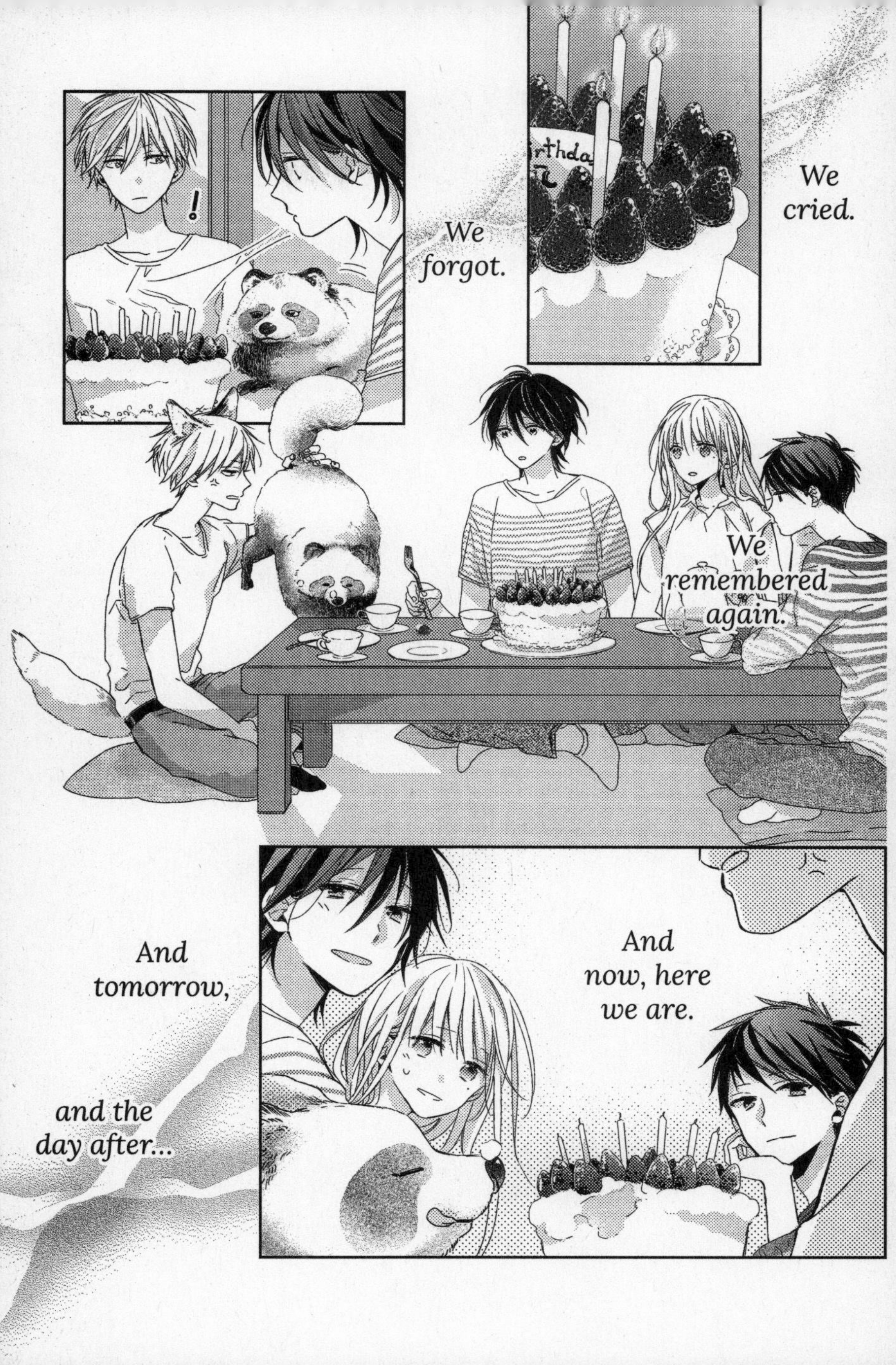

We cried.
We forgot.
!
We remembered again.
And now, here we are.
And tomorrow,
and the day after...

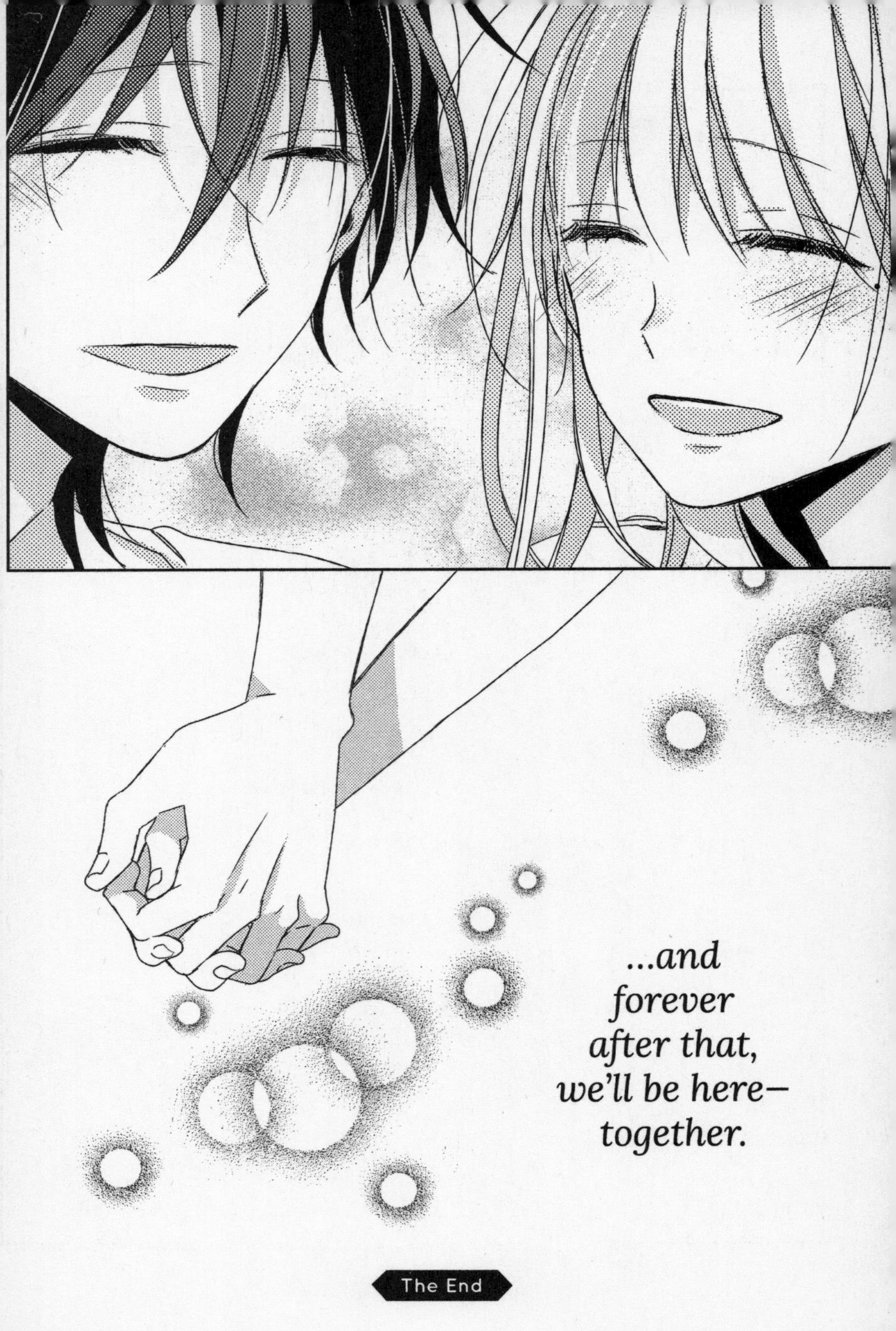
...and forever after that, we'll be here—together.
The End

Bonus Chapter

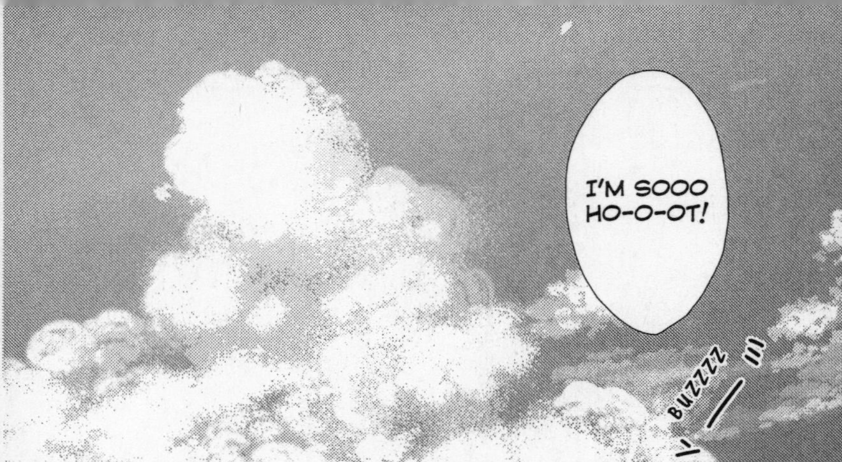
I'M SOOO HO-O-OT!
BUZZZZ
BUZZZZ
I DON'T WANNA COOK!
だら LAZE
Right?
...
だら SLUMP

That Wolf-Boy is Mine!

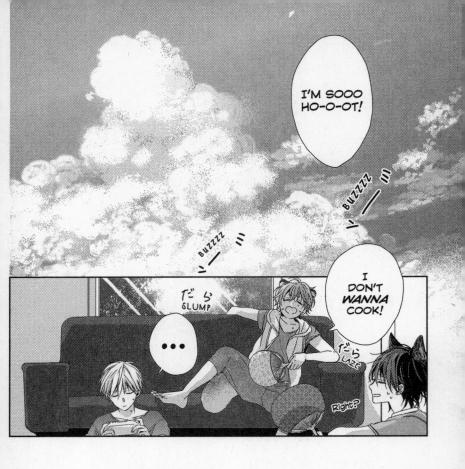

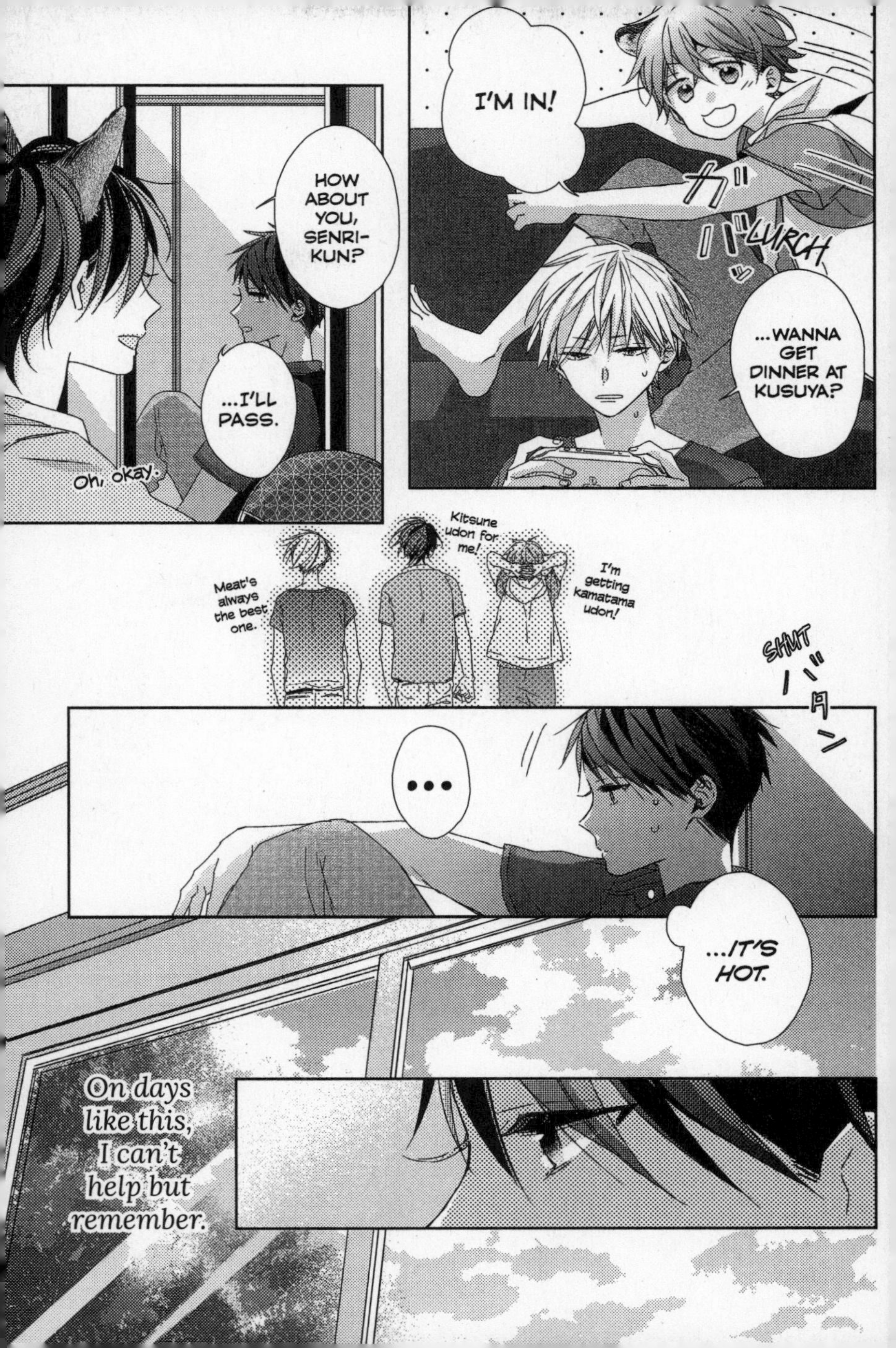
...WANNA GET DINNER AT KUSUYA?
LURCH
I'M IN!
HOW ABOUT YOU, SENRI-KUN?
...I'LL PASS.
Oh, okay.
I'm getting kamatama udon!
Kitsune udon for me!
Meat's always the best one.
SHUT
...
...IT'S HOT.
On days like this, I can't help but remember.

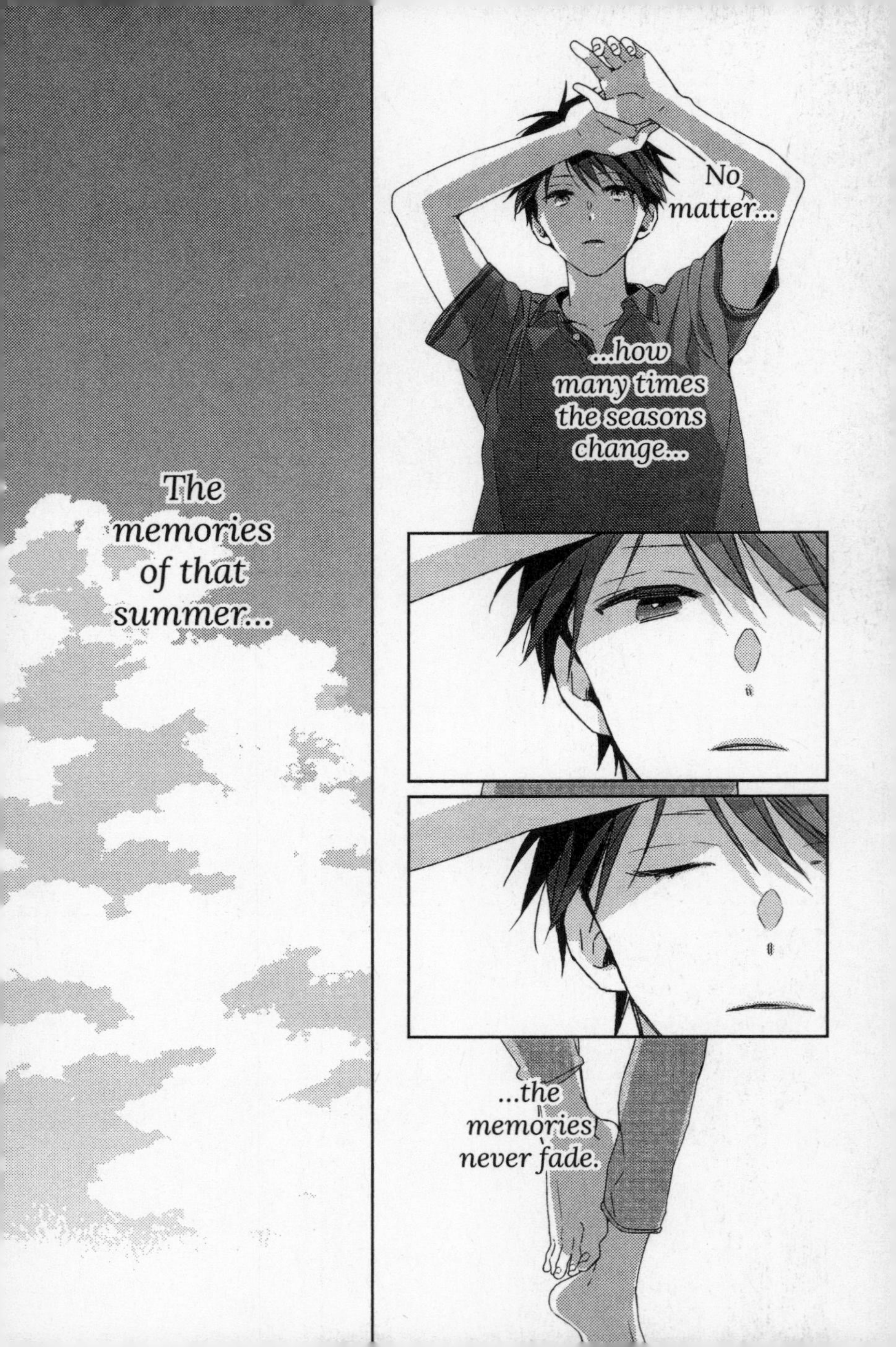
No matter...
...how many times the seasons change...
...the memories never fade.
The memories of that summer...

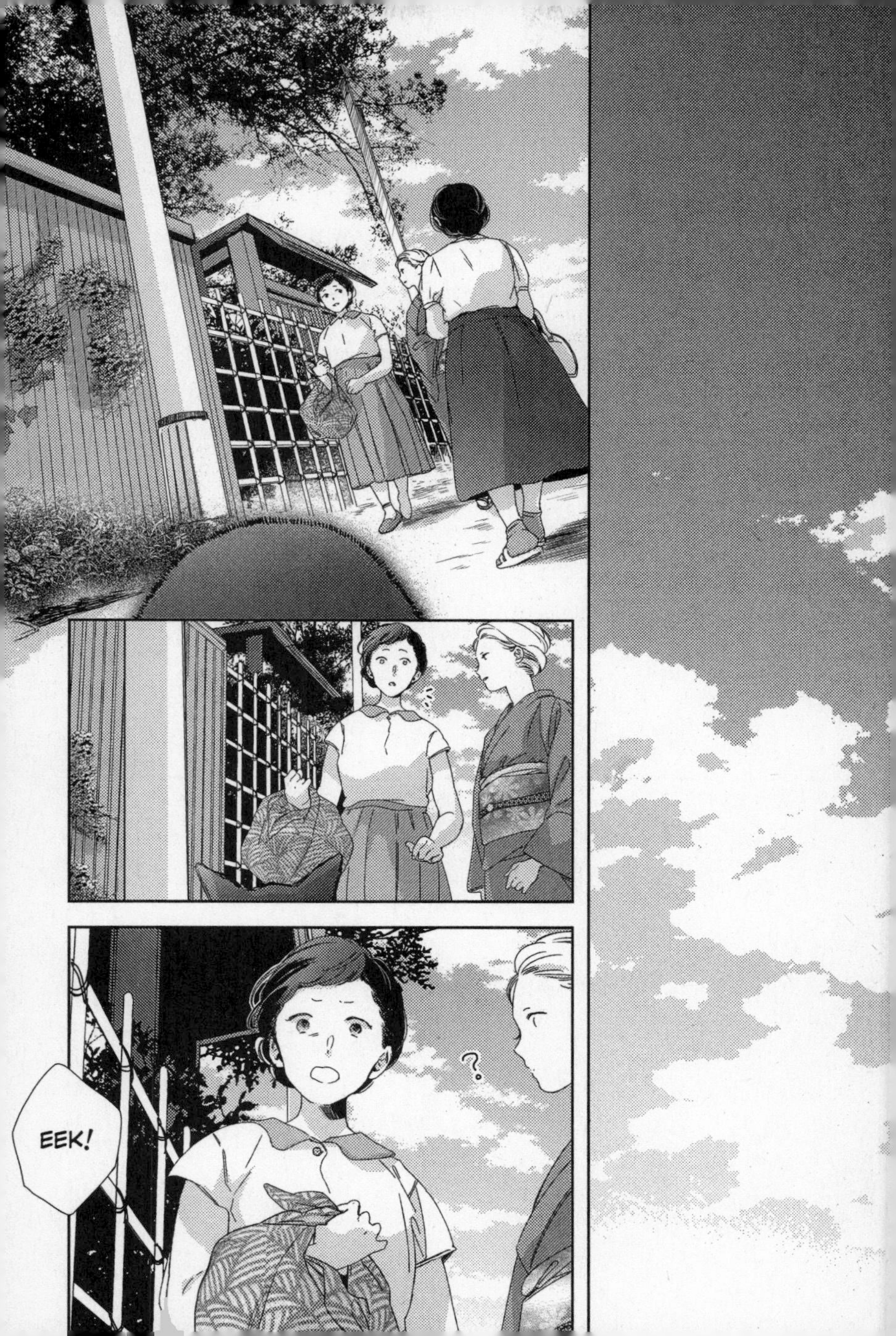
?
EEK!

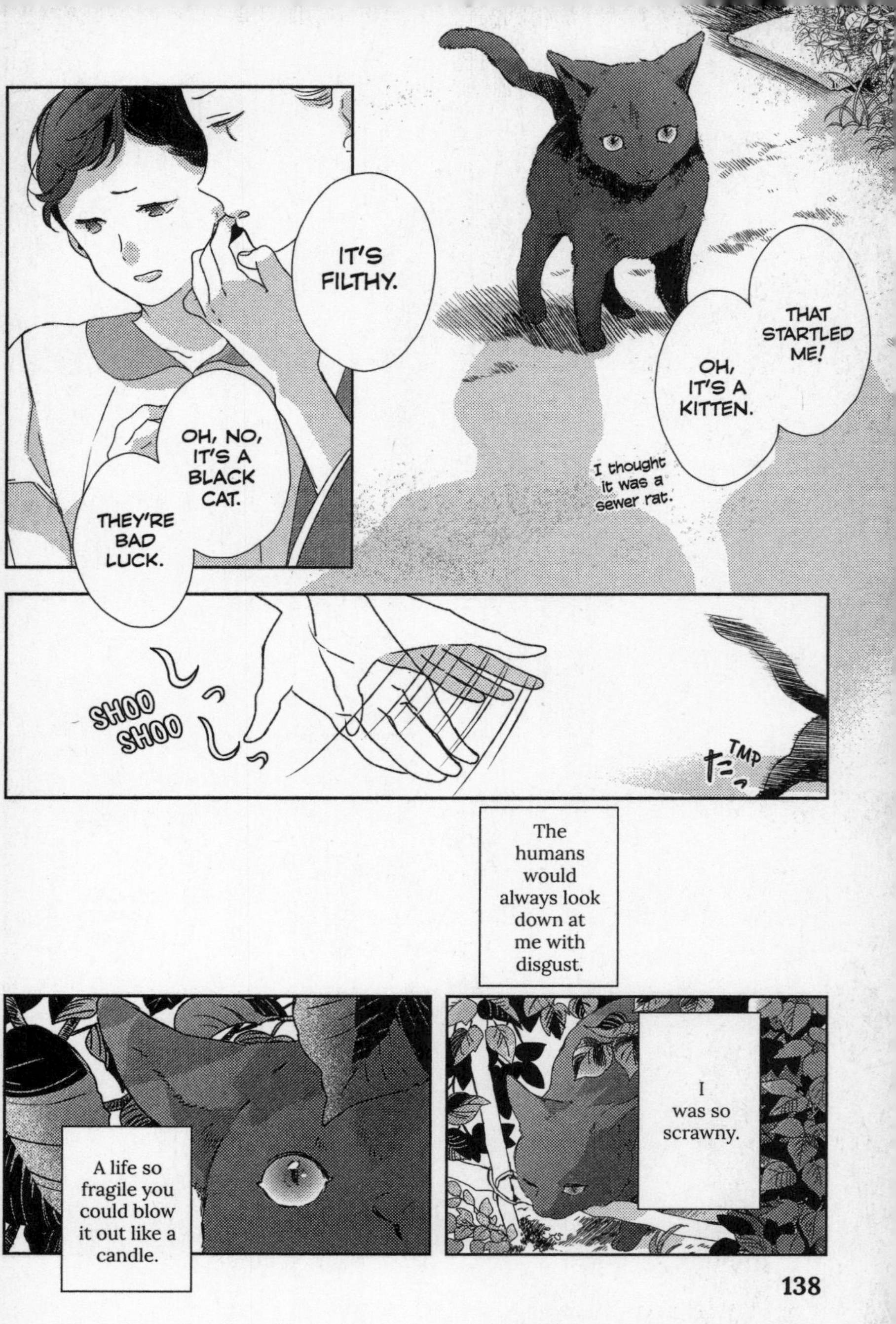
THAT STARTLED ME!
OH, IT'S A KITTEN.
I thought it was a sewer rat.
IT'S FILTHY.
OH, NO, IT'S A BLACK CAT.
THEY'RE BAD LUCK.
TMP
SHOO SHOO
The humans would always look down at me with disgust.
I was so scrawny.
A life so fragile you could blow it out like a candle.

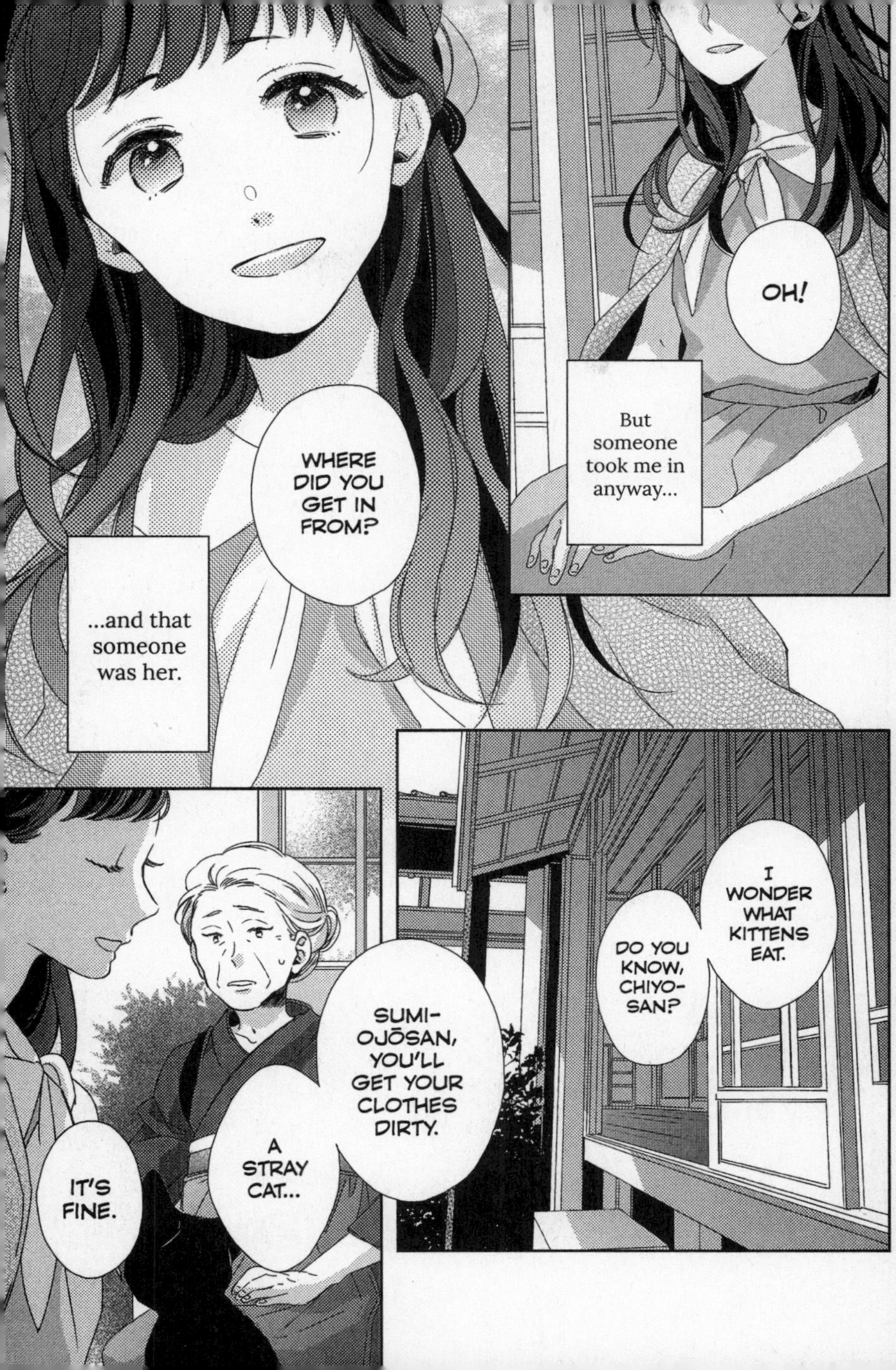
OH!
But someone took me in anyway...
WHERE DID YOU GET IN FROM?
...and that someone was her.
I WONDER WHAT KITTENS EAT.
DO YOU KNOW, CHIYO-SAN?
SUMI-OJŌSAN, YOU'LL GET YOUR CLOTHES DIRTY.
A STRAY CAT...
IT'S FINE.

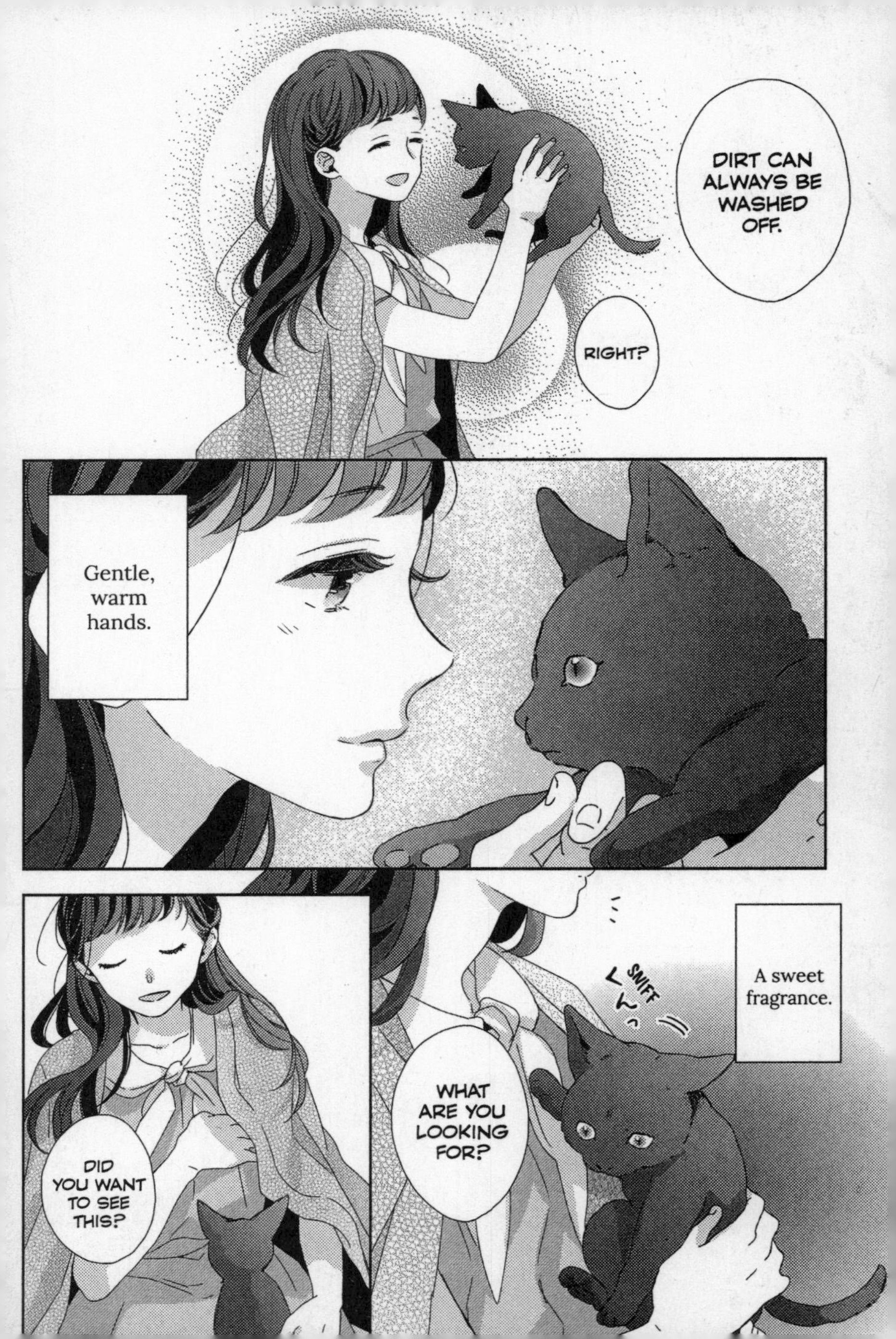
DIRT CAN ALWAYS BE WASHED OFF.
RIGHT?
Gentle, warm hands.
A sweet fragrance.
SNIFF
WHAT ARE YOU LOOKING FOR?
DID YOU WANT TO SEE THIS?

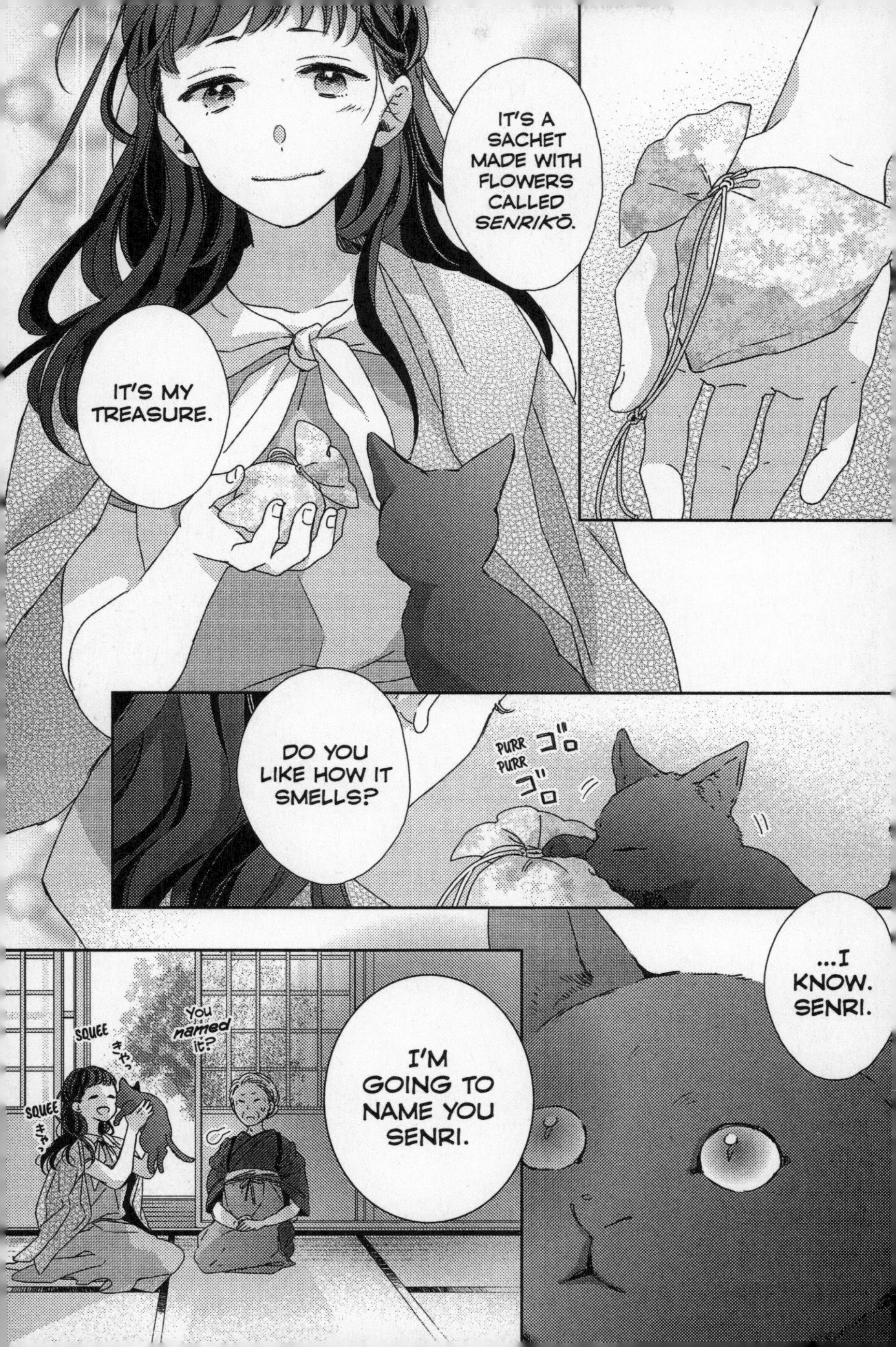
IT'S A SACHET MADE WITH FLOWERS CALLED *SENRIKŌ*.
IT'S MY TREASURE.
DO YOU LIKE HOW IT SMELLS?
PURR ゴロ
PURR ゴロ
...I KNOW. SENRI.
I'M GOING TO NAME YOU SENRI.
You *named* it?
SQUEE きゃっ
SQUEE きゃっ

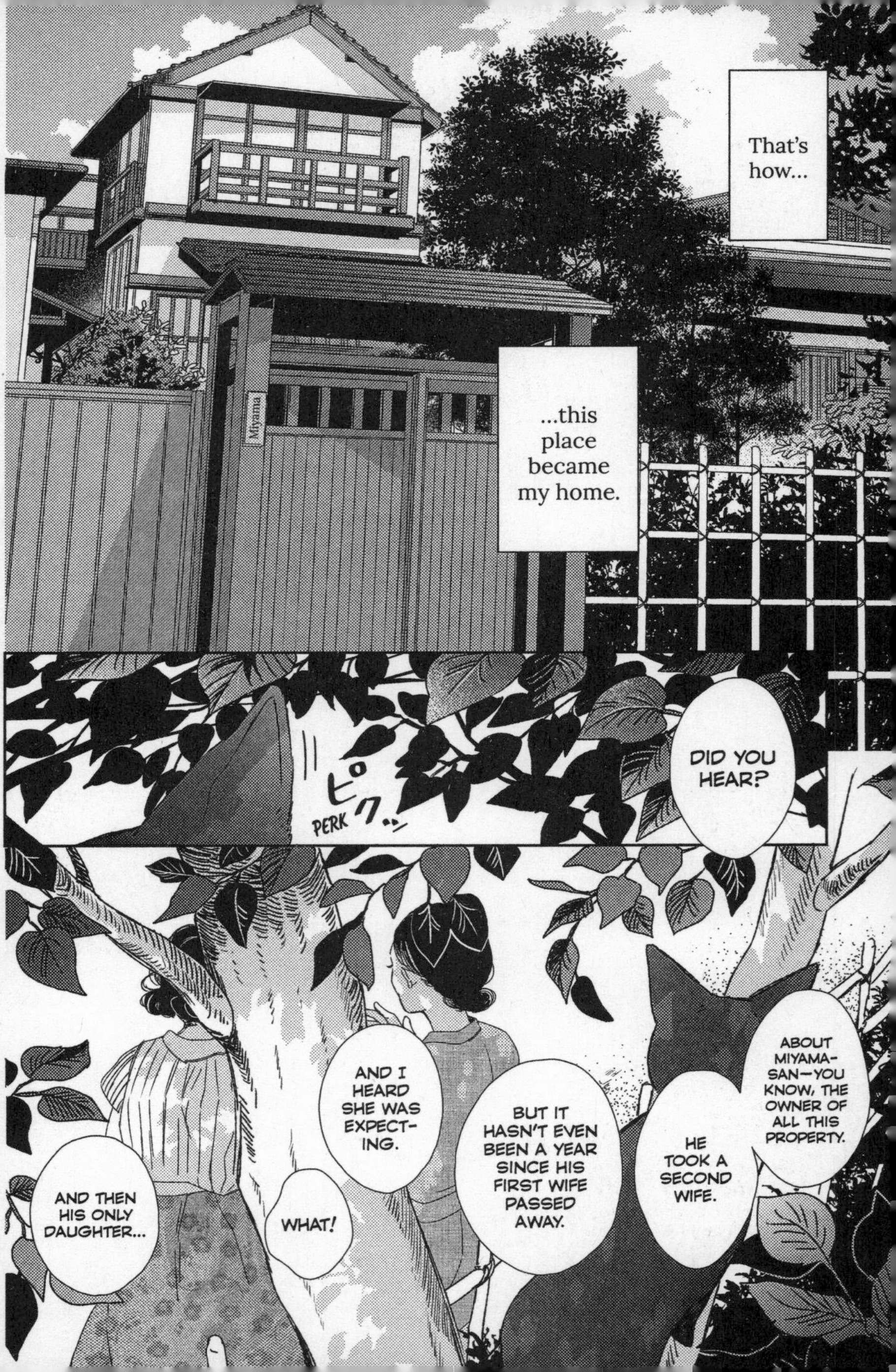
That's how...
...this place became my home.
Miyama
DID YOU HEAR?
ピクッ
PERK
ABOUT MIYAMA-SAN—YOU KNOW, THE OWNER OF ALL THIS PROPERTY.
HE TOOK A SECOND WIFE.
BUT IT HASN'T EVEN BEEN A YEAR SINCE HIS FIRST WIFE PASSED AWAY.
AND I HEARD SHE WAS EXPECTING.
WHAT!
AND THEN HIS ONLY DAUGHTER...

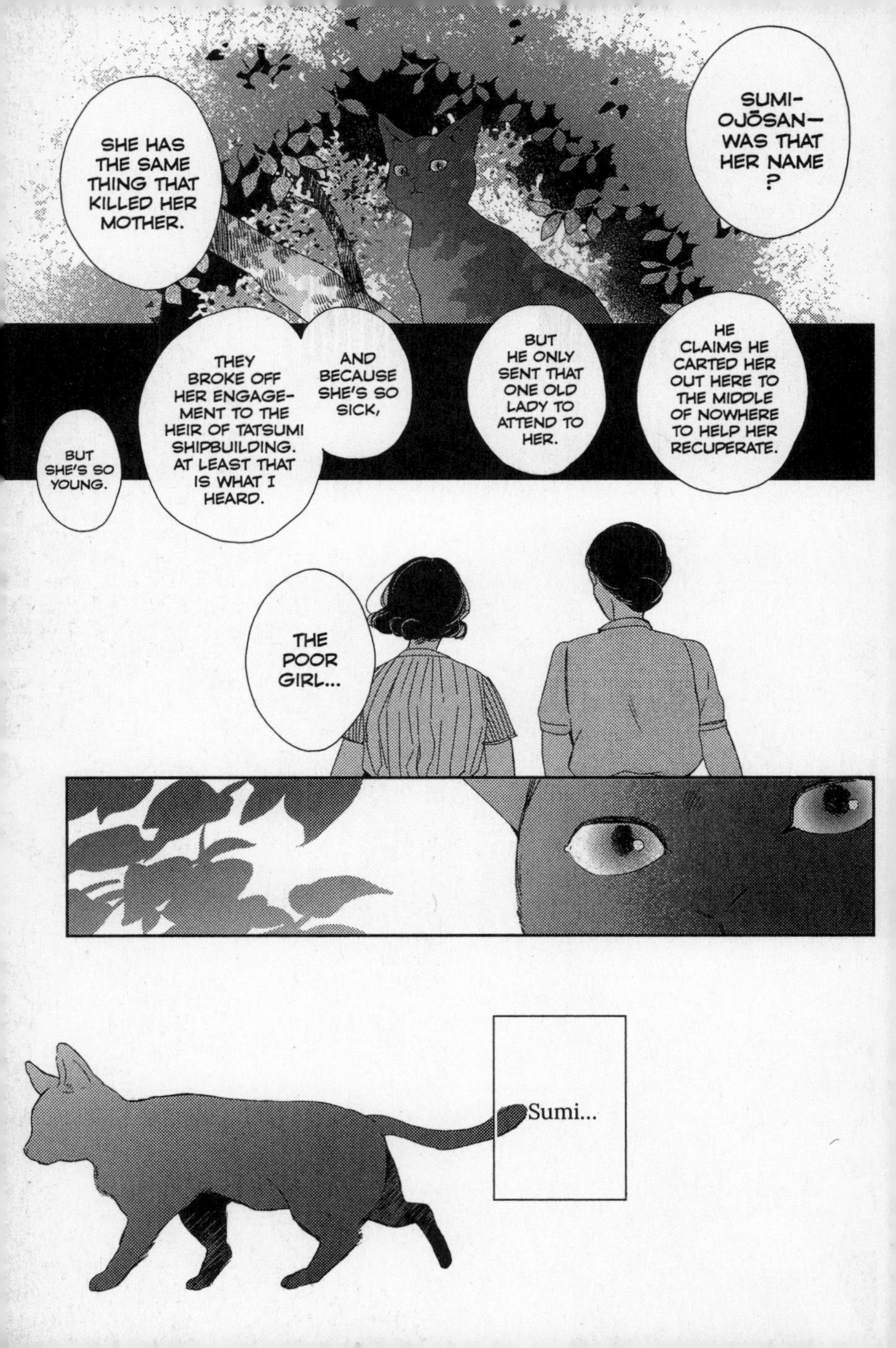
SUMI-OJŌSAN—WAS THAT HER NAME?
SHE HAS THE SAME THING THAT KILLED HER MOTHER.
HE CLAIMS HE CARTED HER OUT HERE TO THE MIDDLE OF NOWHERE TO HELP HER RECUPERATE.
BUT HE ONLY SENT THAT ONE OLD LADY TO ATTEND TO HER.
AND BECAUSE SHE'S SO SICK,
THEY BROKE OFF HER ENGAGEMENT TO THE HEIR OF TATSUMI SHIPBUILDING. AT LEAST THAT IS WHAT I HEARD.
BUT SHE'S SO YOUNG.
THE POOR GIRL...
Sumi...

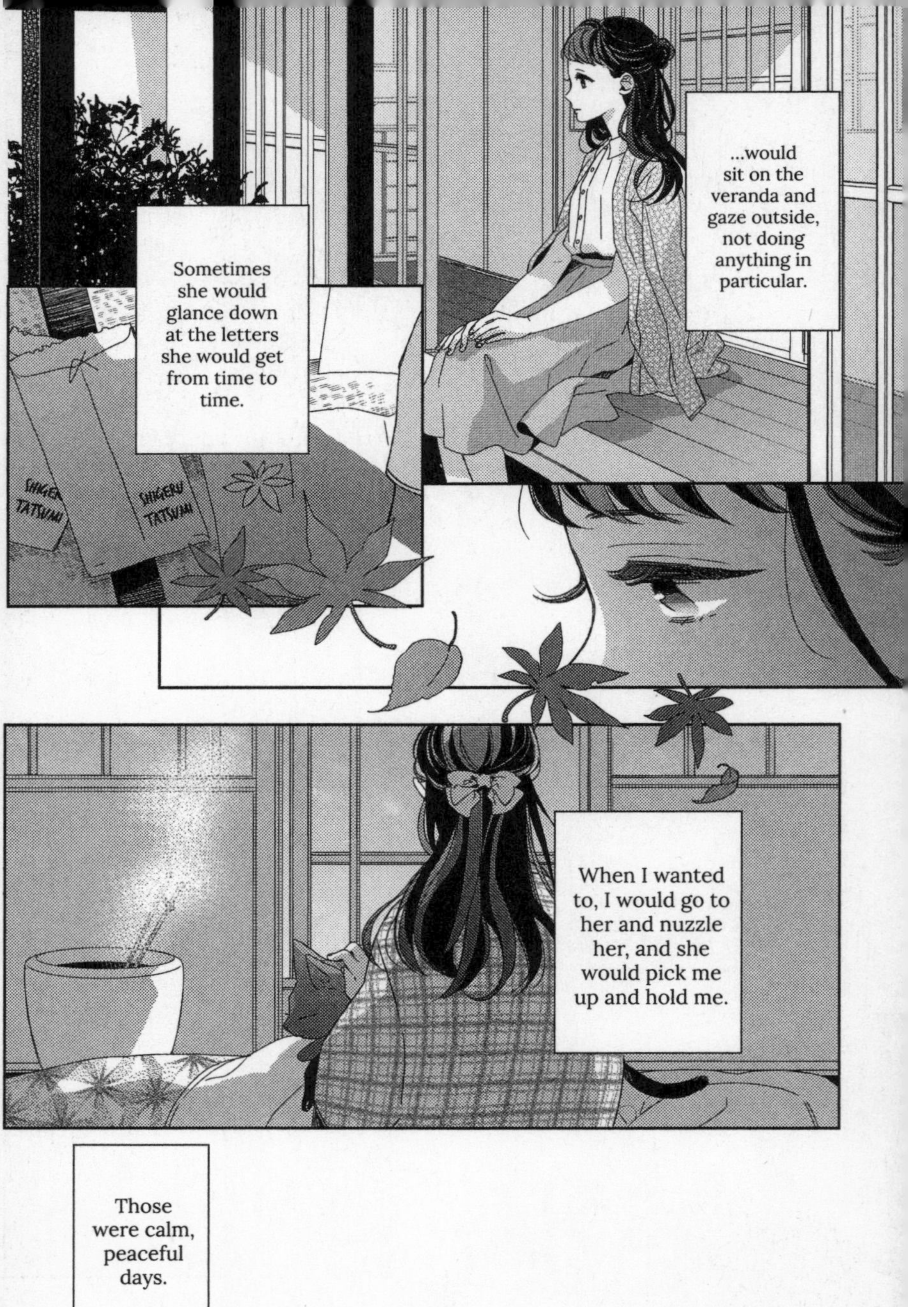
...would sit on the veranda and gaze outside, not doing anything in particular.
Sometimes she would glance down at the letters she would get from time to time.
SHIGERU TATSUMI
SHIGERU TATSUMI
When I wanted to, I would go to her and nuzzle her, and she would pick me up and hold me.
Those were calm, peaceful days.

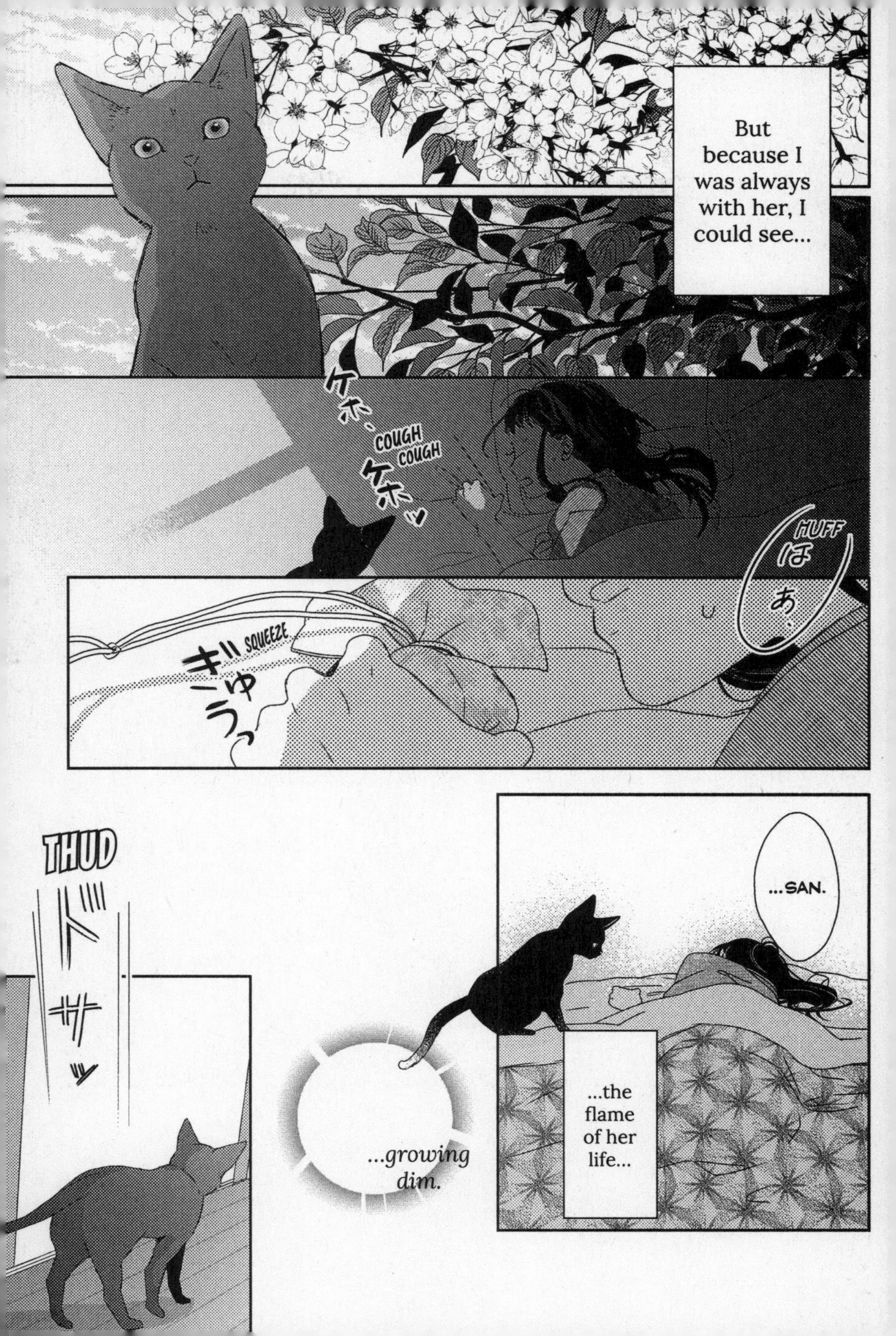
But because I was always with her, I could see...
COUGH COUGH
HUFF
SQUEEZE
...SAN.
...the flame of her life...
...growing dim.
THUD

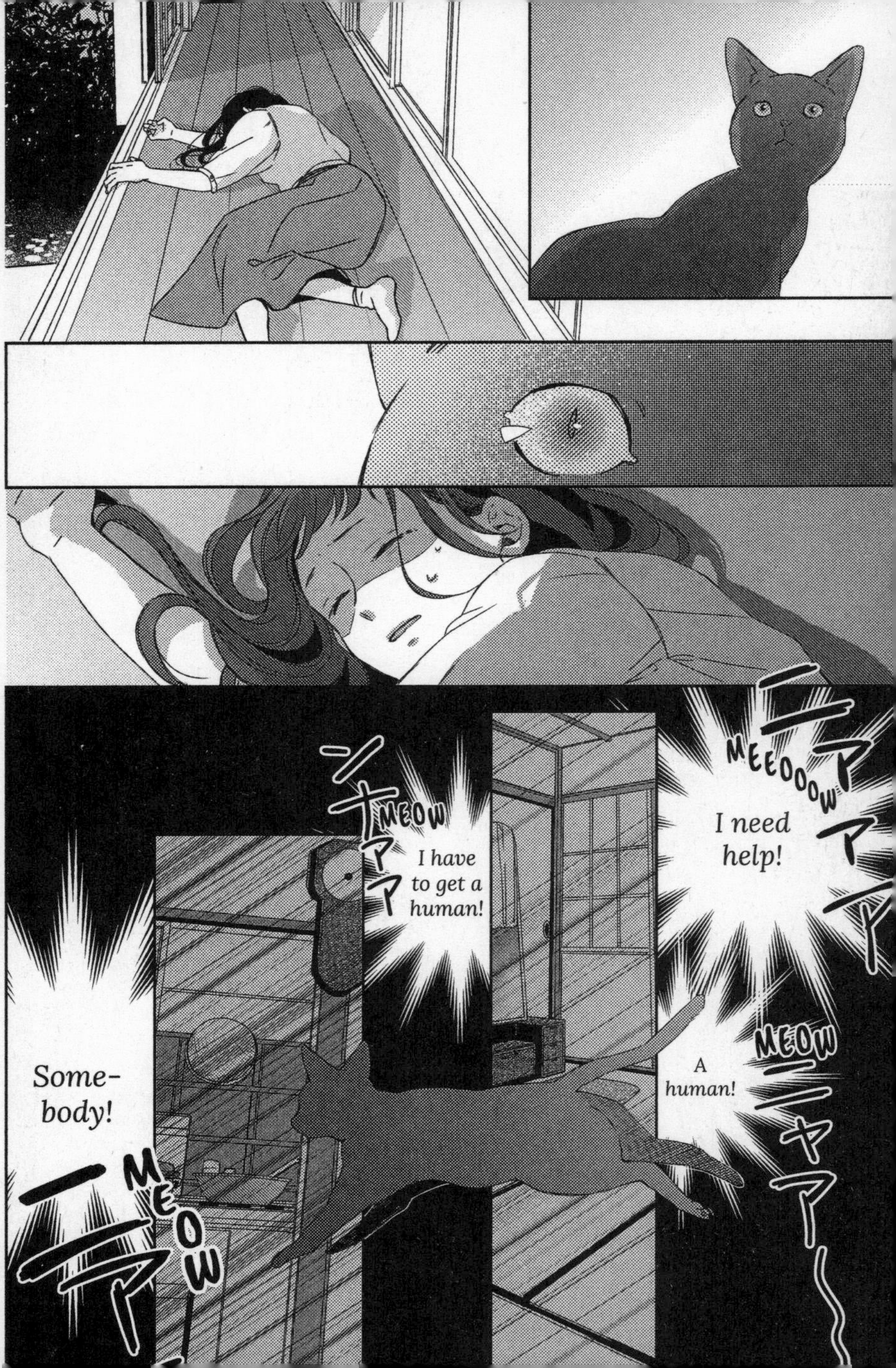
MEEOOOW
I need help!
MEOW
A human!
MEOW
I have to get a human!
Some-body!
MEOW

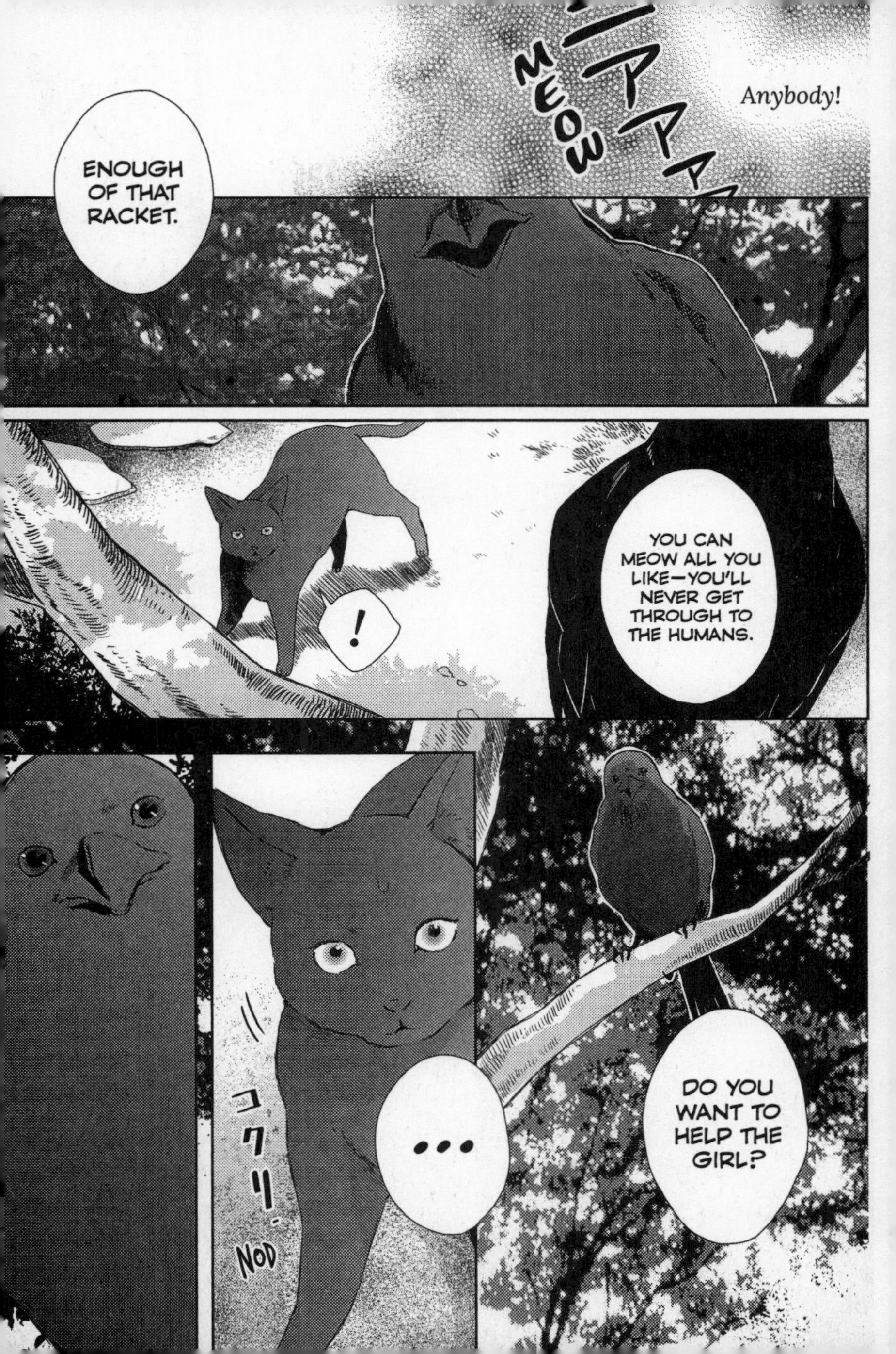
Anybody!
MEOW
ENOUGH OF THAT RACKET.
YOU CAN MEOW ALL YOU LIKE—YOU'LL NEVER GET THROUGH TO THE HUMANS.
!
DO YOU WANT TO HELP THE GIRL?
...
コクリ
NOD

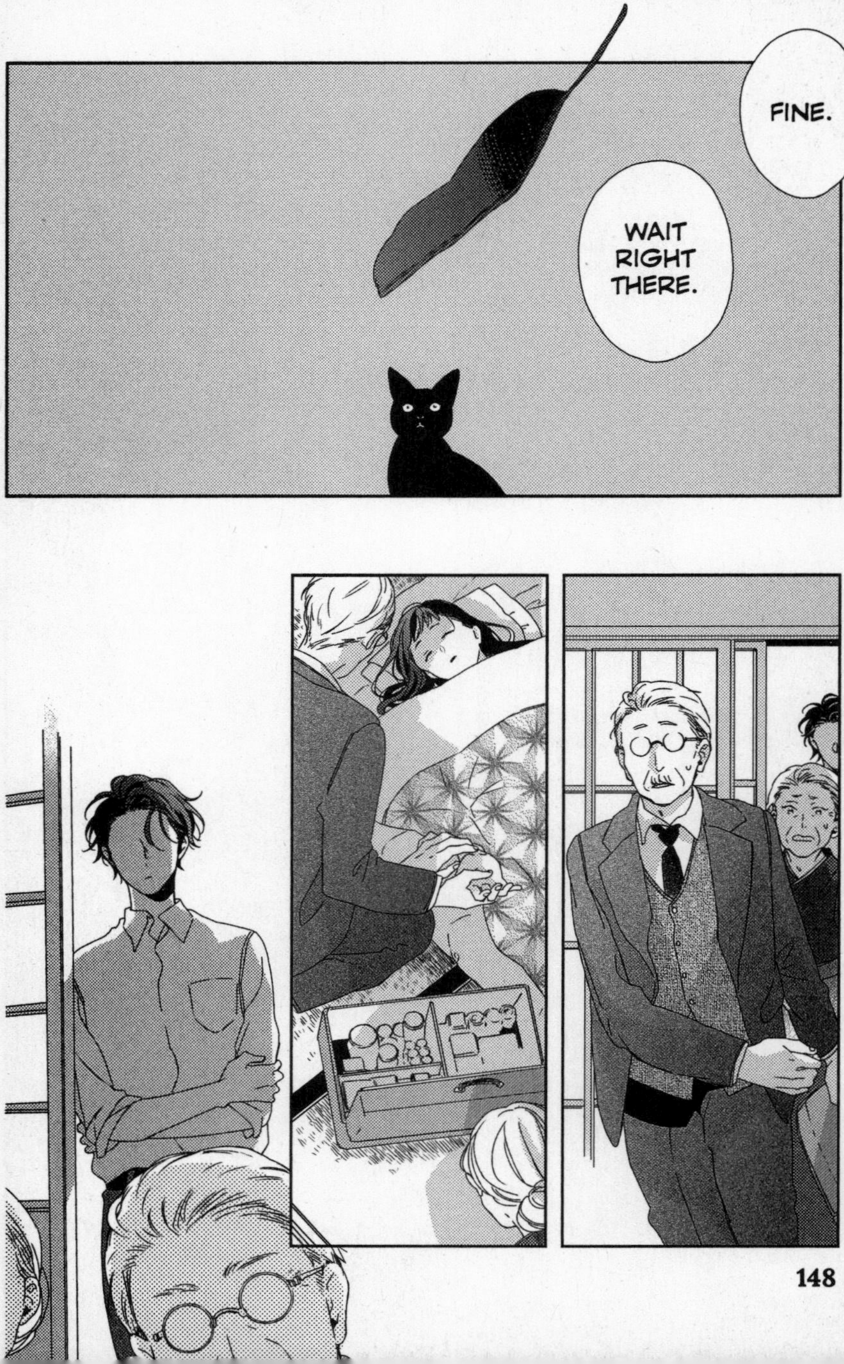
FINE.
WAIT RIGHT THERE.

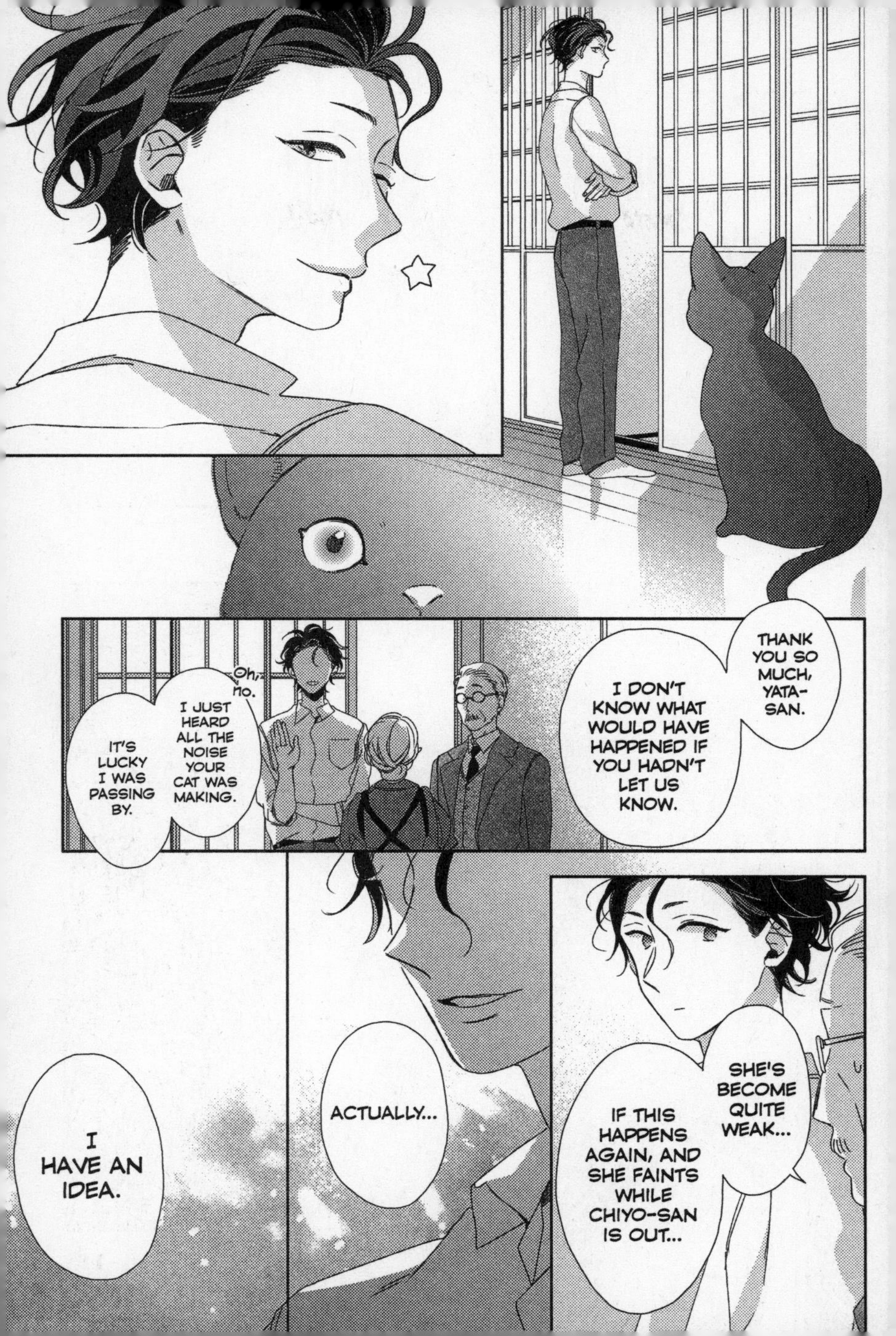
THANK YOU SO MUCH, YATA-SAN.
I DON'T KNOW WHAT WOULD HAVE HAPPENED IF YOU HADN'T LET US KNOW.
Oh, no.
I JUST HEARD ALL THE NOISE YOUR CAT WAS MAKING.
IT'S LUCKY I WAS PASSING BY.
SHE'S BECOME QUITE WEAK...
IF THIS HAPPENS AGAIN, AND SHE FAINTS WHILE CHIYO-SAN IS OUT...
ACTUALLY...
I HAVE AN IDEA.

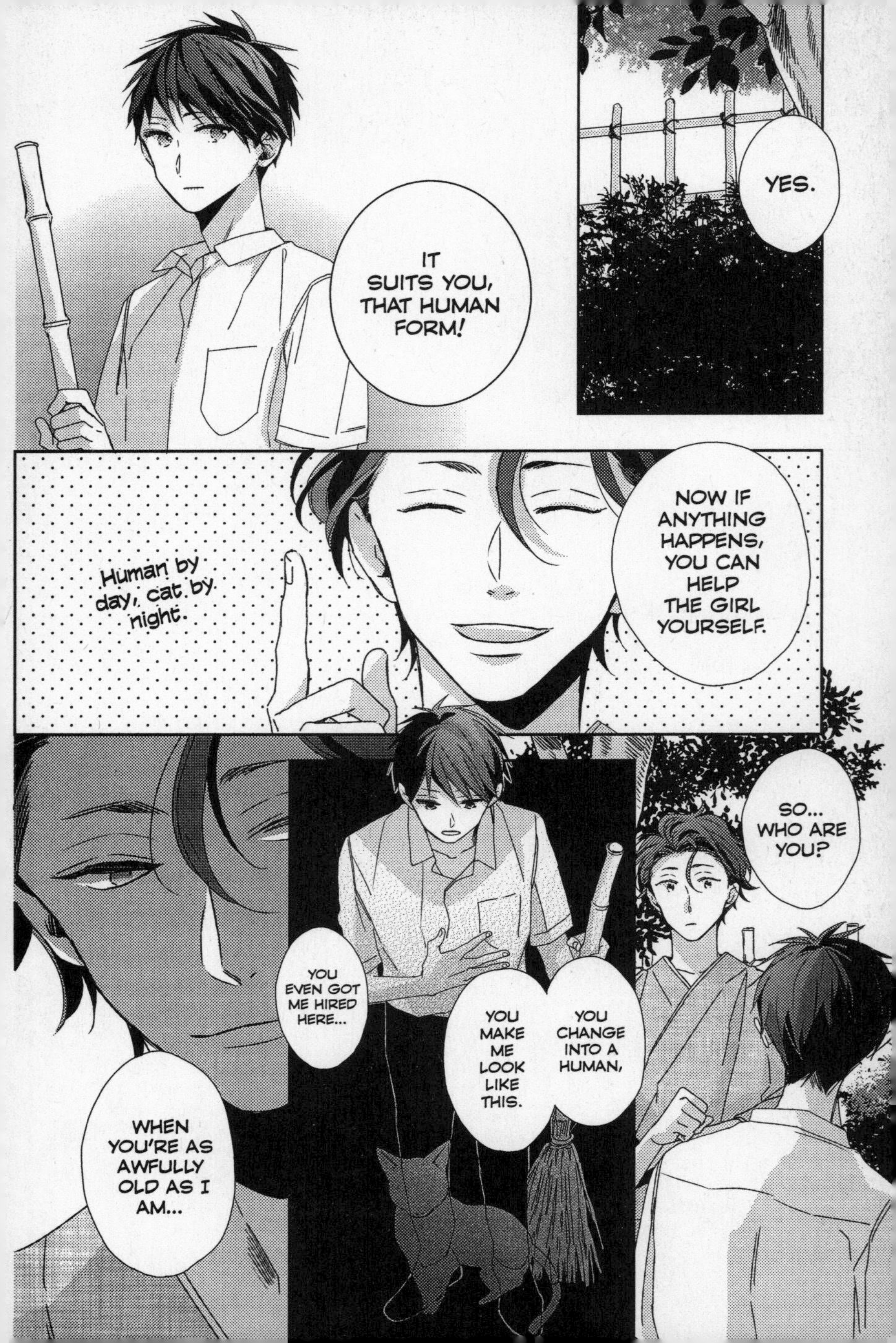
YES.
IT SUITS YOU, THAT HUMAN FORM!
NOW IF ANYTHING HAPPENS, YOU CAN HELP THE GIRL YOURSELF.
Human by day, cat by night.
SO... WHO ARE YOU?
YOU CHANGE INTO A HUMAN,
YOU MAKE ME LOOK LIKE THIS.
YOU EVEN GOT ME HIRED HERE...
WHEN YOU'RE AS AWFULLY OLD AS I AM...

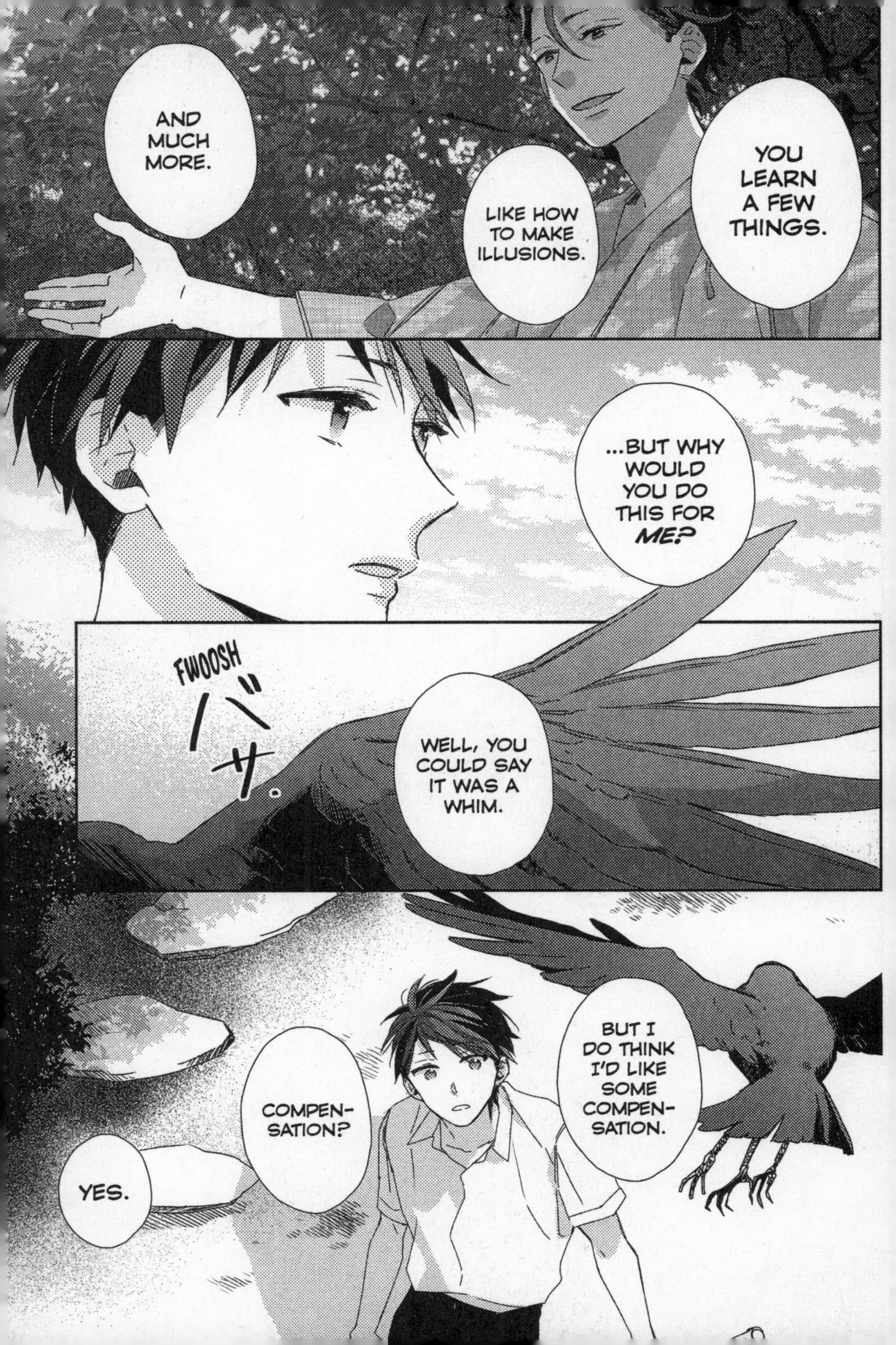
YOU LEARN A FEW THINGS.
LIKE HOW TO MAKE ILLUSIONS.
AND MUCH MORE.
...BUT WHY WOULD YOU DO THIS FOR *ME?*
FWOOSH
バサ
WELL, YOU COULD SAY IT WAS A WHIM.
BUT I DO THINK I'D LIKE SOME COMPEN-SATION.
COMPEN-SATION?
YES.

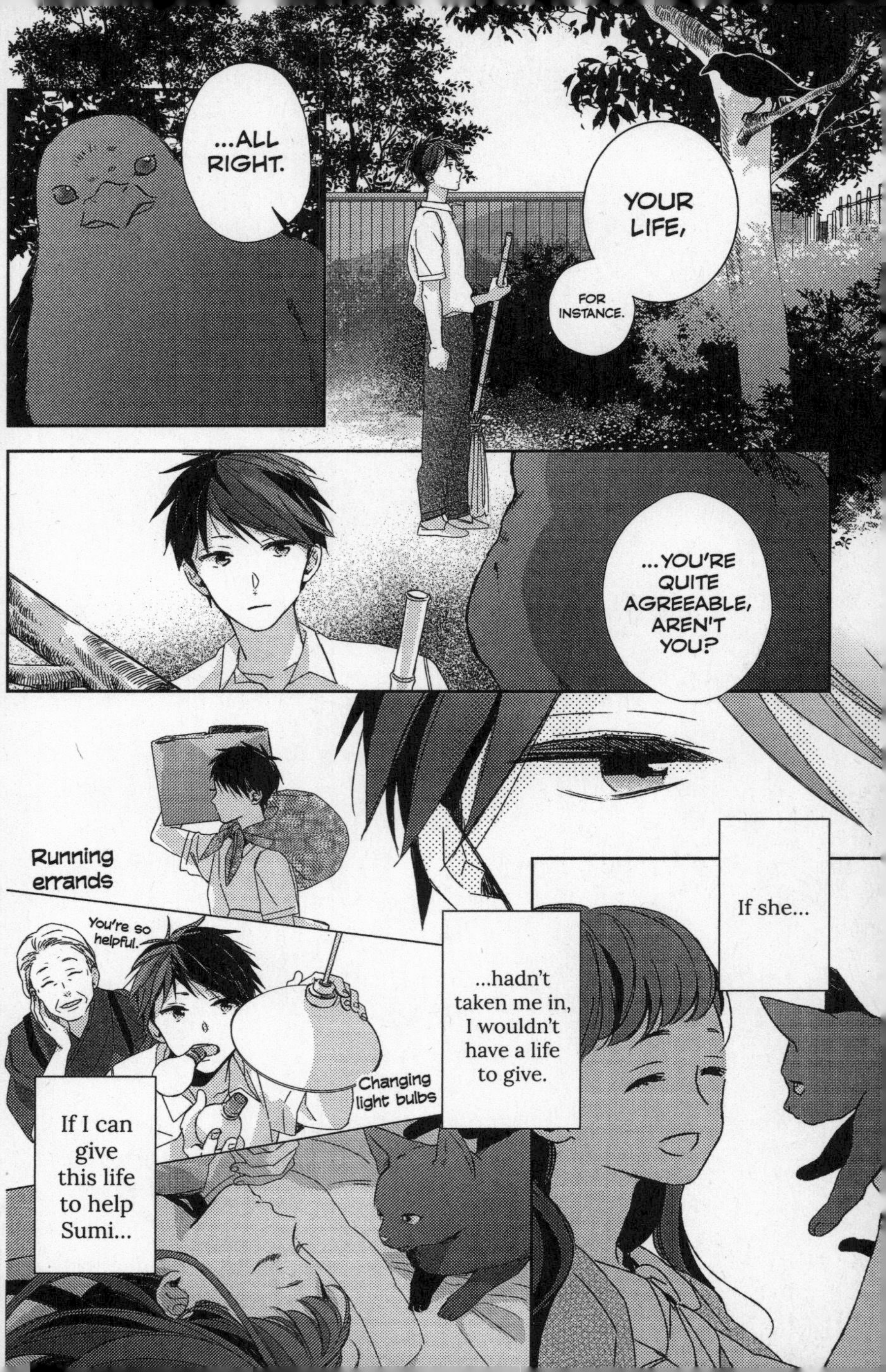
YOUR LIFE,
FOR INSTANCE.
...ALL RIGHT.
...YOU'RE QUITE AGREEABLE, AREN'T YOU?
If she...
...hadn't taken me in, I wouldn't have a life to give.
Running errands
You're so helpful.
Changing light bulbs
If I can give this life to help Sumi...

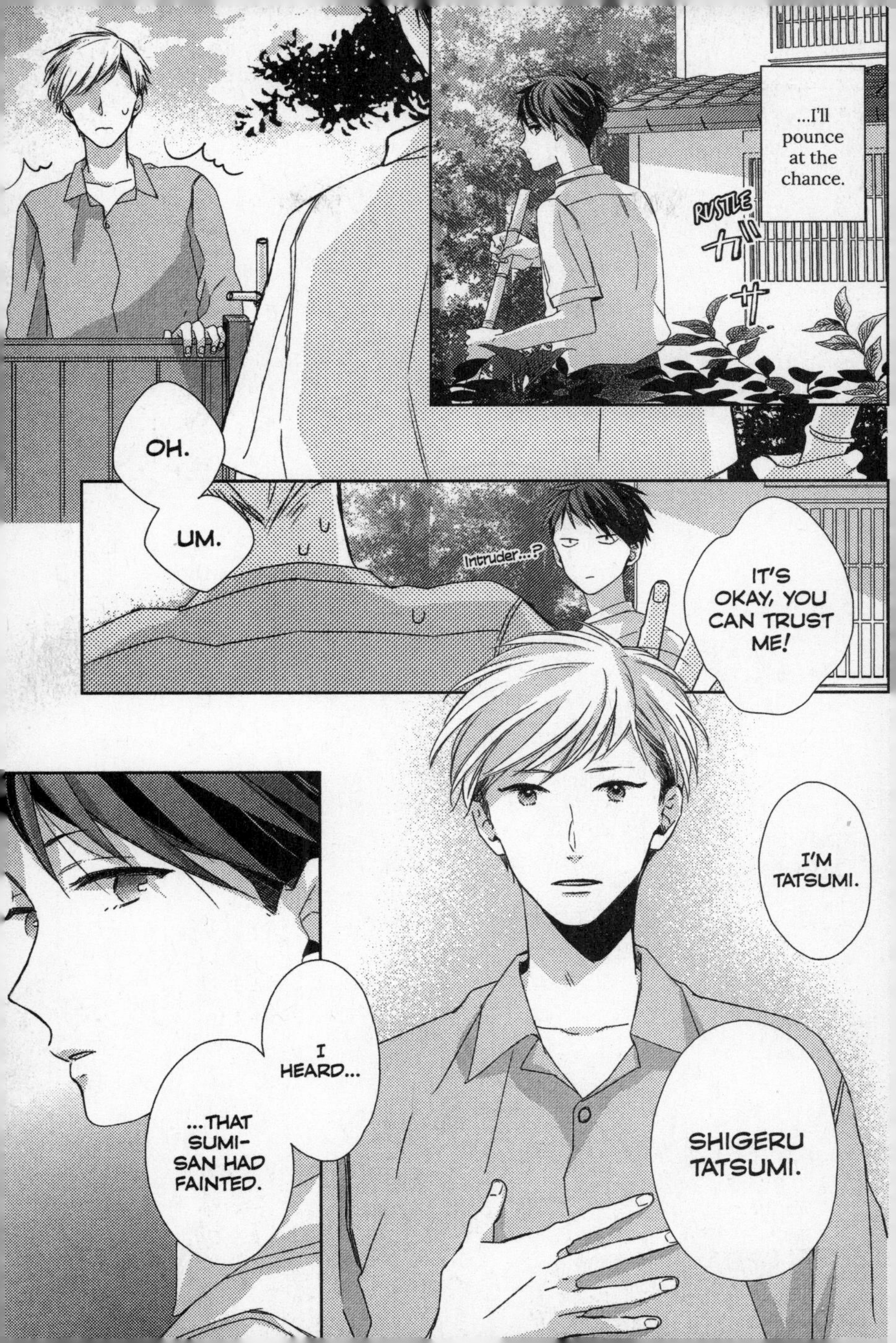

...I'll pounce at the chance.
RUSTLE
カサ
OH.
UM.
IT'S OKAY, YOU CAN TRUST ME!
Intruder...?
I'M TATSUMI.
SHIGERU TATSUMI.
I HEARD...
...THAT SUMI-SAN HAD FAINTED.

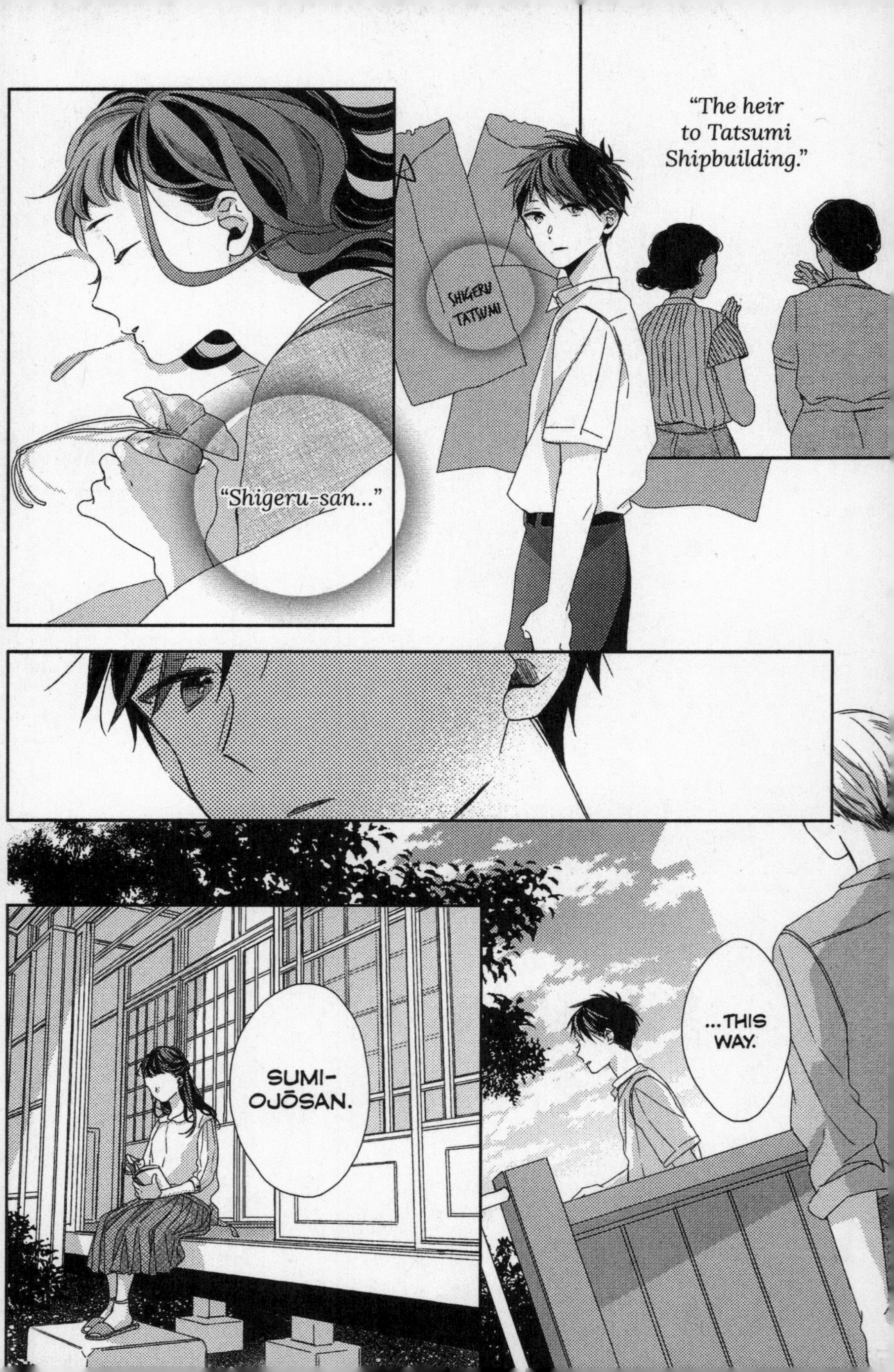
"The heir to Tatsumi Shipbuilding."
SHIGERU TATSUMI
"Shigeru-san..."
...THIS WAY.
SUMI-OJŌSAN.

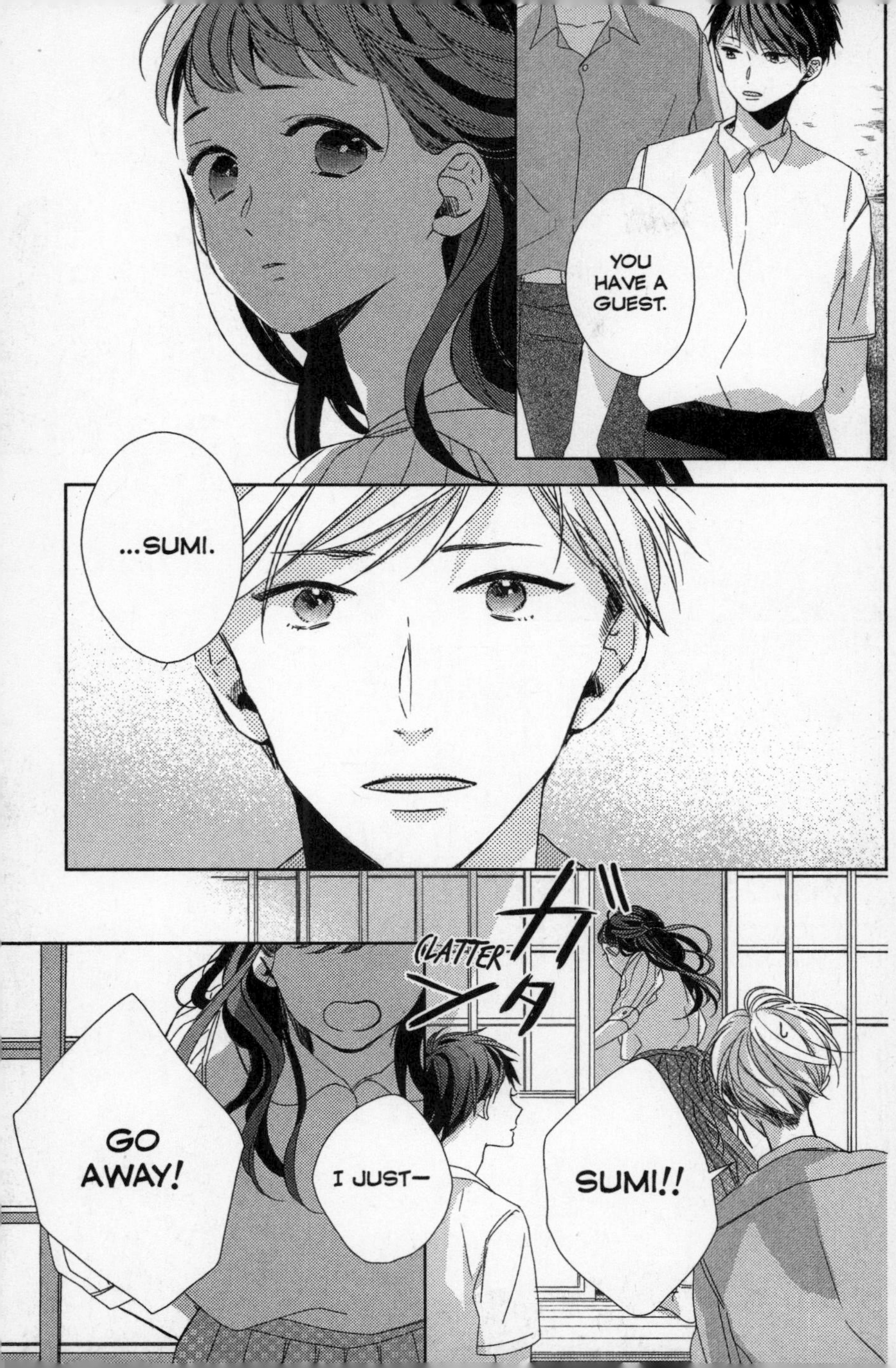
YOU HAVE A GUEST.
...SUMI.
CLATTER
SUMI!!
I JUST—
GO AWAY!

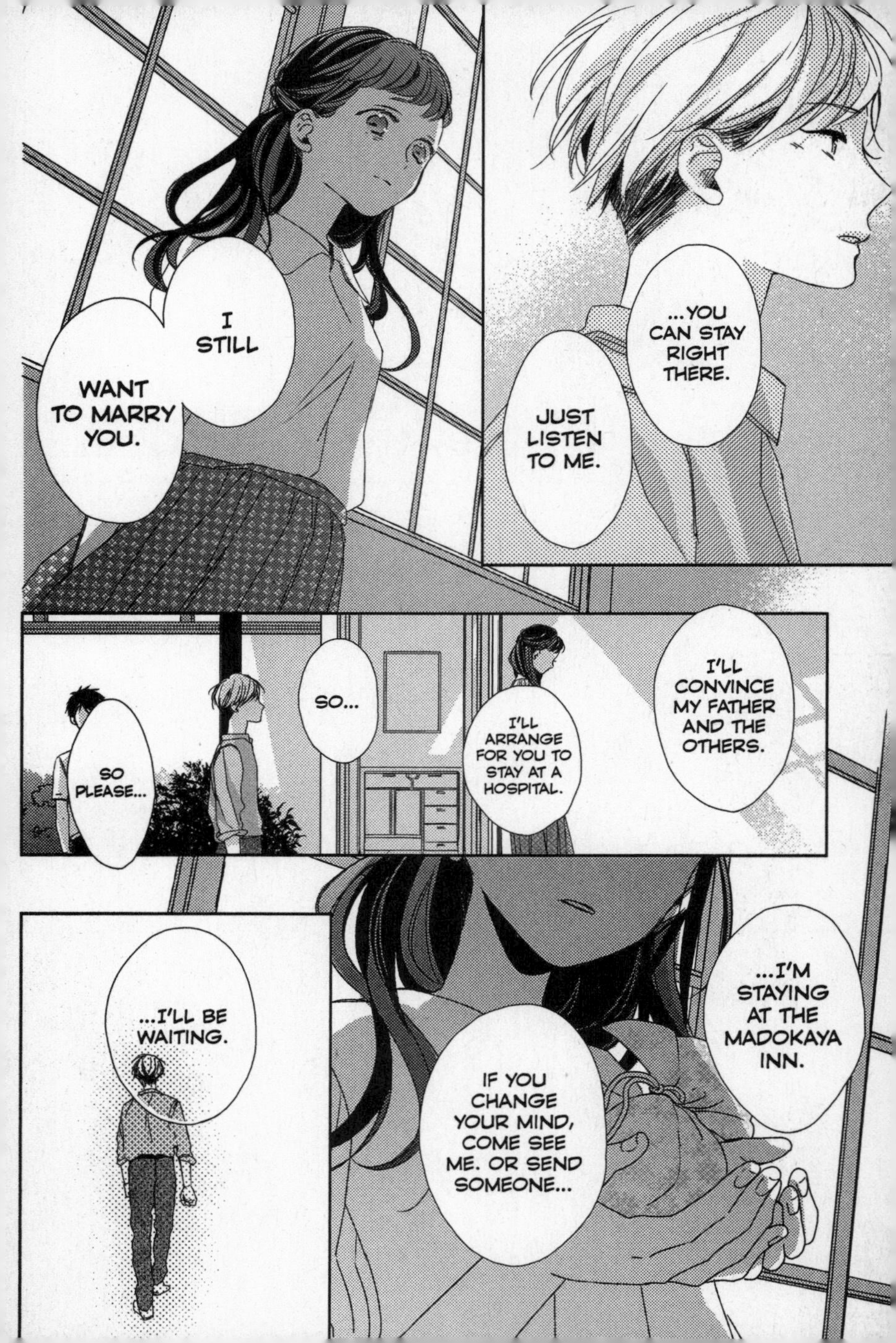
...YOU CAN STAY RIGHT THERE.
JUST LISTEN TO ME.
I STILL
WANT TO MARRY YOU.
I'LL CONVINCE MY FATHER AND THE OTHERS.
I'LL ARRANGE FOR YOU TO STAY AT A HOSPITAL.
SO...
SO PLEASE...
...I'M STAYING AT THE MADOKAYA INN.
IF YOU CHANGE YOUR MIND, COME SEE ME. OR SEND SOMEONE...
...I'LL BE WAITING.

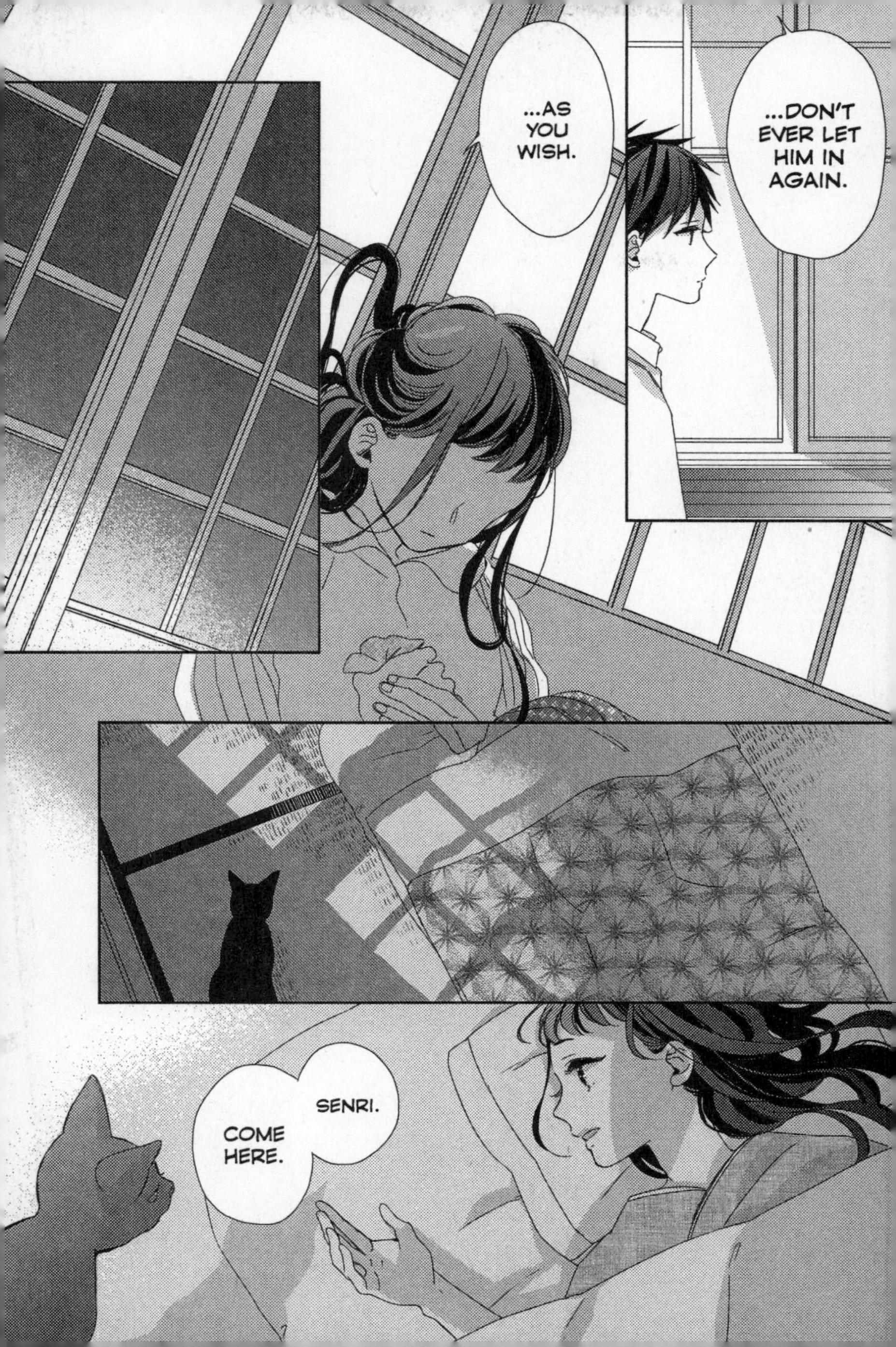
...DON'T EVER LET HIM IN AGAIN.
...AS YOU WISH.
SENRI.
COME HERE.

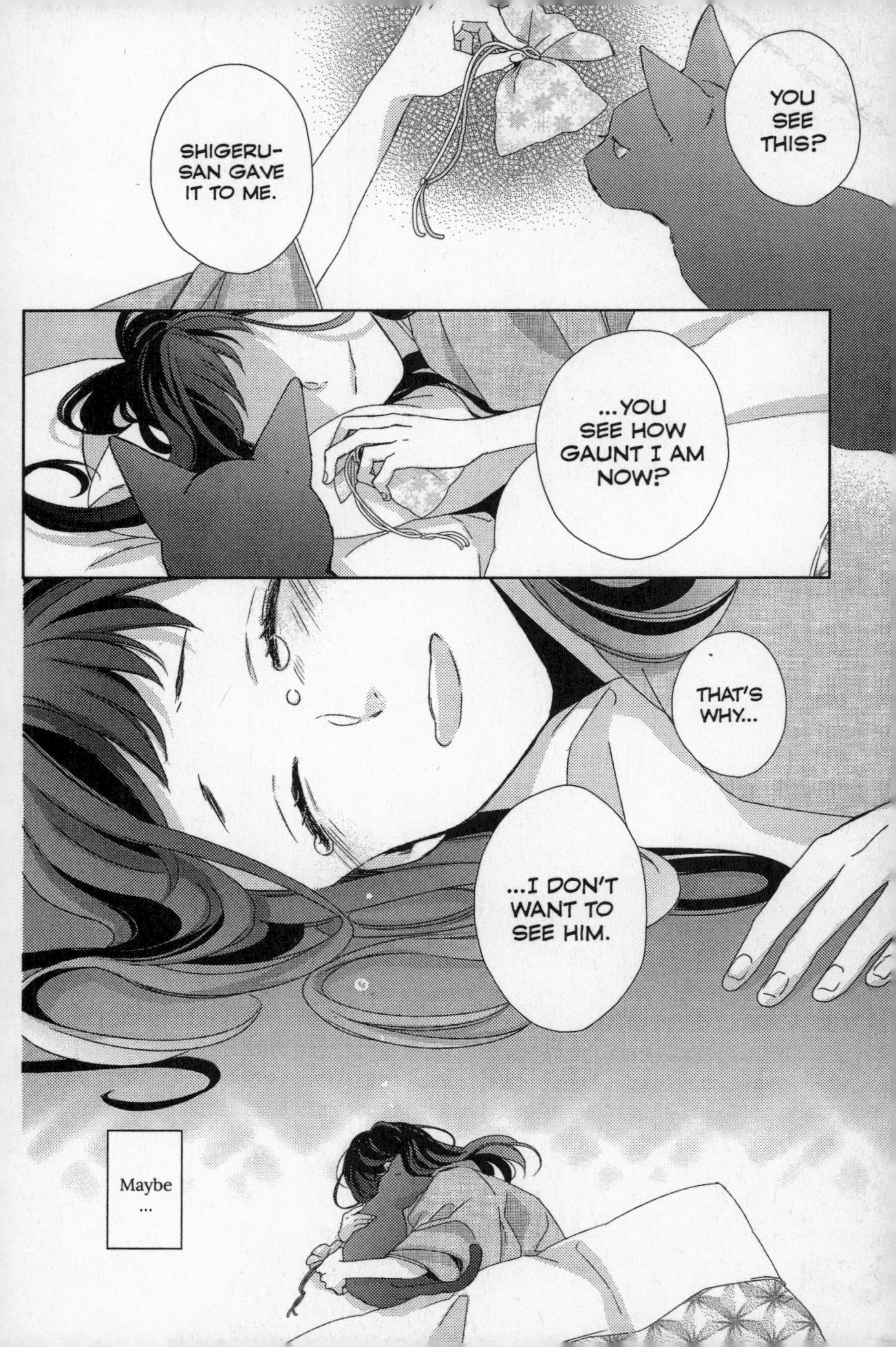
YOU SEE THIS?
SHIGERU-SAN GAVE IT TO ME.
...YOU SEE HOW GAUNT I AM NOW?
THAT'S WHY...
...I DON'T WANT TO SEE HIM.
Maybe ...

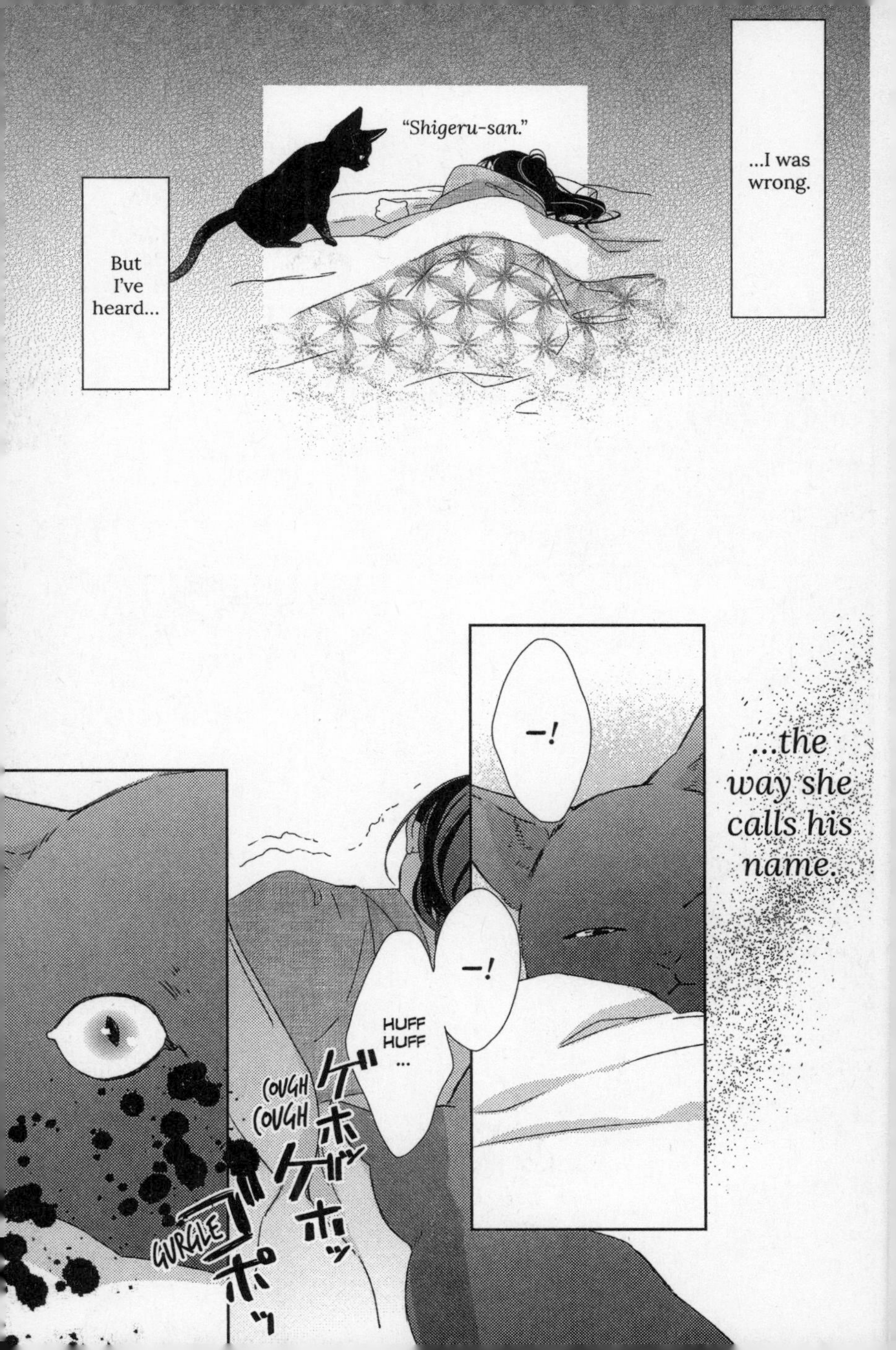
...I was wrong.
"Shigeru-san."
But I've heard...
...the way she calls his name.
—!
—!
HUFF HUFF ...
ゲホッ ゲホッ
COUGH COUGH
ゴポッ
GURGLE

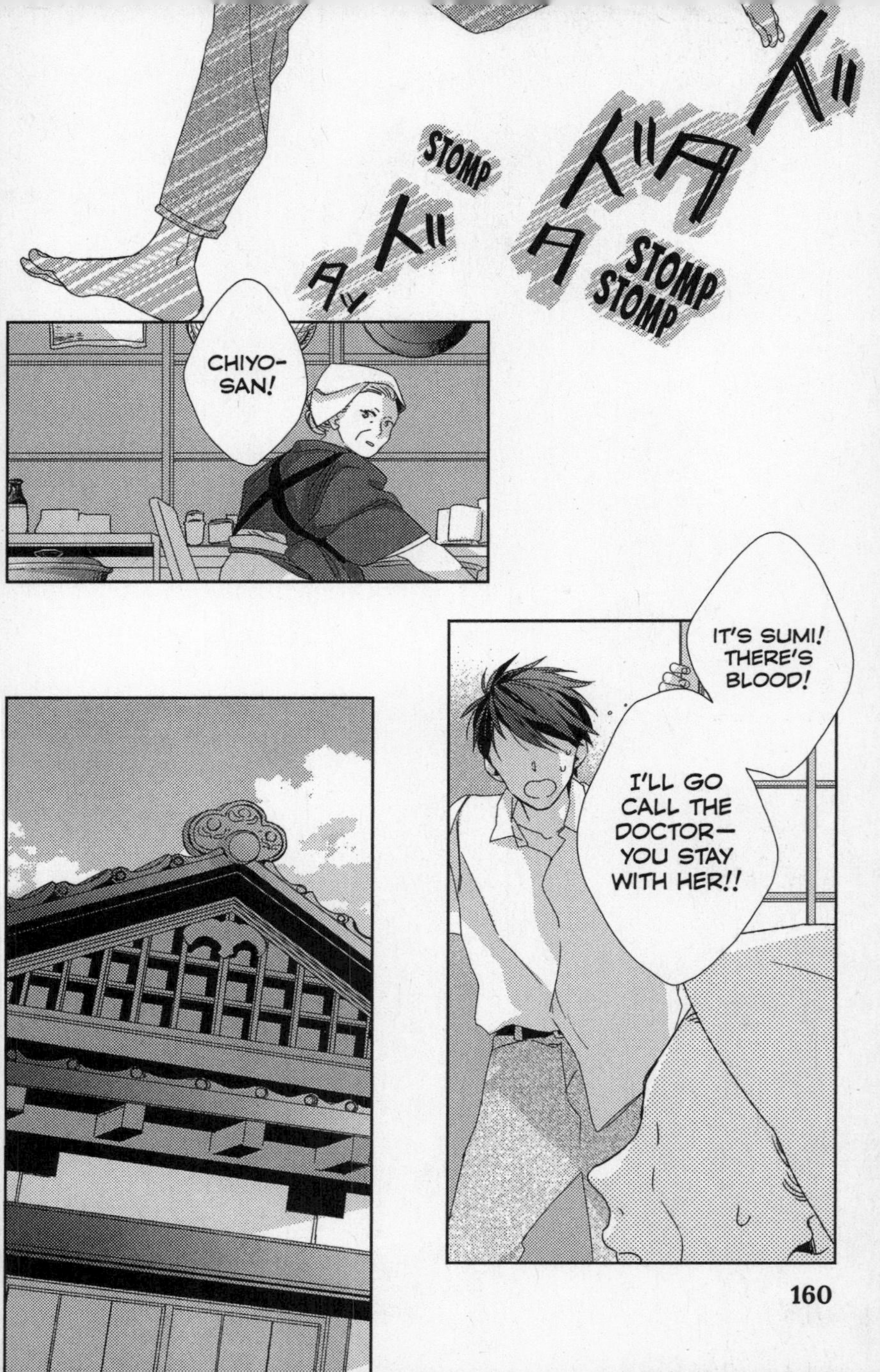
STOMP
STOMP STOMP STOMP
CHIYO-SAN!
IT'S SUMI! THERE'S BLOOD!
I'LL GO CALL THE DOCTOR— YOU STAY WITH HER!!

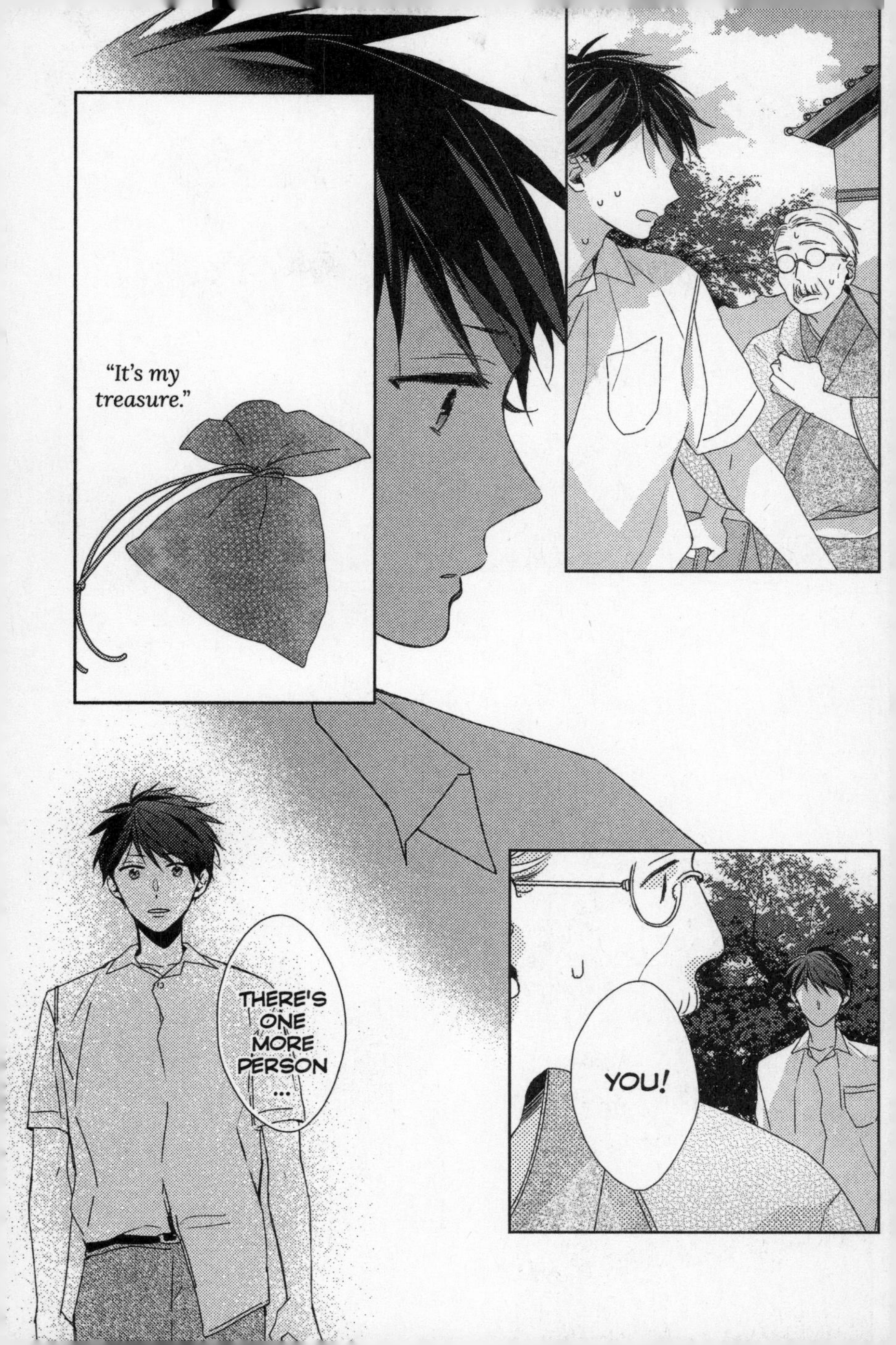
"It's my treasure."
YOU!
THERE'S ONE MORE PERSON ...

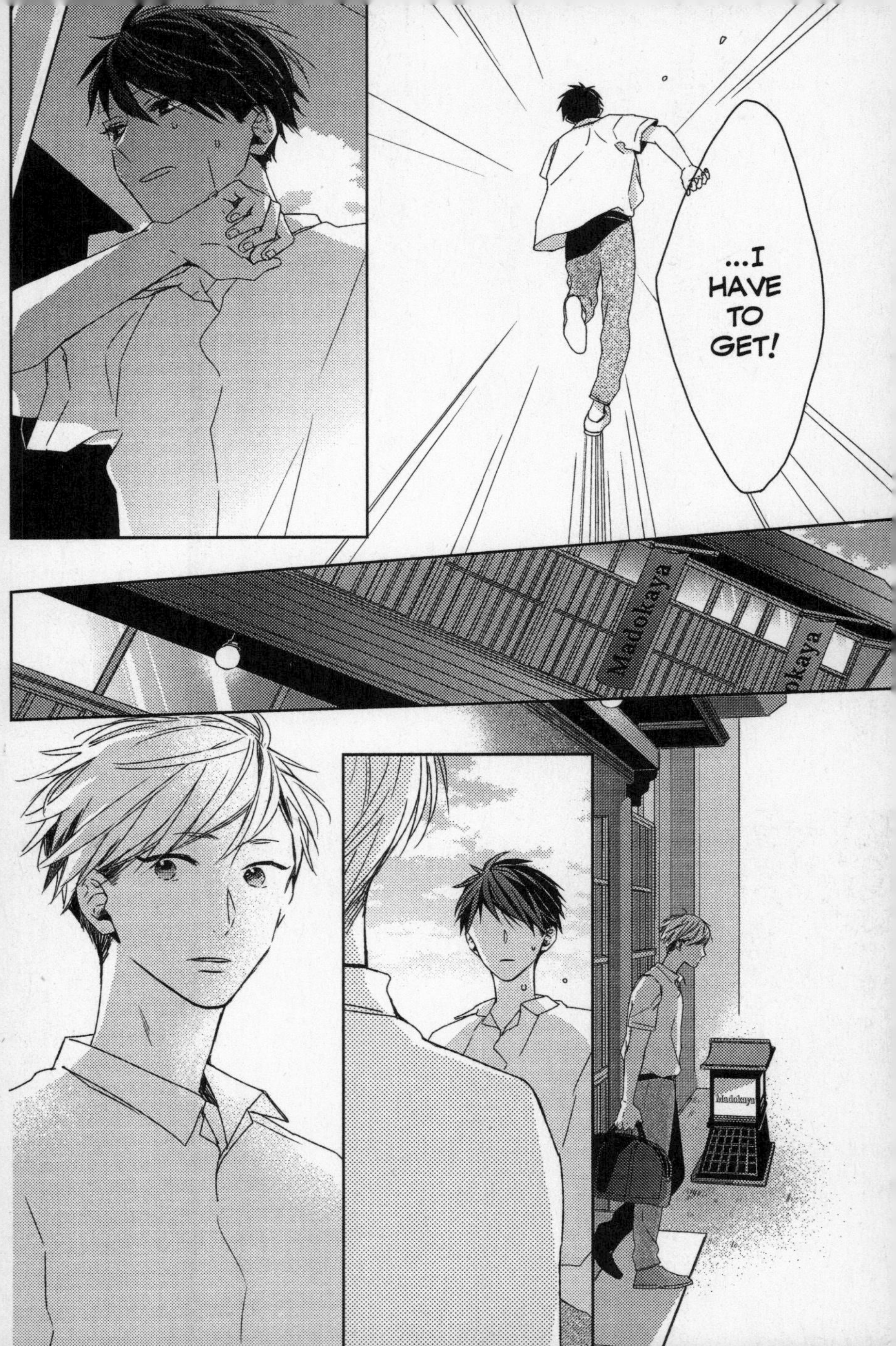
...I HAVE TO GET!
Madokaya
Madokaya
Madokaya

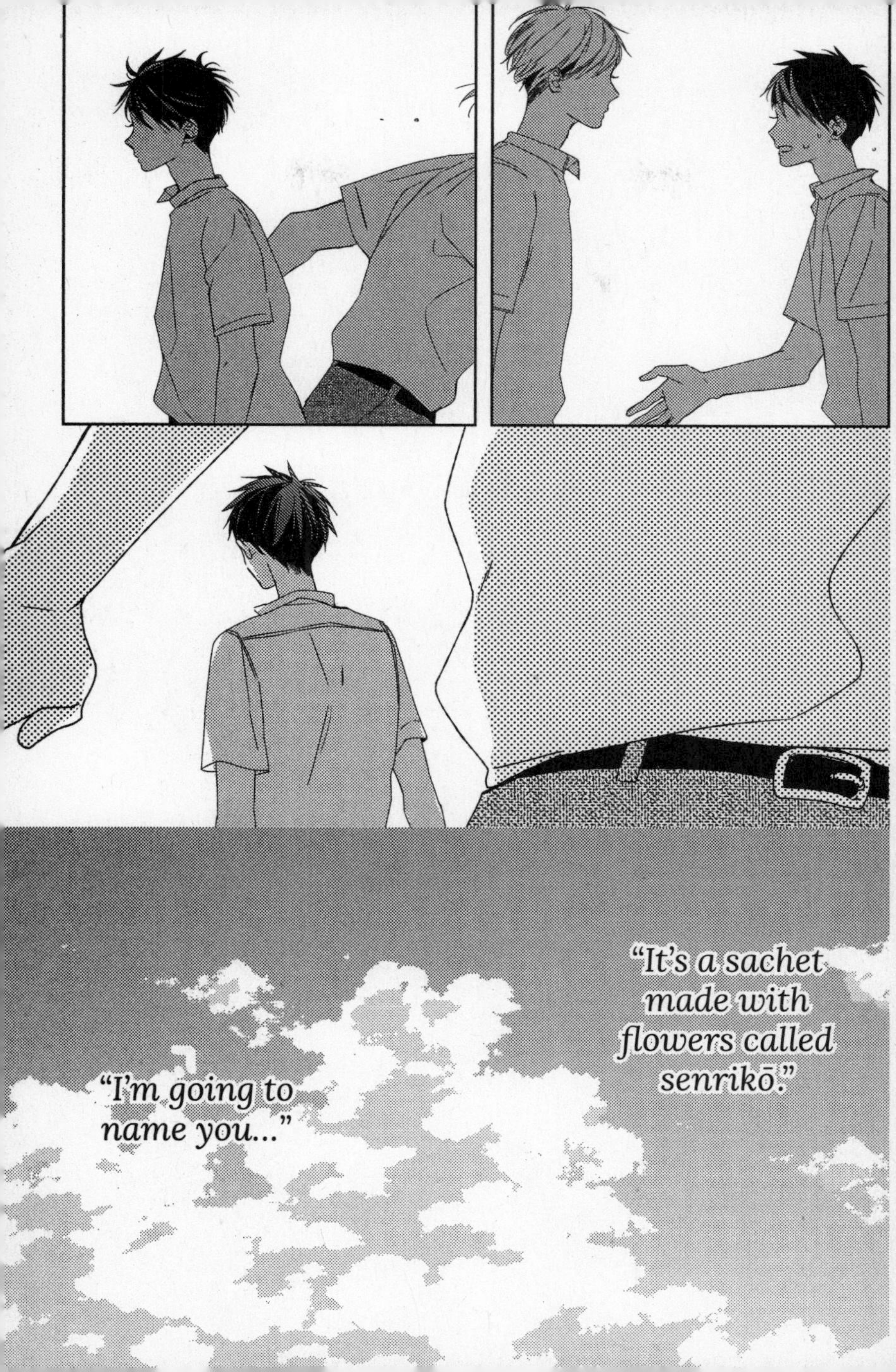
"It's a sachet made with flowers called senrikō."
"I'm going to name you..."

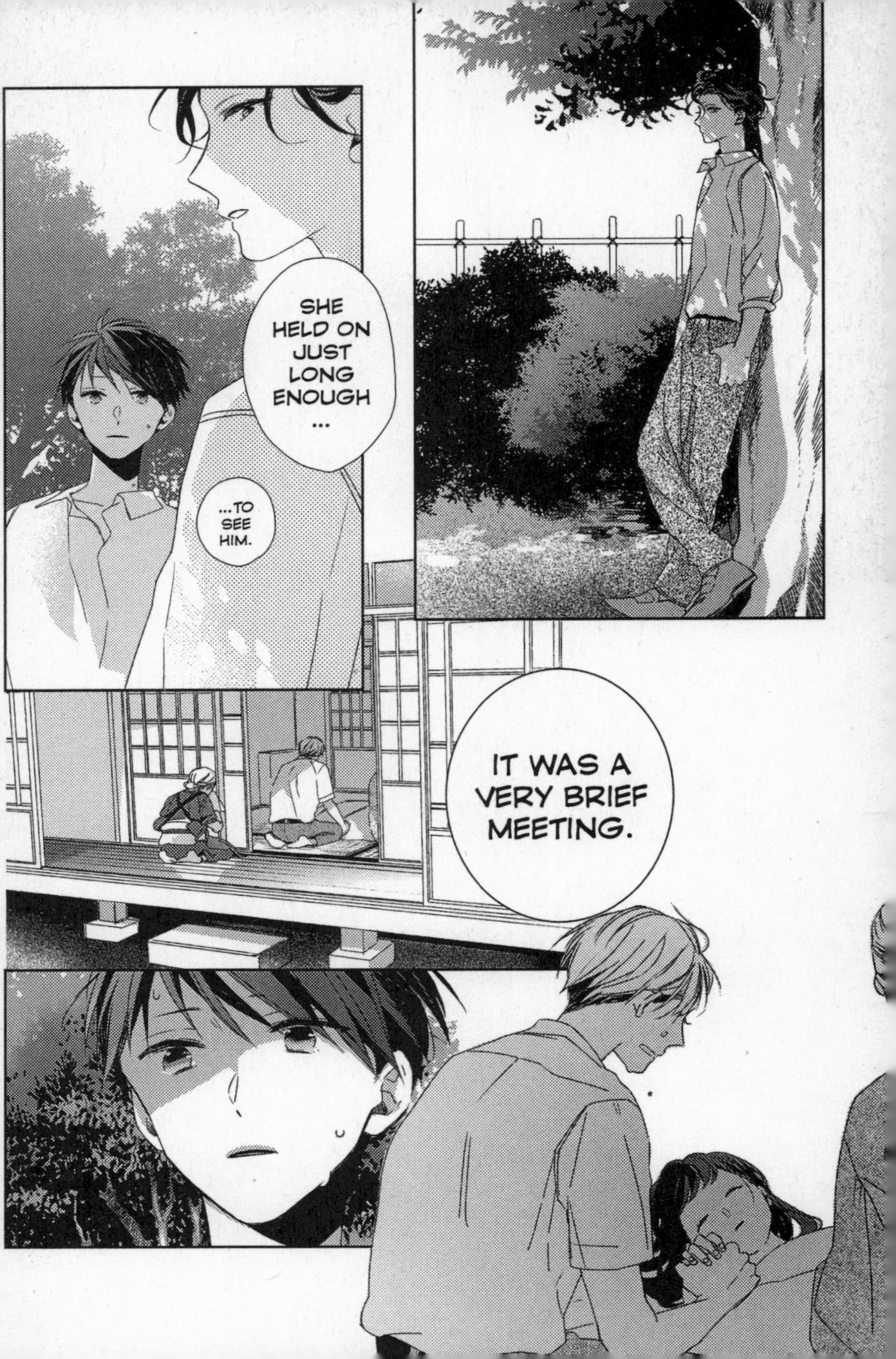
SHE HELD ON JUST LONG ENOUGH ...
...TO SEE HIM.
IT WAS A VERY BRIEF MEETING.

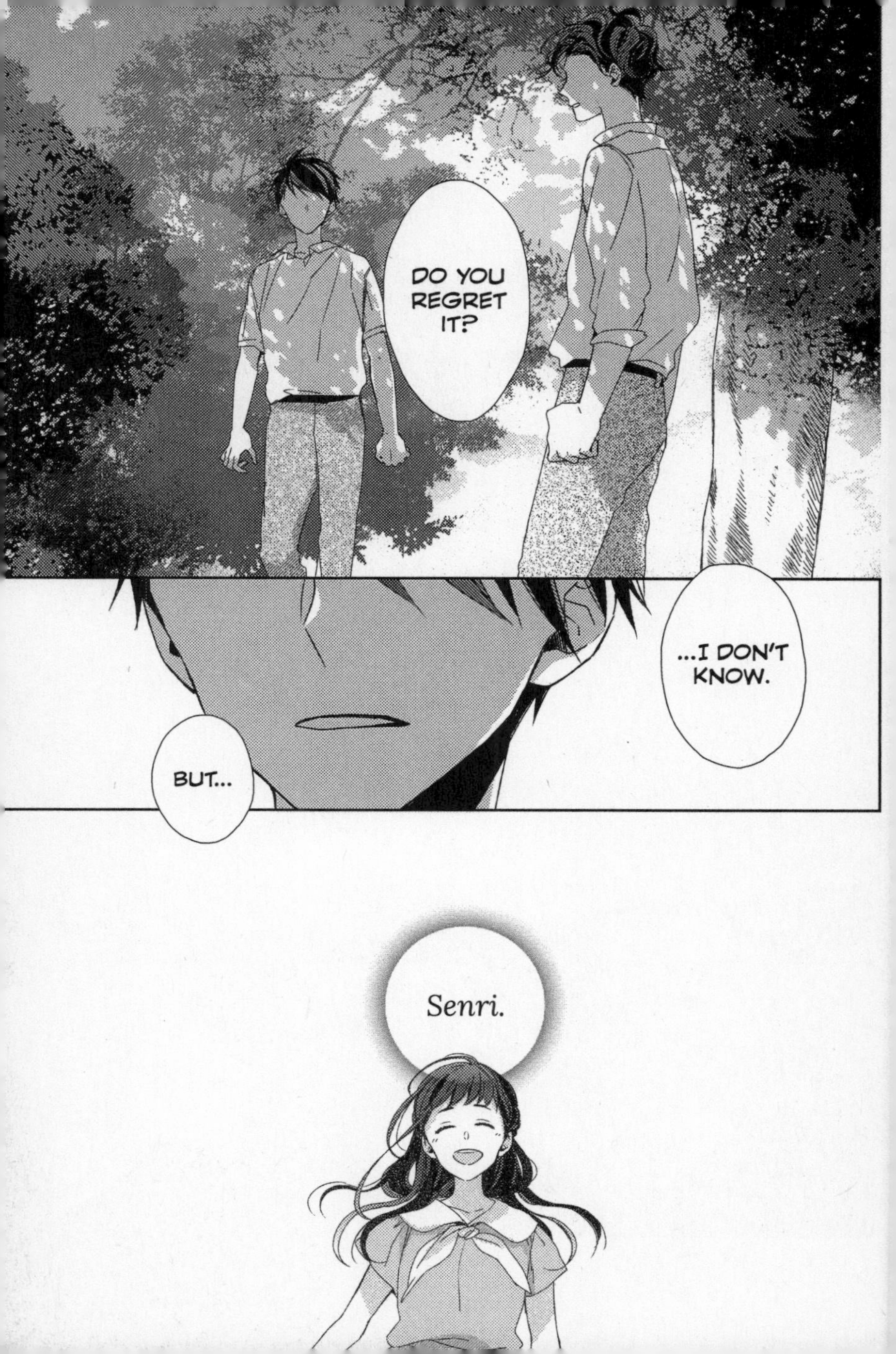
DO YOU REGRET IT?
...I DON'T KNOW.
BUT...
Senri.

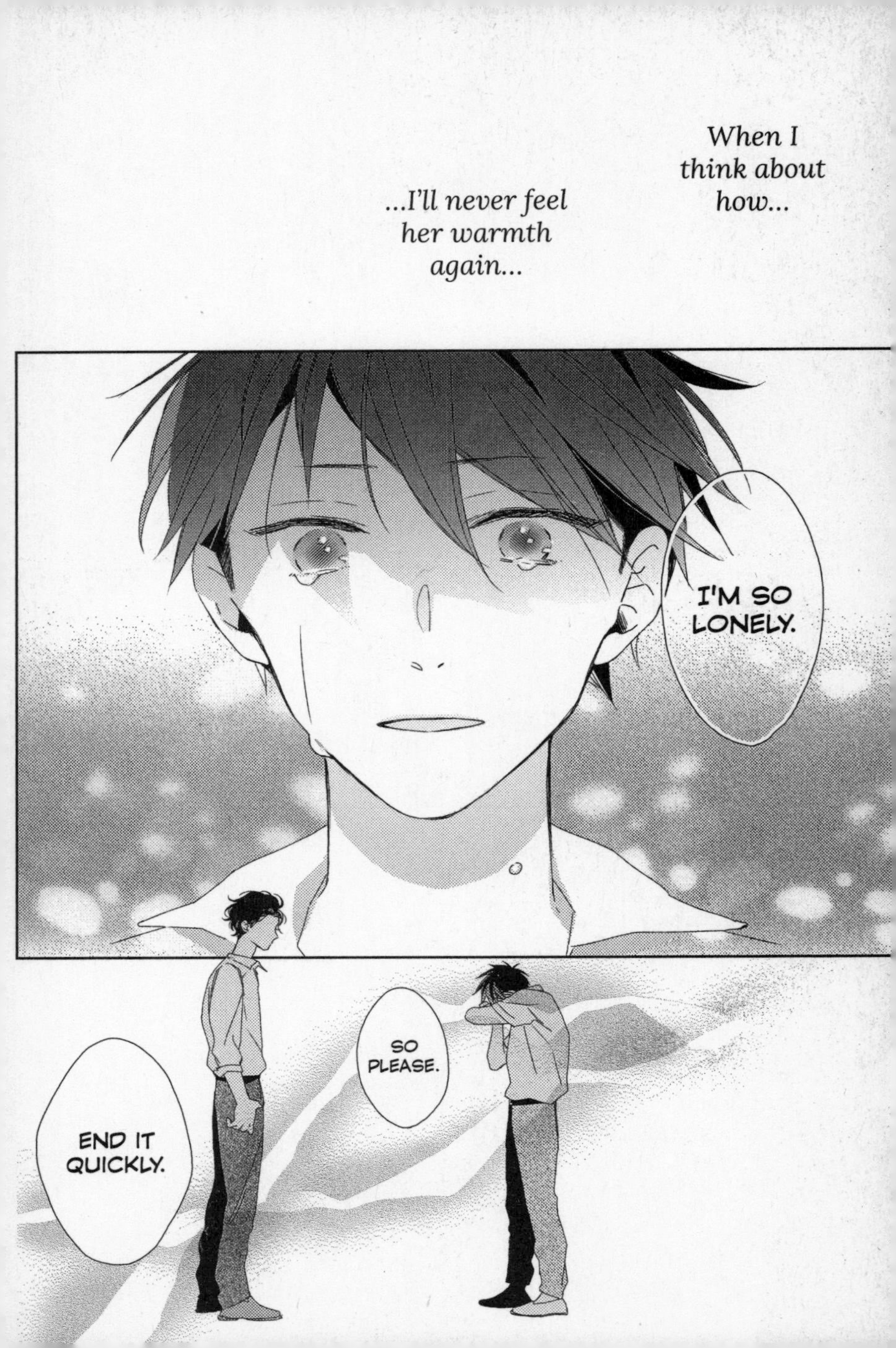
When I think about how...
...I'll never feel her warmth again...
I'M SO LONELY.
SO PLEASE.
END IT QUICKLY.

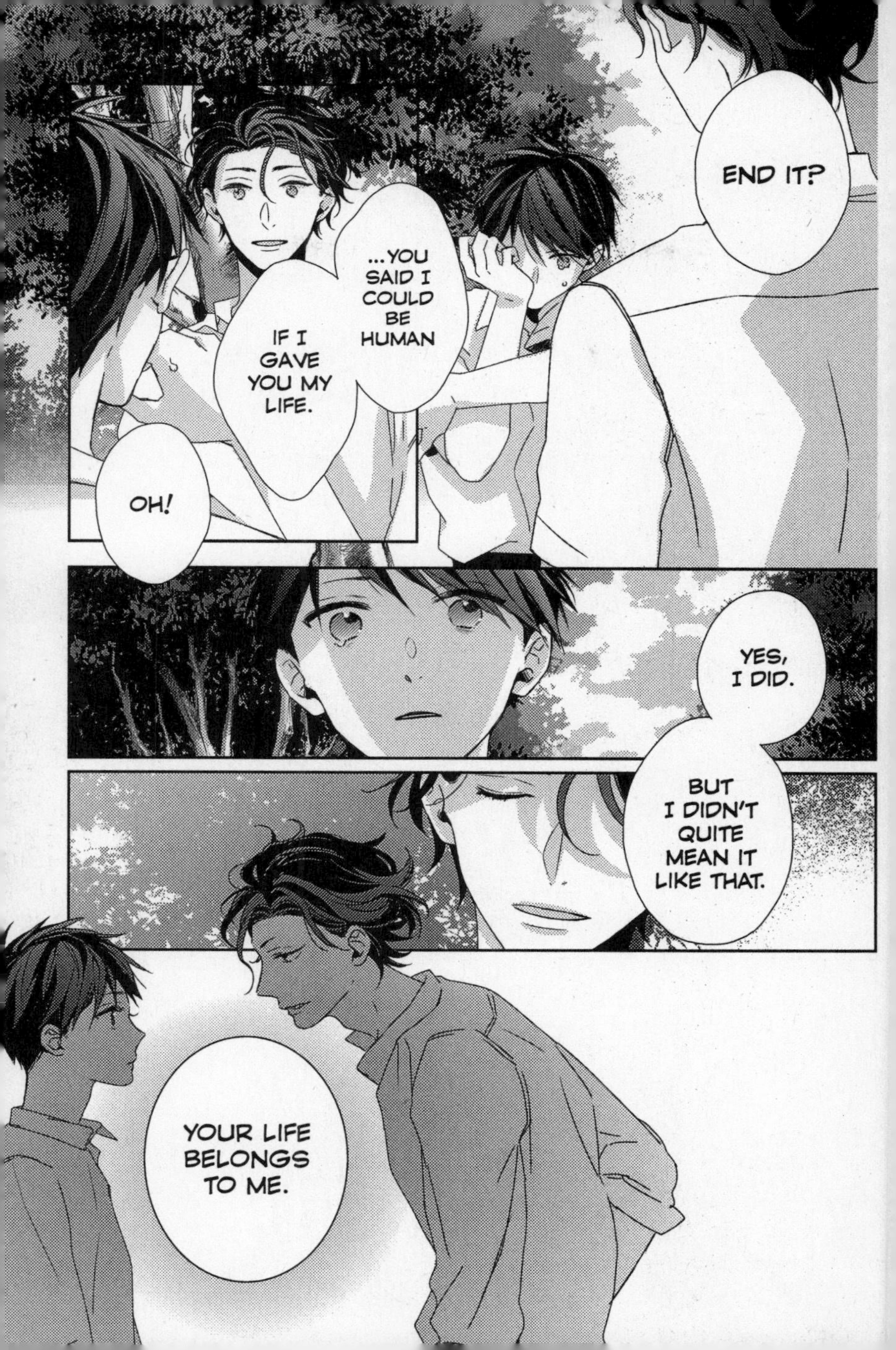
END IT?
...YOU SAID I COULD BE HUMAN
IF I GAVE YOU MY LIFE.
OH!
YES, I DID.
BUT I DIDN'T QUITE MEAN IT LIKE THAT.
YOUR LIFE BELONGS TO ME.

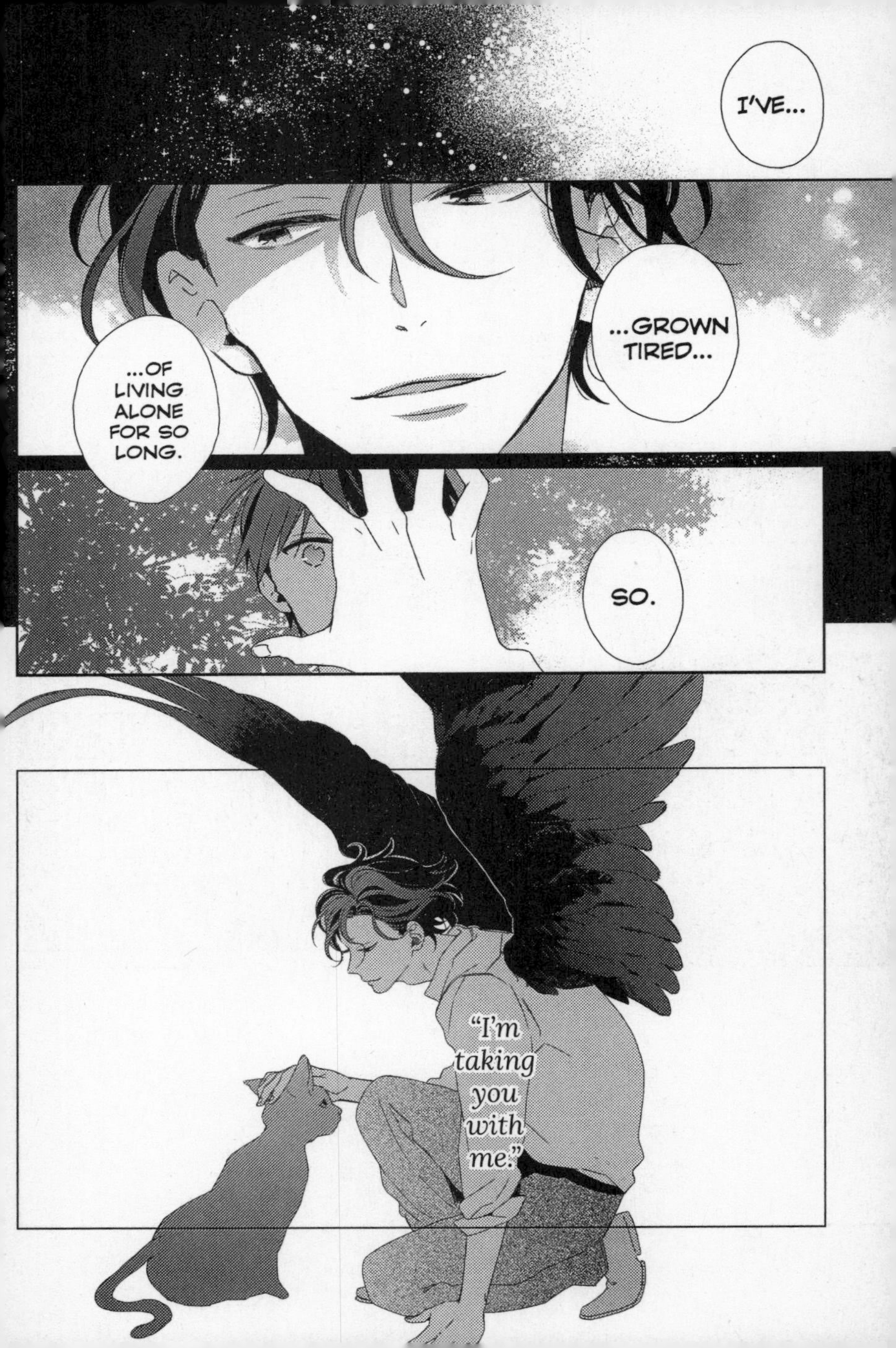
I'VE...
...GROWN TIRED...
...OF LIVING ALONE FOR SO LONG.
SO.
"I'm taking you with me."

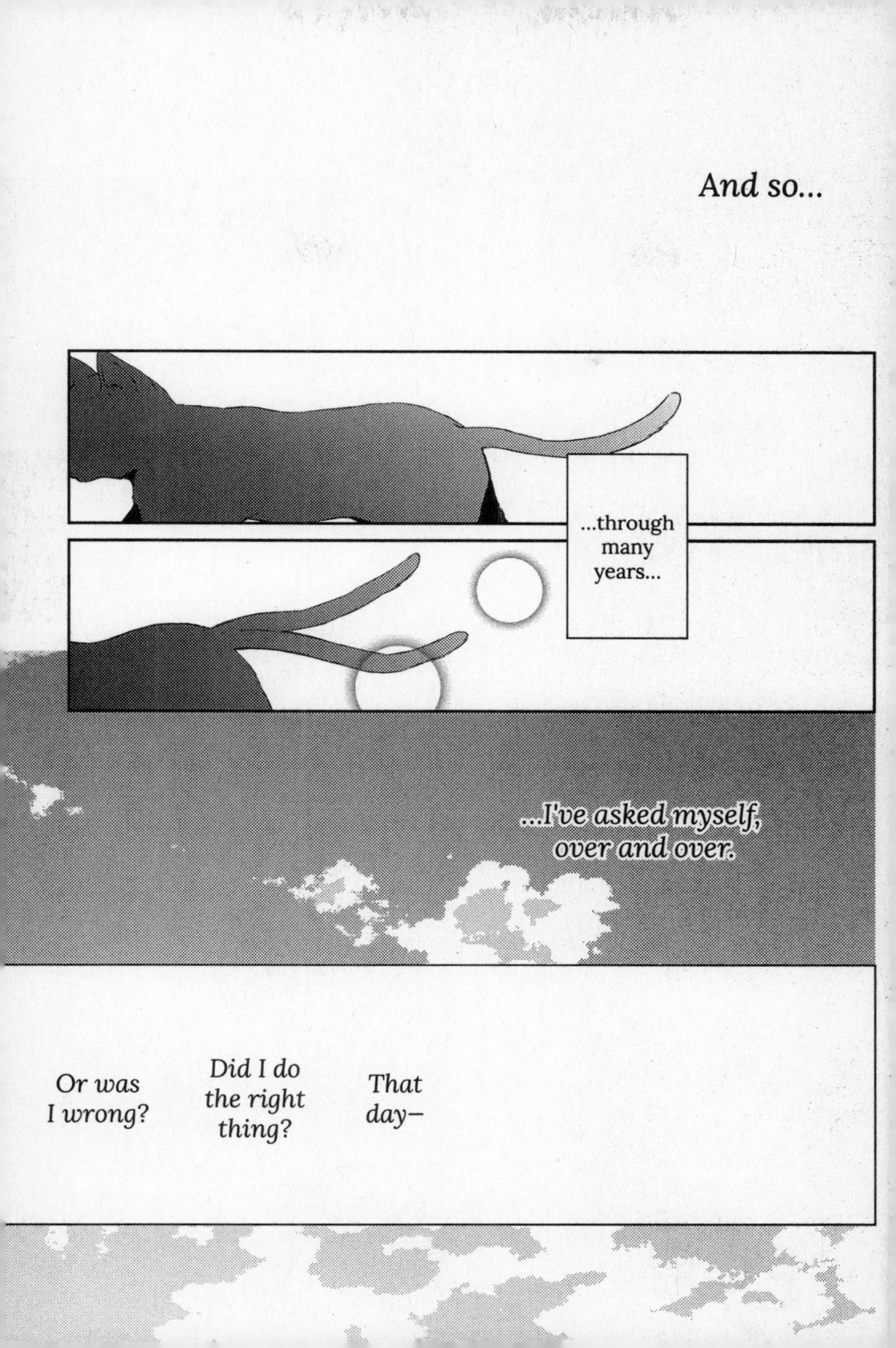

And so...

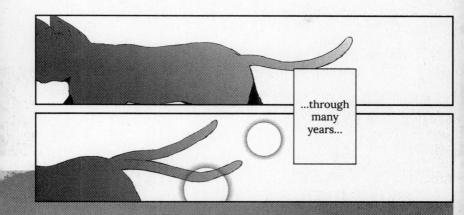

...through
many
years...

...I've asked myself,
over and over.

Or was
I wrong?

Did I do
the right
thing?

That
day—

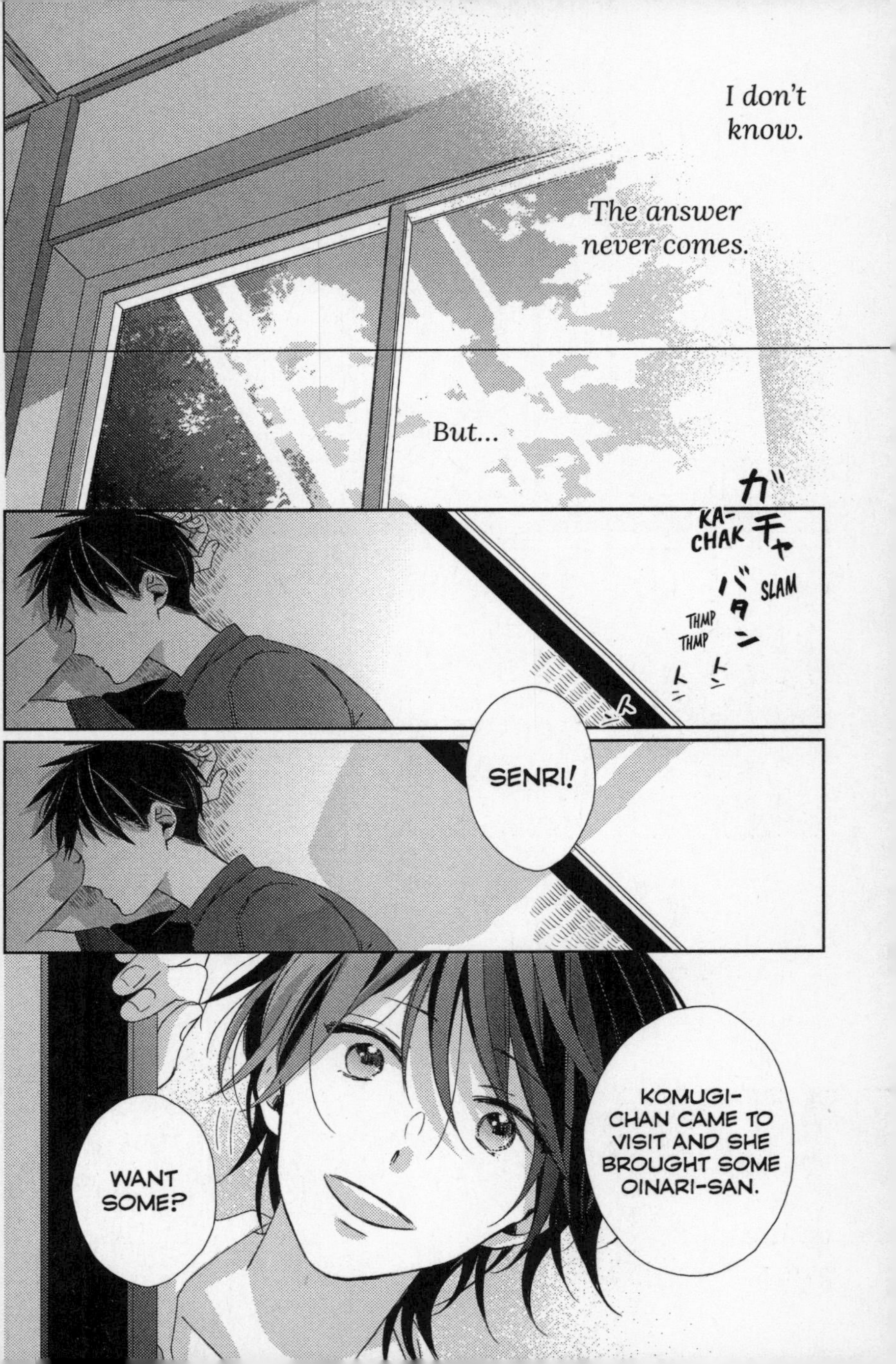
I don't know.
The answer never comes.
But...
ガチャ KA-CHAK
バタン SLAM
トントン THMP THMP
SENRI!
KOMUGI-CHAN CAME TO VISIT AND SHE BROUGHT SOME OINARI-SAN.
WANT SOME?

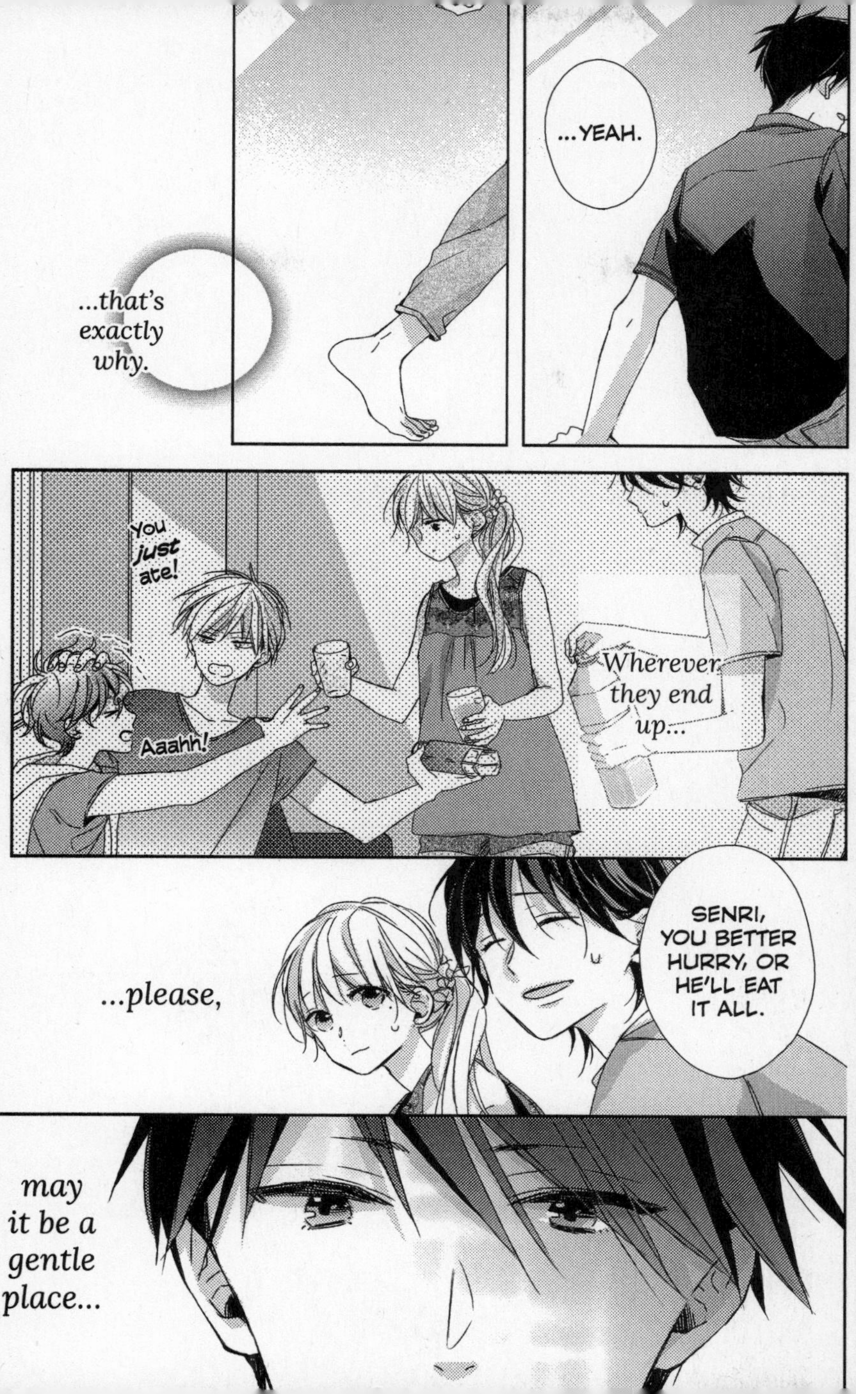
...YEAH.
...that's exactly why.
Wherever they end up...
You just ate!
Aaahh!
SENRI, YOU BETTER HURRY, OR HE'LL EAT IT ALL.
...please,
may it be a gentle place...

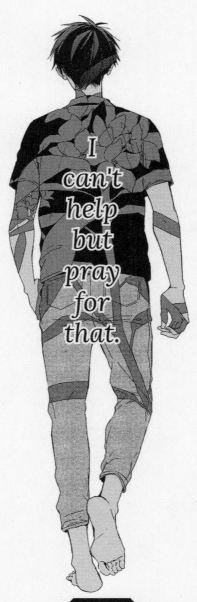

I
can't
help
but
pray
for
that.

The End

That Wolf-Boy is Mine!

That Wolf-Boy's Epilogue

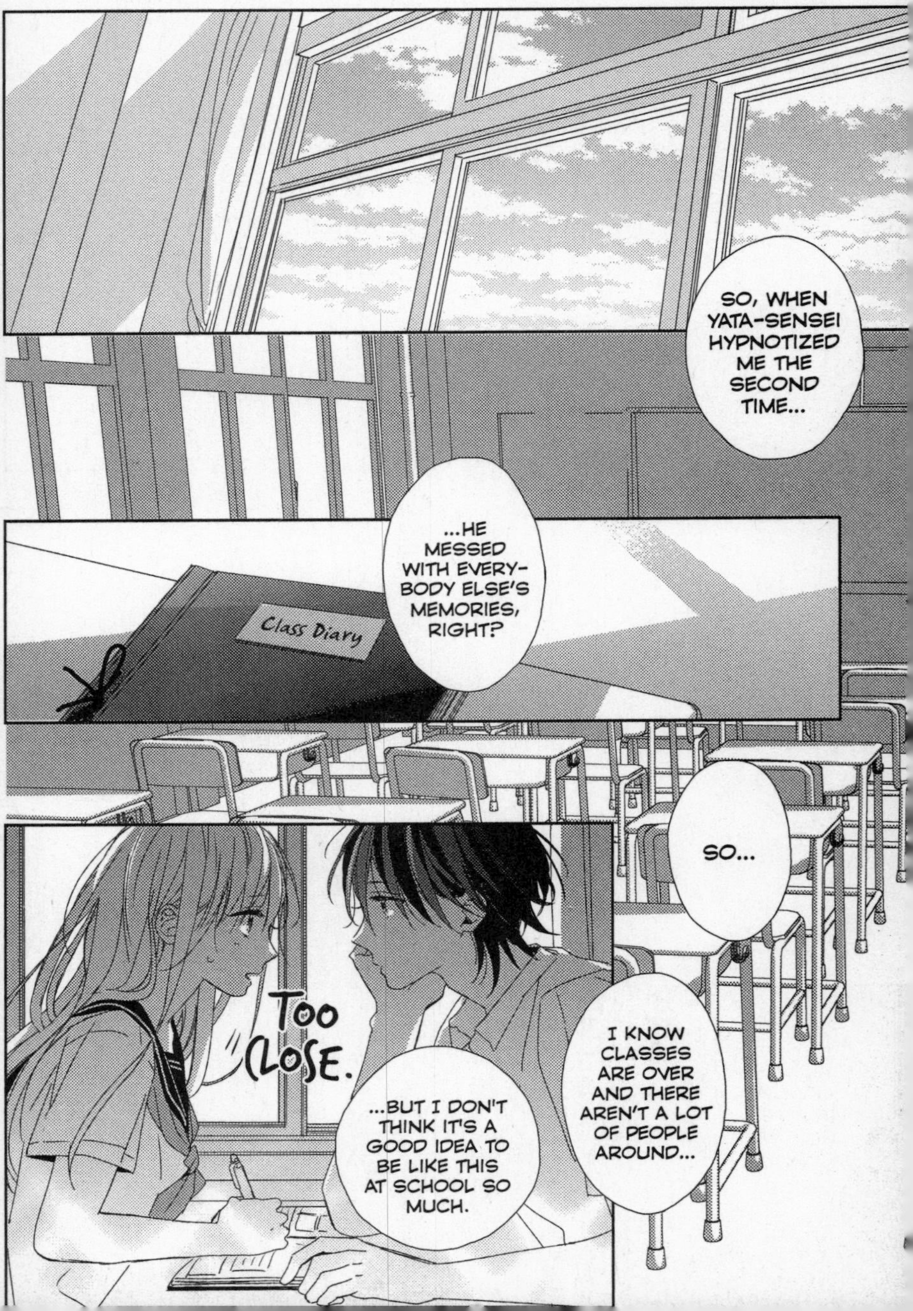
SO, WHEN YATA-SENSEI HYPNOTIZED ME THE SECOND TIME...
...HE MESSED WITH EVERY-BODY ELSE'S MEMORIES, RIGHT?
Class Diary
SO...
I KNOW CLASSES ARE OVER AND THERE AREN'T A LOT OF PEOPLE AROUND...
...BUT I DON'T THINK IT'S A GOOD IDEA TO BE LIKE THIS AT SCHOOL SO MUCH.
TOO CLOSE.

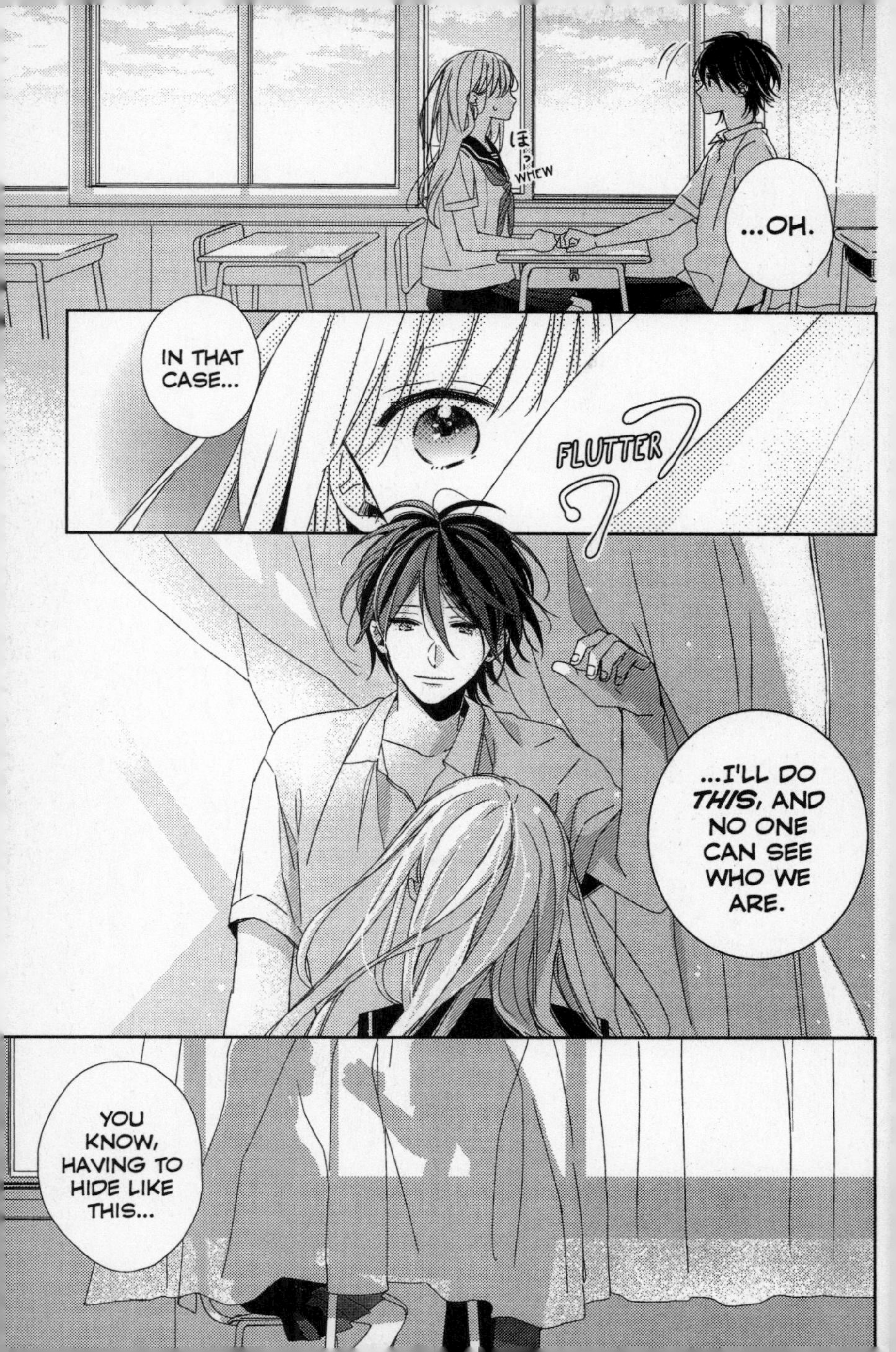
...OH.
ほっ
WHEW
IN THAT CASE...
FLUTTER
...I'LL DO *THIS*, AND NO ONE CAN SEE WHO WE ARE.
YOU KNOW, HAVING TO HIDE LIKE THIS...

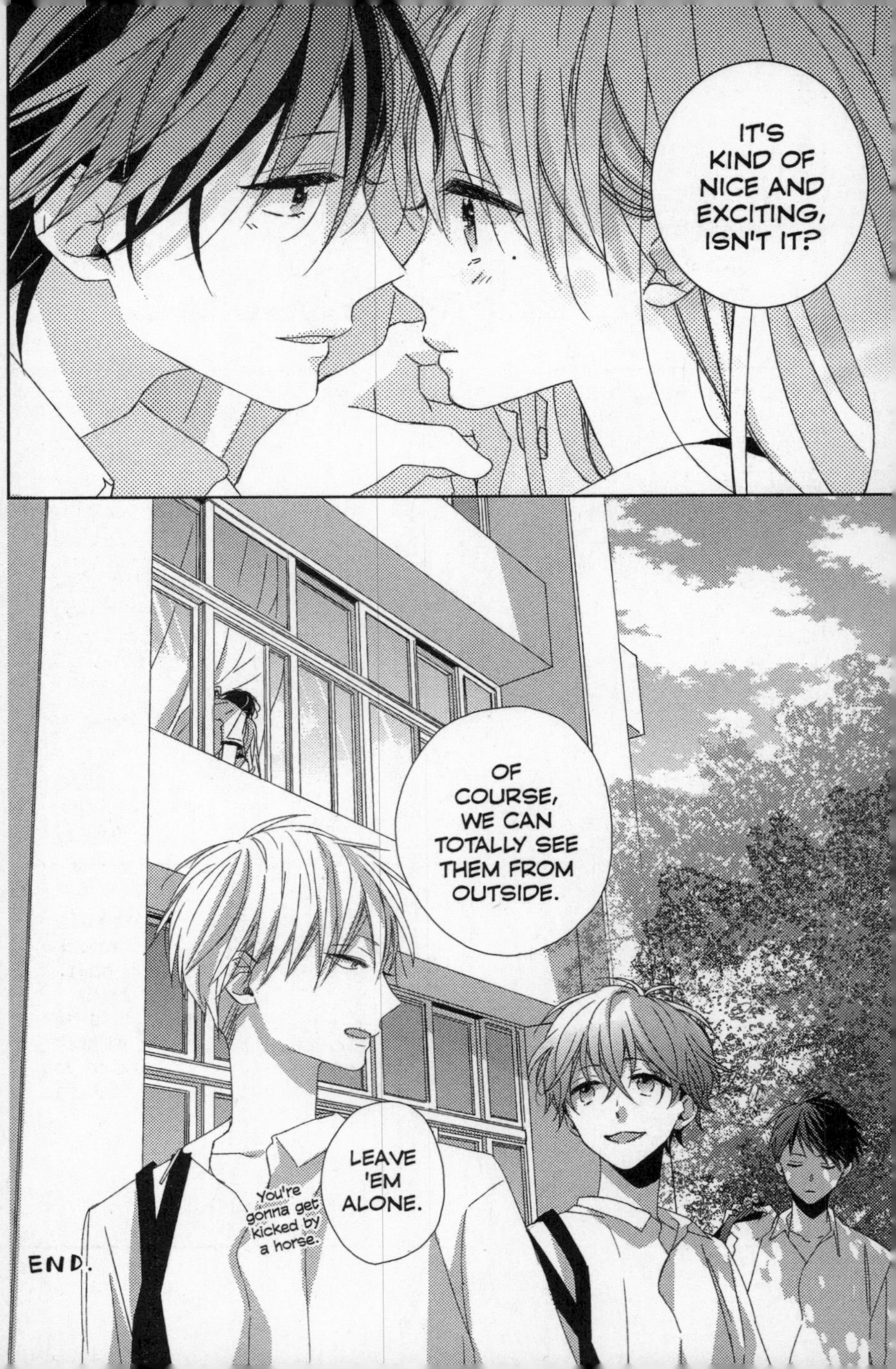
IT'S KIND OF NICE AND EXCITING, ISN'T IT?
OF COURSE, WE CAN TOTALLY SEE THEM FROM OUTSIDE.
LEAVE 'EM ALONE.
You're gonna get kicked by a horse.
END.

Afterword

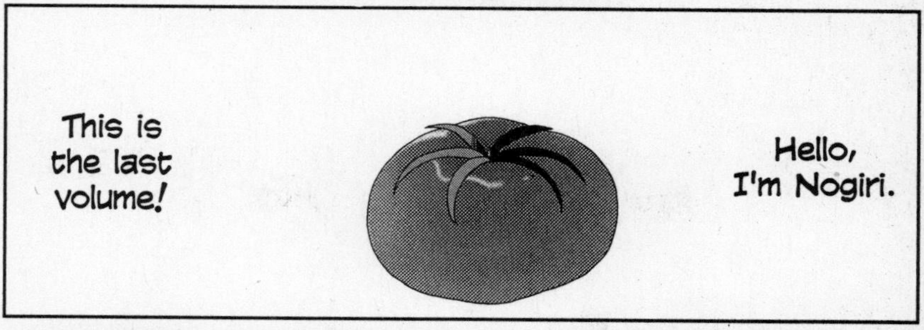
Hello, I'm Nogiri.
This is the last volume!

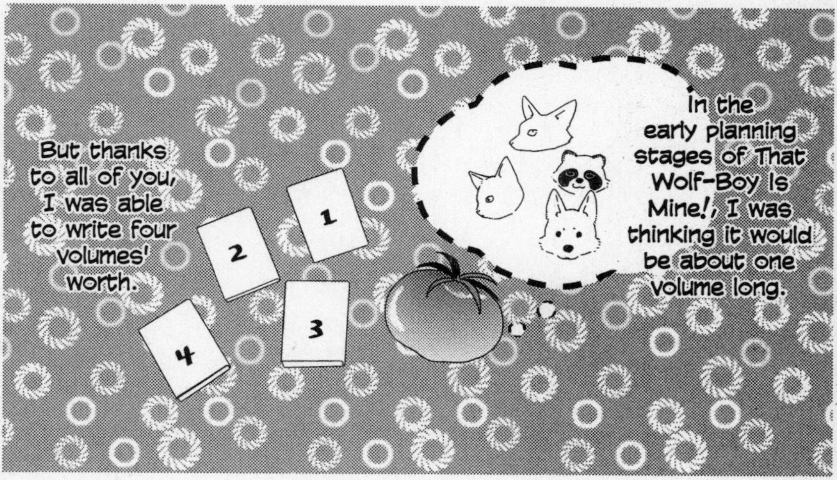
In the early planning stages of That Wolf-Boy Is Mine!, I was thinking it would be about one volume long.
But thanks to all of you, I was able to write four volumes' worth.

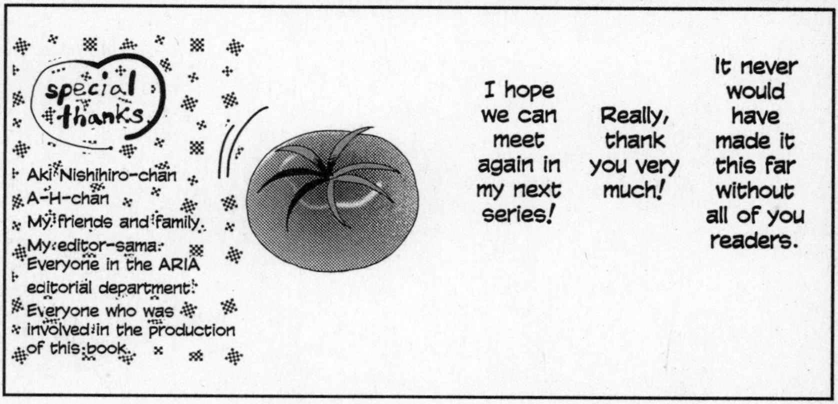
It never would have made it this far without all of you readers.
Really, thank you very much!
I hope we can meet again in my next series!
special thanks
Aki Nishihiro-chan
A-H-chan
My friends and family
My editor-sama
Everyone in the ARIA editorial department
Everyone who was involved in the production of this book

Translation Notes

Family Tomb, page 107
In Japan, one tombstone is often enough for one family. This is because the bodies of the deceased are usually cremated, and their ashes are placed in urns. These vessels are kept in a chamber under the tombstone.

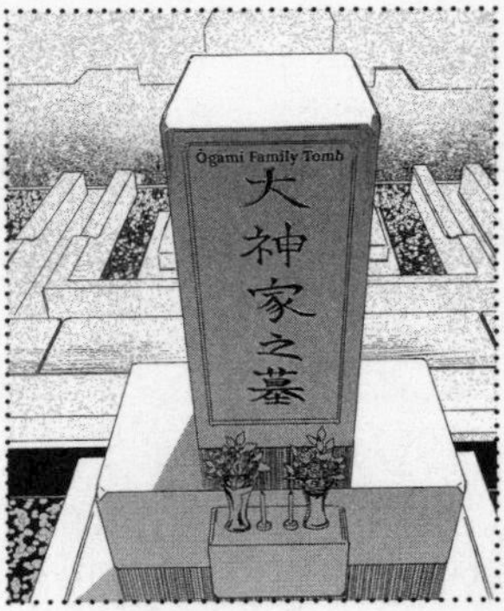
Ōgami Family Tomb
大神家之墓

Kamatama udon, page 135
Kamatama udon, also known as Kagawa style, is udon in a raw egg sauce. Although the eggs will definitely offer protein, they're not exactly "meat," so with Aoshi ordering egg udon and Yū ordering udon topped with bean curd, Rin feels the need to remind them both that meat is the superior choice–especially since they're all carnivores.

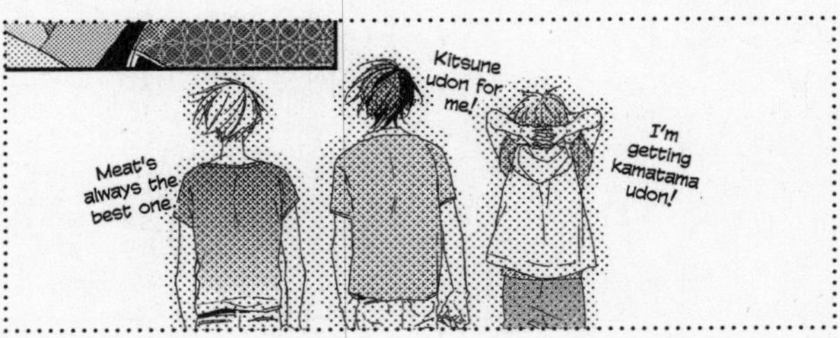
I'm getting kamatama udon!
Kitsune udon for me!
Meat's always the best one.

Ojōsan, page 139
This is a term of respect used when addressing a young woman. It is most frequently used to refer to young women from well-to-do families and implies a certain level of class or social status.

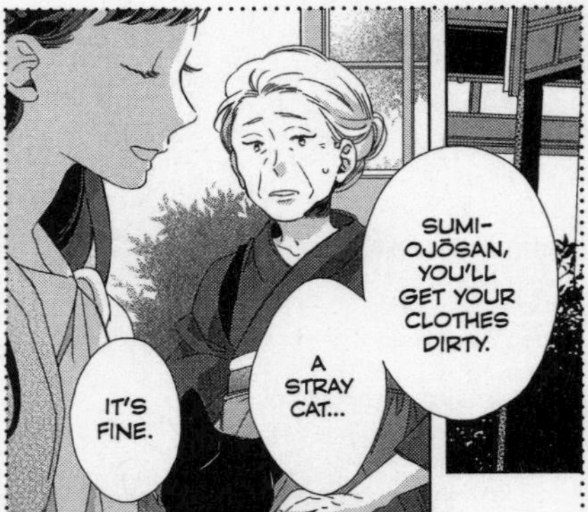
SUMI-OJŌSAN, YOU'LL GET YOUR CLOTHES DIRTY.
A STRAY CAT...
IT'S FINE.

Senrikō, page 141
This is the name of a type of cherry blossom. It means "fragrant over a long distance."

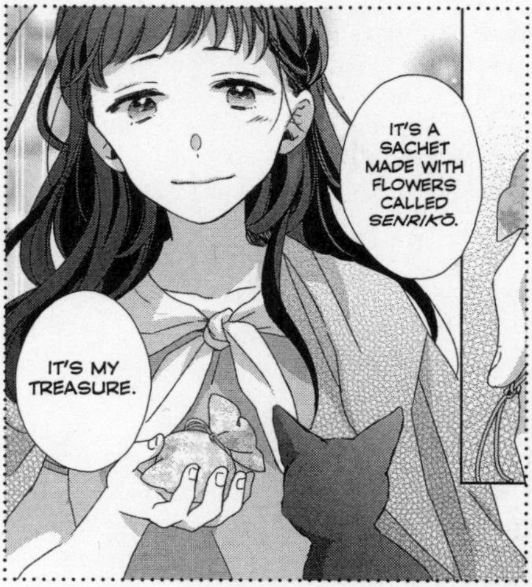
IT'S A SACHET MADE WITH FLOWERS CALLED *SENRIKŌ*.
IT'S MY TREASURE.

Kicked by a horse, page 176
According to a saying from the Edo era, this is the fate awaiting any who would be so rude as to thwart a couple who are in love.

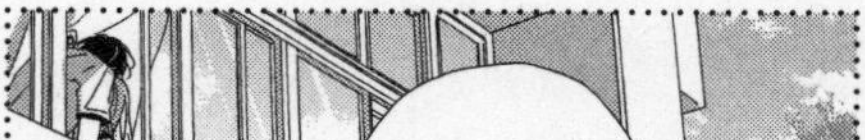
OF COURSE, WE CAN TOTALLY SEE THEM FROM OUTSIDE.
LEAVE 'EM ALONE.
You're gonna get kicked by a horse.

a Silent Voice

KC
KODANSHA COMICS

"The word heartwarming was made for manga like this."
—Manga Bookshelf

"A harsh and biting social commentary... delivers in its depth of character and emotional strength." -Comics Bulletin

"A very powerful story about being different and the consequences of childhood bullying... Read it."
—Anime News Network

Shoya is a bully. When Shoko, a girl who can't hear, enters his elementary school class, she becomes their favorite target, and Shoya and his friends goad each other into devising new tortures for her. But the children's cruelty goes too far. Shoko is forced to leave the school, and Shoya ends up shouldering all the blame. Six years later, the two meet again. Can Shoya make up for his past mistakes, or is it too late?

Available now in print and digitally!

Mei Tachibana has no friends — and says she doesn't need them!

But everything changes when she accidentally roundhouse kicks the most popular boy in school! However, Yamato Kurosawa isn't angry in the slightest—in fact, he thinks his ordinary life could use an unusual girl like Mei. But winning Mei's trust will be a tough task. How long will she refuse to say, "I love you"?

My Little Monster

OPPOSITES ATTRACT...MAYBE?

Haru Yoshida is feared as an unstable and violent "monster." Mizutani Shizuku is a grade-obsessed student with no friends. Fate brings these two together to form the most unlikely pair. Haru firmly believes he's in love with Mizutani and she firmly believes he's insane.

KC KODANSHA COMICS

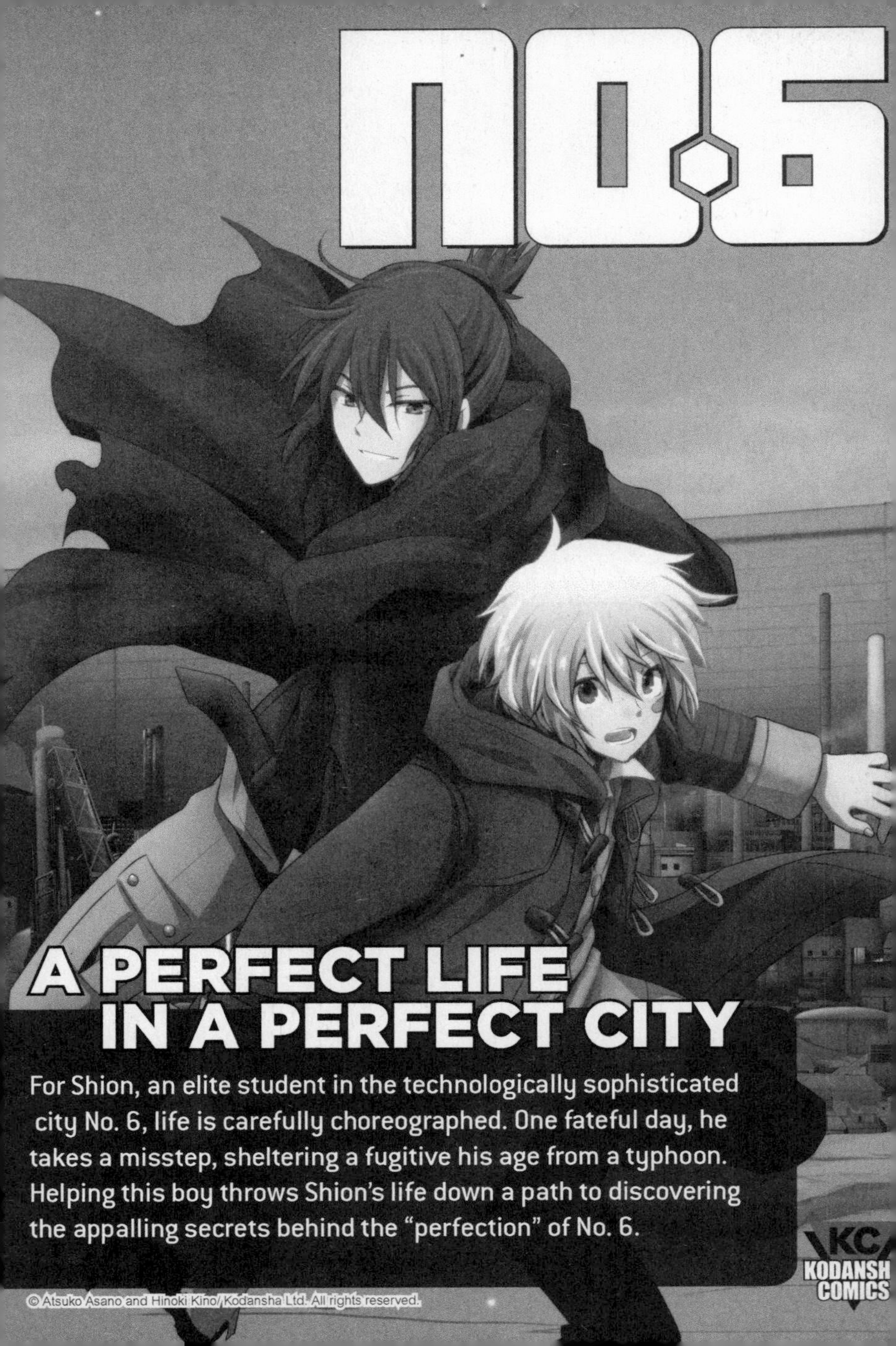
NO.6
A PERFECT LIFE
IN A PERFECT CITY
For Shion, an elite student in the technologically sophisticated city No. 6, life is carefully choreographed. One fateful day, he takes a misstep, sheltering a fugitive his age from a typhoon. Helping this boy throws Shion's life down a path to discovering the appalling secrets behind the "perfection" of No. 6.
KC
KODANSH
COMICS
© Atsuko Asano and Hinoki Kino/Kodansha Ltd. All rights reserved.

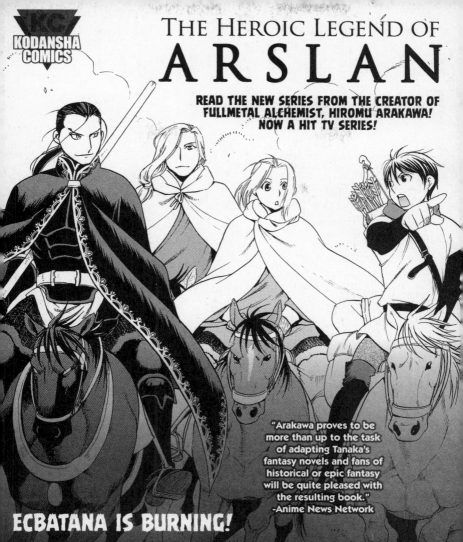

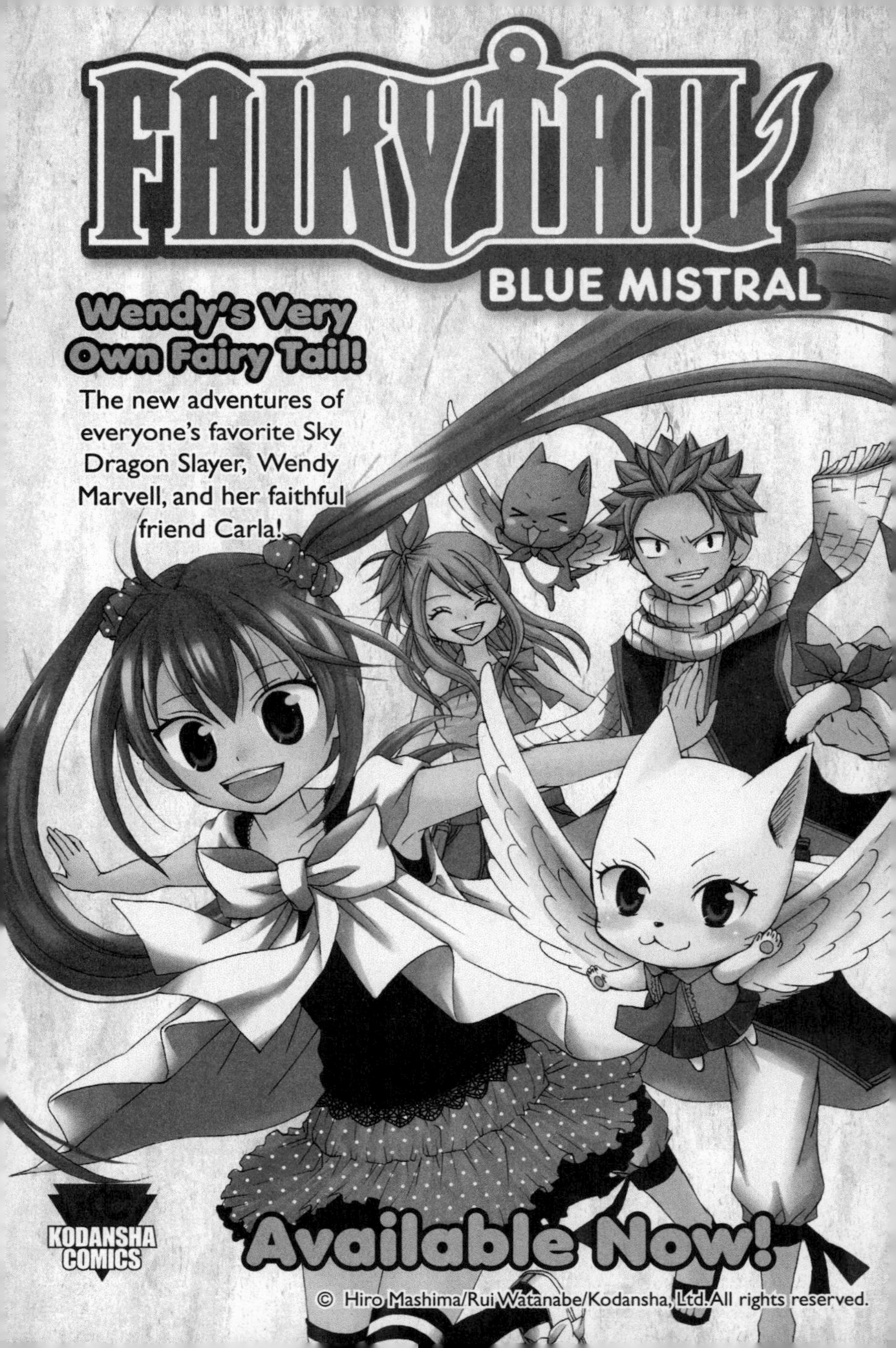
FAIRY TAIL
BLUE MISTRAL
Wendy's Very Own Fairy Tail!
The new adventures of everyone's favorite Sky Dragon Slayer, Wendy Marvell, and her faithful friend Carla!
KODANSHA COMICS
Available Now!
© Hiro Mashima/Rui Watanabe/Kodansha, Ltd. All rights reserved.

Fairy Tail takes place in a world filled with magic. 17-year-old Lucy is a wizard-in-training who wants to join a magic guild so that she can become a full-fledged wizard. She dreams of joining the most famous guild, known as Fairy Tail. One day she meets Natsu, a boy raised by a dragon which vanished when he was young. Natsu has devoted his life to finding his dragon father. When Natsu helps Lucy out of a tricky situation, she discovers that he is a member of Fairy Tail, and our heroes' adventure together begins.

FAIRY TAIL

MASTER'S EDITION

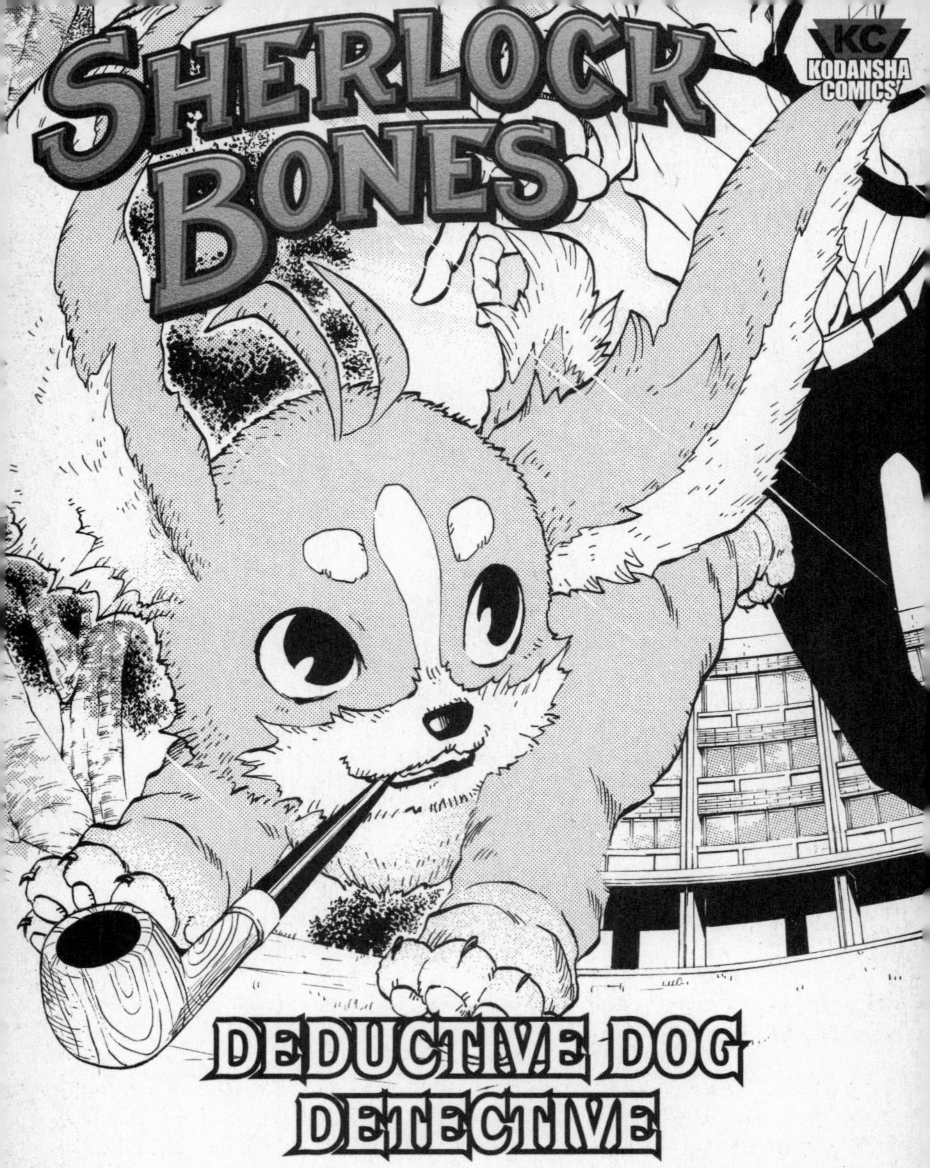
SHERLOCK BONES
KC KODANSHA COMICS

DEDUCTIVE DOG DETECTIVE

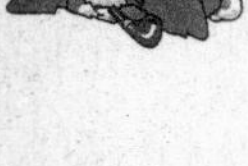

When Takeru adopts a new pet, he's in for a surprise—the dog is none other than the reincarnation of Sherlock Holmes. With no one else able to communicate with Holmes, Takeru is roped into becoming Sherdog's assistant, John Watson. Using his sleuthing skills, Holmes uncovers clues to solve the trickiest crimes.

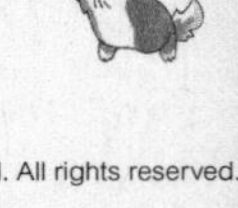

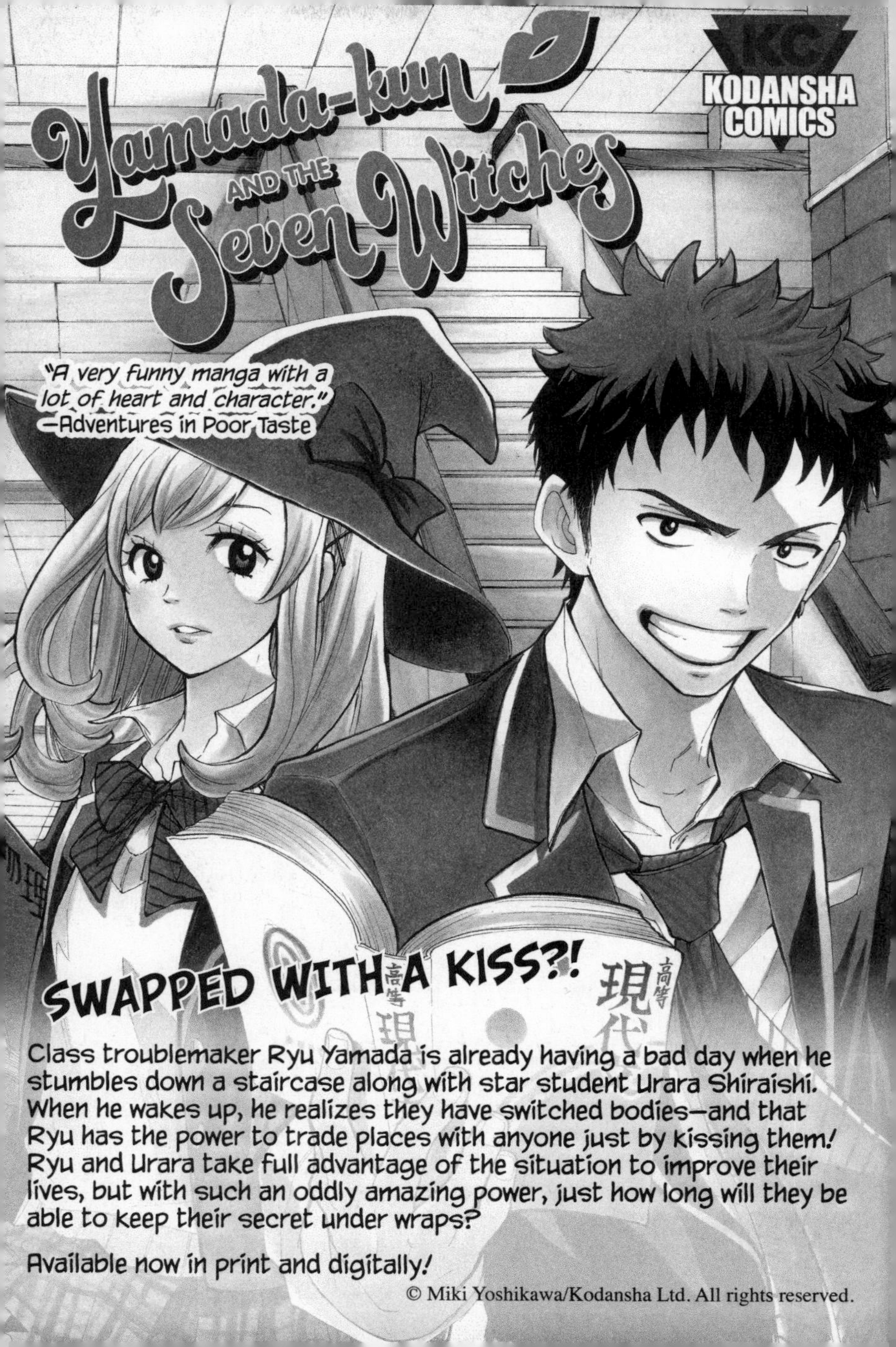
KODANSHA COMICS
Yamada-kun AND THE Seven Witches
"A very funny manga with a lot of heart and character."
—Adventures in Poor Taste
SWAPPED WITH A KISS?!
Class troublemaker Ryu Yamada is already having a bad day when he stumbles down a staircase along with star student Urara Shiraishi. When he wakes up, he realizes they have switched bodies—and that Ryu has the power to trade places with anyone just by kissing them! Ryu and Urara take full advantage of the situation to improve their lives, but with such an oddly amazing power, just how long will they be able to keep their secret under wraps?
Available now in print and digitally!
© Miki Yoshikawa/Kodansha Ltd. All rights reserved.

DEVIL SURVIVOR

AFTER DEMONS BREAK THROUGH INTO THE HUMAN WORLD, TOKYO MUST BE QUARANTINED. WITHOUT POWER AND STUCK IN A SUPERNATURAL WARZONE, 17-YEAR-OLD KAZUYA HAS ONLY ONE HOPE: HE MUST USE THE "COMP," A DEVICE CREATED BY HIS COUSIN NAOYA CAPABLE OF SUMMONING AND SUBDUING DEMONS, TO DEFEAT THE INVADERS AND TAKE BACK THE CITY.

BASED ON THE POPULAR VIDEO GAME FRANCHISE BY ATLUS!

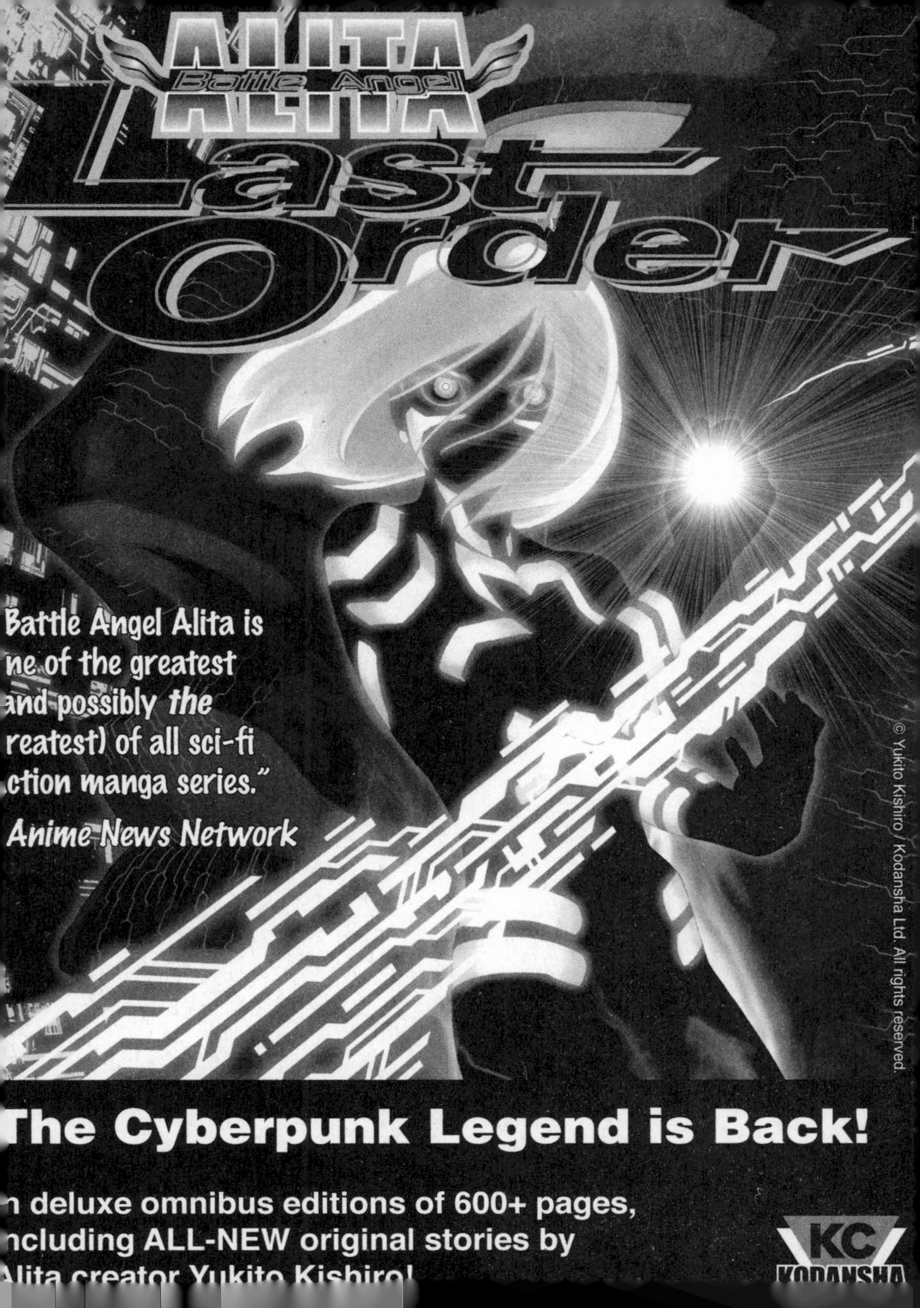

ALITA
Battle Angel
ALITA
Last Order
Battle Angel Alita is
ne of the greatest
and possibly *the*
reatest) of all sci-fi
ction manga series."
Anime News Network
© Yukito Kishiro / Kodansha Ltd. All rights reserved.
The Cyberpunk Legend is Back!
n deluxe omnibus editions of 600+ pages,
ncluding ALL-NEW original stories by
lita creator Yukito Kishiro!
KC
KODANSHA

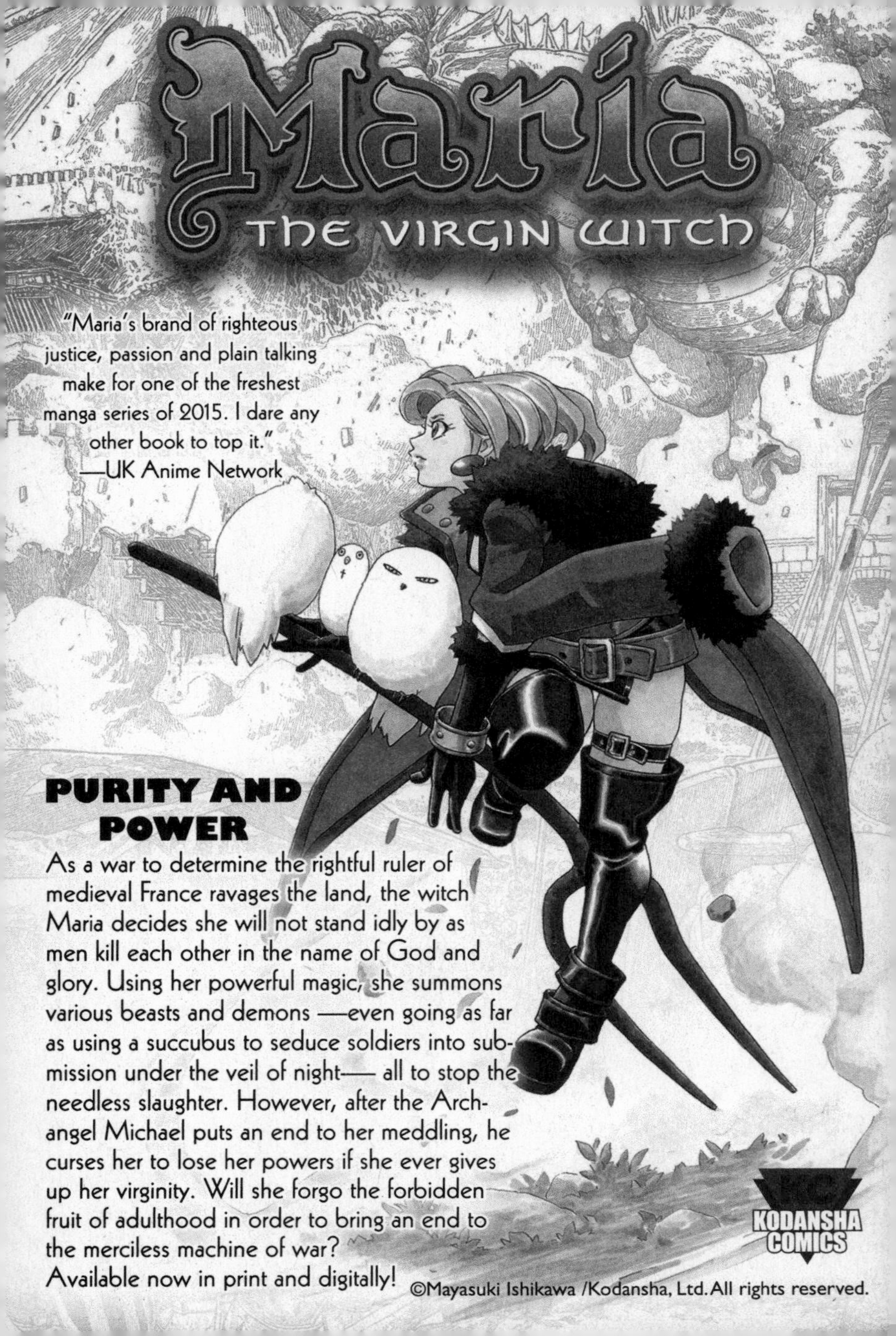
Maria
THE VIRGIN WITCH
"Maria's brand of righteous justice, passion and plain talking make for one of the freshest manga series of 2015. I dare any other book to top it."
—UK Anime Network
PURITY AND POWER
As a war to determine the rightful ruler of medieval France ravages the land, the witch Maria decides she will not stand idly by as men kill each other in the name of God and glory. Using her powerful magic, she summons various beasts and demons —even going as far as using a succubus to seduce soldiers into submission under the veil of night— all to stop the needless slaughter. However, after the Archangel Michael puts an end to her meddling, he curses her to lose her powers if she ever gives up her virginity. Will she forgo the forbidden fruit of adulthood in order to bring an end to the merciless machine of war?
Available now in print and digitally!
KODANSHA COMICS
©Mayasuki Ishikawa /Kodansha, Ltd. All rights reserved.

SANKAREA

undying love

"I ONLY LIKE ZOMBIE GIRLS."

Chihiro has an unusual connection to zombie movies. He doesn't feel bad for the survivors – he wants to comfort the undead girls they slaughter! When his pet passes away, he brews a resurrection potion. He's discovered by local heiress Sanka Rea, and she serves as his first test subject!

A Kodansha Comics Trade Paperback Original
That Wolf-Boy is Mine! volume 4 copyright © 2016 Yoko Nogiri
English translation copyright © 2017 Yoko Nogiri

Published in the United States by Kodansha Comics, an imprint of
Kodansha USA Publishing, LLC, New York.

Publication rights for this English edition arranged through
Kodansha Ltd, Tokyo.

ISBN 978-1-63236-403-6

Printed in the United States of America.

www.kodanshacomics.com

9 8 7 6 5 4 3 2 1
Translation: Alethea and Athena Nibley
Lettering: Sara Linsley
Editing: Megan McPherson and Haruko Hashimoto
Kodansha Comics edition cover design by Phil Balsman